For Girls ONLY

the ultimate guide to being a girl

For Girls ONLY

the ultimate guide to being a girl

by Sylvaine Jaoui
illustrated by Manu Boisteau
edited by Andrea Bussell

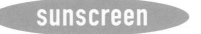

Library of Congress Cataloging-in-Publication Data
Jaoui, Sylvaine.
For girls only / by Sylvaine Jaoui ; illustrated by Manu Boisteau.
p. cm. — (Sunscreen)
ISBN 978-0-8109-8432-5 (Harry N. Abrams, Inc.)
1. Teenage girls—Psychology. 2. Teenage girls—Health and hygiene. 3.
Beauty, Personal. 4. Grooming for girls. 5. Interpersonal relations in adolescence. 6. Adolescence. I. Title.
HQ798.J36 2010
646.70083'42—dc22
2009022934

Text copyright © 2010 Sylvaine Jaoui
Illustrations copyright © 2010 Manu Boisteau

Translated by Nicholas Elliott

Book series design by Higashi Glaser Design

Printed and bound in China
10 9 8 7 6 5 4 3 2 1

Amulet Books are available at special discounts when purchased in quantity
for premiums and promotions as well as fundraising or educational use.
Special editions can also be created to specification. For details, contact
specialmarkets@abramsbooks.com or the address below.

ABRAMS
THE ART OF BOOKS SINCE 1949

115 West 18th Street
New York, NY 10011
www.abramsbooks.com

contents

BOYS, CLOTHES,
GOSSIP, CRUSHES,
LOVE, BODY IMAGE,
SECRETS, SIBLINGS,
TATTOOS, PIERCINGS,
MAKEUP, BOYS,
CLOTHES, GOSSIP,
CRUSHES, LOVE.

What do you call someone who:

- Spends hours in the bathroom

- Obsesses about her nose or hips or skin in the mirror

- Is terrified of the first kiss

- Will always be loyal to her best friend

- Thinks about getting a piercing or tattoo or trying a new hairstyle

- Loves secrets

- Has a hard time understanding her parents

- Dreams of finding Prince Charming

- Doesn't know how to get the boys at school to notice her

- Fights with her older sister

- Talks on the phone with her friends for hours

Here's the answer: a girl!

Girls come in all shapes and sizes. Some like makeup, some like sports. Some confide in their parents, some wouldn't dream of telling them what they're really thinking. Some love to flirt with boys, some feel sick with worry at the thought, or could care less. What's the bottom line? Girls are marvelously complicated. And this book is here to help you better understand yourselves as you're dealing with the chaos of being a teenager, and to give you some important tips on how to make life a bit easier.

clothes

Your wardrobe is important, right? You check out what the girls at school are wearing when you pass them in the hallway. And you notice when they covet your new knockoff handbag while you're in line for lunch. When you go shopping at the start of the season, you try to spot the hottest trends and be the first at school to wear them. Or you buy those crazy low-rider jeans because everyone else started wearing them and you want to be just as cool. Sometimes you even buy clothes not necessarily because you like them, but because you are trying to fit in. Choice in clothes is a way for people to identify themselves—especially for teens. Dressing in a certain fashion is a way to tell people, "I'm just like you, so don't reject me." Or "I like the same TV shows or music that you do."

Fitting in can be really stressful. So you don't think twice about taking all the money you got for Christmas or your birthday, or that you saved up from extra chores or babysitting, and spending it all on expensive distressed jeans or that striped boho scarf that looks hand-knit. Let's be honest—as you swipe your mom's credit card or fork over the cash, the only thing on your mind is the moment you show up at school or someone's party wearing your new purchase and seeing the heads turn.

It's nothing to be ashamed of—we all do it. Girls love clothes and fashion because wearing something cool makes us feel more confident about ourselves or seductive to other people. Everyone wants to be loved and adored.

But maybe you're bored with the usual jeans and T-shirts that you see at school every day and you don't really want to look like everyone else. Sometimes you think that the girl in the avant-garde outfit or with the retro haircut looks a little weird, but her unique flair also makes her cool or special, too. Remember: it's not always *what* you wear, but *how* you wear it. *Nothing* is more attractive than confidence. Being noticed isn't just about the amazing peasant blouse you're wearing, but also about how you carry yourself in it. Use your clothes not just as an opportunity to show your friends that you belong, but also as a way to express who *you* are. You have your own personality. Why not let your look reflect it? Feel like combining a romantic silk top with some rock-and-roll black leather boots—go for it! You can be your own fashion designer or personal stylist.

gossip

Why do girls like to gossip? We could approach this question in a scientific manner and explain that the language centers in the brain are not the same in males as they are in females. Not only are they one-third larger in girls' brains than they are in boys', but also the left hemisphere, where language is centered, develops earlier in girls than in boys. This is actually why girls learn to talk earlier and better than their male playmates. We could pass that information along, but does it really explain why girls love to talk so much? Let's bypass science and try to use some feminine intuition.

How do boys talk? They use short and simple sentences. For boys, language is about passing along information or answering a question in the most basic way. Speaking is a practical tool used for dealing with daily situations.

Now think about how girls talk. You should probably sit down, because the answer is going to take a while. Like their male counterparts, girls speak to transmit information or answer a question. But that's not where it stops. For a girl, language is a way to express feelings—joy, sadness, discouragement, surprise, confusion. Her conversation with her girlfriends will include every last detail about how sad she was when Chad broke up with her, or how delighted she was when Howard waited for her after math class.

When boys hear the way girls talk to one another, they either get bored or ask the question "What is the point you're trying to get across?" They don't

Susan told Andrea that Jammi told Maggie that you told Scott that I have a crush on him!

understand that girls like to listen, to be there for one another, to share in the good news, or to understand every little detail. Boys want to cut to the chase or find a quick solution to the issue at hand; girls want to be heard and understood. And the common truth is, believe it or not, girls just *like* to talk.

It sounds so simple, and it is. Sometimes girls just talk for the sake of talking! It's how we're wired. It's fun to share things with our friends and talk about clothes and boys and what happened on *Gossip Girl*. It makes us feel connected to others and helps us to relate better. But while gossiping might come naturally to girls, you have to remember how it makes you feel when someone gossips about you. No one likes to feel exposed or talked about, so you should never talk about others in a way that could be hurtful.

marking
your body

As recently as ten or fifteen years ago, most people considered piercing a barbaric ritual inherited from the punk movement. Having rings through your eyebrows was seen as an aggressive, hard-core fashion statement. But attitudes have started to change. You might even be thinking of following in a friend's footsteps and getting a little loop on the side of your nose or a stud in your tongue. What makes you want to have all these little "holes" in your head?

The first, most obvious answer is that you like how it looks. You want to be beautiful and you think body piercing is a way of achieving that. It's a way of decorating your body, just as you do with makeup and clothes. It's a form of body art, of creating an image of yourself. Piercing is just another accessory that gives you style. And when you pick up a magazine and see some actress, singer, or model with a belly-button piercing, you want to look like her, too. Like any other fashion accessory, a piercing or tattoo allows you to be part of a community.

Another reason, which may be the most important, is that marking your body can be a declaration of independence. Tattoos and piercings, just like

a drastic new haircut or color, often serve as a way of claiming your body for yourself. We mark our bodies to show that we are free to do what we want with them. Often, this is a way of telling our parents that our childhood is ending and that we are able to think for ourselves.

But be careful: piercing and tattooing permanently change your body. In addition to the risk of infection (or even more serious illnesses if basic hygienic practices aren't followed), what you think looks cool today might look pretty silly when you're in college. That barbell in your eyebrow or dragon tattoo on your back that you thought was so tough might be awfully amusing to your grandkids.

Fact No. 1

If you wear glasses, don't leave them at home on a first date.

true love

Having grown up hearing children's stories of Prince Charming saving young damsels in distress, girls have come to believe that reality is like a fairy tale. They have no trouble identifying with legendary heroines: Sleeping Beauty, Cinderella, Snow White . . . the list goes on and on.

So, from an early age, we imagine that's how real life must be, and we dream of that moment when Prince Charming will ride in on his white stallion and take us off into the sunset. Maybe a white stallion isn't involved in your fantasy, but you still imagine you'll show up alone and shy at a party one night and suddenly a boy—I mean a prince—will be overcome by your beauty and run to your side. He is handsome and intelligent, rich and funny, and offers to take you for a ride on his private jet or in his brand-new red Ferrari or . . . STOP!

Have you ever encountered a fourteen-year-old boy with a driver's license, a private jet, or a Ferrari? It's great to dream—it makes us feel good, and in some cases fantasizing is how we start to imagine how we can get what we want. But beware: dreams can sometimes be hazardous to your heart and health.

If you keep fantasizing about life, you lose your ability to see reality for what it really is. You can become blinded by illusions and sometimes not see the good, real things that are right in front of your face. How many girls

choose to maintain virtual relationships on the computer rather than face

real life? Or how many girls fantasize about movie stars, singers, or other

"unattainable guys" from whom the most they'll ever get is an autograph?

Since there's no real relationship with these guys, there's no chance of being

disappointed or hurt. And since there's no chance to get to know them and see

who they really are, they remain perfect. And *no one* is perfect. Remember:

living is about taking chances, including the chance to be happy. And unless

you take the time to get to know someone and risk getting hurt, you'll never

know what kind of relationship you're capable of and how much joy another

person can bring you.

The other danger in fantasizing too much is that you might compare your

real boyfriend, if you have one, to an unattainable ideal, and blame him for

not measuring up. The slightest gap between our fantasy and reality can be a major disappointment. Not too many guys can live up to all our expectations. If he chooses to stay after school and play basketball with his friends instead of seeing a movie with you, it's a major drama. He didn't notice your new low-rider jeans—proof he doesn't love you. The dream of a constantly loving and attentive Prince Charming winds up ruining your life.

Here's the brutal truth: Prince Charming doesn't exist. However, the one who does exist—and who you should make sure not to miss—is a boy who is charming. Even if he doesn't show up on a white stallion (isn't a skateboard cooler anyway?), he might be the one who can make you happy now.

dealing with
dad

In childhood, a girl's father is often her ideal man—the one she looks up to and is just like the one she plans to someday marry. But adolescence brings a different perspective. The myth of the perfect man takes a hard hit. As you grow older, you realize that your dad is just a regular guy. He doesn't know everything, he can't defend you from the entire world, and sometimes he's even downright wrong! A gaping chasm has opened between the superhero you have built up in your head and the reality of the normal man who picks you up from cheerleading practice.

Dad, I promise I'll call you every hour on the hour to tell you how the party is.

And I'll be home at twelve sharp.

This new perception can sometimes turn girls against their fathers. If Daddy can't do *every*thing, then maybe he can't do *any*thing. The relationship changes. And as with every change in a family, everyone has to be aware of what everyone else is going through. For fathers, this can be particularly tough. When you were a little girl, you needed a larger-than-life image of your dad to help build your own identity. But now you need to accept that your father is an ordinary guy. And you have to make room for the future guys in your life.

A natural distance starts to occur between you and your dad. But even though that distance is natural, it can also be painful. The most important thing is for Dad to remain a part of your life. While your relationship is changing and you might need some healthy space, you also need to know that he loves you unconditionally and is looking out for you. He was the first man to tell you how special you are, and his opinion about you and your life still carries great weight. So when he dares to criticize your boyfriends or frowns upon your outfits, it bugs you.

You need to realize that in the eyes of a father, even though you're growing up, you're still a little angel to be kept safe from harm. Your dad knows exactly what boys are like (he is one!) and he worries they'll break your heart. He may even be right about some of the boys in your life, but since you want to learn life lessons on your own, you probably tell him to mind his own business and stop being so protective. But try to cut Dad a little bit of slack—he's trying to accept the fact that you're becoming a woman. And his watchful eye can also help you feel more confident and secure as you go through the many changes of being a teenager.

the
tease

The tease actually plays an important role in the world of girls. What people hold against her is her compulsive need to tempt any boy who comes within a million miles of her. You know the girl: tight jeans, low-cut shirt, batting eyelashes. You hate the way she smiles innocently at the boys and pretends like she's a helpless victim. Or the way she makes suggestive comments and throws herself all over any member of the male species. Somehow the boys rush to carry her books or help her with her homework. They seem to be automatically pulled in by her sex appeal.

Her favorite thing is to go for boys who are already taken. They provide her with a chance to show she's the sexiest girl of all. In order to demonstrate her power, she'll try anything to steal your boyfriend. If you're friends with a tease, you always have to be on your guard. She might care about your friendship, but sadly, her triumph over men is more important. She needs male attention in order to feel better about herself.

Though you might think the tease is a parasite we'd be better off without, she serves a purpose. First of all, she's a model for how to deal with boys—or rather how *not* to deal with them. You can learn a lot by watching a tease, both tricks that always work and techniques that always fall flat. It might be useful information for you to see how the boys swoon when a tease tosses her hair or smiles adoringly! But it's important to know that games ultimately don't pay off when trying to catch a boy's attention. None of her quick tricks can make a relationship work in the long run.

Fact No. 2

If you eat a burger and fries for dinner, ordering a diet soda to go with them is not watching your weight.

big
sisters

You share the same parents, you once shared the same toys, and you continue to share the best laugh attacks. She's the person who knows you best. She immediately notices when your eyes are sparkling or when your chin starts to quiver, signaling tears are to follow. When you were little, you admired her. You tried on her clothes and you sprayed yourself with her new perfume. You did what she said because she protected you. You imitated her.

She also did everything first. She was the first one to slam the door in your dad's face and scream, "I don't care!"; the first one to wear makeup and fashionable clothes; the first one to go out with a boy. She was your role model. But sometimes you don't want a model, because you need to do things your own way or be the first one to accomplish something all by yourself. She might be the older one, but now you're growing up, too.

There comes a time when you don't feel like being defined by your relationship to your sister anymore. You want to be yourself. Outside of your family, the rest of the world gives you this opportunity. The outside world does not compare you to your sister—you can be the best at dance, math, making jokes, charming boys, whatever you want.

But being at home isn't so easy. When your big sister tells you what to do or treats you like a child, sometimes you rebel. You don't want to always be forced into the little-sister role. You want her to recognize you as her equal.

It's only natural that you don't want your big sister to boss you around anymore, and therefore some big fights might be occurring. You might say some nasty things back and forth to each other, but it's important to read between the lines. When she makes you feel like a child or orders you around, she might really be trying to say, "Don't you love me like you used to? You used to idolize me but now you don't listen to me at all!" And when you ignore her or yell at her to stop making you feel like a baby, you might really be saying, "I will always look up to you, but I want you to be proud of my own accomplishments and see me as more grown-up."

Some parts of the big sister/little sister dynamic will always be there—probably for the rest of your life. She will want to nurture you and look out for you, and you will look to her for her opinion and encouragement. But as you both grow older, your friendship will grow, too. And as you go down different paths and make your own decisions, you will learn to lean on each other as equals.

the
future

Getting married and starting a family might be far in the future, but it's still a major concern of yours. Unlike boys, who probably don't worry about wives or babies at all, teenage girls start envisioning their future lives early on. You wonder: What kind of wedding dress do I want? What will my husband look like? What will I name my children? Where will we live? Even if it's all a fun fantasy, the idea of marriage and motherhood is part of how girls think about their futures from a relatively early age.

Why are girls and boys so different this way? Well, education plays a significant role. Just take a look at the toys made specifically for girls and you'll realize the message they deliver: dolls to coddle and take care of like a mommy in training, toy dishes setting the stage for dinner or tea parties, frilly pink things to make you think you have to be pretty all the time. From an early age, society teaches girls to acquire the qualities of a dedicated mother and good housewife.

At school, we're expected to be organized and take better care of our notebooks, have nice penmanship, and be nicer to our classmates. A boy who gets in a fight during recess is considered to be a tough little guy who knows what he wants. But a girl who fights back and speaks her mind is often considered bad. Girls are supposed to be gentle and motherly.

And though people say society has evolved so that men and women are equal, 80 percent of housework (grocery shopping, cooking, laundry, cleaning, etc.) is still done by women. The same lack of balance applies to child care: fathers dedicate an average of twelve hours and forty-one minutes per week to their children, while mothers devote twenty-five hours and thirty-seven minutes. With a model like this, it's not surprising that girls are trained to think about marriage and children. We're taught to believe that family life will take up a significant amount of our time in the future.

But many girls don't want the traditional "female role" of mother and wife. And there's no reason why you should have to go down that path if you don't want to. Marriage and parenthood might work for lots of people, but it's not a requirement of adulthood. However, what is a requirement is being able to stay true to yourself and following the road that makes you happy. Lots of people choose the traditional path because they think that's what society expects of them or they are afraid to stand out. It's fine if you're fantasizing about your perfect white wedding dress and a picket fence, but if you want to walk down the aisle in leather pants while a rock band plays behind you, well that's cool, too! Or maybe eloping in Las Vegas is more your style, or never marrying at all. Maybe you want five kids or maybe you have no desire to be a parent. Being an adult is about making your own decisions and being the person you want to be, because no one else can live your life for you.

the
beauty myth

It's a mystery. How come that girl who doesn't make the slightest effort to be fashionable or who isn't particularly pretty or sexy (at least as far as other girls can tell) gets all the boys without even trying? What is it about her that makes her so attractive?

All you need to do is turn on the TV or pick up a magazine to see there are established beauty standards. Currently, tall, thin women are seen as beautiful. Throw in some blond hair, big boobs, and full lips—even better! Ambitious actresses and models try to stick to this image as closely as possible. Women even have plastic surgery such as breast implants or silicone injections to try to achieve an unattainable standard of beauty. But the truth is, not everyone looks like Angelina Jolie or Blake Lively. And you don't need to.

Every time period has its own standards. In the nineteenth century, American women were supposed to be pudgy, with pearl-white skin and small feet. In the seventies, the stick figure was in: no butt and no breasts. In North Africa in the early twentieth century, girls old enough to get married ate bread dipped in olive oil to make sure they were beautifully fat on their wedding day. If you look at women in Renaissance paintings, you'll see they had round figures that would make many of us today self-conscious in our jeans. In short, beauty varies from one era to the next, and one country

to the next. We're taught what is beautiful by society, and then we try to emulate it.

OK, fine, you get that part, but how come boys still like certain girls right from the start? And sometimes these aren't the girls who look like supermodels but the ones who seem to possess some other kind of mysterious quality.

Well, you've answered your own question. Maybe the girl doesn't match her era's beauty standards—she may even reject its codes by refusing to wear sexy clothes or work out to make her body look a certain way. But she has her own unique beauty and she's proud of it. Being relaxed and comfortable in your own skin always makes a greater impression than a push-up bra or highlights. Confidence in yourself and security in who you are is the greatest turn-on.

What sets the confident, unique girls apart from the traditionally attractive ones is charm. Charm is invisible—you can't get it at the makeup counter or the hair salon or the plastic surgeon's office. It doesn't cost a thing, and its effects are magical. It doesn't matter if a girl has a couple extra pounds around the middle, frizzy hair, or a big nose—she's still attractive if she's comfortable with her own looks and proud of them. Isn't it reassuring to know that while you might not look like Halle Berry, you still have the potential to always be charming? So flaunt the characteristics that make you who you are and embrace the fabulous you!

party time!

Where most boys take two minutes to throw on a pair of jeans, a T-shirt, and sneakers, when girls have to choose an outfit for a party or event, they spend hours debating what to wear and trying on clothes. A girl's bedroom before a party could look like a disaster zone—numerous pairs of balled-up jeans on the floor, half-unbuttoned dresses thrown across the bed, inside-out T-shirts sprawled out everywhere. Why? Because parties are the ideal opportunity for girls to test two fundamental things.

The first is whether they can attract boys. It's totally normal to fantasize about meeting a boy at a party and getting a date. Sometimes you even plan your outfit or hairstyle weeks in advance in hopes of standing out or looking cool. You think if you look a certain way, all the boys will fall at your feet.

The second reason girls take such care in preparing their outfits is to impress other girls. Sometimes you spend more time at a party sizing up the other girls than you do looking for cute boys. Unfortunately, looking good can be a competition among girls, and winning this game can sometimes be more important than getting a guy to ask you to dance.

While boys might settle rivalries with their fists, girls face off with more subtle weapons. This doesn't mean the battle is any less ferocious! Criticism of your outfit or some girl telling you your jeans look too tight is often more damaging than a punch in the nose. So what's the best way to make yourself feel confident and beautiful when you go to your next party?

Let's face it, sometimes getting ready for the party can be more fun than the party itself. If you don't trust your mother's or sister's advice, now is the time to call in the experts: your friends! Get ready for the party together—your friends will love coming over for a wardrobe consultation and will expect you to do the same. Have a little pre-party: put on your favorite music, lay out your outfit selections, select your potential perfume or makeup options, and start trying it all on! You can help your friends apply eyeliner or fix one another's hair, and the best part is you get to hang out and talk with your friends. You'll see they have all the same insecurities and fears that you do. They worry about whether or not their butt looks good in their jeans and whether their lip gloss is the right shade, too. Now is the time to have fun and support one another. And if you're with your friends, any party will be a success.

keepsakes

If Brad Pitt gave you an autograph, you'd probably tape it up on the wall over your bed, right? Do you sometimes rip photos of celebrities out of magazines and keep them in your drawer so you can gaze at them in private? Do you ever search out videos endlessly on YouTube so you can watch your favorite rock stars in concert, singing your favorite song to you over and over? If you do these things for your celebrity crush, it's not so hard to believe that you might behave this way with your crush at school. Maybe he lent you his pencil in math class and you sneakily put it in your purse so you could keep it. Maybe you bought a certain CD because you know it's his favorite band. Maybe you even grabbed a note he wrote out of the trash so you could study his handwriting and see what he said.

To boys, this sounds crazy. Why would girls want to keep meaningless little objects? Isn't a thrown-away piece of paper just some garbage? The truth is, for girls, these objects mean something. They are reminders of the person and clues to who he might be inside. Girls want to create a bond with the people they admire or have crushes on. These keepsakes help us to feel a connection to someone and to fantasize about our potential love story with him. Also, if we don't really know what the object of our affection is like, these mementos help him feel more real to us.

Another reason for holding on to these little treasures is to show them to other girls. Keepsakes act as living proof of a "relationship." You want to tell your girlfriends every detail of your date from Friday night—so of course you keep the stub of your movie ticket! You show them the text messages he sent you asking you out. Or maybe you keep a dried flower from the corsage you wore to the homecoming dance. Each object will recall a place, a day, or an event, allowing us to put what we experienced into words. Our girlfriends—the audience—will listen breathlessly (and a little enviously) to our passionate tales.

There's nothing wrong with having keepsakes. But remember, you can't keep everything. And what's even more exciting than keeping a photograph of the captain of the football team under your pillow is actually talking to him and seeing if he's worth your time. How about spending time with your new boyfriend instead of just rereading all his e-mails?

Fact No. 3

Never laugh at a boy when he asks you out. Because your laughter could cause many tears.

I guess you can give me your heart

YES!

saying no

The answer is simple. If you don't want to do something with a boy, you should say no to his offer. There are no obligations on the road to love. For something to happen, both people have to want it. A boy's desire to do something, *anything*, should never take precedence over a girl's desire not to do it. Whether we're talking about having a soda, going on a date to the school dance, kissing, touching, or anything more, if you don't want to do it, just say NO!

And if you think that saying yes when you don't want to is a way of being nice or not hurting someone's feelings, you're wrong. It's wrong because you aren't being true to yourself and because you're deceiving someone else. Why lead someone on or let someone think you feel a certain way if you don't—it's only going to cause more trouble for you later. As hard as saying no might be, it's better to get it all out in the open right from the start. Everyone is responsible for knowing what he or she wants, not for making everyone else happy.

Life isn't about being nice, it's about being true. Boy-girl relations may have changed over the years, but girls are often still stuck in the role of wanting to be nice and not hurting someone else, to their own peril. Girls often have a difficult time stating what they want for themselves. All these reasons can make it hard to say no.

On the other hand, it's also possible that you simply aren't ready yet for what a boy is proposing. In this case, the answer can be different. Maybe it's not a flat-out no, but "I'd like to wait," or "I'm not ready for that yet." Whether it's kissing, touching, or more, girls may feel the need to know a boy better, to trust him, and be sure of their feelings for him before going further. Whatever the reason may be, it's valid. No means no. If the boy doesn't want to wait, it means he isn't worthy of whatever the girl was getting ready to one day give him.

Some young guys like to pretend they're "lady-killers." They imitate what they think are macho attitudes and expressions because they think they'll impress girls this way. They also might make girls feel bad about themselves for saying no. Any boy who suggests a girl is immature or inadequate for saying no, or who gets angry and tries to force a girl to do something because his own "needs" are more important than hers, is a big loser. Girls should not be abused by this type of behavior, EVER! Boys usually act this way because they are insecure with themselves or their own ability to attract girls. If a boy was so sure of himself, he wouldn't try to force you to do anything.

Can I?

If I let you kiss me, then will you like me?

There's no timetable. Everyone is ready for different things at different times. So once again, all you need to do is be true to yourself.

self-
consciousness

Self-consciousness is a bad feeling you experience because you're uncomfortable with your appearance. You hide because you feel like you don't look how you're supposed to. Modesty, on the other hand, is a conscious choice: "I don't show my body to others because I don't want to, or because I don't feel the need to reveal myself that much." Though the result may outwardly be the same, these two ideas are different. Your own level of modesty is whatever is right for you. Some girls feel comfortable in form-fitting jeans and tops, others don't. Some girls feel comfortable changing for gym class in front of others, and some girls need to go change in private in the bathroom stall.

A few years back, you were always delighted to go to the pool with your friends. All you thought about was underwater sneak attacks and triple back-flip championships. Times have changed. The idea of being seen in a bathing suit may well have become a real source of anxiety for you. The problem isn't so much that boys might see you, but that *everybody* is looking at you. You'd love to strut along the edge of the pool, pretending like you don't care how you look, but instead you cover up and stand back, afraid that people are criticizing you.

It's the same thing at home. To avoid any comments from your family (even if they're compliments), some girls start wearing oversize sweaters or T-shirts and lock themselves in the bathroom when they need to change their clothes. They can't stand people coming into their room without knocking, for fear that they'll be caught undressing. They're disturbed by their changing bodies: hair growing in new places, hips and breasts getting bigger and rounder. These changes are all totally normal—it's what every girl goes through to become a woman—but sometimes it makes you feel like an alien.

Remember: boys go through this, too. Their voices start to change, they suddenly need to shave (or worry because they don't), and suddenly their feet outgrow the rest of their body. Some guys grow tall and muscular, others feel scrawny and inadequate. Sometimes it's comforting to know that everyone is feeling like her or his body is out of control. Everyone is trying to get to know a new body. And as with every new encounter, you need time to adapt and change. You have to get used to yourself and get to know yourself. Don't be shy to take a good look at yourself and to make the adjustments you need to feel good in your new body. For example, maybe some of the clothes you used to wear don't look right anymore and you need to try new things. Or maybe now you can finally hold up that strapless dress you always wanted. In any event, you need to find what is right for you.

Fact No. 4

Beware of homemade
beauty remedies

getting your
period

There are times when girls wish they could be boys, because boys seem to have it so easy. . . . Even though we were all impatient to get our periods, so that we could join the group who already had them, we soon regretted that we now had to calculate whether or not we could accept an invitation to go to the swimming pool. Along with getting our periods came days of cramps and feeling bloated, and even the occasional mood swing.

If you look at it scientifically, your period is just the elimination of a mucus membrane, lining the wall of the uterus, which would have housed an impregnated egg if it had been fertilized. But in a girl's day-to-day life, everything is a lot more complicated. Menstruation is a totally normal thing, yet it always seems to be veiled in secrecy. When you think about, it's really silly that girls use funny expressions to refer to their periods, as if they were ashamed of them. It doesn't help that many of the advertisements you see on TV or in magazines can make you feel like having your period is some kind of curse. Getting your period is a biological reality, and every woman has to deal with it. There's nothing to hide or feel embarrassed about.

Though it's natural to be a little modest about your body and totally under-standable that you don't want to broadcast that you've got your period to the entire school, it's about time that girls today relaxed a little and were able to experience that time of the month as nothing more than a slightly uncomfort-able physiological phenomenon.

dealing with

mom

Lately, she's been really hard to take. Hardly an hour goes by without her making some kind of comment about the state of your room, the clothes you wear, or how much time you spend on the phone with your girl-friends. Even worse, you just want a little space but feel like it's impossible to have any privacy at home.

Until recently, you did whatever your mother told you. Sometimes you negotiated a little, but she always had the last word. But now you're older and you have more and more trouble tolerating her telling you what to do. You're becoming independent. You feel like it's your life and you're the one who knows what's good for you. This is a new situation for both of you. Your mother is sud-denly faced with a teenager who is behaving in a new, rebellious way, and you are suddenly feeling the need to act out and stand up for yourself in ways you haven't before.

When Mom's comments are about your body, tension hits an all-time high—"You're wearing too much makeup," "You can't go out dressed like that," "Who was that boy you were with downstairs?" There comes a point where you no longer hear these words as the advice of a protective mother and you fire right back. Yet there is often truth in what your mother tells you (certain makeup styles, outfits, or company you're keeping can do you more harm than good), and she has only your best interest in mind. But there are different ways of saying things, and sometimes mothers don't choose their words very well. Because they're afraid that you won't listen, they tend to give orders, and if there's one thing you can't take anymore, it's when she butts into your private life. So the two of you square off for a fight when a calm discussion could have led to agreement.

This new situation requires some adjustments. Although you feel like suddenly you and your mom can't relate to each other anymore, it's important to note that you actually now have more in common. You and your mother share the same gender and feminine sensibility. Your mother is an adult, and you're now becoming one. While your newfound independence might threaten your mom or make her feel like she doesn't know you anymore, this is also a time when you really need her to lean on. Because you're becoming a woman and going through so many changes (and becoming more like her in some ways), her reassurances could really mean a lot and she can answer many of your questions.

Sometimes a rivalry can also exist between mothers and daughters. It can be hard for a mother to see her daughter in sexy clothes or flirting with boys, because you used to be an innocent little girl. Similarly, daughters sometimes want to compete with their mothers to show that they are women, too. Having two women around can be difficult, but now is the time to learn from each other. Your mother can become a real friend and confidante in a way she wasn't before. She can tell you about fights she had with her best friend when she was in high school, or tell you how nervous she was when she went on her first date.

Who better than a mother to teach her daughter about getting her period, buying the right bra, first loves, and broken hearts? Never forget that before she was a mom, she was once a teenage girl. She experienced the times of doubt, anger, and excitement you're going through. No doubt she also had run-ins with her own mom. She understands a lot more than you think.

Of course, there are some things you don't want to discuss with your mother and that you prefer to talk about only with your friends. But remember, sometimes only a single glance from your mom when you're on your way out of the bathroom in a new outfit will make you feel beautiful and tell you she's proud of you. And even if the next minute she's yelling at you because your skirt is too short, no one understands you like she does.

Fact No. 5

No pair of shoes is ever worth suffering for!

first
kiss

Do you worry about your first kiss? Do you think about which way to turn your head or how to use your tongue or, most important, if you will be good at it? Sure, there are books and magazine articles and Web sites, but there's no perfect formula for how to kiss. Everyone has different styles. And until you're in the moment, you won't know exactly how to prepare for it.

Of course, it's totally normal to be scared of the first time. Every girl has her own story. There's the one who has her first kiss in a movie theater and finds it disgusting and never wants to try it again. And sometimes you think you like someone until he kisses you and then you realize you don't like him romantically at all! Another girl might kiss her crush at a party and see stars and hearts and rainbows. Or maybe a girl kisses her boyfriend good night after the school dance and suddenly wishes she could kiss someone else. There are as many stories as you have friends. Kissing a boy is such a big deal because for most girls it's the first intimate physical contact they've had with someone in a romantic way. It's based on your desire (you know, those butterflies in your stomach) and provides both of you with a new kind of pleasure. It also teaches you something new about yourself—what you like or don't like or what you may be looking for.

Though there are no foolproof recipes for kissing a boy, there's one thing you have to remember for your first kiss: only do it when you're really ready.

You shouldn't kiss someone just because your friends might have done it already. Instead, you have to take your time and carefully choose the one with whom you'll share this moment. First kisses are important: even if you'll kiss other guys in the future, this one will always have a special place in your memory. So pick a boy who's worthy! The essential condition for a successful kiss is desire. You should want to kiss him and not ever have to force yourself. (Because then it will be totally gross.) Always *feel* that it's the right time. If it's the right time, it's sure to be *much* more fun.

Kissing someone you love is like breathing. Do you ask yourself how to breathe? Do you tell yourself, "I need to inhale and exhale to make sure I don't suffocate?" No. Your body doesn't need your brain for that. It's the same for kissing: things happen naturally. A girl who's in love doesn't need to think about where to put her tongue or how to tilt her head. If you're in the moment, it will just flow, and everything will be fine.

unhealthy
comparisons

As girls enter adolescence and their bodies begin to change (on average, an additional six inches and twenty pounds), they sometimes feel like they're seeing an alien when they look at themselves in the mirror. Their bodies no longer look like the ones they've known all their lives. This can make them feel uncomfortable, or worse, many girls start not liking themselves anymore. Suddenly, all they see is a bump on their nose they didn't have before or a flat chest while other girls are filling up their bras. The good news is that you are not alone. All girls feel this way at some point during adolescence. Girls complain that their butts are too big or not big enough. Or they complain about whatever other features they're worried about. But the thing to remember is just because you can't see past your bra size or how many pimples are on your chin, the truth is, you're the only person who is scrutinizing yourself this closely. Most people are so worried about their own insecurities, they're not even noticing the fact that you're having a bad hair day.

As if comparing yourself to your friends wasn't bad enough, you also have glossy magazines and hip television shows telling you what's beautiful. You know it's not realistic to try to look like a model (let's face it, there are very few women who actually work as models), but you can't help wishing you did look like them. You see their perfect skin, long legs, lack of cellulite, flat stomachs, gorgeous hair, and flawless faces, and you think something must be wrong with you. After obsessing over magazines for years, some girls come to think there's only one way to be beautiful: plastic surgery. Round out the tip of your nose, add a cup size to your breasts, do a little tuck here and there . . . STOP!

Before you start thinking that models just naturally look so perfect, there's something you need to know. The models that you see in the pages of magazines don't really exist. Most magazine covers are actually digital creations. In real life, models are just like the rest of us, with greasy hair, the occasional zit in the middle of their forehead, and boyfriends who dump them. But unlike us, when they get their picture taken, they're handed over to an army of hair dressers, makeup artists, and stylists who get paid a lot of money to make them look good and cover up their every flaw. And once they look as good as they can, their photos are still airbrushed so that their faces are without any flaws and the dimples in their thighs disappear.

OK, you get that part, but you still think they've got it easier than you do. But at what price? Diets, appetite suppressants, anorexia, and the constant threat of being let go by the modeling agency if they put on the slightest bit of weight or if their look isn't "in" anymore. That doesn't sound like a very fun job, does it? Perhaps models are trained to be even more insecure than the rest of us.

So what can we girls do?

We can make the most of the bodies we have. We can learn how to display our bodies at their best and cleverly adapt our look to maximize our assets and minimize our flaws. Sometimes we even attract people with the very features we're most insecure about. Yup, that bump on your nose, the round hips, big butt, flat chest, or prominent forehead might be exactly what somebody likes about you or thinks sets you apart from all the rest. Sometimes our imperfections are exactly what make us beautiful.

And here's another secret: boys don't just like the skinny girls they see in magazines. Five or ten pounds will not make the difference in whether or not a boy wants to go out with you. Boys like curves and think they're sexy—so don't go on a juice fast because you think you need to suffer to get a date.

your
best friend

Your best friend is a very important player in your life. She is your confidante, the sister you choose for yourself (unlike the one your parents stuck you with!), and her opinion means the world to you. You can tell her anything and share everything. She revels in your successes and comforts you when you're down. You fantasize about boys together and criticize the ones

who hurt you. She knows you better than anyone (considering how much time you spend on the phone or IMing, that's no surprise).

Sometimes the outside world or the hallways of school can be a really scary place, or even a hostile one. Your best friend is your ally. You know she will always defend you and be on your side. With just a knowing smile or certain look, she can comfort you and assure you that you're not alone.

If someone asked you why you chose her out of the sea of girls around you, you might be able to explain exactly how and why you became best friends, or maybe it just naturally happened over time and you can't really explain it at all.

The point is, you don't look for a best friend, you find her. When you two get to know each other and hang out, it all just clicks. It's a powerful feeling and a real relationship that demands availability, attention, and loyalty. Obviously, with that level of emotional investment, just as in romantic love, there can sometimes be turbulence—miscommunications, disagreements, and the danger of "breaking up."

Even if you love your best friend better than anyone, it's not unusual for you to "un-love" her from time to time. Maybe she was too busy to hear about that bad math test, or she had a date with a boy she didn't tell you about, or she made a slightly cutting comment about your makeup. Sometimes these little things can make you feel betrayed and you reevaluate the whole relationship! Suddenly, the girl you would have trusted with anything no longer seems

worthy. You yell and cry because she wasn't there when you needed her or you feel like she's leaving you out.

Why does this feel so terrible? Because she is your best friend! She understands you best, so when she lets you down, it feels like the greatest loss. It's like that old saying "You only hurt the ones you love." It's because she does know you so well and cares about you so much that she has the power to also hurt you deeply. If you didn't love each other, there wouldn't be anything to lose. And remember: you can't know so much about someone and share everything and still agree all the time. It's only because you understand each other so well that sometimes tensions can rise. The good news is, most fights are temporary, and if you keep talking and put yourselves in each other's shoes, you can always reconcile when you hit a rough patch.

be
yourself

Have you ever rolled your eyes at a girl in class when you notice how her thong is intentionally pulled up high out of her jeans? Or do you ever snicker at girls your age who wear provocative clothing or makeup? You notice how the boys stare at a colorful bra strap that hangs out under a girl's tank top or how their eyes follow the string of that obvious thong and land on the most fleshy part of the body. You think to yourself, why do they need to dress that way? Why is attracting boys so important all the time? And what's so wrong with normal white cotton underwear?

Or maybe you are that girl who buys a leopard-print thong and makes sure the class can see it peeking out from under your clothes. Maybe it makes you feel powerful or more mature than the other girls. Some girls feel sexy or grown-up if they show off their clothes or what's underneath, but does it really make them more sophisticated or more of a woman than the rest? No.

When your body changes during adolescence and you no longer look like a little girl, you wonder who you are and ask yourself lots of questions about your femininity. Sometimes you need things like hot pink underwear or a lace bra to make you feel more attractive. You're also starting to feel the need to be looked at and to entice guys. You want them to give you attention. But you also might sometimes feel like hiding under a baggy T-shirt or jean jacket.

Sometimes being a girl is a real pain . . .

Everyone wants to feel desirable sometimes. Maybe you think if you buy the whole Victoria's Secret catalog then people will stop seeing you as a little girl and look at you as a woman. This is all perfectly normal. But make sure the things you choose to wear will show off your best assets and will not make a show of you. You can wear the clothes that make you happy, but be true to yourself and not to some idea of what girls are supposed to look like to attract boys.

Our grandmothers' generation fought hard for women to freely express themselves and be in control of their bodies and to stop being considered as objects. Of course, clothes and underwear seem harmless enough, but they shouldn't turn us into caricatures. It's not your low-cut neckline or your heels that make you desirable, it's who you are and how you feel about yourself that do. Clothes and accessories just give you a helping hand.

Femininity isn't measured by the size of a Wonderbra or the length of your eyelashes. It's not about whether you wear sexy panties or boy shorts, because we're all the same underneath. It's our hearts and minds that set us apart from the others, and as we said before, femininity doesn't come in a bottle that you can buy in a department store. Being attractive or sexy is much more mysterious than that thong peeking out of your jeans. Confidence in who you really are is more powerful than any perfume.

Fact No. 6

Size is just a number. Don't break a sweat trying to fit into a size 6 because you think the number sounds good. Buy a pair of jeans that fits you right, and if you don't like the size on the tag, just cut it out.

suggestions for further reading

Books

Bell, Ruth. *Changing Bodies, Changing Lives: A Book for Teens on Sex and Relationships*. New York: Three Rivers Press, 1998.

Burningham, Sarah O'Leary. *How to Raise Your Parents: A Teen Girl's Survival Guide*. San Francisco: Chronicle Books, 2008.

———. *Boyology: A Teen Girl's Crash Course in All Things Boy*. San Francisco: Chronicle Books, 2009.

Ford, Amanda. *Be True to Yourself: A Daily Guide for Teenage Girls*. Berkeley, CA: Conari Press, 2000.

Fox, Annie and Ruth Kirschner. *Too Stressed To Think? A Teen Guide to Staying Sane When Life Makes You Crazy*. Minneapolis, MN: Free Spirit Publishing, Inc., 2005.

Haag, Pamela. *Voices of a Generation: Teenage Girls on Sex, School, and Self*. New York: Marlowe and Company, 2000.

Weston, Carol. *Girltalk: All the Stuff Your Sister Never Told You*. New York: HarperCollins Publishers, 2004.

Web sites

www.coolnurse.com

www.girlshealth.gov

www.gogirlworld.org

www.gURL.com

kidshealth.org

www.teenhealthfx.com

www.youngwomenshealth.org

index

Fodor's 2010

BOSTON

Where to Stay and Eat
for All Budgets

Must-See Sights
and Local Secrets

Ratings You Can Trust

Fodor's Travel Publications   New York, Toronto, London, Sydney, Auckland
www.fodors.com

FODOR'S BOSTON 2010
Editor: Kelly Kealy

Editorial Contributors: Katie Hamlin

Writers: Diane Bair, Bethany Cassin Beckerlegge, Susan MacCallum-Whitcomb, Pamela Wright

Production Editor: Carrie Parker
Maps & Illustrations: David Lindroth, Inc.; Mapping Specialists, *cartographers*; Bob Blake, Rebecca Baer, *map editors*; William Wu, *information graphics*
Design: Fabrizio LaRocca, *creative director*; Guido Caroti, Siobhan O'Hare, *art directors*; Tina Malaney, Chie Ushio, Ann McBride, Jessica Walsh, *designers*; Melanie Marin, *senior picture editor*
Cover Photo: (Copley Square, Back Bay) James Lemass
Production Manager: Amanda Bullock

ISBN 978–1–4000–0858–2

ISSN 0882-0074

SPECIAL SALES
This book is available at special discounts for bulk purchases for sales promotions or premiums. Special editions, including personalized covers, excerpts of existing books, and corporate imprints, can be created in large quantities for special needs. For more information, write to Special Markets/Premium Sales, 1745 Broadway, MD 6-2, New York, New York 10019, or e-mail specialmarkets@randomhouse.com.

AN IMPORTANT TIP & AN INVITATION
Although all prices, opening times, and other details in this book are based on information supplied to us at press time, changes occur all the time in the travel world, and Fodor's cannot accept responsibility for facts that become outdated or for inadvertent errors or omissions. So **always confirm information when it matters,** especially if you're making a detour to visit a specific place. Your experiences—positive and negative—matter to us. If we have missed or misstated something, **please write to us.** We follow up on all suggestions. Contact the Boston editor at editors@fodors.com or c/o Fodor's at 1745 Broadway, New York, NY 10019.

PRINTED IN THE UNITED STATES OF AMERICA

10 9 8 7 6 5 4 3 2 1

Be a Fodor's Correspondent

Your opinion matters. It matters to us. It matters to your fellow Fodor's travelers, too. And we'd like to hear it. In fact, we need to hear it.

When you share your experiences and opinions, you become an active member of the Fodor's community. That means we'll not only use your feedback to make our books better, but we'll publish your names and comments whenever possible. Throughout our guides, look for "Word of Mouth," excerpts of your unvarnished feedback.

Here's how you can help improve Fodor's for all of us.

Tell us when we're right. We rely on local writers to give you an insider's perspective. But our writers and staff editors—who are the best in the business—depend on you. Your positive feedback is a vote to renew our recommendations for the next edition.

Tell us when we're wrong. We're proud that we update most of our guides every year. But we're not perfect. Things change. Hotels cut services. Museums change hours. Charming cafés lose charm. If our writer didn't quite capture the essence of a place, tell us how you'd do it differently. If any of our descriptions are inaccurate or inadequate, we'll incorporate your changes in the next edition and will correct factual errors at fodors.com immediately.

Tell us what to include. You probably have had fantastic travel experiences that aren't yet in Fodor's. Why not share them with a community of like-minded travelers? Maybe you chanced upon a beach or bistro or B&B that you don't want to keep to yourself. Tell us why we should include it. And share your discoveries and experiences with everyone directly at fodors.com. Your input may lead us to add a new listing or highlight a place we cover with a "Highly Recommended" star or with our highest rating, "Fodor's Choice."

Give us your opinion instantly at our feedback center at www.fodors.com/feedback. You may also e-mail editors@fodors.com with the subject line "Boston Editor." Or send your nominations, comments, and complaints by mail to Boston Editor, Fodor's, 1745 Broadway, New York, NY 10019.

You and travelers like you are the heart of the Fodor's community. Make our community richer by sharing your experiences. Be a Fodor's correspondent.

Happy Traveling!

Tim Jarrell, Publisher

CONTENTS

MAPS

ABOUT THIS BOOK

Our Ratings

Sometimes you find terrific travel experiences and sometimes they just find you. But usually the burden is on you to select the right combination of experiences. That's where our ratings come in.

As travelers we've all discovered a place so wonderful that its worthiness is obvious. And sometimes that place is so unique that superlatives don't do it justice: you just have to be there to know. These sights, properties, and experiences get our highest rating, **Fodor's Choice,** indicated by orange stars throughout this book.

Black stars highlight sights and properties we deem **Highly Recommended,** places that our writers, editors, and readers praise again and again for consistency and excellence.

By default, there's another category: any place we include in this book is by definition worth your time, unless we say otherwise. And we will.

Disagree with any of our choices? Care to nominate a place or suggest that we rate one more highly? Visit our feedback center at www.fodors.com/feedback.

Budget Well

Hotel and restaurant price categories from ¢ to $$$$ are defined in the opening pages of our restaurant and hotel chapters. For attractions, we always give standard adult admission fees; reductions are usually available for children, students, and senior citizens. Want to pay with plastic? **AE, D, DC, MC, V** following restaurant and hotel listings indicate whether American Express, Discover, Diners Club, MasterCard, and Visa are accepted.

Restaurants

Unless we state otherwise, restaurants are open for lunch and dinner daily. We mention dress only when there's a specific requirement and reservations only when they're essential or not accepted—it's always best to book ahead.

Hotels

Hotels have private bath, phone, TV, and air-conditioning and operate on the European Plan (aka EP, meaning without meals), unless we specify that they use the Continental Plan (CP, with a continental breakfast), Breakfast Plan (BP, with a full breakfast), or Modified American Plan (MAP, with breakfast and dinner) or are all-inclusive (including all meals

and most activities). We always list facilities but not whether you'll be charged an extra fee to use them.

Many Listings
★	Fodor's Choice
★	Highly recommended
✉	Physical address
✛	Directions
⌖	Mailing address
☎	Telephone
🖷	Fax
⊕	On the Web
✐	E-mail
🎫	Admission fee
☉	Open/closed times
Ⓜ	Metro stations
▤	Credit cards

Hotels & Restaurants
🏨	Hotel
⌯	Number of rooms
⚱	Facilities
❢⦶	Meal plans
✕	Restaurant
⌂	Reservations
⚲	Smoking
🍺	BYOB
✕🏨	Hotel with restaurant that warrants a visit

Outdoors
⌘	Golf
⛺	Camping

Other
☺	Family-friendly
⇨	See also
✉	Branch address
☞	Take note

WHEN TO GO

Weather-wise, **late spring and fall** are the optimal times to visit Boston. Aside from mild temperatures, the former boasts blooming gardens throughout the city; and the latter (specifically from mid-September to early November) sees the surrounding countryside ablaze with brilliantly colored foliage. At both times, however, you should expect crowds.

Autumn, for instance, lures hordes of hopeful leaf-peepers. Students must be factored into the mix as well. More than 250,000 of them flood into Boston and Cambridge each September; then pull out again in May and June. So hotels and restaurants, especially during move-in and move-out weekends, can be packed.

The good news is that this is a four-season destination. Summer brings sailboats to Boston Harbor, concerts to the Esplanade, and café tables to assorted sidewalks. It also brings the most reliable sunshine. If you're dreaming of a classic shore vacation, summer is prime. (Of course, others also know this—which makes advance planning imperative.)

Even winter has its pleasures. The cultural season heats up when it's cold, and Boston sports a festive glow over the holidays, thanks to the thousands of lights strung around the Common, Public Garden, and Commonwealth Avenue Mall. During the post-Christmas period, temperatures continue to fall. But penny-pinchers will be pleased to know that lodging prices do, too.

Climate

Like other northeastern American cities, Boston can be uncomfortably hot and humid in summer and frigid in winter. Yet the saying here is "if you don't like the weather, just wait a moment." A gray, overcast day can quickly turn sunny and warm—or vice versa. Hence, it's best to come prepared for unseasonable spells at anytime of year.

WHAT'S WHERE

1 Beacon Hill. While important landmarks abound here in Brahmin territory, the gaslighted streets lined with classic Federal-style town houses are worth the strolling effort themselves. Two of the loveliest are Chestnut and Mt. Vernon (the latter opens onto leafy Louisburg Square, where Louisa May Alcott once wrote and John Kerry now lives).

2 The Old West End. Since urban renewal, little evidence of the old days remains save for Massachusetts General Hospital and the imposing Charles Street Jail (now the Liberty Hotel). While it's no longer a thriving immigrant enclave, it's still got the hands-on Museum of Science and TD Banknorth Garden, home of Boston's pro hockey and basketball teams and known to locals as the "Gah-den."

3 Government Center. Architects wax poetic about the Brutalist and Bauhaus structures that are the focal point of Government Center; most others just think they're ugly. Head straight to Faneuil Hall and the trio of restored market buildings that share its name. Inside Faneuil Hall Marketplace are boutiques, bars, and a food court; outside, find street performers and souvenir vendors. On Friday and Saturday, nearby Haymarket's

open-air stalls offer a less-touristy alternative.

4 The North End. Though small, Boston's oldest residential neighborhood is crammed full of history. Copp's Hill Burying Ground attests to the North End's Puritan past, and Paul Revere House and Old North Church evoke the Revolutionary Age. Yet for all the Americana, this often feels like an Italian village due to an immigration influx that began in the late 1800s. Look for *salumerias* (cured meat shops, or delis), social clubs, and authentic Italian restaurants.

5 Charlestown. The Bunker Hill Monument is a towering tribute to one of the pivotal battles of 1775, and the USS *Constitution*—the oldest commissioned ship in the U.S. fleet—is a towering tangle of masts and rigging. When Old Ironside's home was transformed in 1974 from a hardscrabble naval yard into a National Historic Site, townies moved into restored shipbuilders' quarters, and neighborhood restaurateurs went upscale.

6 Downtown. Historical places like the Old South Meeting House and Old State House are still wedged incongruously between office towers, but the Theater District (think Opera House

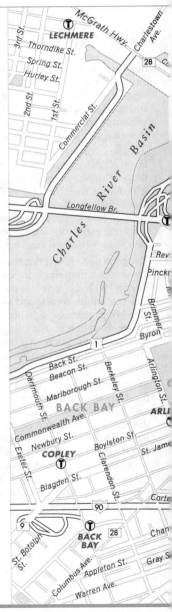

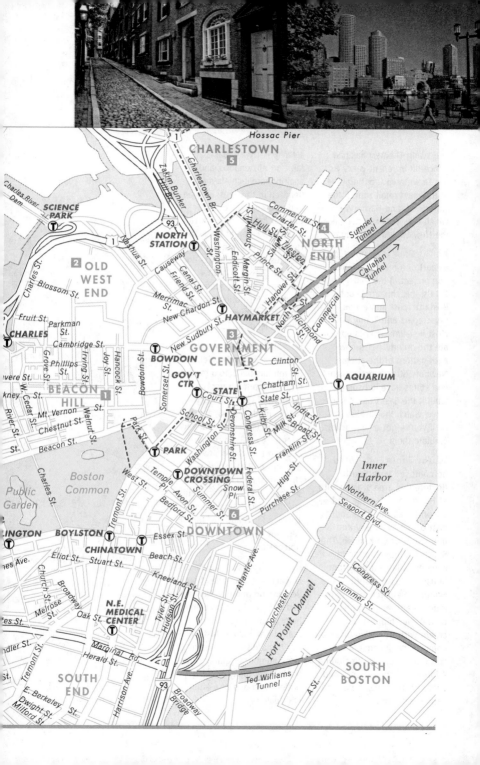

WHAT'S
WHERE

and Wang Theater) has had a face-lift in recent years, as has Downtown Crossing (one of the main retail zones), the waterfront, and HarborWalk—which runs past key sites like the New England Aquarium.

7 The Back Bay. Developed as part of a marsh reclamation project in the mid-1800s, this chic area contains Boston's most impressive skyscrapers and Trinity Church. Most first-time visitors apreciate the orderly, not-a-cowpath pattern of the streets. Newbury Street's many high-end stores have led some to label it the East Coast's Rodeo Drive; watch the fashionistas or, if you've got deep pockets, emulate them.

8 The South End. Not to be confused with South Boston, this area starts south of Huntington Avenue and encompasses the area southeast of the Back Bay and due south of Chinatown. The South End has enough lavishly embellished bowfront houses to earn a spot in the National Register of Historic Places—and enough style to win the "hippest hood" crown with its active arts community, dynamic multicultural population (including a large gay contingent), and some of the city's most innovative restaurants.

9 The Fenway. Baseball fans, art aficionados, and aspiring intellectuals meet head-on in the Fens: a meandering green space that is the first link in Frederick Law Olmsted's Emerald Necklace. Here you'll find Fenway Park, the Museum of Fine Arts and Isabella Stewart Gardner Museum, and a peppering of academic institutions including Boston University and Harvard Medical School.

10 South Boston and the Streetcar Suburbs. South Boston has become a magnet for museum hoppers: The Institute of Contemporary Art debuted in 2006, and the Children's Museum reopened after a $45-million redo in 2007. At this writing, the Boston Tea Party Ships & Museum should reopen in summer 2010. Further afield are the Arnold Arboretum in Jamaica Plain and the John F. Kennedy Library & Museum in Dorchester.

11 Cambridge. A separate city across the Charles from Boston and home to Harvard and MIT, Cambridge has long been a haven for writers, radicals, and iconoclasts. The city has a disproportionately large number of quirky cafés, bookshops, funky clothing outlets, and one-of-a-kind craft galleries.

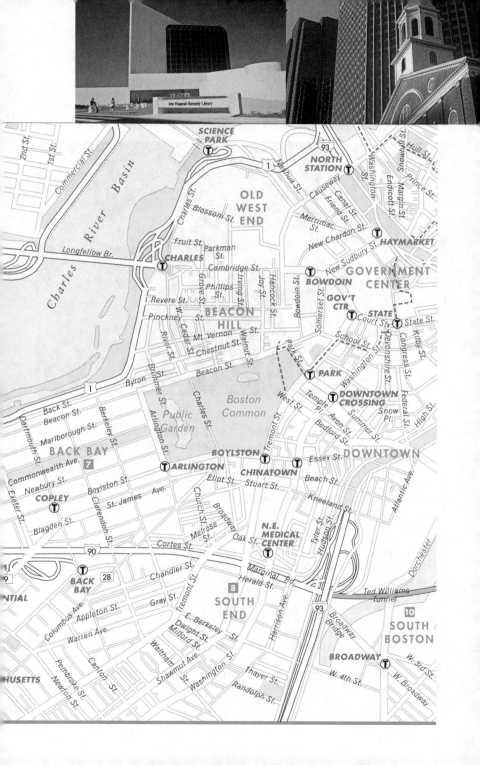

QUINTESSENTIAL BOSTON

History 101

Boston may no longer be the "Hub of the Universe," yet it *is* the undisputed epicenter of American history. Much of the political ferment that spawned the nation took place here, and visitors are often awed by the concentration of sites. Locals, on the other hand, take them in stride. Sure, they revere Revere as much as the next guy. But to Bostonians, the past isn't abstract. Rather, it is woven into the fabric of daily life. Families routinely picnic on the same Common where Puritans grazed their cows; and the faithful still worship in Old North Church, where two lanterns were fatefully hung on the night of April 18, 1775. Community activists, similarly, follow Sam Adams's example by debating hot topics in Faneuil Hall; while bookworms continue to gravitate, as Ralph Waldo Emerson and his transcendentalist buddies did, to the Boston Public Library.

Cultural Encounters

The 17th-century Puritans dubbed Boston the City on a Hill; 18th-century patriots called it the Cradle of Liberty. To 19th-century arts lovers, however, it was the highly cultured Athens of America. Today Boston still packs quite a cultural punch. For instance, Symphony Hall (a Victorian showpiece with unparalleled acoustics) is widely considered to be one of the world's finest concert venues. And that's just the tip of the artistic iceberg. As part of the Fenway Cultural District, Symphony Hall counts among its neighbors such venerable institutions as the New England Conservatory of Music, the Huntington Theatre Company, the Mary Baker Eddy Library, the Isabella Stewart Gardner Museum, and the Museum of Fine Arts. All offer free public access during the annual "Opening Our Doors Day" in October and at various other points in the year.

Boston is a welcoming city, big on heart and beauty. But fitting in here involves more than dropping your Rs and taking the T (as the Massachusetts Bay Transportation Authority is affectionately called). To understand Boston, you must first understand what makes Bostonians tick ...

The Red Sox

The "Red Sox Nation" doesn't have a representative at the U.N, but its citizens couldn't be more fervent if they did. Though Bostonians are wild about their football, hockey, and basketball teams, only the Sox can bring the entire town to its feet—or its knees. Want to see what the fuss is about? Tickets to watch the 2004 and 2007 World Series winners are hard to come by, so savvy fans reserve online ASAP. Procrastinators may get lucky at the Fenway Park ticket office next to Gate A, which opens at 10 AM. If you strike out there, a limited number of tickets are sold at Gate C two hours before game time. Alternately, you can sidle up to a guy holding out tickets just after game time, and haggle. Once inside, be prepared to don a Red Sox cap, down a Fenway frank, and sing along to "Sweet Caroline," in the eighth inning.

Wicked Good Food

Boston's independent restaurant scene is on par with New York, San Francisco, and Chicago. So while history buffs look back fondly on a certain tea party, foodies simply look forward to dinner. For all the talk of cod and beans, the area lays claim to a long line of "celebrity chefs:" M. Sanzian (remembered largely as the inventor of Boston cream pie) made quite a stir in the mid-1800s and, a century later, Julia Child launched a culinary revolution from her Cambridge kitchen. These days it's Todd English, Lydia Shire, Ming Tsai, Gordon Hamersley, Jasper White, and Michael Schlow who make eating out a gastronomic adventure. The ideal time to taste their wares and try up-and-coming competitors is during Restaurant Week (held in August and March) when more than 100 participating eateries prepare three-course prix-fixe menus for as little as $20.

IF YOU LIKE

City Walks

In a compact place where streets often evolved from cow paths and colonial lanes, driving is no simple task—which may explain why the first U.S. subway was built here in 1897. Still, "America's Walking City" is best seen on foot. So grab some good shoes and start exploring.

See Red. The logical first step is to follow the red stripe that marks the famed Freedom Trail (⇨ "Following the Freedom Trail" box in Chapter 1). Starting in Boston Common, this 2½-mi path winds through the city connecting 16 Revolutionary-era sites; among them, Paul Revere's home and Samuel Adams's burial place. Join one of the free National Park Service tours or honor the patriots' spirit by doing the route independently.

Go Green. In 1878 renowned landscape architect Frederick Law Olmsted started work on the Emerald Necklace—six jewel-like parks strung together by a greenway. Though the Common and Public Garden predate his designs, they're connected to them by the Commonwealth Avenue Mall, creating an urban oasis that extends 7 mi past meadows, manicured flowerbeds, and marshy ponds from Downtown to Dorchester. ☎617/522–2700 ⊕www.emeraldnecklace.org.

Take a Walk on the Waterside. Boston's 47-mi HarborWalk allows convenient access to favorite waterfront attractions (like the New England Aquarium), plus picturesque piers, working wharves, even urban beaches. If you only have an hour, download HarborWalk's free audio guide and stroll from Christopher Columbus Park to the new Institute of Contemporary Art on Fan Pier. ☎617/482–1722 ⊕www.bostonharborwalk.com.

Sports

In Beantown you can mark off the seasons by checking the sports lineup. Avid spectators know that the "Boys of Summer" arrive in spring and that the bearish Bruins come out of hibernation in the fall. However, it's easy to get a sports fix in any season.

Touch Base. Small but mighty Fenway, the oldest major league park, is a pilgrimage site for baseball fans, and year-round tours (☎617/226–6666 ⊕boston.redsox.mlb.com) provide the ultimate insider's view. You'll get a firsthand look at the press box, dugout seats, Pesky's Pole, and—when schedules permit—the fabled Green Monster. It's as close as you'll get to this beloved field without being drafted into the MLB.

Visit the Secret Garden. Prefer Bobby Orr or Larry Bird over Ted Williams? Seek out the Sports Museum (☎617/624–1234 ⊕www.sportsmuseum.org) in TD Banknorth Garden. The Bruins and Celtics get home advantage here (one popular exhibit, for example, is a hockey penalty box). But there's also artwork, equipment, and archival footage relating to Boston's other pro teams, as well as Olympic medalists and Marathon winners.

Have a Ball. Football fans will get a kick out of visiting Gillette Stadium in Foxborough. It is home turf for the Super Bowl–winning New England Patriots and the focal point of Patriot Place (⊕www.patriot-place.com): a new state-of-the-art entertainment complex that houses interactive football-theme exhibits and the Patriots Hall of Fame.

Multicultural Experiences

The Brits who founded Boston back in 1630 understandably get a lot of press. Nevertheless, they represent only the first of many immigrant groups who helped shape this city. So don't leave without seeing some of its lively ethnic enclaves.

Get Your Irish Up. All the Boston Celtics aren't basketball players. For proof, simply take the Irish Heritage Trail (☎ *617/696–9880* ⊕ *www.irishheritagetrail.com*). It's a self-guided, 3-mi walk covering sites associated with prominent Irish-Americans from John Hancock (who knew!?) to JFK, as well as the everyday folks who were forced from their homeland by the 1840s Potato Famine. Afterward, down a pint in their memory at an authentic Irish pub.

Orient Yourself. Though it covers only a few blocks, Boston's densely populated Chinatown ranks as the country's third largest. Chinatown is now developing its own heritage trail and offering youth-led tours (☎ *617/482–2380* ⊕ *www.asiancdc.org*). Another fun way to experience this colorful quarter is through its equally colorful celebrations. Chinese New Year promises dragon parades and firecrackers, while the August Moon Festival features lion dancing and lanterns.

Chow Bella. Red sauce has been simmering in the North End since the Italian immigrants moved here in the 1880s. The demographic is changing (today only 40% of residents claim Italian descent), but you only have to look at the thriving restaurants to see that *la vita* is still *dolce* in Boston's Little Italy. A tasteful market tour will teach you the finer points of local cuisine (☎ *617/523–6032* ⊕ *www.micheletopor.com*).

Getting Out on the Water

This city has long been defined by its coast and waterways. The original colonists were drawn here largely because of Boston's natural harbor, and local commerce and culture have remained inextricably bound to it.

Set Sail. June through September, you can relive the Golden Age of Sail aboard the *Liberty Clipper,* a replica two-masted gaff-rigged schooner that operates daytime harbor tours and romantic sunset cruises from Long Wharf. Rather hoist your own jib or perhaps even paddle your own canoe? Affordable rental boats are readily available both on the harborfront and along the Charles River. (⇨ *Boating in Chapter 6*).

Watch Whales. Whale-watching excursions, organized by the **New England Aquarium** (☎ *617/973–5206* ⊕ *www.neaq.org*), run from April through October. At Stellwagen Bank (30 mi offshore) an onboard naturalist susses out humpbacks, finbacks, minkes, and more. While these supersize mammals come mainly to feed, some seem happy to perform. If you're lucky, one might breach, blow, or give you a wave with its massive flipper.

Enjoy Ferry Tales. One of the city's top values is the $10–$12 round-trip ride from Long Wharf to Boston Harbor Islands National Park. May to October you can hop the Harbor Express ferry (☎ *617/222–6999* ⊕ *www.harborexpress.com*) for Georges Island, where hiking and beachcombing opportunities abound. Ranger-led tours of the island's pre–Civil War fort are also offered, and intrepid types can take advantage of a complimentary water shuttle to outlying islets.

ON THE CALENDAR

There is *always* something happening around Boston. We've rounded up the top annual events. But for a fuller selection consult the **Greater Boston Convention & Visitors Bureau** (☎888/733–6277 ⊕*www.bostonusa.com*) or the **Massachusetts Office of Travel & Tourism** (☎800/227–6277 ⊕*www.mass-vacation.com*). Local papers like the *Boston Globe* (⊕*www.boston.com*) and the *Phoenix* (⊕*www.thephoenix.com*) are also reliable resources. Both Web sites have searchable event listings.

WINTER November	Celebrate Turkey Day the contemporary way by viewing the parade at **America's Hometown Thanksgiving Celebration** (☎508/746–1818 ⊕*www.usathanksgiving.com*) in Plymouth. Or go retro at **Plimoth Plantation** (☎508/746–1622 ⊕*www.plimoth.org*). The re-created Pilgrim village has a theme exhibit and serves a praiseworthy dinner.
December	Dust off your tricorn hat. The **Boston Tea Party Reenactment** (☎617/482–6439 ⊕*www.oldsouthmeetinghouse.org*) kicks off at the Old South Meeting House, and festivities are free to anyone in colonial garb. Bostonians turn out in force for the city's **First Night Celebration** (☎617/542–1399 ⊕*www.firstnight.org*), a full day and night of arts-oriented alcohol-free activities. Some 250 performances, held at scores of venues indoors and out, culminate with fireworks over Boston Harbor.
January	Why wait for St. Paddy's Day? Irish (and Scottish and Breton and Quebecois . . .) eyes start smiling in mid-January when the **Boston Celtic Music Festival** (☎617/492–7679 ⊕*www.bcmfest.com*) is staged in local clubs.
February	Oenophiles have a reason to rejoice when the **Boston Wine Expo** (☎877/946–3976 ⊕*www.wineexpoboston.com*) opens at the Seaport World Trade Center. More than 400 wineries pop their corks at America's largest consumer wine show. Even if the Bruins let you down (again!) you can still enjoy the annual **Beanpot Hockey Tournament** (☎617/624–1000 ⊕*www.beanpothockey.com*) between area college teams.
SPRING April	On Patriots' Day (the third Monday in April), the prestigious **Boston Marathon** (☎617/236–1652 ⊕*www.bostonmarathon.org*) fills the streets from rural Hopkinton to the Back Bay. Go to "Heartbreak Hill" and watch competitors sprint, stride, or limp up this make-or-break section of the 26-mi course.

	May	Everyone "makes way for ducklings" in the Mother's Day **Duckling Parade** (☎*617/723–8144* ⊕*www.friendsofthepublic garden.org*) as costumed children waddle from Beacon Hill to the Public Garden.
SUMMER	June	Rowing shells are replaced by supersize vessels decorated with dragon heads and tails when the **Hong Kong Dragon Boat Festival** (⊕*www.bostondragonboat.org*) takes over the Charles River. For more than a quarter-century, the **Rockport Chamber Music Festival** (☎*978/546–7391* ⊕*www.rcmf.org*) has lured music lovers to this picturesque seaside town 45 mi north of Boston.
	July	During Boston's weeklong **Harborfest** (☎*617/227–1528* ⊕*www. bostonharborfest.com*), hundreds of events—many of them free—take place along the waterfront and Downtown. The celebration includes kiddy activities, concerts, walking tours, and the USS *Constitution* Turnaround Cruise, plus a **Chowderfest** on City Hall Plaza. **Boston Pops Concert & Fireworks Display** (☎*888/484–7677* ⊕*www.july4th.org*) ends Harborfest with a bang on Independence Day. The free star-spangled musical extravaganza at the Hatch Shell draws huge crowds, but you can avoid the worst of them by attending the preview concert on the evening of July 3 instead. Zydeco, fado, raga, rockabilly—you'll hear them all northwest of Boston at the **Lowell Folk Festival** (☎*978/970–5200* ⊕*www.lowellfolkfestival.org*). America's largest free folk event tunes up the last weekend of the month.
FALL	September	Experience reel life at the **Boston Film Festival** (☎*617/523–8388* ⊕*www.bostonfilmfestival.org*). Whether you're jazzed up or feeling blue, there's a late-September festival for you. The **Beantown Jazz Festival** (⊕*www.beantownjazz.org*) brings music to the South End; while the **Boston Blues Festival** (⊕*www.bluestrust.com*) caps Blues Week with concerts at the Hatch Shell.
	October	College crew teams—and spectators bearing blankets and beer—come from all over for the **Head of the Charles Regatta** (☎*617/868–6200* ⊕*www.hocr.org*). It's the world's largest two-day rowing event. Salem is bewitching during **Haunted Happenings** (☎*978/744–3663* ⊕*www.hauntedhappenings. com*), a series of candlelighted tours, witch trial reenactments, and other themed events climaxing on Halloween.

GREAT ITINERARIES

BOSTON IN 4 DAYS

Clearly every traveler moves at a different pace. One might pass a contented hour in the massive Museum of Fine Arts; another might have to be forcibly removed at closing time. Nevertheless, in four days you should be able to hit the city highlights without feeling rushed. If you're lucky enough to have a few vacation days to spare, you can put them to good use exploring nearby communities.

Day 1: Hit the Trail

About 3 million visitors walk the Freedom Trail every year—and there's a good reason why: taken together, the route's 16 sites offer a crash course in colonial history. That makes the trail a "must" in Bostonian terms, so you might as well tackle it sooner rather than later. Linger wherever you like, leaving time for lunch in bustling Quincy Market. (Its food court is a good place to sample at least one of Boston's edible holy trinity: lobster, clams, and "chowdah.") Next, follow the redbrick road into the North End, where you'll find Old North Church and Paul Revere's former home (Boston's oldest house, it was constructed almost 100 years before he moved in). After wandering the neighborhood's narrow streets, dine in one of Little Italy's authentic eateries. Or—if you still have time and shoe leather left—keep going across the Charlestown Bridge. See the USS *Constitution*, visit the new Battle of Bunker Hill Museum; then catch the MBTA water shuttle back to Downtown.

Day 2: Head for the Hill

Named for the light that topped it in the 17th century, Beacon Hill originally stood a bit taller until earth was scraped off its peak and used as landfill not far away. What remains—namely gas street lamps, shady trees, brick sidewalks, and stately Brahmin brownstones—evokes old Boston. When soaking up the ambience, don't forget to take in some of Beacon Hill's "official" attractions. After all, major sites from Boston's various theme trails, including the Massachusetts State House, the Boston Athenaeum, the African Meeting House, and the Granary Burying Ground, are here. Afterward, stroll over to the Common and the Public Garden (America's oldest public park and oldest botanical garden respectively). Both promise greenery and great people-watching. If shopping is more your bag, cruise for antiques along Charles Street, the thoroughfare that separates them. In the evening, chow down on chow mein in the affordable eateries of Chinatown or go upscale at hot new restaurants in the Theater District.

Day 3: Get an Overview

From the Back Bay, you can cover a lot of Boston's other attractions in a single day. Start at the top (literally) by seeing 360-degree views from the Prudential Center's Skywalk Observatory. Once you understand the lay of the land, just plot a route based on your interests. Architecture aficionados can hit the ground running at the neoclassical Public Library and Romanesque Trinity Church. Shoppers, conversely, can opt for the stores of Newbury Street and Copley Place (a high-end mall anchored by Neiman Marcus). Farther west in the Fens, other choices await. Art connoisseurs might view the collection at the world-class Museum of Fine Arts (with 350,000 *objets d'art* spanning 3,000 years it could take some time!) or the more manageably sized Isabella Stewart Gardner Museum. Quirky, carnival-like Fenway Park beckons baseball fans to the other side of the Fens. Depending

on your taste—and the availability of tickets—cap the day with a Symphony Hall concert or a Red Sox game.

Day 4: On the Waterfront

Having spent so much time focusing on the old, why not devote a day to something new in the burgeoning Seaport District? Begin at the Institute of Contemporary Art (ICA) on Fan Pier. Boston's first new art museum in almost a century boasts a bold cantilevered design that makes the most of its waterside location. It makes the most of its art collection, too, by offering special programs that appeal even to little tykes and hard-to-please teens. Of course, keeping kids engaged may prove difficult considering that the new and improved Children's Museum is located close by. Check out its innovative exhibits or continue on to that old waterfront favorite, the New England Aquarium, which celebrates its 40th birthday in 2009. Highlights include the Giant Ocean Tank, hands-on tidal pools, an engaging sea lion show, and scores of happy-footed penguins. Outside the facility you can sign on for a harbor cruise, whale-watching trip, or ferry ride to the Boston Harbor Islands.

BEYOND BOSTON PROPER

Day 1: Explore Cambridge

From pre-Revolutionary times, Boston was the region's commercial center and Cambridge was the 'burbs: a place more residential than mercantile, with plenty of room to build the nation's first English-style, redbrick university. Not surprisingly the heart of the community—geographically and otherwise—is still Harvard Square. It would be easy enough to while away a day here browsing the shops, lounging at a café, then wandering over to the riverbank to watch crew teams practice. But Harvard Square is also the starting point for free student-led campus tours (⊕ *www.harvard.edu* has details), as well as for strolls along Brattle Street's "Tory Row" (No. 105 was occupied by both Washington *and* Longfellow). If the heady academic atmosphere leaves you hungry for learning, return across the river to see the Science Museum. Sitting astride the Charles River Dam, it's especially popular with children. Alternately, spend the evening like a true Cantabrigian by taking in a concert or lecture at Sanders Theatre.

Day 2: Step Back in Time

You only have to travel a short distance to visit historic places you read about in grade school. For a side trip to the 17th century, head 35 mi southeast to Plymouth. The famed rock doesn't live up its hype. But Plimoth Plantation (an open-air museum re-creating life among Pilgrims) and *Mayflower II* are well worth the trip. A second option is to veer northwest to see Revolutionary-era sites in Lexington (now a well-to-do bedroom community). Start at the National Heritage Museum for a recap of the events that started the whole shebang; then proceed to Battle Green where "the shot heard round the world" was fired. After stopping by Minute Man National Historic Park, bookworms may continue to Concord to tour the homes of literary luminaries like Ralph Waldo Emerson, Louisa May Alcott, and Nathaniel Hawthorne. Conclude your novel excursion with a walk around Walden Pond, where Henry David Thoreau wrote one of the founding documents of the ecology movement.

GREAT ITINERARIES

TIPS

❶ When walking from one end of town to the other seems too arduous, do as the Bostonians do and take the T. Public transit will put you within a block of almost anywhere you want to go, and an MBTA Link-Pass ($9 per day, $15 per week) allows for unlimited travel on subways, local buses, and inner-harbor ferries, as well as some commuter trains.

❷ You can usually buy Symphony Hall tickets online or through your hotel concierge. But in-the-know locals get rush seats (unused subscriber tickets put on sale an hour before curtain time). Since the Sox are in a league of their own, scoring ball tickets is trickier. If you're empty-handed, watch the action at Game On!—a two-story sports bar attached to Fenway Park.

❸ For a traditional lunch "North of Boston," try Longfellow's Wayside Inn in Sudbury. (On-site you'll see an 18th-century gristmill and the school Mary attended with her little lamb.) If you don't want to have miles to go before you sleep, book into Concord's Colonial Inn rather than returning to Boston: it was a Thoreau family residence before becoming a hostelry in 1889.

❹ Die-hard sightseers might consider taking a pass—a "Go Boston" Pass (☎ *800/ 887–9103* ⊕ *www.goboston.com*). Sold in one-day to one-week increments, it's priced from $54.99 and covers dozens of attractions, tours, and excursions. CityPass (☎ *888/330–5008* ⊕ *www.citypass.com*) sells a similar product covering five key sites for $44.

Day 3: A Shore Thing

Anyone eager to taste the salt air or feel the surge of the sea should consider taking a day trip to the North Shore towns of Salem and Gloucester. The former has a Maritime National Historic Site—complete with vintage wharves and warehouses—that proves there is more to the notorious town than just witchcraft; while the latter (America's oldest seaport and, after *The Perfect Storm*, perhaps its most identifiable) demonstrates that men *still* go down to the sea in ships. Prefer to just beach yourself? Nature lovers can flock to Crane Beach in Ipswich, about an hour north of Boston. Part of a 1,200-acre wildlife refuge, it includes 4 mi of sand rimmed by scenic dunes. For a quick sand-in-every-crevice experience take either the MBTA's Harbor Express ferry south to Nantasket Beach in Hull or the commuter train north to Manchester-by-the-Sea's Singing Beach where the sand has such a high silica content that it actually sings (or at least squeaks) when you walk on it.

Exploring Boston

WORD OF MOUTH

"For us, the Freedom Trail was a don't miss. We also loved going to a Red Sox game, but tickets are hard to come by. The duck tour is good for a quick overview of the city. Don't forget to get some cannoli and gelato!"

—volcanogirl

"You should definitely walk through the Boston Common and Public Garden– and make sure to check out the Make Way for Ducklings statue, which is near the corner of Beacon and Charles Streets."

—ats16

Updated
by Bethany
Cassin
Beckerlegge

There's history and culture around every bend in Boston—skyscrapers nestle next to historic hotels while modern marketplaces line the antique cobblestone streets. But to Bostonians, living in a city that blends yesterday and today is just another day in their beloved Beantown.

And though you might be tempted, it's difficult to fit a stereotype to this city because of Boston's many layers. The deepest layer is the historical one, the place where musket-bearing revolutionaries vowed to hang together or hang separately. The next tier, a dense spread of Brahmin fortune and fortitude, might be labeled the Hub. The Hub saw only journalistic accuracy in the label "the Athens of America" and felt only pride in the slogan "Banned in Boston." Over that layer lies Beantown, home to the Red Sox faithful and the raucous Bruins fans who crowded the old Boston "*Gah*-den"; this is the city whose ethnic loyalties account for its many distinct neighborhoods. Crowning these layers are the students who throng the area's universities and colleges every fall, infuriating some but pleasing many with their infusion of high spirits and money from home.

BEACON HILL AND BOSTON COMMON

Past and present home of the old-money elite, contender for the "Most Beautiful" award among the city's neighborhoods, and hallowed address for many literary lights, Beacon Hill is Boston at its most Bostonian. The redbrick elegance of its narrow streets sends you back to the 19th century just as surely as if you had stumbled into a time machine. But Beacon Hill residents would never make the social faux pas of being out of date. The neighborhood is home to hip boutiques and trendy restaurants, frequented by young, affluent professionals rather than D.A.R. matrons.

Once the seat of the Commonwealth's government, Beacon Hill was called "Trimountain" and later "Tremont" by early colonists because of its three summits: Pemberton, Mt. Vernon Hill, and Beacon Hill, named for the warning light set on its peak in 1634. In 1799 settlers leveled out the ground for residences, using it to create what is now Charles Street; by the early 19th century the crests of the other two hills were also lowered.

When the fashionable families decamped for the "new" development of the Back Bay starting in the 1850s, enough residents remained to ensure that the south slope of the Hill never lost its Brahmin character.

By the mid-20th century, most of the multistory single-family dwellings on Beacon Hill were converted to condominiums and apartments, which are today among the most expensive in the city.

REASONS TO GO

■ **The Freedom Trail.** Walk along Paul Revere's fated path for a glimpse of living American history.

■ **Posh Purchases.** Strap on some stilettos and join the quest for fashionable finds on Newbury Street, Boston's answer to Manhattan's 5th Avenue.

■ **Red-Sox Nation.** Boston's baseball team is the one thing that will bring the entire city to its feet—or its knees. Few baseball fans, Red Sox faithful or not, can deny the mystique of one of the game's most hallowed grounds—Fenway Park.

■ **Painted Glory.** Gaze at paintings, listen to concerts, and stare down statuary at the beautiful Isabella Stewart Gardner Museum. While away hours upon hours at the Museum of Fine Arts, contemplating the works of French masters Edouard Manet, Camille Passarro, and Pierre-Auguste Renoir; and American painters such as Mary Cassatt, Childe Hassam, John Singer Sargent, and Edward Hopper.

Beacon Hill is bounded by Cambridge Street on the north, Beacon Street on the south, the Charles River Esplanade on the west, and Bowdoin Street on the east.

A good place to begin an exploration of Beacon Hill is at the Boston Common Visitor Information Center (⇨ below), where you can buy a map or a complete guide to the Freedom Trail.

Ranger-led tours leave from the **National Park Service Visitor Center** (⊠ *15 State St. 02109-3502* ☎*617/242–5642* ⊕*www.nps.gov/bost*) from mid-April through November.

TIMING Beacon Hill, one of the more-compact areas of Boston, can be easily explored in an afternoon; add an extra few hours if you wish to linger on the Common and in the shops on Charles Street or tour the Black Heritage Trail. In winter the cobblestone streets can be difficult to navigate, but the neighborhood is especially pretty during the holidays—the Common is alive with Christmas lights, and on Christmas Eve carolers and bell ringers fill Louisburg Square. Other seasons bring other pleasures, from cherry blossoms on the Common in spring to free summer concerts on the nearby Esplanade.

Numbers in the margin correspond to the Beacon Hill & Boston Common map.

TOP ATTRACTIONS

🄳 **Acorn Street.** Surely the most photographed street in the city, Acorn is
★ Ye Olde Colonial Boston at its best. For drivers, the cobblestone street may be Boston's roughest ride (and so narrow that only one car can squeeze through at a time). Delicate row houses line one side, and on the other are the doors to Mt. Vernon's hidden gardens. Once the homes of 19th-century artisans and tradesmen, these little jewels are now every bit as prestigious as their larger neighbors on Chestnut and Mt. Vernon streets.

C **Boston Common.** Nothing is more

Fodor'sChoice central to Boston than the Com-

★ mon, the oldest public park in the United States and undoubtedly the largest and most famous of the town commons around which New England settlements were traditionally arranged. Boston Common is not built on landfill like the adjacent Public Garden, nor is it the result of 19th-century park planning, as are Frederick Law Olmsted's Fens and Franklin Park; it started as 50 acres where the freemen of Boston could graze their cattle. (Cows were banned in 1830.) Dating from 1634, it's as old as the city around it. Latin names are affixed to many of the Common's trees; it was once expected that proper Boston schoolchildren be able to translate them.

> **HISTORIC BY LAW**
>
> The classic face of Beacon Hill comes from its brick row houses, nearly all built between 1800 and 1850. Even the sidewalks are brick and will remain so by public fiat; in the 1940s, residents staged an uncharacteristic sit-in to prevent conventional paving. Since then, public law, the Beacon Hill Civic Association, and the Beacon Hill Architectural Commission have maintained tight control over everything from the gas lamps to the colors of front doors.

The **Central Burying Ground** (⊠ *Boylston St. near Tremont* T *Boylston*) may seem an odd feature for a public park, but remember that in 1756, when the land was set aside, this was a lonely corner of the Common. It's the final resting place of Tories and Patriots alike, as well as many British casualties of the Battle of Bunker Hill. The most famous person buried here is Gilbert Stuart, the portraitist best known for his likenesses of George and Martha Washington; he died a poor man in 1828. The Burying Ground is open daily 9–5. On Tremont Street near Boylston stands the 1888 **Boston Massacre Memorial;** the sculpted hand of one of the victims has a distinct shine from years of sightseers' caresses. The Common's highest ground, near the park's Parkman Bandstand, was once called Flagstaff Hill. It's now surmounted by the **Soldiers and Sailors Monument,** honoring Civil War troops. The Common's only body of water is the **Frog Pond,** a tame and frog-free concrete depression used as a children's wading pool during steamy summer days and for ice-skating in winter. It marks the original site of a natural pond that inspired Edgar Allan Poe to call Bostonians "Frogpondians." In 1848 a gushing fountain of piped-in water was created to inaugurate Boston's municipal water system.

On the Beacon Street side of the Common sits the splendidly restored **Robert Gould Shaw 54th Regiment Memorial,** executed in deep-relief bronze by Augustus Saint-Gaudens in 1897. It commemorates the 54th Massachusetts Regiment, the first Civil War unit made up of free blacks, led by the young Brahmin Robert Gould Shaw. He and half of his troops died in an assault on South Carolina's Fort Wagner; their story inspired the 1989 movie *Glory.* The monument—first intended to depict only Shaw until his abolitionist family demanded it honor his regiment as well—figures in works by the poets John Berryman and Robert Lowell, both of whom lived on the north slope of Beacon Hill in the 1940s. In Lowell's moving poem "For the Union Dead"

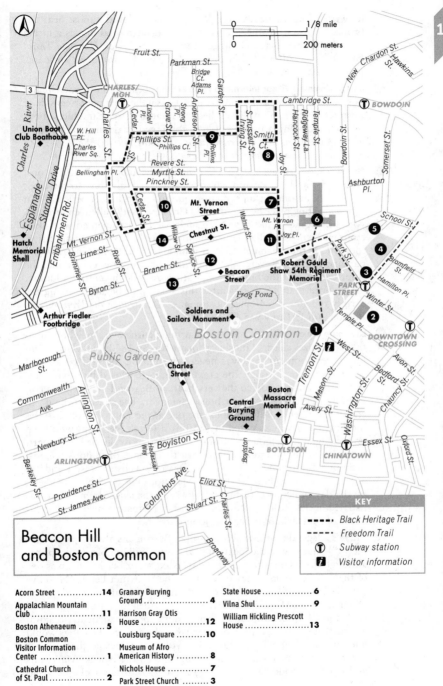

Beacon Hill
and Boston Common

KEY

- - - - Black Heritage Trail
- - - - Freedom Trail
Ⓣ Subway station
ⓘ Visitor information

he writes, "at the dedication, William James could almost hear the bronze Negroes breathe." This magnificent memorial makes a fitting first stop on the Black Heritage Trail (⇨ *"The Black Heritage Trail" box, below*). ✉ *Bounded by Beacon, Charles, Tremont, and Park Sts., Beacon Hill* Ⓣ *Park St.*

❶ **Boston Common Visitor Information Center.** This center, run by the Greater Boston Convention and Visitors Bureau, is on the Tremont Street side of Boston Common. It's well supplied with stacks of free pamphlets about Boston, including a useful guide to the Freedom Trail, which begins in the Common. ✉ *147 Tremont St., Beacon Hill* ☎ *888/733–2678* ⊕ *www.bostonusa.com* ☉ *Mon.–Sat. 8:30–5, Sun. 10–6* Ⓣ *Park St.*

❹ **Granary Burying Ground.** "It is a fine thing to die in Boston," A. C. Lyons,

★ an essayist and old Boston wit, once remarked, alluding to the city's cemeteries, among the most picturesque and historic in America. If you found a resting place here at the Old Granary, as it's called, chances are your headstone would have been impressively ornamented with skeletons and winged skulls. Your neighbors would have been impressive, too: among them Samuel Adams, John Hancock, Benjamin Franklin's parents, and Paul Revere. Note the winged hourglasses carved into the stone gateway of the burial ground; they are a 19th-century addition, made more than 150 years after this small plot began receiving the earthly remains of colonial Bostonians. ✉ *Entrance on Tremont St., Beacon Hill* ☉ *Daily 9–5* Ⓣ *Park St.*

❿ **Louisburg Square.** One of the most charming corners in a neighborhood
★ that epitomizes charm, Louisburg Square was an 1840s model for townhouse development that was never repeated on the Hill because of space restrictions. Today, the grassy square—enclosed by a wrought-iron fence and considered the very heart of Beacon Hill—belongs collectively to the owners of the houses facing it. The statue at the north end of the green is of Columbus, the one at the south end of Aristides the Just; both were donated in 1850 by a Greek merchant who lived on the square. The houses, most of which are now divided into apartments and condominiums, have seen their share of famous tenants, including author and critic William Dean Howells at Nos. 4 and 16, and the Alcotts at No. 10 (Louisa May not only lived but died here, on the day of her father's funeral). In 1852 the singer Jenny Lind was married in the parlor of No. 20. Louisburg Square is also the current home of Massachusetts Senator John Kerry.

There's a legend that Louisburg (proper Bostonians always pronounce the "s") Square was the location of the Rev. William Blaxton's spring, although there's no water there today. Blaxton, or Blackstone, was one of the first Bostonians, having come to the Shawmut Peninsula to live with his books and his apple trees in the mid-1620s, after the group with whom he arrived from England disbanded. When the Puritans, who had settled in Charlestown, found their water supply inadequate, Blaxton invited them to move across the river, where he assured them they would find an "excellent spring." Just a few years later, he sold them all but 6 acres of the peninsula he had bought from the Native Americans and left for Rhode Island, seeking greater seclusion; a plaque at 50

Beacon Street commemorates him. ⊠*Between Mt. Vernon and Pickney Sts., Beacon Hill* Ⓣ*Park St.*

⑧ Museum of Afro American History. Ⓒ Ever since runaway slave Crispus Attucks became one of the famous victims of the Boston Massacre of 1770, the African-American community of Boston has played an important part in the city's history. Throughout the 19th century, abolition was the cause célèbre for Boston's intellectual elite, and during that time, blacks came to thrive in neighborhoods throughout the city. The Museum of Afro American History was established in 1964 to promote this history. The umbrella organization includes a trio of historic sites: the Abiel Smith School;

Fodor'sChoice
★

SECRET GARDENS

Strolling through Beacon Hill, you might be sorely tempted to sneak a peek into those glorious private gardens that are just barely visible behind sheltering walls and wrought-iron gates. Rather than risk arrest, time your visit for the third Thursday in May when about a dozen of them open to the public. The self-guided **Hidden Gardens of Beacon Hill tour** (☎*617/227–4392* ⊕*www.beaconhillgardenclub.org*), an event that's happened annually since 1929, costs $30 when you purchase tickets in advance.

the African Meeting House; and the African Meeting House on the island of Nantucket, off the coast of Cape Cod. Park Service personnel continue to lead tours of the **Black Heritage Trail** (⇨ *"The Black Heritage Trail" box*), starting from the Shaw Memorial. The museum is the site of activities, including lectures, children's storytelling, and concerts focusing on black composers.

A few years ago the museum honored the 200th anniversary of the **African Meeting House,** the oldest black church building still standing in the United States, with a major restoration that returned the house to its 1855 appearance. The centerpiece of Beacon Hill's African-American community, the Meeting House was constructed almost entirely with African-American labor, using funds raised in both the white and the black communities. The facade is an adaptation of a design for a town house published by the Boston architect Asher Benjamin. In 1832 the New England Anti-Slavery Society was formed here under the leadership of William Lloyd Garrison. When the black community began to migrate at the end of the 19th century to the South End and Roxbury, the building became a synagogue. In 1972 it was purchased by the Museum of Afro American History, but that year a fire destroyed the slate roof and original pulpit. After its reconstruction, it was designated a historic site in 1974 and reopened in 1987.

In keeping with the big anniversary celebration, the **Abiel Smith School** will display the writings of Frederick Douglass, original printings of the poet Phillis Wheatley, and copies of William Lloyd Garrison's antislavery newspaper, the *Liberator*. The two-floor exhibit will also hold the findings of an archaeological dig, including photos, fine china, and a rare pulpit. The school operated from 1835 to 1855, educating a total of about 200 students. ⊠*46 Joy St., Beacon Hill* ☎*617/725–0022* ⊕*www.afroammuseum.org* ⊠*Free, $5 suggested donation* ⊗ *Mon.–Sat. 10–4* Ⓣ*Charles/MGH.*

WORTH NOTING

 Appalachian Mountain Club. The bowfront mansion that serves as the headquarters of one of New England's oldest environmental institutions draws nature lovers from all over the world. The club is a reliable source of useful information on outdoor recreation throughout the region, including cross-country skiing and hiking. (You don't have to be a member to use its resources.) Architecturally, the building is notable for its carved cornices and oriel window decorated with vines and gargoyles. ⊠ *5 Joy St., Beacon Hill* ☎ *617/523–0636* ⊕ *www.outdoors. org* ⊙ *Weekdays 9–5* Ⓣ *Park St.*

Beacon Street. Some New Englanders believe wealth is a burden to be borne with a minimum of display. Happily, the early residents of Beacon Street were not among them. They erected many fine architectural statements, from the magnificent State House to grand patrician mansions. Here are some of the most important buildings of Charles Bulfinch, the ultimate designer of the Federal style in America: dozens of bowfront row houses, the Somerset Club, and the glorious Harrison Gray Otis House.

After the **Boston Athenaeum,** Beacon Street highlights begin at No. 34, originally the Cabot family residence and until 1996 the headquarters of Little, Brown and Company, once a mainstay of Boston's publishing trade. At 33 Beacon Street is the **George Parkman House,** its gracious facade hiding more than a few secrets. One of the first sensational "trials of the century" involved the murder of Dr. George Parkman, a wealthy landlord and Harvard benefactor. He was bludgeoned to death in 1849 by Dr. John Webster, a Harvard medical professor and neighborhood acquaintance who allegedly became enraged by Parkman's demands that he repay a personal loan. At the conclusion of the trial, the professor was hanged; he's buried in an unmarked grave on Copp's Hill in the North End. Parkman's son lived in seclusion in this house overlooking the Common until he died in 1908. The building is now used for civic functions.

Notice the windows of the twin **Appleton-Parker Houses,** built by the pioneering textile merchant Nathan Appleton and a partner at Nos. 39 and 40. These are the celebrated purple panes of Beacon Hill; only a few buildings have them, and they are incredibly valuable. Their amethystine mauve color was the result of the action of the sun's ultraviolet light on the imperfections in a shipment of glass sent to Boston around 1820. The mansions aren't open to the public.

The quintessential snob has always been a Bostonian—and the **Somerset Club,** at 42 Beacon Street, has always been the inner sanctum of blue-nose Cabots, Lowells, and Lodges. The mansion is a rare intrusion of the granite Greek Revival style into Beacon Hill. The older of its two buildings was erected in 1819 by David Sears and designed by Alexander Parris, the architect of Quincy Market. A few doors down is the grandest of the three houses Harrison Gray Otis built for himself during Boston's golden age.

➎ Boston Athenaeum. One of the cofounders of the Boston Athenaeum is credited with coining an expression that has made politicians and

1

newspaper editorialists rejoice ever since: in an 1819 letter, William Tudor first compared Boston with Athens because of its many cultural and educational institutions; Bostonians now jealously guard the title "Athens of America." Tudor, the first editor of the *North American Review,* would surely have cited the Athenaeum, one of the oldest libraries in the country, as partial proof. Founded in 1807 from the seeds sown by the Anthology Club (headed by Ralph Waldo Emerson's father), it moved to its present imposing quarters—modeled after Palladio's Palazzo da Porta Festa in Vicenza, Italy—in 1849. Only 1,049 proprietary shares exist for membership in this cathedral of scholarship, and most have been passed down for generations; the Athenaeum is, however, open for use by qualified scholars, and yearly memberships are open to all by application.

The first floor is open to the public and houses an art gallery with rotating exhibits, marble busts, porcelain vases, lush oil paintings, and books. The children's room is also open for the public to browse or read a story in secluded nooks overlooking the Granary Burying Ground. Take the guided tour to spy one of the most marvelous sights in the world of Boston academe, the fifth-floor Reading Room. With two levels of antique books, comfortable reading chairs, high windows, and assorted art, the room appears straight out of a period movie, rather than a modern scholarly institution. ■TIP➔ **Only eight people can fit in the tiny elevator to the fifth floor, so call at least 24 hours in advance to reserve your spot on the tour.** Among the Athenaeum's holdings are most of George Washington's private library and the King's Chapel Library, sent from England by William III in 1698. With a nod to the Information Age, an online catalog contains records for more than 600,000 volumes. The Athenaeum extends into 14 Beacon Street. ✉*10½ Beacon St., Beacon Hill* ☎*617/227–0270* ⊕*www.bostonathenaeum. org* ✆*Free* ⊘*Mon. 9–8, Tues.–Fri. 9–5:30, Sat. 9–4. Tours Tues. and Thurs. at 3* Ⓣ*Park St.*

② **Cathedral Church of St. Paul.** Though it looks a bit like a bank, St. Paul's is actually the first Boston structure built in the Greek Revival style (1820). It was established by a group of wealthy and influential patriots who wanted a wholly American Episcopal parish—the two existing Episcopal churches, Christ Church (Old North) and Trinity, were both founded before the Revolution—that would contrast with the existing colonial and "gothick" structures around town. The building was to be topped with an entablature showing St. Paul preaching to the Corinthians—but the pediment remains uncarved, as Bishop Henry Sherrill instead used the money to start the clergy pension program for the national Episcopal church. ✉*138 Tremont St., Beacon Hill* ☎*617/482–5800* ⊕*www.stpaulboston.org* ⊘*Weekdays 9–5. Services Sun. at 8* AM*, 10* AM*, and 12:30 (in Cantonese); Mon. at 1, and Fri. at 1 (Ju'mah; Muslim Friday Prayers). Luncheon concerts Oct.–May, Wed. at 12:15* Ⓣ*Park St.*

■ DID YOU KNOW?

Beacon Hill's north slope played a key part in African-American history. A community of free blacks lived here in the 1800s; many worshipped at the African Meeting House, established in 1805 and still standing. It came to be

Following the Freedom Trail

More than a route of historic sites, the Freedom Trail is a 2½-mi walk into history, bringing to life the events that exploded on the world during the Revolution. Its 16 way stations allow you to reach out and touch the very wellsprings of U.S. civilization. (And for those with a pinch of Yankee frugality, only three of the sites charge admission.) Follow the route marked on your maps, and keep an eye on the sidewalk for the red stripe that marks the trail.

Follow the red-brick road in Boston to 16 historic sites with national significance.

It takes a full day to complete the entire route comfortably. The trail lacks the multimedia bells and whistles that are quickly becoming the norm at historic attractions, but on the Freedom Trail, history speaks for itself.

Begin at Boston Common. Get your bearings at the Visitor Information Center on Tremont Street, then head for the **State House,** Boston's finest piece of Federalist architecture. Several blocks away is the **Park Street Church,** whose 217-foot steeple is considered by many to be the most beautiful in all of New England.

Reposing in the church's shadows is the **Granary Burying Ground,** final resting place of Samuel Adams, John Hancock, and Paul Revere. A short stroll to Downtown brings you to **King's Chapel,** built in 1754 and a hotbed of Anglicanism during the colonial period. Follow the trail past the statue of Benjamin Franklin to the **Old Corner Bookstore** site, where Hawthorne, Emerson, and Longfellow were published. Nearby is the **Old South Meeting House,** where pretempest arguments, heard in 1773, led to the Boston Tea Party. Overlooking the site of the Boston Massacre is the earliest-known public building in Boston, the **Old State House,** a Georgian beauty.

Cross the plaza to **Faneuil Hall** and explore its upstairs Assembly Room, where Samuel Adams fired the indignation of Bostonians during those times that tried men's souls. Find your way back to the red stripe and follow it into the North End.

Stepping into the **Paul Revere House** takes you back 200 years—here are the hero's own saddlebags, a toddy warmer, and a pine cradle made from a molasses cask. Nearby Paul Revere Mall is a tranquil rest spot. Next to the Paul Revere House is one of the city's oldest brick buildings, the **Pierce-Hichborn House.**

Next, tackle a place guaranteed to trigger a wave of patriotism: the **Old North Church** of "One if by land, two if by sea" fame—sorry, the 154 creaking stairs leading to the belfry are out-of-bounds for visitors. Then head toward **Copp's Hill Burying Ground,** cross the bridge over the Charles, and check out that revered icon the **USS Constitution,** "Old Ironsides."

The photo finish? A climb to the top of the **Bunker Hill Monument** for the incomparable vistas. Finally, head for the nearby Charlestown water shuttle, which goes directly to the downtown area, and congratulate yourself: you've just completed a unique crash course in American history.

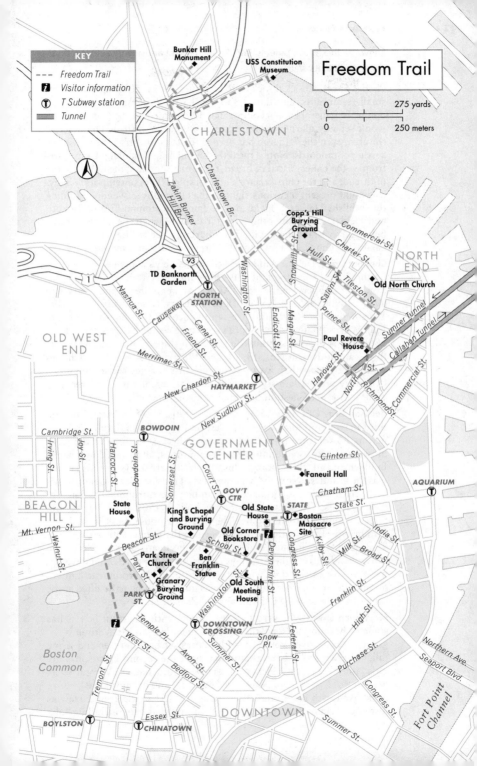

Freedom Trail

0   275 yards

0   250 meters

Bunker Hill Monument

USS Constitution Museum 🛈

CHARLESTOWN

Zakim Bunker Hill Br.

Charlestown Br.

Copp's Hill Burying Ground

Commercial St.

Charter St.

NORTH END

Hull St.

Snowhill St.

Salem St.

Tileston St.

Old North Church

TD Banknorth Garden

Washington St.

Prince St.

Margin St.

Endicott St.

Hanover St.

Sumner Tunnel

Callahan Tunnel

NORTH STATION Ⓣ

Paul Revere House

North St.

Richmond St.

Commercial St.

Nashua St.

Causeway

Canal St.

Friend St.

Merrimac St.

New Chardon St.

HAYMARKET Ⓣ

OLD WEST END

Irving St.

Joy St.

Hancock St.

Cambridge St.

BOWDOIN Ⓣ

Somerset St.

New Sudbury St.

GOVERNMENT CENTER

Clinton St.

Faneuil Hall

Chatham St.

AQUARIUM Ⓣ

BEACON HILL

Mt. Vernon St.

Walnut St.

Bowdoin St.

State House

Beacon St.

Court St.

GOV'T CTR Ⓣ

King's Chapel and Burying Ground

Old State House

State St.

STATE Ⓣ

Boston Massacre Site

India St.

Milk St.

Broad St.

Park Street Church

Granary Burying Ground

Park St.

PARK ST. Ⓣ

Ben Franklin Statue

School St.

Old Corner Bookstore 🛈

Devonshire St.

Congress St.

Kilby St.

Washington St.

Old South Meeting House

Franklin St.

High St.

🛈

Boston Common

Tremont St.

Temple Pl.

West St.

Avon St.

DOWNTOWN CROSSING Ⓣ

Snow Pl.

Summer St.

Federal St.

Purchase St.

Congress St.

Northern Ave.

Seaport Blvd.

Bedford St.

BOYLSTON Ⓣ

Essex St.

CHINATOWN Ⓣ

DOWNTOWN

Summer St.

Fort Point Channel

known as the "Black Faneuil Hall" for the fervent antislavery activism that
started within its walls.

Charles Street. Chockablock with antiques shops, clothing boutiques,
small restaurants, and flower shops, Charles Street more than makes
up for the general lack of commercial development on Beacon Hill. You
won't see any glaring neon; in keeping with the historic character of
the area, even the 7-Eleven has been made to conform to the prevailing
aesthetic standards. Notice the old-fashioned signs hanging from storefronts—the bakery's loaf of bread, the florist's topiary, the tailor's spool
of thread, and the chiropractor's human spine. The contemporary activity would present a curious sight to the elder Oliver Wendell Holmes,
the publisher James T. Fields (of the famed Bostonian firm of Ticknor
and Fields), and many others who lived here when the neighborhood
belonged to establishment literati. Charles Street sparkles at dusk from
gas-fueled lamps, making it a romantic place for an evening stroll.

Chestnut Street. Delicacy and grace characterize virtually every structure
on this street, from the fanlights above the entryways to the wrought-
iron boot scrapers on the steps. Author and explorer Francis Parkman
lived here, as did the lawyer Richard Henry Dana (who wrote *Two
Years Before the Mast*), and 19th-century actor Edwin Booth, brother of
John Wilkes Booth. Edwin Booth's sometime residence, 29A, dates from
1800 and is the oldest house on the south slope of the Hill. Also note
the **Swan Houses,** at Nos. 13, 15, and 17, commissioned from Charles
Bulfinch by Hepzibah Swan as dowry gifts for her three daughters.
Complete with Adam-style entrances, marble columns, and recessed
arches, they are Chestnut Street at its most beautiful.

⑫ **Harrison Gray Otis House.** Harrison Gray Otis, a U.S. senator, Boston's
third mayor, and one of the Mt. Vernon Proprietors (a group of pros-
perous Boston investors), built in rapid succession three of the city's
most splendidly ostentatious Federal-era houses, all designed by Charles
Bulfinch and all still standing. This, the third Harrison Gray Otis House,
was the grandest. Now the headquarters of the American Meteorologi-
cal Society, the house was once freestanding and surrounded by English-
style gardens. The second Otis house, built in 1800 at 85 Mt. Vernon
Street, is now a private home. The first Otis house, built in 1796 on
Cambridge Street, is the only one open to the public. Otis moved into
45 Beacon Street in 1805 and stayed until his death in 1848. His tenure
thus extended from the first days of Beacon Hill's residential development almost to the time when many of the Hill's prominent families
decamped for the Back Bay, which was just beginning to be filled at the
time of Otis's death. ⊠ *45 Beacon St., Beacon Hill.*

Mt. Vernon Street. Mt. Vernon Street, along with Chestnut Street, has
some of Beacon Hill's most distinguished addresses. Mt. Vernon is the
grander of the two, however, with houses set back farther and rising
taller; it even has a freestanding mansion, the second Harrison Gray
Otis House, at No. 85. Henry James once wrote that Mt. Vernon Street
was "the only respectable street in America," and he must have known,
as he lived with his brother William at No. 131 in the 1860s. He was
just one of many literary luminaries who resided here, including Julia

CLOSE UP

1

The Black Heritage Trail

Until the end of the 19th century the north side of opulent Beacon Hill contained a vibrant community of free blacks—more than 8,000 at its peak—who built houses, schools, and churches that stand to this day. In the African Meeting House, once called the Black Faneuil Hall, orators rallied against slavery. The streets were lined with black-owned businesses. The black community has since shifted to other parts of Boston, but the 19th-century legacy can be rediscovered on the Black Heritage Trail.

Established in the late 1960s, the self-guiding trail stitches together 14 sites in a 1½-mi walk. Park rangers give tours daily Memorial Day through Labor Day at 10 AM, noon, and 2 PM, and from Labor Day to Memorial Day at 2 PM, starting from the Shaw Memorial in Boston Common. To tour on your own, pick up brochures from the **Museum of Afro American History** (⊠ 46 Joy St., Beacon Hill) or the **National Park Service Visitor Center** (⊠ 15 State St., Beacon Hill).

Start at the stirring **Robert Gould Shaw 54th Regiment Memorial** in Boston Common. Shaw, a young white officer from a prominent Boston abolitionist family, led the first black regiment to be recruited in the North during the Civil War. From here, walk up Joy Street to 5–7 Pinckney Street to see the 1797 **George Middleton House**, Beacon Hill's oldest existing home built by blacks. Nearby, the **Phillips School** at Anderson and Pinckney streets was one of Boston's first integrated schools. The **John J. Smith House**, 86 Pinckney, was a rendezvous point for abolitionists and escaping slaves, and the **Charles Street Meeting House**, at Mt. Vernon and Charles streets, was

once a white Baptist church and later a black church and community center. In 1876 the building became the site of the **African Methodist Episcopal Church,** which was the last black institution to leave Beacon Hill, in 1939. The **Lewis and Harriet Hayden House** at 66 Phillips Street, the home of freed slaves turned abolitionists, was a stop on the Underground Railroad. Harriet Beecher Stowe, author of Uncle Tom's Cabin, visited here in 1853 for her first glimpse of fugitive slaves. The Haydens reportedly kept a barrel of gunpowder under the front step, saying they'd blow up the house before they'd surrender a single slave. At **2 Phillips Street,** John Coburn, cofounder of a black military company, ran a gaming house, described as a "private place for gentlemen."

The five residences on **Smith Court** are typical of African-American Bostonian homes of the 1800s, including No. 3, the 1799 clapboard house where William C. Nell, America's first published black historian and a crusader for school integration, boarded from 1851 to 1865. At the corner of Joy Street and Smith Court is the **Abiel Smith School,** the city's first public school for black children. The school's exhibits interpret the ongoing struggle started in the 1830s for equal school rights. Next door is the venerable **African Meeting House,** which was the community's center of social, educational, and political activity. The ground level houses a gallery; in the airy upstairs, you can imagine the fiery sermons that once rattled the upper pews.

Ward Howe, who composed "The Battle Hymn of the Republic" and lived at No. 32, and the poet Robert Frost, who lived at No. 88.

❼ Nichols House. The only Mt. Vernon Street home open to the public, the Nichols House was built in 1804 and attributed to Charles Bulfinch. It became the lifelong home of Rose Standish Nichols (1872–1960), Beacon Hill eccentric, philanthropist, peace advocate, and one of the first female landscape designers. Although the Victorian furnishings passed to Miss Nichols by

WHO'S CHARLIE?

When riding the rails in Boston, look out for Charlie, a poor soul immortalized in the 1950s Kingston Trio hit "M.T.A." He "never returned" from the subway for lack of a nickel needed for his departure fare. Charlie lives on—in odd faceless form—as the mascot of the MBTA's new "CharlieCard" ticket system (metal tokens were phased out in 2006).

descent, she added a number of colonial-style pieces to the mix, such as an American Empire rosewood sideboard and a bonnet-top Chippendale highboy. The result is a delightful mélange of styles. Nichols made arrangements in her will for the house to become a museum, and knowledgeable volunteers from the neighborhood have been playing host since then. To see the house, you must take a tour (included in the price of admission). ⊠*55 Mt. Vernon St., Beacon Hill* ☎*617/227–6993* ⊕*www.nicholshousemuseum.org* ☜*$7* ☉*Apr.–Oct., Tues.–Sat. 11–4; Nov.–Mar., Thurs.–Sat. 11–4. First tour at 11, tours on ½ hr thereafter; last tour starts at 4* Ⓣ*Park St.*

❸ Park Street Church. If this Congregationalist church at the corner of Tremont and Park streets could sing, what a joyful song it would be. Inside the church, which was designed by Peter Banner and erected in 1809–10, Samuel Smith's hymn "America" was first sung on July 4, 1831. The country's oldest musical organization, the Handel & Haydn Society, was founded here in 1815; in 1829 William Lloyd Garrison began his long public campaign for the abolition of slavery here. The distinguished steeple is considered by many critics to be the most beautiful in New England. Just outside the church, at the intersection of Park and Tremont streets (and the main subway crossroads of the city), is **Brimstone Corner.** Does the name refer to the fervent thunder of the church's preachers, the fact that gunpowder was once stored in the church's crypt, or the story that preachers once scattered burning sulfur on the pavement to attract the attention of potential churchgoers? Historians can't agree. ⊠*1 Park St., Beacon Hill* ☎*617/523–3383* ⊕*www.parkstreet.org* ☉*Tours mid-June–Aug., Tues.–Fri. 9–4, Sat. 9–3. Sun. services at 8:30, 11, 4, and 6* Ⓣ*Park St.*

Park Street Station. One of the first four stops on the first subway in America, Park Street Station was part of the line that originally ran only as far as the present-day Boylston stop. It was opened for service in 1897 against the warnings of those convinced it would make buildings along Tremont Street collapse. The copper-roof kiosks are National Historic Landmarks—outside them cluster flower vendors, street musicians, and partisans of causes and beliefs ranging from Irish nationalism to Krishna Consciousness. The station is the center of Boston's subway system; "inbound" trains are always traveling toward Park Street. ✉*Park and Tremont Sts., Beacon Hill.*

**NEED A
BREAK?**

There are two **Starbucks** on the 3/10-mi-long Charles Street—but hold out for **Panificio Bakery** (✉*144 Charles St., Beacon Hill* ☎*617/227–4340),* a cozy neighborhood hangout and old-fashioned Italian café. Soups and pizzas are made on the premises; for quick fortification, go for one of the Mediterranean sandwiches, or apply your sweet tooth to a raspberry turnover with a cappuccino.

❻ State House. On July 4, 1795, the surviving fathers of the Revolution were on hand to enshrine the ideals of their new Commonwealth in a graceful seat of government designed by Charles Bulfinch. Governor Samuel Adams and Paul Revere laid the cornerstone; Revere would later roll the copper sheathing for the dome.

Bulfinch's neoclassical design is poised between Georgian and Federal; its finest features are the delicate Corinthian columns of the portico, the graceful pediment and window arches, and the vast yet visually weightless golden dome (gilded in 1874 and again in 1997). During World War II, the dome was painted gray so that it would not reflect moonlight during blackouts and thereby offer a target to anticipated Axis bombers. It's capped with a pinecone, a symbol of the importance of pine wood, which was integral to the construction of Boston's early houses and churches—as well as the State House itself.

Inside the building are Doric Hall, with its statuary and portraits; the Hall of Flags, where an exhibit shows the battle flags from all the wars in which Massachusetts regiments have participated; the Great Hall, an open space used for state functions that houses 351 flags from the cities and towns of Massachusetts; the governor's office; and the chambers of the House and Senate. The Great Hall contains a giant, modernistic clock designed by New York artist R. M. Fischer. Its installation in 1986 at a cost of $100,000 was roundly slammed as a symbol of legislative extravagance. There's also a wealth of statuary, including figures of Horace Mann, Daniel Webster, and a youthful-looking President John F. Kennedy in full stride. Just outside Doric Hall is 1999s "Hear Us," a series of six bronze busts honoring the contributions of women to public life in Massachusetts. But perhaps the best known piece of artwork in the building is the carved wooden *Sacred Cod,* mounted in the Old State House in 1784 as a symbol of the commonwealth's maritime wealth. It was moved, with much fanfare, to Bulfinch's structure in 1798. By 1895, when it was hung in the new House chambers, the representatives had begun to consider the Cod their unofficial mascot—so much so that when *Harvard Lampoon* wags "codnapped" it in 1933, the House refused to meet in session until the fish was returned, three days later. ✉*Beacon St. between Hancock and Bowdoin Sts., Beacon Hill* ☎*617/727–3676* ⊕*www.state.ma.us/sec/trs/trsidx.htm* ✆*Free* ⊙ *Weekdays 9–5. Tours 10–4; call ahead to schedule* Ⓣ*Park St.*

❾ Vilna Shul. As the oldest synagogue in Boston, this historic treasure is the focus of both renovation and research. The two-story brick building was completed in 1919 by Jews from Vilna, in what is now Lithuania.

Modeled after the medieval synagogues of Europe, it's the last surviving example of the more than 50 synagogues that once dotted Beacon Hill. The building, abandoned in 1985 after the congregation dropped to a single member, was bought by the Boston Center for Jewish Heritage, which is overseeing its ongoing restoration. Above the doorway gleams renewed gilded Hebrew lettering; the hand-carved ark and the stained-glass Star of David are worth a peek; and murals depicting traditional Sephardic themes are being uncovered from beneath seven layers of paint.

> **FRUGAL FUN**
>
> Take a cue from locals and sign up for one of the Boston Park Rangers' programs. Top picks include a visit to the city stables to meet the Mounties and their horses, regularly scheduled readings of Robert McCloskey's *Make Way for Ducklings* in Boston's Public Garden, and city scavenger hunts geared for families. Contact Boston Parks and Recreation ☎617/635-7487 ⊕ *www.cityof boston.gov/parks/parkrangers/.*

Three skylights flood it with natural light. ✉*14–18 Phillips St., Beacon Hill* ☎*617/523-2324* ⊕*www.vilnashul.com* ✉*Donations accepted* ⊙ *Wed., Thurs., and Fri. 11–5, Sun. 1–5* Ⓣ*Charles/MGH.*

❸ **William Hickling Prescott House.** A modest but engaging house museum has been installed in this 1808 Federal structure designed by Asher Benjamin. Now the headquarters for the Massachusetts Society of Colonial Dames of America, the house was the home of noted historian William Hickling Prescott from 1845 to 1859. Some rooms are furnished with period furniture, including the former study with Prescott's desk and "noctograph," which helped the nearly blind scholar write. (He was blinded in one eye by a flying crust of bread during a food fight at Harvard.) Ask about Prescott's secret staircase, which allowed him to escape into his study from boring guests in the parlor. The house also has a fine costume collection. ✉*55 Beacon St., Beacon Hill* ☎*617/742-3190* ⊕*www.nscda.org/ma/william_hickling_prescott_house.htm* ✉*$5* ⊙*Tours May–Oct., Wed., Thurs., and Sat. noon–4* Ⓣ*Park St., Charles/MGH.*

THE OLD WEST END

Just a few decades ago, this district—separated from Beacon Hill by Cambridge Street—resembled a typical medieval city: thoroughfares that twisted and turned, maddening one-way lanes, and streets that were a veritable hive of people. Then, progress—or what passes for progress—all but eliminated the thriving Irish, Italian, Jewish, and Greek communities to make room for a mammoth project of urban renewal, designed in the 1960s by I. M. Pei.

Today little remains of the *Old* West End except for a few brick tenements and a handful of monuments, including the first house built for Harrison Gray Otis. The biggest surviving structures in the Old West End with any real history are two public institutions, Massachusetts General Hospital and the former Suffolk County Jail, which dates from

1849 and was designed by Gridley Bryant. The onetime prison is now part of the luxurious, and wryly named, Liberty Hotel.

Behind Massachusetts General and the sprawling Charles River Park apartment complex (famous among Storrow Drive commuters as the place with signs reading IF YOU LIVED HERE, YOU'D BE HOME NOW) is a small grid of streets recalling an older Boston. Here are furniture and electric-supply stores, a discount camping-supply house (Hilton's Tent City), and many of the city's most popular watering holes. The main drag here is Causeway Street. North Station and the area around it, on Causeway between Haverhill and Canal streets, provide service to commuters from the northern suburbs and cheap brews to local barflies, and can be jammed when there's a game at the TD Banknorth Garden, the home away from home for loyal Bruins and Celtics fans.

In addition to the Garden, the innovative Museum of Science is one of the more-modern attractions of the Old West End. The newest addition to the area's skyline is the Leonard P. Zakim Bunker Hill Bridge, which spans the Charles River just across from the TD Banknorth Garden.

Numbers correspond to the Old West End map.

TOP ATTRACTIONS

6

Museum of Science. With 15-foot lightning bolts in the Theater of Electricity and a 20-foot-long *Tyrannosaurus rex* model, this is just the place to ignite any child's scientific curiosity. Occupying a compound of buildings north of Massachusetts General, the museum sits astride the Charles River Dam. More than 550 exhibits cover astronomy, astrophysics, anthropology, progress in medicine, computers, the organic and inorganic earth sciences, and much more. The emphasis is on hands-on education. For instance, at the "Investigate!" exhibit children explore such scientific principles as gravity by balancing objects—there are no wrong answers here, only discoveries. Children can learn the physics behind everyday play activities such as swinging and bumping up and down on a teeter-totter in the "Science in the Park" exhibit. Other displays include "Light House," where you can experiment with color and light, and the perennial favorite, "Dinosaurs: Modeling the Mesozoic," which lets kids become paleontologists and examine dinosaur bones, fossils, and tracks.

The **Charles Hayden Planetarium** (☎617/723–2500), with its sophisticated multimedia system based on a Zeiss planetarium projector, produces exciting programs on astronomical discoveries. Laser light shows, with laser graphics and computer animation, are scheduled Thursday through Sunday evenings. The shows are best for children older than five. Admission to the planetarium is $4 if you paid the admission for the museum and $9 for the planetarium alone. The Museum of Science includes the **Mugar Omni Theater** (☎617/723–2500), a five-story dome screen. The theater's state-of-the-art sound system provides extra-sharp acoustics, and the huge projection allows the audience to practically experience the action on-screen. Try to get tickets in advance online or over the phone. Admission for shows is $9 (or $4 if you paid the admission for the museum). Call or check the museum's Web site for showtimes. Although the museum is usually viewed as a family

Fodor's Choice
★

DUCK TOURS

With its colorful duck vehicles Boston Duck Tours is a Boston fixture, taking more than half a million people a year on unique, amphibious tours of the city: Boylston Street, Tremont Street, and the River Charles, all in one 80-minute trip. Tours depart from the Prudential Center and the Museum of Science, and run seven days a week, rain or shine, from late March to late November (all ducks are heated). Tickets are $29.95 for adults and $20 for ages 3–11. They sell out fast so reserve early. ☎ 617/267–3825 ⊕ www.bostonducktours.com.

DUCK TALK

"Take a duck tour. If you do this at the start of your trip (book online)

it'll give you a good idea of the layout of the city and an overview of the history (the guides/drivers are great and entertaining)." —highflyer

". . . Unless you have a highly developed sense of irony, I cannot imagine that you or anyone else between 14 and 44 would enjoy the duck tours. Take your grandchildren when the time comes. On the other hand, the Swan Boats in the Public Garden are charming." —Ackislander

"Oh, c'mon, Ackislander . . . take a look on the Duck Tours next time they go by, and you'll probably see 14- to 44-year-olds on it, camping it up. Undoubtedly with highly developed senses of irony." —Cassandra

destination, a more-adult crowd appears on Friday nights from 6 to 10 for the **Science Street Café,** where you can sip a martini and enjoy better-than-usual museum food to the sounds of live music. Afterward, stroll through near-empty exhibit halls for a late viewing or climb up to the Gilliland Observatory for a romantic up-close glimpse of the nighttime sky. ⊠ *Science Park at the Charles River Dam, Old West End* ☎ *617/723–2500* ⊕ *www.mos.org* ⊠ *$19* ⊙ *July 5–Labor Day, Sat.–Thurs. 9–7, Fri. 9–9; After Labor Day–July 4, Sat.–Thurs. 9–5, Fri. 9–9* Ⓣ *Science Park.*

WORTH NOTING

❷ **Harrison Gray Otis House.** This is the first of three houses built for and bearing the name of Harrison Gray Otis, Boston's third mayor and a prominent citizen and developer. It's now the headquarters for the Society for the Preservation of New England Antiquities (SPNEA), an organization that owns and maintains dozens of properties throughout the region. The society restored the 1796 house; two of the floors are open as a museum. The furnishings, textiles, wall coverings, and even the interior paint, specially mixed to match old samples, are faithful to the Federal period, circa 1790–1810. You may be surprised to see the bright and vivid colors favored in those days. The dining room is set up as though Harry Otis were about to come in and pour a glass of Madeira. But Otis lived here only four years before moving to more-sumptuous digs, designed by Charles Bulfinch, on Beacon Hill. A corner of the museum details the house's history after Otis moved out. A second-floor room brings to life the home's days as a late-19th-century boardinghouse, and a hallway display describes the "champoo baths" of former resident Mrs. Mott. Thought a quack in her time, she actually

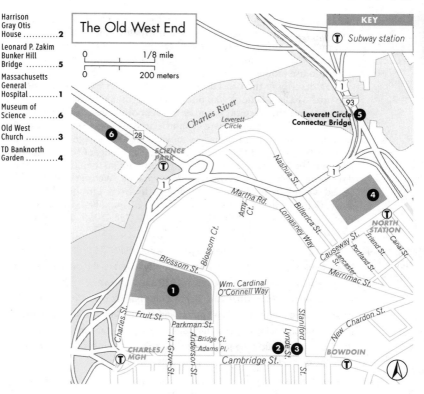

promoted the first aromatherapy saunas. A summertime Beacon Hill walking tour originates here. ✉ *141 Cambridge St., Old West End* ☎ *617/227–3957* ✪ *www.historicnewengland.org* 💲 *$8* ⊙ *Tours on hr and ½ hr Wed.–Sun. 11–4:30* Ⓣ *Charles/MGH, Bowdoin.*

⑤ Leonard P. Zakim Bunker Hill Bridge. Dedicated in October 2002, the Zakim Bridge is the newest Boston landmark, part of the "Big Dig" construction project. The 1,432-foot-long bridge, designed by Swiss bridge architect Christian Menn, is the widest cable-stayed hybrid bridge ever built and the first to use an asymmetrical design. The towers evoke the Bunker Hill Monument, and the distinctive fan shape of the cables gives the bridge a modern flair. The bridge was named after Lenny Zakim, a local civil-rights activist who headed the New England Region of the Anti-Defamation League and died of cancer in 1999; and the Battle of Bunker Hill, a defining moment in U.S. history. One of the best spots to view the bridge is from the Charlestown waterfront across the river. The best viewing is at night, when the illuminated bridge glows blue. ✉ *Old West End.*

① Massachusetts General Hospital. Incorporated in 1811, MGH has traditionally been regarded as the nation's premier general hospital. The domed, granite **Bulfinch Pavilion** was designed in 1818 by Boston's leading architect, Charles Bulfinch. It was in the hospital's **amphitheater**

(⊠ *Main entrance on N. Grove St.; turn right after coffee shop*) that, on October 16, 1846, Dr. John Collins Warren performed the first operation on a patient anesthetized by ether; the place was promptly nicknamed the "Ether Dome." You may visit the amphitheater today when it's not in use (admission free; open daily 9–5) and see the fourth-floor display describing the procedure that made modern surgery possible. Harvard Medical School was once on the grounds of Massachusetts General, and the hospital is today the school's oldest teaching affiliate. It was in a laboratory here around Thanksgiving 1849 that one of Boston's most notorious murders took place. Dr. George Parkman, a wealthy landlord and Harvard benefactor, was bludgeoned to death by Dr. John Webster after an argument over an unpaid loan. After several days of mystery over Parkman's disappearance, Webster's doom was sealed when part of the victim's jaw was discovered in the laboratory stove. Other grisly evidence turned up in the cesspool beneath Webster's privy. ⊠ *55 Fruit St., Old West End* ☎ *617/726–2000* ⊕ *www.mgh. harvard.edu* Ⓣ *Charles/MGH.*

■ **NEED A BREAK?**
Harvard Gardens (⊠ *316 Cambridge St., Beacon Hill* ☎ *617/523–2727*), a Beacon Hill legend, was the first bar in the city to get its liquor license after the repeal of Prohibition. It opened in 1930 and was owned by the same family until the 1990s. Once considered a dive bar, it's become much more upscale with a menu of gourmet pizzas and sandwiches and scrumptious brunch fare, including a spectacular Bloody Mary. The tuna melt on tandoori bread is a solid base for a day's exploring. The place is often packed with doctors and nurses enjoying post-shift drinks.

❸ **Old West Church.** Built in 1806 to a design of the builder and architect Asher Benjamin, this imposing United Methodist church stands, along with the Harrison Gray Otis House next door, as a reminder of the days when the area was a fashionable district. The church was a stop on the Underground Railroad, and it was the first integrated congregation in the country, giving open seating to blacks and whites alike just before 1820. In the early 1960s, when the church served as a public library and polling place, Congressman John F. Kennedy voted here. Free organ concerts are held here Tuesday at 8 PM in June, July, and August. ⊠ *131 Cambridge St., Old West End* ☎ *617/227–5088* ⊕ *www.oldwestchurch.org* ◷ *Tues. 10:30–1, Wed. 1:30–4, and Thurs. 10:30–4, but call to confirm. Sun. services at 11 AM* Ⓣ *Bowdoin, Government Center.*

❹ **TD Banknorth Garden.** Diehards still moan about the loss of the old Boston Garden, a much more intimate venue than this mammoth facility, which opened in 1995. Well, now they've got the next best thing. A decade after it opened as the FleetCenter, the home of the Celtics (basketball) and Bruins (hockey) is once again known as the Garden. Okay, so it's got the name of a bank attached now, but to locals it's once again just the good old "Gah-den." The original—which opened in 1928 and was famously the only indoor court in the National Basketball Association where games could be called on account of rain—is fondly remembered as the playing grounds for the likes of Larry Bird

HIGH-TECH HIDE AND SEEK

Geocaching—finding hidden caches using GPS coordinates posted on the Web—is a fun way to explore a neighborhood, and it turns out that Boston is full of buried treasure with more than 3,900 caches hidden throughout the area.

What's in a cache? There's always a logbook with information from the cache's founder, and notes from fellow discoverers. Often the cache contains a small treasure, anything from maps, books, jewelry, games, and more. We know one lucky cache discoverer who found a gift certificate to one of the finest restaurants in Boston. Get coordinates for Boston caches at www.geocaching.com.

and Bobby Orr. Still, the new Garden, with its air-conditioning, comfier seats, improved food selection, a 1,200-vehicle parking garage, and nearly double the number of bathrooms, has won grudging acceptance. After all, the Bruins now play on a regulation-size rink, and there are no obstructed views—though the place is so big you might need binoculars. The Garden occasionally offers public-skating sessions in the winter months; call ahead for hours and prices. The fifth and sixth levels of the TD Banknorth Garden house the **Sports Museum of New England** (⊠ *Use west premium seating entrance* ☎*617/624–1234* ⊕*www.sportsmuseum.org*), where displays of memorabilia and photographs showcase the history and the legends behind Boston's obsession with sports. Take a behind-the-scenes tour of locker and interview rooms in the off-season, or test your sports knowledge with interactive games. You can even see how you stand up to life-size statues of sports heroes Carl Yastrzemski and Larry Bird. The museum is open daily 11–5, with admission allowed only on the hour. Last entrance is at 3 PM on most days, 2 PM on game days; admission is $6. ⊠*Causeway St. at Canal St., Old West End* ☎*617/624–1000* ⊕*www.tdbanknorthgarden.com* Ⓣ*North Station.*

GOVERNMENT CENTER

This is a section of town Bostonians love to hate. Not only does Government Center house what they can't fight—City Hall—but it also contains some of the bleakest architecture since the advent of poured concrete. But though the stark, treeless plain surrounding City Hall has been roundly jeered for its user-unfriendly aura, the expanse is enlivened by feisty political rallies, free summer concerts, and the occasional festival. On the corner of Tremont and Court streets, the bleakness is partly mitigated by the local landmark Steaming Kettle, a gilded kettle cast in 1873 that once boiled around the clock. (It now marks a Starbucks.)

A GOOD WALK

The modern, stark expanse of Boston's **City Hall ❶** and the twin towers of the **John F. Kennedy Federal Office Building ❷** are an introduction to Boston in its urban-renewal stage. But just across Congress Street is **Faneuil Hall ❸**, a site of political speech making since Revolutionary times, and just beyond that is **Quincy Market ❹**, where you can shop (and eat) until you drop. For more Bostonian fare, walk back toward Congress Street to **Blackstone Block ❺** and the city's oldest restaurant, the **Union Oyster**

House ❻. (Fashionable ladies take note: The cobblestones are treacherous if you're wearing heels.) Near the restaurant is the **Holocaust Memorial ❼**, a six-tower construction of glass and steel. Follow Marshall Street north and turn right onto Blackstone Street to pass **The Haymarket ❽**, a flurry of activity on Friday and Saturday with open-air stalls selling produce and other foodstuffs. To sample Italian goodies, make your way to the North End via the pedestrian walkways that lead to Salem and Hanover streets.

More historic buildings are just a little farther on: 18th-century Faneuil Hall and the frenzied Quincy Market.

The curving six-story Center Plaza building, across from the Government Center T stop and the broad brick desert of City Hall Plaza, echoes the much older Sears Crescent, a curved commercial block next to the Government Center T stop. The Center Plaza building separates Tremont Street from the higher ground to the west: Pemberton Square and the old and "new" courthouses.

Although the $14 billion Central Artery/Tunnel project—the Big Dig—is essentially finished, the plan to turn old construction zones into parkland is still underway. The Rose Kennedy Greenway, as the stretch of parks is called, is slowly sprouting green, although they still lack the finishing touches. But after billions of dollars spent and a decade of traffic snarls, Bostonians are finally seeing the good side of the Big Dig. Traffic is flowing better and the roads aren't quite so confusing. The pedestrian ways in this area are also better marked, but don't feel shy about asking a local for help getting where you're going—you may still need it!

Numbers correspond to the Government Center & the North End map.

TIMING You can easily spend several hours hitting the stores, boutiques, and historic sites of the Faneuil Hall and Quincy Market complex. On Friday and Saturday, you can try to forge a path through the packed crowds at the Haymarket farmers' market (wear good walking shoes, as the cobblestones get slippery with trampled produce). Nearly everything is open on Sunday.

TOP ATTRACTIONS

 Blackstone Block. Between North and Hanover streets, near the Haymarket, lies the Blackstone Block, now visited mostly for its culinary landmark, the **Union Oyster House.** Named for one of Boston's first

1

settlers, William Blaxton, or Blackstone, it's the city's oldest commercial block, for decades dominated by the butcher trade. As a tiny remnant of old Boston, the Blackstone Block remains the city's "family attic"— to use the winning metaphor of critic Donlyn Lyndon: more than three centuries of architecture are on view, ranging from the 18th-century Capen House to the modern Bostonian Hotel. A colonial-period warren of winding lanes surrounds the block.

Facing the Blackstone Block, in tiny **Union Park,** framed by Congress Street and Dock Square, are two bronze figures, one seated on a bench and the other standing eye to eye with passersby. Both represent James Michael Curley, the quintessential Boston pol and a questionable role model for urban bosses. It's just as well that he has no pedestal. Also known as "the Rascal King" or "the Mayor of the Poor," and dramatized by Spencer Tracy in *The Last Hurrah* (1958), the charismatic Curley was beloved by the city's dominant working-class Irish for bringing them libraries, hospitals, bathhouses, and other public-works projects. His career got off to a promising start in 1903, when he ran—and won—a campaign for alderman from the Charles Street Jail, where he was serving time for taking someone else's civil-service exam. Over the next 50 years he dominated Boston politics, serving four nonconsecutive terms as mayor, one term as governor, and four terms as congressman. No one seemed to mind the slight glitch created when his office moved, in 1946, to the federal penitentiary, where he served five months of a 6- to 18-month sentence for mail fraud: he was pardoned by President Truman and returned to his people a hero.

❸ Faneuil Hall. The single building facing Congress Street is the real Faneuil
★ Hall, though locals often give that name to all five buildings in this shopping complex. Bostonians pronounce it *Fan*-yoo'uhl or *Fan*-yuhl. Like other Boston landmarks, Faneuil Hall has evolved over many years. It was erected in 1742, the gift of wealthy merchant Peter Faneuil, who wanted the hall to serve as both a place for town meetings and a public market. It burned in 1761 and was immediately reconstructed according to the original plan of its designer, the Scottish portrait painter John Smibert (who lies in the Granary Burying Ground). In 1763 the political leader James Otis helped inaugurate the era that culminated in American independence when he dedicated the rebuilt hall to the cause of liberty.

In 1772 Samuel Adams stood here and first suggested that Massachusetts and the other colonies organize a Committee of Correspondence to maintain semiclandestine lines of communication in the face of hardening British repression. In later years the hall again lived up to Otis's dedication when the abolitionists Wendell Phillips and Charles Sumner pleaded for support from its podium. The tradition continues to this day: in presidential-election years, the hall is the site of debates between contenders in the Massachusetts primary.

Faneuil Hall was substantially enlarged and remodeled in 1805 according to a Greek Revival design of the noted architect Charles Bulfinch; this is the building you see today. Its purposes remain the same: the balconied Great Hall is available to citizens' groups on presentation

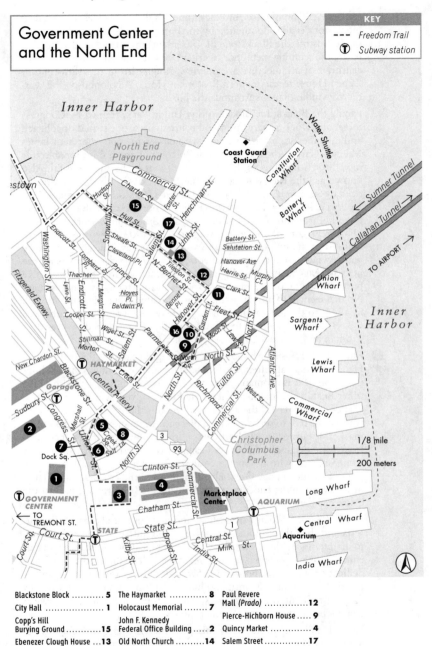

Government Center and the North End

KEY

--- Freedom Trail

Ⓣ Subway station

Inner Harbor

North End Playground

Coast Guard Station

Constitution Wharf

Water Shuttle

Commercial St.

Battery Wharf

Sumner Tunnel

Callahan Tunnel

TO AIRPORT

Union Wharf

Inner Harbor

Sargents Wharf

Lewis Wharf

Commercial Wharf

Christopher Columbus Park

AQUARIUM

Long Wharf

Central Wharf

Aquarium

India Wharf

of a request signed by a required number of responsible parties; it also plays host to regular concerts.

Inside Faneuil Hall are dozens of paintings of famous Americans, including the mural *Webster's Reply to Hayne,* Gilbert Stuart's portrait of Washington at Dorchester Heights. Park rangers give informational talks about the history and importance of Faneuil Hall on the hour and half hour. The rangers are a good resource, as interpretive plaques are few. On the building's top floors are the headquarters and museum of the **Ancient & Honorable Artillery Company of Massachusetts** (☎617/227–1638). Founded in 1638, it's the oldest militia in the Western Hemisphere, and the third oldest in the world, after the Swiss Guard and the Honorable Artillery Company of London. Its status is now strictly ceremonial, but it's justly proud of the arms, uniforms, and other artifacts on display. Admission is free. The museum is open weekdays 9 to 3:30. Brochures about Faneuil Hall's history, distributed by the National Park Service, make lighthearted references to the ongoing commercialism nearby by reprinting a 1958 ditty by Francis Hatch: "Here orators in ages past / Have mounted their attacks / Undaunted by proximity / Of sausage on the racks." Faneuil Hall has always sat in the middle of Boston's main marketplace: when such men as Andrew Jackson and Daniel Webster debated the future of the Republic here, the fragrances of bacon and snuff—sold by merchants in **Quincy Market** across the road—greeted their noses. Today, the aroma of coffee wafts through the hall from a snack bar. The shops at ground level sell New England bric-a-brac. ⊠ *Faneuil Hall Sq., Government Center* ☎*617/523–1300* ⊕*www.cityofboston.gov/freedomtrail/faneuilhall. asp* ⬛*Free* ☉*Great Hall daily 9–5; informational talks every ½ hr. Shops Mon.–Saturday 10* AM*–9* PM*, Sunday noon–6* PM. Ⓣ*Government Center, Aquarium, State.*

➐ **Holocaust Memorial.** At night, its six 50-foot-high glass-and-steel towers
Fodor'sChoice glow like ghosts. During the day the monument seems at odds with
★ the 18th-century streetscape of Blackstone Square behind it. Shoehorned into the north end of Union Park, the Holocaust Memorial is the work of Stanley Saitowitz, whose design was selected through an international competition; the finished memorial was dedicated in 1995. Recollections by Holocaust survivors are set into the glass-and-granite walls; the upper levels of the towers are etched with 6 million numbers in random sequence, symbolizing the Jewish victims of the Nazi horror. Manufactured steam from grates in the granite base makes for a particularly haunting scene after dark. ⊠ *Union St. near Hanover St.,* Ⓣ *Government Center.*

➍ **Quincy Market.** Not everyone likes Quincy Market, also known as Faneuil Hall Marketplace; some people prefer grit to polish, and disdain the shiny cafés and boutiques. But there's no denying that this pioneer effort at urban recycling set the tone for many similar projects throughout the country, and that it has brought tremendous vitality to a once-tired corner of Boston. Quincy Market continues to attract huge crowds of tourists and locals throughout the year. In the early '70s, demolition was a distinct possibility for the decrepit buildings. Fortunately, the primitive idea that urban renewal was always best accomplished with a bulldozer was beginning to yield to the more-progressive concept of reuse. With the participation of the Boston Redevelopment Authority, architect Benjamin Thompson planned a renovation of Quincy Market, and the Rouse Corporation of Baltimore undertook its restoration, which was completed in 1976. Try to look beyond the shop windows to the grand design of the

market buildings themselves; they represent a vision of the market as urban centerpiece, an idea whose time has certainly come again.

The market consists of three block-long annexes: **Quincy Market, North Market,** and **South Market,** each 535 feet long and across a plaza from Faneuil Hall. The structures were designed in 1826 by Alexander Parris as part of a public-works project instituted by Boston's second mayor, Josiah Quincy, to alleviate the cramped conditions of Faneuil Hall and clean up the refuse that collected in Town Dock, the pond behind it. The central structure, made of granite, with a Doric colonnade at either end and topped by a classical dome and rotunda, has kept its traditional market-stall layout, but the stalls now purvey international and specialty foods: sushi, frozen yogurt, bagels, calzones, sausage-on-a-stick, Chinese noodles, barbecue, and baklava, plus all the boutique chocolate-chip cookies your heart desires. This is perhaps Boston's best locale for grazing; the hardest part is choosing what to sample.

Along the arcades on either side of the Central Market are vendors selling sweatshirts, photographs of Boston, and arts and crafts—some schlocky, some not—along with a couple of patioed bars and restaurants. The North and South markets house a mixture of chain stores and specialty boutiques. Quintessential Boston remains here only in Durgin Park, opened in 1826 and known for its plain interior, brassy waitresses, and large portions of traditional New England fare.

A greenhouse flower market on the north side of Faneuil Hall provides a splash of color; at Christmastime, trees along the cobblestone walks are strung with thousands of sparkling lights. In summer, up to 50,000 people a day descend on the market; the outdoor cafés are an excellent spot to watch the hordes if you can find a seat. Year-round the pedestrian walkways draw street performers, and rings of strollers form around magicians and musicians. ⊠*Bordered by Clinton, Commercial, and Chatham Sts., Government Center* ☎*617/523–1300* ⊕*www.faneuilhallmarketplace.com* ۞*Mon.–Sat. 10–9, Sun. noon–6. Restaurants and bars generally open daily 11* AM–2 AM; *food stalls open earlier* Ⓣ*Government Center, Aquarium, State.*

❻ Union Oyster House. Billed as the oldest restaurant in continuous service in the United States, the Union Oyster House first opened its doors as the Atwood & Bacon Oyster House in 1826. Charles Forster of Maine was the first American to use the curious invention of the toothpick on these premises. And John F. Kennedy was also among its patrons; his

1

favorite booth has been dedicated to his memory. The charming facade is constructed of Flemish bond brick and adorned with Victorian-style signage. With its scallop, clam, and lobster dishes—as well as the de rigueur oyster—the menu hasn't changed much from the restaurant's early days (though the prices have). ⊠ *41 Union St., Government Center* ☏ *617/227–2750* ⊕ *www.unionoysterhouse.com* ⊙ *Sun.–Thurs. 11–9:30, Fri. and Sat. 11–10; bar open until midnight* Ⓣ *Haymarket.*

NEED A BREAK?

If all that snacking has you craving something more substantial, you might want to sample Boston's Irish heritage at the **Black Rose** (⊠ *160 State St., Government Center* ☏ *617/742–2286* ⊕ *www.irishconnection.com/black rose.html*); take a right at the far end of the South Market. The bar-restaurant features traditional Irish fare and live music seven nights a week.

WORTH NOTING

❶ **City Hall.** Over the years, various plans—involving gardens, restaurants, music, and hotels—have been floated to make this a more-people-friendly site. Possibly the only thing that would ameliorate Bostonians' collective distaste for the chilly Government Center is tearing it down. But for the moment, City Hall, an upside-down ziggurat design on a brutalist redbrick plaza remains in commission. The design, by Kallman, McKinnell, and Knowles, confines administrative functions to the upper floors and places offices that deal with the public at street level. ⊠ *Congress St. at North St., Government Center* Ⓣ *Government Center.*

❽ **The Haymarket.** Loud, self-promoting vendors pack this exuberant maze of a marketplace at Marshall and Blackstone streets on Friday and Saturday from 7 AM until mid-afternoon (all vendors will likely be gone by 5 at the latest). Pushcart vendors hawk fruits and vegetables against a backdrop of fish, meat, and cheese shops. The accumulation of debris left every evening has been celebrated in a whimsical 1976 public-arts project—Mags Harries's *Asaroton,* a Greek word meaning "unswept floors"—consisting of bronze fruit peels and other detritus smashed into pavement. Another Harries piece, a bronze depiction of a gathering of stray gloves, tumbles down between the escalators in the Porter Square T station in Cambridge. At Creek Square, near the Haymarket, is the **Boston Stone.** Set into the brick wall of the gift shop of the same name, this was a marker long used as milepost zero in measuring distances from Boston. ⊠ *Marshall and Blackstone Sts., Government Center* Ⓣ *Government Center* ⊙ *Fri. and Sat. 7 AM–mid-afternoon.*

❷ **John F. Kennedy Federal Office Building.** Looming up at the northwest edge of City Hall Plaza, these twin towers are noted structures for architecture aficionados: they were designed by the founder of the Bauhaus movement, Walter Gropius, who taught at Harvard toward the end of his illustrious career. Gropius's house, designed by him in textbook Bauhaus style, is in nearby suburban Lincoln.

THE NORTH END

The warren of small streets on the northeast side of Government Center is the North End, Boston's Little Italy. In the 17th century the North End *was* Boston, as much of the rest of the peninsula was still under water or had yet to be cleared. Here the town bustled and grew rich for a century and a half before the birth of American independence. Now visitors can get a glimpse into Revolutionary times while filling up on some of the most scrumptious pastries and pastas to be found in modern Boston.

Today's North End is almost entirely a creation of the late 19th century, when brick tenements began to fill up with European immigrants—first the Irish, then Central European Jews, then the Portuguese, and finally the Italians. For more than 60 years the North End attracted an Italian population base, so much so that one wonders whether wandering Puritan shades might scowl at the concentration of Mediterranean verve, volubility, and Roman Catholicism here. This is Boston's haven not only for Italian restaurants but also for Italian groceries, bakeries, boccie courts, churches, social clubs, cafés, and street-corner debates over home-team soccer games. ■TIP➔ **July and August are highlighted by a series of street festivals, or** *feste,* **honoring various saints, and by local community events that draw people from all over the city.** A statue of St. Agrippina di Mineo—which is covered with money when it's paraded through the streets—is a crowd favorite.

Although hordes of tourists follow the redbrick ribbon of the Freedom Trail through the North End, the jumbled streets retain a neighborhood feeling, from the grandmothers gossiping on fire escapes to the laundry strung on back porches. Gentrification diluted the quarter's ethnic character by filling it with yuppies. But linger for a moment along Salem or Hanover streets and you can still hear people speaking with Abruzzese accents. If you wish to study up on this fascinating district, head for the North End branch of the Boston Public Library on Parmenter Street, where a bust of Dante acknowledges local cultural pride.

TIMING Allow two hours for a walk through the North End, longer if you plan on dawdling in a café. This part of town is made for strolling, day or night. Many people like to spend part of a day at nearby Quincy Market, then head over to the North End for dinner—the district has an impressive selection of traditional and contemporary Italian restaurants. Families should note that on Saturday afternoons from May through October the Paul Revere House schedules some of the most delightful events for children in the city. And on Sunday, try to catch the ringing of the bells of the Old North Church after the 11 AM service; Paul Revere rang them on Sabbath mornings as a boy.

Numbers correspond to the Government Center & the North End map.

TOP ATTRACTIONS

🅑 **Copp's Hill Burying Ground.** An ancient and melancholy air hovers like a fine mist over this colonial-era burial ground. The North End graveyard incorporates four cemeteries established between 1660 and 1819. Near

A GOOD WALK

Walking is the best way to view the sights of the North End. Parking is for residents only and even then is practically nonexistent, so most people arrive by T (Haymarket or Government Center). ■ TIP→ **If you come by car, your best bet is to find a garage near Haymarket and Quincy Market (try the lot at 75 State Street and validate your parking with a purchase at Quincy Market);** from there you can follow the red stripe of the Freedom Trail to **Salem Street**. Once there, turn right on Cross Street and left on **Hanover Street**, the North End's main thoroughfare. From Hanover, turn right on Parmenter Street and left on North Street, following the Freedom Trail into North Square to reach the venerable brick **Pierce-Hichborn House** ❾ and, beside

it, the contrasting **Paul Revere House** ❿. Take Prince Street back to Hanover Street and continue on Hanover to reach **St. Stephen's** ⓫, the only remaining church designed by the influential architect Charles Bulfinch. Directly across the street is the Prado, or **Paul Revere Mall** ⓬, dominated by a statue of the patriot on horseback. At the end of the mall is the **Old North Church** ⓮, of "one if by land, two if by sea" fame, from which twin lanterns warned of the invading British on the night of Revere's legendary ride. Continue following the Freedom Trail to Hull Street and **Copp's Hill Burying Ground** ⓯, the resting place of many Revolutionary heroes. Then head back to Hanover Street for a well-deserved cappuccino and cannoli.

the Charter Street gate is the tomb of the Mather family, the dynasty of church divines (Cotton and Increase were the most famous sons) who held sway in Boston during the heyday of the old theocracy. Also buried here is Robert Newman, who crept into the steeple of the Old North Church to hang the lanterns warning of the British attack the night of Paul Revere's ride. Look for the tombstone of Captain Daniel Malcolm; it's pockmarked with musket-ball fire from British soldiers, who used the stones for target practice. Across the street at 44 Hull is the **narrowest house in Boston**—it's a mere 10 feet across. ⊠ *Intersection of Hull and Snowhill Sts., North End* ⊗ *Daily 9–5* Ⓣ *North Station.*

⓰ **Hanover Street.** This is the North End's main thoroughfare, along with the smaller and narrower Salem Street. It was named for the ruling dynasty of 18th- and 19th-century England; the label was retained after the Revolution, despite a flurry of patriotic renaming (King Street became State Street, for example). Hanover's business center is thick with restaurants, pastry shops, and Italian cafés; on weekends, Italian immigrants who have moved to the suburbs return to share an espresso with old friends and maybe catch a soccer game broadcast via satellite. Hanover is one of Boston's oldest public roads, once the site of the residences of the Rev. Cotton Mather and the colonial-era patriot Dr. Joseph Warren, as well as a small dry-goods store run by Eben D. Jordan— who went on to launch the Jordan Marsh department stores.

NEED A
BREAK?

Caffe Vittoria (✉ *290–296 Hanover St., North End* ☎ *617/227-7606*) is rightfully known as Boston's most traditional Italian café. Gleaming brass, marble tabletops, and one of the city's best selections of grappa keep the place packed with locals. Fill a takeaway box with cannoli and other mouthwatering Italian pastries at **Mike's Pastry** (✉ *300 Hanover St., North End* ☎ *617/742-3050*). If you're lucky enough to snag a table, linger over the cappuccino or try one of the many flavors of gelato.

⑭ Fodor'sChoice ★ **Old North Church.** Standing at one end of the **Paul Revere Mall** is a church famous not only for being the oldest one in Boston (built in 1723) but for housing the two lanterns that glimmered from its steeple on the night of April 18, 1775. This is Christ Church, or the Old North, where Paul Revere and the young sexton Robert Newman managed that night to signal the departure by water of the British regulars to Lexington and Concord. Newman, carrying the lanterns, ascended the steeple (the original tower blew down in 1804 and was replaced; the present one was put up in 1954 after the replacement was destroyed in a hurricane) while Revere began his clandestine trip by boat across the Charles.

DID YOU
KNOW?

Longfellow's poem aside, the Old North Church lanterns were not a signal *to* Paul Revere but *from* him to Charlestown across the harbor.

Although William Price designed the structure after studying Christopher Wren's London churches, the Old North—which still has an active Episcopal congregation (including descendants of the Reveres)—is an impressive building in its own right. Inside, note the gallery and the graceful arrangement of pews (reserved in colonial times for the families that rented them); the bust of George Washington, pronounced by the Marquis de Lafayette to be the truest likeness of the general he ever saw; the brass chandeliers, made in Amsterdam in 1700 and installed here in 1724; and the clock, the oldest still running in an American public building. The pews—No. 54 was the Revere family pew—are the highest in the United States because of the little charcoal-burning foot warmers (used to accommodate parishioners back when). Try to visit when changes are rung on the bells, after the 11 AM Sunday service; they bear the inscription, WE ARE THE FIRST RING OF BELLS CAST FOR THE BRITISH EMPIRE IN NORTH AMERICA. On the Sunday closest to April 18, descendants of the patriots reenact the raising of the lanterns in the church belfry during a special evening service.

Behind the church is the **Washington Memorial Garden,** where volunteers cultivate a plot devoted to plants and flowers favored in the 18th century. The garden is studded with several unusual commemorative plaques, including one for the Rev. George Burrough, who was hanged in the Salem witch trials in 1692; it was his great-grandson, Robert Newman, who carried the famous pair of lanterns to the steeple. In another niche hangs the "Third Lantern," dedicated in 1976 to mark the country's bicentennial celebration. ✉ *193 Salem St., North End* ☎ *617/523-6676* ⊕ *www.oldnorth.com* ⊙ *Jan. and Feb., Tues.–Sun. 10–4; Mar.–May, daily 9–5; June–Oct., daily 9–6; Nov. and Dec., daily 10–5. Sun. services at 9 and 11 AM* Ⓣ *Haymarket, North Station.*

WORTH NOTING

⑬ Ebenezer Clough House. Built in 1712, this house is now the only local survivor of its era aside from Old North, which stands nearby. Picture the streets lined with houses such as this, with an occasional grander Georgian mansion and some modest wooden-frame survivors of old Boston's many fires—this is what the North End looked like when Paul Revere was young. The home is privately owned and not open to the public. ⊠ *21 Unity St., North End.*

⑩ Paul Revere House. It's an interesting coincidence that the oldest house standing in downtown Boston should also have been the home of Paul Revere, patriot activist and silversmith, as many homes of famous Bostonians have burned or been demolished over the years. The Revere house could easily have become one of them back when it was just another makeshift tenement in the heyday of European immigration. It was saved from oblivion in 1902 and restored to an approximation of its original 17th-century appearance.

Originally on the site was the parsonage of the Second Church of Boston, home to the Rev. Increase Mather, the Second Church's minister. Mather's house burned in the great fire of 1676, and the house that Revere was to occupy was built on its location about four years later, nearly a hundred years before Revere's 1775 midnight ride through Middlesex County. Revere owned it from 1770 until 1800, although he lived there for only 10 years and rented it out for the next two decades. Pre-1900 photographs show it as a shabby warren of storefronts and apartments. The clapboard sheathing is a replacement, but 90% of the framework is original; note the Elizabethan-style overhang and leaded windowpanes. A few Revere furnishings are on display here, and just gazing at his silverwork—much more of which is displayed at the Museum of Fine Arts—brings the man alive.

Special events are scheduled throughout the year, many designed with children in mind. During the first weekend in December, the staff dresses in period costume and serves apple-cider cake and other colonial-era goodies. From May through October, you might encounter a silversmith practicing his trade, a dulcimer player entertaining a crowd, or a military-reenactment group in full period regalia. And if you go to the house on Patriots' Day, chances are you'll bump into a fife-and-drum corps.

The immediate neighborhood also has Revere associations. The little park in North Square is named after Rachel Revere, his second wife, and the adjacent brick **Pierce-Hichborn House** once belonged to relatives of Revere. The garden connecting the Revere house and the Pierce-Hichborn House is planted with flowers and medicinal herbs favored in Revere's day. ⊠ *19 North Sq., North End* ☎ *617/523–2338* ⊕ *www. paulreverehouse.org* ⊠ *$3.50, $5.50 with Pierce-Hichborn House* ⊙ *Jan.–Mar., Tues.–Sun. 9:30–4:15; Nov. and Dec., and 1st 2 wks of Apr., daily 9:30–4:15; mid-Apr.–Oct., daily 9:30–5:15* Ⓣ *Haymarket, Aquarium, Government Center.*

⑫ Paul Revere Mall *(Prado).* This makes a perfect time-out spot from the Freedom Trail. Bookended by two landmark churches—Old North

Paul Revere's Ride

Test: Paul Revere was (1) a patriot whose midnight ride helped ignite the American Revolution; (2) a part-time dentist; (3) a silversmith who crafted tea services; (4) a printer who engraved the first Massachusetts state currency; or (5) a talented metallurgist who cast cannons and bells. The only correct response is "all of the above." But there's much more to this outsize Revolutionary hero—bell ringer for the Old North Church, founder of the copper mills that still bear his name, and father of 16 children.

Although his life spanned eight decades (1734–1818), Revere is most famous for that one night, April 18, 1775, when he became America's most celebrated Pony Express rider. *"Listen, my children, and you shall hear / Of the midnight ride of Paul Revere"* are the opening lines of Henry Wadsworth Longfellow's poem, which placed the event at the center of American folklore. Longfellow may have been an effective evangelist for Revere, but he was an indifferent historian.

Revere wasn't the only midnight rider. As part of the system set in motion by Revere and William Dawes Jr., also dispatched from Boston, there were at least several dozen riders so that the capture of any one of them wouldn't keep the alarm from being sounded. It's also known that Revere never looked for the lantern signal from Charlestown. He told Robert Newman to hang two lanterns from Old North's belfry since the Redcoats were on the move by water, but by that time, Revere was already being rowed across the Charles River to begin his famous ride.

Revere and Dawes set out on separate routes but had the same mission: to warn patriot leaders Samuel Adams and John Hancock that British regular troops were marching to arrest them, and alarm the countryside along the way. The riders didn't risk capture by shouting the news through the streets—and they never uttered the famous cry "The British are coming!," since Bostonians still considered themselves British. When Revere arrived in Lexington a few minutes past midnight and approached the house where Adams and Hancock were lodged, a sentry challenged him, requesting that he not make so much noise. "Noise!" Revere replied. "You'll have noise enough before long."

Despite Longfellow's assertion, Revere never raised the alarm in Concord, for he was captured en route. He was held and questioned by the British patrol, and eventually released, without his horse, to walk back to Lexington in time to witness part of the battle on Lexington Green.

Poetic license aside, this tale has become part of the collective American spirit. Americans dote on hearing that Revere forgot his spurs, only to retrieve them by tying a note to his dog's collar, then awaiting its return with the spurs attached. The resourcefulness he showed in using a lady's petticoat to muffle the sounds of his oars while crossing the Charles is greatly appreciated. Little wonder that these tales resonate in the hearts and imagination of America's citizenry, as well as in Boston's streets on the third Monday of every April, Patriots' Day, when Revere's ride is reenacted—in daylight—to the cheers of thousands of onlookers.

and St. Stephen's—the mall is flanked by brick walls lined with bronze plaques bearing the stories of famous North Enders. An appropriate centerpiece for this enchanting cityscape is Cyrus Dallin's equestrian **statue of Paul Revere**. Despite his depictions in such statues as this, the gentle Revere was stocky and of medium height—whatever manly dash he possessed must have been in his eyes rather than his physique. That physique served him well enough, however, for he lived to be 83 and saw nearly all of his Revolutionary comrades buried. ⊠*Bordered by Tileston, Hanover, and Unity Sts., North End* ⊤*Haymarket, Aquarium, Government Center.*

❾ Pierce-Hichborn House. One of the city's oldest brick buildings, this structure, just to the left of the Paul Revere House, was once owned by Nathaniel Hichborn, a boatbuilder and Revere's cousin on his mother's side. Built about 1711 for a window maker named Moses Pierce, the Pierce-Hichborn House is an excellent example of early Georgian architecture. The home's symmetrical style was a radical change from the wood-frame Tudor buildings, such as the Revere House, then common. Its four rooms are furnished with modest 18th-century furniture, providing a peek into typical middle-class life. ⊠*29 North Sq., North End* ☎*617/523–2338* ⌨*$2, $5.50 with Paul Revere House* ☉*Guided tours only; call to schedule* ⊤*Haymarket, Aquarium, Government Center.*

⓫ St. Stephen's. Rose Kennedy, matriarch of the Kennedy clan, was christened here; 104 years later, St. Stephen's held mourners at her 1995 funeral. This is the only Charles Bulfinch church still standing in Boston, and a stunning example of the Federal style to boot. Built in 1804, it was first used as a Unitarian Church; since 1862 it has served a Roman Catholic parish. When the belfry was stripped during a major 1960s renovation, the original dome was found beneath a false cap; it was covered with sheet copper and held together with hand-wrought nails, and later authenticated as being the work of Paul Revere. ⊠*401 Hanover St., North End* ☎*617/523–1230* ☉*Daily 7:30–4:30. Sun. Mass at 11, Sat. at 4:30, Tues.–Fri. at 7:30* AM ⊤*Haymarket, Aquarium, Government Center.*

Salem Street. This ancient and constricted thoroughfare, one of the two main North End streets, cuts through the heart of the neighborhood and runs parallel to and one block west of Hanover. Between Cross and Prince streets, Salem Street contains numerous restaurants and shops. One of the best is Shake the Tree, one of the North End's trendiest boutiques, selling stylish clothing, gifts, and jewelry. The rest of Salem Street is mostly residential, but makes a nice walk to the Copp's Hill Burying Ground.

NEED A BREAK?

The allure of **Bova's Bakery** (⊠*134 Salem St., North End* ☎*617/523–5601*), a neighborhood institution, lies not only in its takeaway Italian breads, calzones, and pastries, but also in its hours: 24 a day (the deli closes at 1 AM, however).

CHARLESTOWN

Boston started here. Charlestown was a thriving settlement a year before colonials headed across the Charles River at William Blaxton's invitation to found the city proper. Today the district's attractions include two of the most visible—and vertical—monuments in Boston: the Bunker Hill Monument, which commemorates the grisly battle that became a symbol of patriotic resistance against the British, and the USS *Constitution*, whose masts continue to tower over the waterfront where she was built more than 200 years ago.

As a neighborhood, Charlestown remains predominantly Irish-American, although gentrification that began in the 1980s continues. Today, despite the inroads made by trendy restaurants such as Todd English's Olives and chic digs such as the Navy Yard condos, the area still suffers a bit from its reputation as an alleged home turf for Irish-led organized crime. A number of bloody murders that remain unsolved—because of the neighborhood's vaunted "code of silence"—haven't helped. But Townies (as old-time Charlestown residents are called) are fiercely proud of their historic, well-maintained streets.

The blocks around the Bunker Hill Monument are a good illustration of a neighborhood in flux. Along streets lined with gas lamps are impeccably restored Federal and mid-19th-century town houses; cheek by jowl are working-class quarters of similar vintage but more-modest recent pasts. Nearby Winthrop Square also has its share of interesting houses. Near the Navy Yard along Main Street is City Square, the beginning of Charlestown's main commercial district, which includes City Square Park, with brick paths and bronze fish sculptures. On Phipps Street is the grave marker of John Harvard, a young minister who in 1638 bequeathed his small library to the fledgling Cambridge College, thereafter renamed in his honor. The precise location of the grave is uncertain, but a monument of 1828 marks its approximate site.

To get to Charlestown, you can walk across the Charlestown Bridge from the North End, or take Bus 93 from the Haymarket T station; it stops three blocks from the Navy Yard entrance. A more-interesting and speedy way to get here is to take the MBTA water shuttle from Long Wharf in downtown Boston, which runs every 15 or 30 minutes year-round.

Numbers correspond to the Charlestown map.

A STICKY SUBJECT

Boston has had its share of grim historic events, from massacres to stranglers, but on the sheer weirdness scale, nothing beats the Great Molasses Flood. In 1919, a steel container of molasses exploded on the Boston Harbor waterfront, killing 21 people and 20 horses. More than 2.3 million gallons of goo oozed onto unsuspecting citizenry, a veritable tsunami of sweet stuff. Some say you can still smell molasses on the waterfront during steamy weather. Smells to us like urban myth!

A GOOD WALK

If you chose to hoof it to Charles-town, follow Hull Street from Copp's Hill Burying Ground to Commercial Street; turn left on Commercial and, two blocks later, right onto the bridge. The entrance to the **Charles-town Navy Yard** ❶ is on your right after crossing the bridge. Just ahead is the Charlestown Navy Yard Visitors Information Center; inside the park gate is the **USS** *Constitution* ❷ and the associated **USS** *Constitution* **Museum** ❸. From here, the red line of the Freedom Trail takes you to the **Bunker Hill Monument** ❹.

TIMING

Give yourself two to three hours for a Charlestown walk; the lengthy Charlestown Bridge calls for endurance in cold weather. You may want to save Charlestown's stretch of the Freedom Trail, which adds considerably to its length, for a second-day outing. You can always save backtracking the historic route by taking the MBTA water shuttle, which ferries back and forth between Charlestown's Navy Yard and downtown Boston's Long Wharf.

TOP ATTRACTIONS

❹ **Bunker Hill Monument.** Three misunderstandings surround this famous
Fodor'sChoice monument. First, the Battle of Bunker Hill was actually fought on
★ Breed's Hill, which is where the monument sits today. (The real Bunker Hill is about ½ mi to the north of the monument; it's slightly taller than Breed's Hill.) Bunker was the original planned locale for the battle, and for that reason its name stuck. Second, although the battle is generally considered a colonial success, the Americans lost. It was a Pyrrhic victory for the British Redcoats, who sacrificed nearly half of their 2,200 men; American casualties numbered 400–600. And third: the famous war cry "Don't fire until you see the whites of their eyes" may never have been uttered by American Colonel William Prescott or General Israel Putnam, but if either one did shout it, he was quoting an old Prussian command made necessary by the notorious inaccuracy of the musket. No matter. The Americans did employ a deadly delayed-action strategy on June 17, 1775, and conclusively proved themselves worthy fighters, capable of defeating the forces of the British Empire.

Among the dead were the brilliant young American doctor and political activist Joseph Warren, recently commissioned as a major general but fighting as a private, and the British Major John Pitcairn, who two months before had led the Redcoats into Lexington. Pitcairn is believed to be buried in the crypt of the Old North Church.

In 1823 the committee formed to construct a monument on the site of the battle chose the form of an Egyptian obelisk. Architect Solomon Willard designed a 221-foot-tall granite obelisk, a tremendous feat of engineering for its day. The Marquis de Lafayette laid the cornerstone of the monument in 1825, but because of a nagging lack of funds, it wasn't dedicated until 1843. Daniel Webster's stirring words at the ceremony commemorating the laying of its cornerstone have gone down in history: "Let it rise! Let it rise, till it meets the sun in his coming.

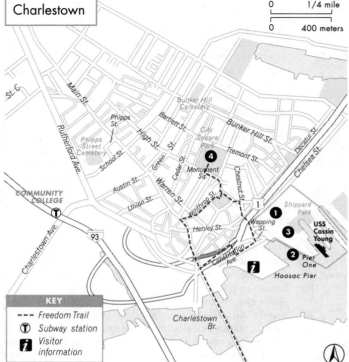

Charlestown

Let the earliest light of the morning gild it, and parting day linger and play upon its summit."

The monument's zenith is reached by a flight of 294 steps. There's no elevator, but the views from the observatory are worth the effort of the arduous climb. A statue of Colonel Prescott stands guard at the base. In the Bunker Hill Museum across the street, artifacts and exhibits tell the story of the battle, while a detailed diorama shows the action in miniature. ☎617/242-5641 ⊕*www.nps.gov/bost/historyculture/bhm. htm.* ⊠*Free* ⊗*Museum daily 9–5, monument daily 9–4:30* ⊤*Community College.*

DID YOU KNOW?

The country's first commercial railway was built in 1826 for the express purpose of hauling the granite for the Bunker Hill obelisk from a quarry in Quincy.

❷ **USS *Constitution*.** Better known as "Old Ironsides," the USS *Constitution* rides proudly at anchor in her berth at the Charlestown Navy
Ⓢ Yard. The oldest commissioned ship in the U.S. fleet is a battlewagon
FodorsChoice of the old school, of the days of "wooden ships and iron men"—when
★ she and her crew of 200 succeeded at the perilous task of asserting the sovereignty of an improbable new nation. Every July 4 and on certain

other occasions she's towed out for a turnabout in Boston Harbor, the very place her keel was laid in 1797.

The venerable craft has narrowly escaped the scrap heap several times in her long history. She was launched on October 21, 1797, as part of the nation's fledgling navy. Her hull was made of live oak, the toughest wood grown in North America; her bottom was sheathed in copper, provided by Paul Revere at a nominal cost. Her principal service was during Thomas Jefferson's campaign against the Barbary pirates, off the coast of North Africa, and in the War of 1812. In 42 engagements, her record was 42–0.

The nickname "Old Ironsides" was acquired during the War of 1812, when shots from the British warship *Guerrière* appeared to bounce off her tough oaken hull. Talk of scrapping the ship began as early as 1830, but she was saved by a public campaign sparked by Oliver Wendell Holmes's poem "Old Ironsides." She underwent a major restoration in the early 1990s, and only about 8%–10% of her original wood remains in place. The keel, the heart of the ship, is original. Today she continues, the oldest commissioned warship afloat in the world, to be a part of the U.S. Navy.

The men and women who look after the *Constitution,* regular navy personnel, maintain a 24-hour watch. Sailors show visitors around the ship, guiding them to her top, or spar, deck, and the gun deck below. Another treat when visiting the ship is the spectacular view of Boston across Boston Harbor. ■ TIP→ **Instead of taking the T, you can get closer to the ship by taking MBTA Bus 92 to Charlestown City Square or Bus 93 to Chelsea Street from Haymarket. Or you can take the Boston Harbor Cruise water shuttle from Long Wharf to Pier 4.** ✉ *Charlestown Navy Yard, 55 Constitution Rd., Charlestown* ☎ *617/242–5670* ⊕ *www.ussconstitution. navy.mil* 🖃 *Free* ☉ *Apr. 1–Oct., Tues.–Sun. 10–5:50; Nov.–Mar. 31, Thurs.–Sun. 10–3:50; last tour at 3:30* Ⓣ *North Station.*

NEED A BREAK? After a blustery walk at the Navy Yard, get a seat by the fireplace and warm yourself with a hearty chowder and Sam Adams draft at the **Warren Tavern.** (✉ *2 Pleasant St., Charlestown* ☎ *617/241–8142* ⊕ *www.warren tavern.com*). Built in 1780, this restored colonial neighborhood pub was once frequented by George Washington and Paul Revere. It was one of the first buildings reconstructed after the Battle of Bunker Hill, which leveled Charlestown. For a meal on the waterfront, try the **Tavern on the Water** (✉ *One 8th St. , Pier 6, Charlestown* ☎ *617/242–8040*) in the Charlestown Navy Yard. It's a neighborhood hangout with outstanding harbor views and the requisite New England seafood dishes.

WORTH NOTING

❶ **Charlestown Navy Yard.** A National Park Service Historic Site since it was decommissioned in 1974, the Charlestown Navy Yard was one of six established to build warships. For 174 years, as wooden hulls and muzzle-loading cannons gave way to steel ships and sophisticated electronics, the yard evolved to meet the navy's changing needs. Here are early-19th-century barracks, workshops, and officers' quarters; a ropewalk (an elongated building for making rope, not open to the public), designed in 1834 by the Greek Revival architect Alexander Parris and used by the navy to turn out cordage for more than 125 years; and one of the oldest operational naval dry docks in the United States. The USS *Constitution* was the first to use this dry dock, in 1833. In addition to the ship itself, check out the *Constitution* Museum, the collections of the Boston Marine Society, and the USS *Cassin Young*, a World War II destroyer typical of the ships built here during that era. At the entrance of the Navy Yard is the **Charlestown Navy Yard Visitors Information Center.** ⊠*55 Constitution Rd., Charlestown* ☎*617/242–5601* ⊕*www. nps.gov/bost/historyculture/cny.htm* ⊙*Visitors Information Center daily 9–5* ⊺*North Station; MBTA Bus 92 to Charlestown City Sq. or Bus 93 to Chelsea St. from Haymarket; or Boston Harbor Cruise water shuttle from Long Wharf to Pier 4.*

USS *Cassin Young*. From a later date than the *Constitution*, this destroyer saw action in Asian waters during World War II. She served the navy until 1960. ⊠*Charlestown Navy Yard, 55 Constitution Rd., Charlestown* ☎*617/242–5601* ⊠*Free* ⊙*Daily 10–4; tours at 11, 2, and 3* ⊺*North Station; MBTA Bus 92 to Charlestown City Sq. or Bus 93 to Chelsea St. from Haymarket; or Boston Harbor Cruise water shuttle from Long Wharf to Pier 4.*

❸ USS *Constitution* Museum. Artifacts and hands-on exhibits pertaining to the USS *Constitution* are on display—firearms, logs, and instruments. One section takes you step-by-step through the ship's most important battles. Old meets new in a video-game battle "fought" at the helm of a ship. ⊠*Adjacent to USS Constitution, Charlestown Navy Yard, Charlestown* ☎*617/426–1812* ⊕*www.ussconstitutionmuseum.org* ⊠*Donations accepted* ⊙*Apr.–Oct., daily 9–6; Nov.–Mar., daily 10–5* ⊺*North Station; MBTA Bus 92 to Charlestown City Sq. or Bus 93 to Chelsea St. from Haymarket; or Boston Harbor Cruise water shuttle from Long Wharf to Pier 4.*

NEED A BREAK? Walking the Freedom Trail is exhausting. Whether Charlestown is your stopping or ending point, take a breather at **Sorelle** (⊠*100 City Sq., Charlestown* ☎*617/242–2125*), a hot little bakery with two locations, delicious sandwiches, and refreshing iced coffees.

DOWNTOWN BOSTON

Boston's commercial and Financial districts—the area commonly called Downtown—are concentrated in a maze of streets that seem to have been laid out with little logic; they are, after all, only village lanes that happen to be lined with modern 40-story office towers. Just as the Great Fire of 1872 swept the old Financial District clear, the Downtown construction in more-recent times has obliterated many of the buildings where 19th-century Boston businessmen sat in front of their rolltop desks. Yet many historic sites remain tucked among the skyscrapers; a number of them have been linked together to make up a fascinating section of the Freedom Trail.

1

The area is bordered by State Street on the north and by South Station and Chinatown on the south. Tremont Street and the Common form the west boundary, and the harbor wharves the eastern edge. Locals may be able to navigate the tangle of thoroughfares in between, but very few of them manage to give intelligible directions when consulted, so you're better off carrying a map.

Washington Street (aka Downtown Crossing) is the main commercial thoroughfare of downtown Boston. It's a pedestrian street once marked by two venerable anchors of Boston's mercantile district, Filene's Basement (now closed for a several-year-long face-lift) and Jordan Marsh (now Macy's). The block reeks of history—and sausage carts. Street vendors, flower sellers, and gaggles of teenagers, businesspeople, and shoppers throng the pedestrian mall outside the two buildings.

Downtown is also the place for some of Boston's most idiosyncratic neighborhoods. The Leather District directly abuts Chinatown, which is also bordered by the Theater District (and the buildings of New England Medical Center) farther west, and to the south, the red light of the once-brazen Combat Zone flickers weakly in a pair of adjacent strip clubs. The Massachusetts Turnpike and its junction with the Southeast Expressway cuts a wide swath through the area, isolating Chinatown from the South End.

TIMING   This section of Boston has a generous share of attractions, so it's wise to save a full day, spending the bulk of it at either the New England Aquarium or the Children's Museum. There are optimum times to catch some sights: the only tours to the top of the U.S. Custom House are at 10 and 4 on sunny days, and a stroll along the waterfront at Rowes Wharf is most romantic at dusk. No need to visit the aquarium at a special hour to catch feeding time—there are five of them throughout the day.

Numbers correspond to the Downtown Boston map.

TOP ATTRACTIONS

⓭ **Children's Museum.** Most children have so much fun here that they don't
☺ realize they're actually learning something. Creative hands-on exhibits
Fodor'sChoice demonstrate scientific laws, cultural diversity, and problem solving.
★ After completing a massive 23,000 square-foot expansion in 2007, the museum has updated a lot of its old exhibitions and added new ones. Some of the most popular stops are also the simplest: bubble-making machinery, the two-story climbing maze, and "Boats Afloat," where children can float wooden objects down a 28-foot-long model of the Fort Point Channel. At the Japanese House you're invited to take off your shoes and step inside a two-story silk merchant's home from Kyoto. The "Boston Black" exhibit stimulates dialogue about ethnicity and community while children play in a Cape Verdean restaurant and the "African Queen Beauty Salon." In the toddler "PlaySpace," children under three can run free in a safe environment. There's also a full schedule of special exhibits, festivals, and performances. ⊠*300 Congress St., Downtown* ☎*617/426–6500* ⊕*www.bostonkids.org* ⊠*$12, Fri. 5–9 $1* ☉*Sat.–Thurs. 10–5, Fri. 10–9* ⓣ*South Station.*

⑪ New England Aquarium. This aquarium challenges you to really imagine life under and around the sea. Seals bark outside the West Wing, its glass-and-steel exterior constructed to mimic fish scales. This facility has a café, a gift shop, and changing exhibits; one exhibit, "Amazing Jellies," features thousands of jellyfish, many of which were grown in the museum's labs. Inside the main facility, you can see penguins, sea otters, sharks, and other exotic sea creatures—more than 2,000 species in all. Some make their home in the aquarium's four-story, 200,000-gallon ocean-reef tank, one of the largest of its kind in the world. Ramps winding around the tank lead to the top level and allow you to view the inhabitants from many vantage points. Don't miss the five-times-a-day feedings; each lasts nearly an hour and takes divers 24 feet into the tank. From outside the glassed-off Aquarium Medical Center, you can watch veterinarians treat sick animals—here's where you can see an eel in a "hospital bed." At the "Edge of the Sea" exhibit children can gingerly pick up starfish and other creatures, while "The Curious George Discovery Corner" is a fun spot for younger kids. Whale-watch cruises leave from the aquarium's dock from April to October, and cost $35.95. Across the plaza is the aquarium's Education Center; it, too, has changing exhibits. The 6½-story-high IMAX theater takes you on virtual journeys from the bottom of the sea to the depths of outer space with its 3-D films. The gift shop seems to have every stuffed aquatic animal ever made. ⊠ *Central Wharf between Central and Milk Sts., Downtown* ☎*617/973–5200* ⊕*www.neaq.org* ☑*$19.95, IMAX $9.95, entrance plus IMAX $25.95* ⊙*July–early Sept., Sun.–Thurs. 9–6, Fri. and Sat. 9–7; early Sept.–June, weekdays 9–5, weekends 9–6* Ⓣ*Aquarium, State.*

WORTH NOTING

❽ Boston Massacre Site. Directly in front of the **Old State House** a circle of cobblestones (on a traffic island) marks the site of the Boston Massacre. It was on the snowy evening of March 5, 1770, that nine British regular soldiers fired in panic upon a taunting mob of more than 75 Bostonians. Five townsmen died. In the legal action that followed, the defense of the accused soldiers was undertaken by John Adams and Josiah Quincy, both of whom vehemently opposed British oppression but were devoted to the principle of fair trial. All but two of the nine regulars charged were acquitted; the others were branded on the hand for the crime of manslaughter. Paul Revere lost little time in capturing the "massacre" in a dramatic engraving that soon became one of the Revolution's most potent images of propaganda. ⊠ *Congress and Court Sts., Downtown* Ⓣ*State.*

⑰ Boston Opera House. Originally the B.F. Keith Memorial Theatre in the days of vaudeville, this venue was designed in beaux arts style by Thomas Lamb and modeled after the Paris Opera House. The theater shut its doors in 1991, but a multimillion-dollar restoration completed in 2004 has brought theater and dance performances back to the Opera House. ⊠*539 Washington St., Downtown* ☎*617/880–2400* ⊕*www. bostonoperahouse.com* Ⓣ*Boylston.*

⑭ Boston Tea Party Ships & Museum. After a lengthy renovation, the museum is, as of this writing, scheduled to reopen in the summer of 2010 (though

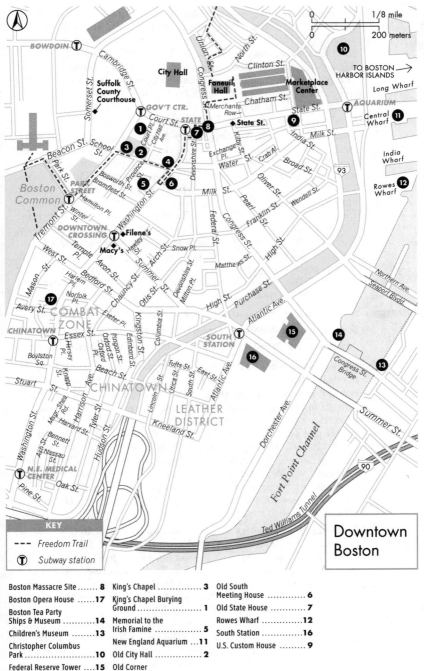

0 | 1/8 mile
0 | 200 meters

1

Downtown Boston

KEY

- - - *Freedom Trail*

Ⓣ *Subway station*

the opening date has been extended more than once). The *Beaver II*, a reproduction of one of the ships forcibly boarded and unloaded the night Boston Harbor became a teapot, is supposed to return to the Fort Point Channel at the Congress Street Bridge and be joined by two tall ships, the *Dartmouth* and the *Eleanor*. Visitors are promised a chance to explore the ships and museum exhibits, meet reenactors, or drink a cup of tea in a new Tea Room. ⊠*Fort Point Channel at Congress St. Bridge, Downtown* ⊕*www.bostonteapartyship.com* ⊙*Check Web site for updated information* Ⓣ*South Station.*

Chinatown. Boston's Chinatown may seem small, but it's said to be the third largest in the United States, after those in San Francisco and Manhattan. Beginning in the 1870s, Chinese immigrants started to trickle in, many setting up tents in a strip they called Ping On Alley. The trickle increased to a wave when immigration restrictions were lifted in 1968. As in most other American Chinatowns, the restaurants are a big draw; on Sunday, many Bostonians head to Chinatown for dim sum. Today the many Chinese establishments—most found along Beach and Tyler streets and Harrison Avenue—are interspersed with Vietnamese, Korean, Japanese, Thai, and Malaysian eateries. A three-story pagoda-style arch at the end of Beach Street welcomes you to the district. ⊠*Bounded (roughly) by Essex, Washington, Marginal, and Hudson* Ⓣ*Chinatown.*

NEED A BREAK?

Never considered bean paste for dessert or eaten a Chinese-style pork bun? Expand your horizons at **Eldo Cake House** (⊠*36–38 Harrison Ave., Downtown* ☎*617/350–7977*), which has both sweet and savory pastries.

❿ **Christopher Columbus Park** *(Waterfront Park)*. It's a short stroll from the Financial District to a view of Boston Harbor. Once a national symbol of rampant pollution, the harbor is making a gradual comeback. This green space bordering the harbor and several of Boston's restored wharves is a pleasant oasis with benches and an arborlike shelter. Lewis Wharf and Commercial Wharf (north of the park), which long lay nearly derelict, had by the mid-1970s been transformed into condominiums, offices, restaurants, and upscale shops. Long Wharf's Marriott hotel was designed to blend in with the old seaside warehouses. In September, the park is home to the Boston Arts Festival. ⊠*Bordered by Atlantic Ave., Commercial Wharf, and Long Wharf, Downtown* Ⓣ*Aquarium.*

Combat Zone. The borders of Chinatown continue to expand, encroaching steadily on the seedy Combat Zone, which has the dubious distinction of being one of the nation's first official red-light districts. It got its name more than 50 years ago when Boston-stationed troops would show up at the local tailor shops for uniform alterations and inevitably tussle with members of other branches of the military here for the same purpose. When the honky-tonk businesses were forced out of what was then Scollay Square to make way for Government Center, they moved into this run-down area. Seeking to contain the spread of vice, city officials created the Lower Washington Street Adult Entertainment District, as Puritan ghosts shuddered. Today the Combat Zone is a shadow of its sleazy self, and the Millennium Place commercial complex on Washington Street has sealed its coffin with Boston's second Ritz-Carlton, a 19-screen Loews theater, a huge spa–fitness center, and luxury condominiums. ⊠*Roughly Washington St., from Boylston St. to a few blocks north.*

⓯ Federal Reserve Tower. On Atlantic Avenue, across from South Station, is this striking aluminum-clad building, designed in 1976 by Hugh Stubbins and Associates. The tower is mainly used for offices, and is not open to the public. ⊠*600 Atlantic Ave., Downtown* ☎*617/973–3000.* Ⓣ*South Station.*

❸ King's Chapel. Both somber and dramatic, King's Chapel looms over the corner of Tremont and School streets. Its distinctive shape wasn't achieved entirely by design; for lack of funds, it was never topped with the steeple that architect Peter Harrison had planned. The first chapel on this site was erected in 1688, when Sir Edmund Andros, the royal governor whose authority temporarily replaced the original colonial charter, appropriated the land for the establishment of an Anglican place of worship. This rankled the Puritans, who had left England to escape Anglicanism and had until then succeeded in keeping it out of the colony.

It took five years to build the solid Quincy-granite structure. As construction proceeded, the old church continued to stand within the rising walls of the new, the plan being to remove and carry it away piece by piece when the outer stone chapel was completed. The builders then went to work on the interior, which remains essentially as they finished it in 1754; it's a masterpiece of proportion and Georgian calm (in fact, its acoustics make the use of a microphone unnecessary for Sunday sermons). The pulpit, built in 1717 by Peter Vintoneau, is the oldest pulpit in continuous use on the same site in the United States. To the right of the main entrance is a special pew once reserved for condemned prisoners, who were trotted in to hear a sermon before being hanged on the Common. The chapel's bell is Paul Revere's largest and, in his judgment, his sweetest sounding. ⊠*Tremont St. at School St., Downtown* ☎*617/227–2155* ⊕*www.kings-chapel.org* ☉*Labor Day–Memorial Day, Sat. 10–4, Sun. 1:30–4; Memorial Day–Labor Day, Mon., Thurs.–Sat., 10–4, Sun. 1:30–4, Tues. and Wed., 10–11:15 and 1:30–4. Year-round music program Tues. 12:15–1; services Sun. at 9:45 and 11, Wed. at 12:15* Ⓣ*Park St., Government Center.*

❶ King's Chapel Burying Ground. Legends linger in this oldest of the city's cemeteries. Glance at the handy map of famous grave sites (posted a short walk down the left path) and then take the path to the right from the entrance and then left by the chapel to the gravestone (1704) of Elizabeth Pain, the model for Hester Prynne in Nathaniel Hawthorne's *The Scarlet Letter.* Note the winged death's head on her stone. Also buried here is William Dawes Jr., who, with Dr. Samuel Prescott, rode out to warn of the British invasion the night of Paul Revere's famous ride (because of Longfellow's stirring poem, Revere is the one who gets all the glory today). Other Boston worthies entombed here—including the first Massachusetts governor, John Winthrop, and several generations of his descendants—were famous for more conventional reasons.

The prominent slate monument between the cemetery and the chapel tells (in French) the story of the Chevalier de Saint-Sauveur, a young officer who was part of the first French contingent that arrived to help the rebel Americans in 1778. He was killed in a riot that began when hungry Bostonians were told they couldn't buy the bread the French were baking for their men, using the Bostonians' own wheat—an awkward situation only aggravated by the language barrier. The chevalier's interment here was probably the occasion for the first Roman Catholic Mass in what has since become a city with a substantial Catholic population. ⊠*Tremont St. at School St., Downtown* ☎*617/227–2155* ⊕*www.cityofboston.gov/freedomtrail/kingschapel.asp* ☉*Late spring–early fall, Mon. and Thurs.–Sat. 10–4; winter, Sat. 10–4* Ⓣ*Park St., Government Center.*

NEED A BREAK?

Fajitas & 'Ritas (⊠*25 West St., Downtown* ☎*617/426–1222*), is a fun stop for a quick dose of Tex-Mex or a liter of frozen margaritas. Service is quick, prices are low, and you can select your nacho toppings.

Leather District. Opposite South Station and inside the angle formed by Kneeland Street and Atlantic Avenue is a corner of Downtown that has been relatively untouched by high-rise development: the old Leather District. It's probably the best place in downtown Boston to get an idea of what the city's business center looked like in the late 19th century. This was the wholesale supply area for raw materials in the days when the shoe industry was a regional economic mainstay; a few leather firms are still here, but most warehouses now contain expensive loft apartments. ⊠*Bordered by Kneeland St., Atlantic Ave., and Lincoln St.* Ⓣ*South Station.*

⑤ Memorial to the Irish Famine. A reminder of the rich immigrant past of this most Irish of American cities consists of two sculptures by artist Robert Shure, one depicting an anguished family on the shores of Ireland, the other a determined and hopeful Irish family stepping ashore in Boston. ⊠*Plaza outside Borders, Washington St. near School St., opposite Old South Meeting House* Ⓣ*State, Downtown Crossing.*

② Old City Hall. Just outside this site sits Richard S. Greenough's bronze statue (1855) of Benjamin Franklin, Boston's first portrait sculpture. Franklin was born in 1706 just a few blocks from here, on Milk Street, and attended the Boston Latin School, founded in 1635 near the City Hall site. (The school has long since moved to Louis Pasteur Avenue, near the Fenway.) As a young man, Franklin emigrated to Philadelphia, where he lived most of his long life. Boston's municipal government settled into the new City Hall in 1969, and the old Second Empire building now houses business offices, not to mention the luxurious Ruth's Chris Steakhouse. ⊠*41–45 School St., Downtown* ⊕*www.oldcityhall.com* Ⓣ*State.*

④ Old Corner Bookstore Site. Through these doors, between 1845 and 1865, passed some of the century's literary lights: Henry David Thoreau, Ralph Waldo Emerson, and Henry Wadsworth Longfellow—even Charles Dickens paid a visit. Many of their works were published here by James T. "Jamie" Fields, who in 1830 had founded the influential

1

firm Ticknor and Fields. In the 19th century the graceful, gambrel-roof early-Georgian structure—built in 1718 on land once owned by religious rebel Anne Hutchinson—also housed the city's leading bookstore. Today, the building is occupied by a jewelry store. ⊠*1 School St., Downtown* Ⓣ*State.*

❻ Old South Meeting House. This is the second-oldest church building in Boston, and were it not for Longfellow's celebration of the Old North in "Paul Revere's Ride," it might well be the most famous. Some of the fieriest of the town meetings that led to the Revolution were held here, culminating in the gathering of December 16, 1773, which was called by Samuel Adams to confront the crisis of three ships, laden with dutiable tea, anchored at Griffin's Wharf. The activists wanted the tea returned to England, the governor would not permit it—and the rest is history. To cries of "Boston Harbor a teapot tonight!" and John Hancock's "Let every man do what is right in his own eyes," the protesters poured out of the Old South, headed to the wharf with their waiting comrades, and dumped £18,000 worth of tea into the water.

One of the earliest members of the congregation was an African slave named Phillis Wheatley, who had been educated by her owners. In 1773 a book of her poems was printed (by a London publisher), making her the first published African-American poet. She later traveled to London, where she was received as a celebrity, but was again overtaken by poverty and died in obscurity at age 31.

The church suffered no small amount of indignity in the Revolution: its pews were ripped out by occupying British troops, and the interior was used for riding exercises by General John Burgoyne's light dragoons. A century later it escaped destruction in the Great Fire of 1872, only to be threatened with demolition by developers. Aside from the windows and doors, the only original interior features surviving today are the tiered galleries above the main floor. The pulpit is a reproduction of the one used by Puritan divines and secular firebrands. Public contributions saved the church.

The exhibition "Voices of Protest" highlights the Old South as a forum for free speech from Revolutionary days to the present, and the 20-minute audio program "If These Walls Could Speak" offers a reenactment of the major events that occurred here. There are also changing exhibits and educational programs, such as the lecture series covering topics from murder cases in Massachusetts to colonial games; it runs Thursday 12:15–1 November to March, and the schedule is available by phone or on the Web. ⊠*310 Washington St., Downtown* ☎*617/482–6439* ⊕*www.oldsouthmeetinghouse.org* ☞*$5* ☺*Apr.–Oct., daily 9:30–5; Nov.–Mar., daily 10–4* Ⓣ*State, Downtown Crossing.*

❼ Old State House. This colonial-era landmark has one of the most recognizable facades in Boston, with its State Street gable adorned by a brightly gilded lion and unicorn, symbols of British imperial power. The original figures were pulled down in 1776. For proof that bygones are bygones, consider not only the restoration of the sculptures in 1880 but also that Queen Elizabeth II was greeted by cheering crowds on July 4, 1976, when she stood on the Old State House balcony (from which the Declaration of Independence was first read in public in Boston and which overlooks the site of the Boston Massacre).

This was the seat of the colonial government from 1713 until the Revolution, and after the evacuation of the British from Boston in 1776 it served the independent Commonwealth until its replacement on Beacon Hill was completed in 1798. John Hancock was inaugurated here as the first governor under the new state constitution.

Like many other colonial-era landmarks, it fared poorly in the years that followed. Nineteenth-century photos show the old building with a mansard roof and signs in the windows advertising assorted businesses. In the 1830s the Old State House served as Boston's City Hall. When demolition was threatened in 1880 because the real estate was so valuable, the Bostonian Society organized a restoration, after which the Old State House reopened with a permanent collection that traces Boston's Revolutionary War history and, on the second floor, exhibits that change every few years.

Immediately outside the Old State House, at 15 State Street, is a **visitor center** run by the National Park Service; it offers free brochures and has restrooms. ⊠ *206 Washington St., at State St., Downtown* ☎ *617/720–1713* ⊕ *www.bostonhistory.org* ⊠ *$5* ⊗ *Daily 9–5* ⊤ *State.*

⑫ Rowes Wharf. Take a Beacon Hill redbrick town house, blow it up to the *n*th power, and you get this 15-story Skidmore, Owings & Merrill extravaganza from 1987, one of the more-welcome additions to the Boston Harbor skyline. From under the complex's gateway six-story arch, you can get great views of Boston Harbor and the yachts docked at the marina. Water shuttles pull up here from Logan Airport—the most intriguing way to enter the city. A windswept stroll along the Harbor-Walk waterfront promenade at dusk makes for an unforgettable sunset on clear days. ⊠ *Atlantic Ave. south of India Wharf* ⊤ *Aquarium.*

⑯ South Station. The colonnaded granite structure is the terminal for all Amtrak trains in and out of Boston. Next door on Atlantic Avenue is the terminal for Greyhound, Peter Pan, and other bus lines. Behind the station's grand 1900s facade, a major renovation project has created an airy, modern transit center. Thanks to its eateries, coffee bars, newsstand, flower stand, and other shops, waiting for a train here can actually be a pleasant experience. ⊠ *Atlantic Ave. and Summer St., Downtown* ⊤ *South Station.*

State Street. During the 19th century, State Street was headquarters for banks, brokerages, and insurance firms; although these businesses have spread throughout the Downtown District, "State Street" still connotes much the same thing as "Wall Street" does in New York. The early commercial hegemony of State Street was symbolized by Long Wharf, built in 1710 and extending some 1,700 feet into the harbor. If today's Long Wharf doesn't appear to be that long, it's not because it has been shortened but because the land has crept out toward its end. State Street once met the water at the base of the Custom House; landfill operations were pursued relentlessly through the years, and the old coastline is now as much a memory as such colonial State Street landmarks as

Governor Winthrop's 1630 house and the Revolutionary-era Bunch of Grapes Tavern, where Bostonians met to drink and wax indignant at their treatment by King George.

❾ **U.S. Custom House.** This 1847 structure resembles a Greek Revival temple that appears to have sprouted a tower. It's just that. This is the work of architects Ammi Young and Isaiah Rogers—at least, the bottom part is. The tower was added in 1915, at which time the Custom House became Boston's tallest building. It remains one of the most visible and best loved in the city's skyline. To appreciate the grafting job, go inside and look at the domed rotunda. The outer surface of that dome was once the roof of the building, but now the dome is embedded in the base of the tower.

The federal government moved out of the Custom House in 1987 and sold it to the city of Boston, which, in turn, sold it to the Marriott Corporation, which has converted the building into hotel space and luxury time-share units, a move that disturbed some historical purists. You can now sip a cocktail in the hotel's Counting Room Lounge, or visit the 26th-floor observation deck. The magnificent Rotunda Room sports maritime prints and antique artifacts, courtesy of the Peabody Essex Museum in Salem. ✉ *3 McKinley Sq., Downtown* ☎ *617/310–6300* Ⓣ *State, Aquarium.*

THE BACK BAY

In the folklore of American neighborhoods, the Back Bay stands with New York's Park Avenue and San Francisco's Nob Hill as a symbol of propriety and high social standing. Before the 1850s it really was a bay, a tidal flat that formed the south bank of a distended Charles River. The filling in of land along the isthmus that joined Boston to the mainland (the Neck) began in 1850 and resulted in the creation of the South End. To the north, a narrow causeway called the Mill Dam (later Beacon Street) was built in 1814 to separate the Back Bay from the Charles. By the late 1800s, Bostonians had filled in the shallows to as far as the marshland known as the Fenway, and the original 783-acre peninsula had been expanded by about 450 acres. Thus the waters of Back Bay became the neighborhood of Back Bay.

Heavily influenced by the then-recent rebuilding of Paris according to the plans of Baron Georges-Eugène Haussmann, the Back Bay planners created thoroughfares that resemble Parisian boulevards. The thorough planning included service alleys behind the main streets to allow provi-

CLOSE UP

Tours Worth Trying

Boston Movie Tours (☎ 866/668–4345 ⊕ www.bostonmovietours.net) takes you to Boston's film and movie hot spots like the South Boston of *The Departed*, the *Ally McBeal* building, the tavern from *Good Will Hunting*, the *Cheers* bar, and Fenway Park, home of the Red Sox and location for movies like *Field of Dreams* and *Fever Pitch*. Guides share filming secrets and trivia from movies like *Legally Blonde* and *Mystic River* along with the best celeb spots in town. Choose between a 90-minute walking tour ($20) or a two- to three-hour theater-on-wheels experience ($35).

Boston Women's Heritage Trail (☎ 617/364–2449 ⊕ www.bwht.org) has nine self-guided walks that highlight remarkable women who played an integral role in shaping the history of Boston and the nation as patriots, intellectuals, abolitionists, suffragists, artists, and writers.

sioning wagons to drive up to basement kitchens. (Today they're used for waste pickup and parking.)

Almost immediately, fashionable families began to decamp from Beacon Hill and the recently developed South End and establish themselves in the Back Bay's brick and brownstone row houses. By 1900 the streets between the Public Garden and Massachusetts Avenue had become the smartest, most desirable neighborhood in all of Boston. An air of permanence and respectability drifted in as inevitably as the tides once had, and the Back Bay mystique was born.

Today the area retains its posh spirit, but mansions are no longer the main draw. Locals and tourists alike flock to the commercial streets of Boylston and Newbury to shop at boutiques, galleries, and the usual mall stores. Many of the bars and restaurants have patio seating and bay windows, making the area the perfect spot to see and be seen while indulging in ethnic delicacies or an invigorating coffee. The Boston Public Library, Symphony Hall, and numerous churches ensure that high culture is not lost amid the frenzy of consumerism.

Note: One of the main thoroughfares, Huntington Avenue, which stretches from Copley Square past the Museum of Fine Arts, has technically been renamed the Avenue of the Arts. However, old habits die hard, particularly with Bostonians; everyone still calls it Huntington.

TIMING   If you're not looking to max out your credit cards, then you can hurry past the boutiques and cover the Back Bay in about two hours. Allow at least half a day for a leisurely stroll with frequent stops on Newbury Street and the shops at Copley Place and the Prudential Center. The reflecting pool at the Christian Science Church is a great time-out spot. Around the third week of April, magnolia time arrives, and nowhere do the flowers bloom more magnificently than along Commonwealth Avenue. In May the Public Garden bursts with color, thanks to its flowering dogwood trees and thousands of tulips. Set aside a Sunday to enjoy the district's many historic churches. To stay oriented, remem-

A GOOD WALK

A walk through the Back Bay properly begins with the **Boston Public Garden ❶**, the oldest botanical garden in the United States. After wandering its meandering pathways, venture into the Back Bay through the gate at Arlington and Commonwealth Avenue. Turn left, and then right on Newbury Street. Ahead are **Emmanuel Church ❺** at No. 15 and the **Church of the Covenant ❻** at No. 67. At the Church of the Covenant, follow Berkeley back to Commonwealth Avenue ("Comm Ave." to natives). One block to your left is the **First Baptist Church ❼**. From here you can continue down the Commonwealth Avenue Mall to view its sumptuous mansions all the way to Massachusetts Avenue. Then, or at any point before you hit Mass Ave. (as the locals refer to it), you can turn south to reach **Newbury Street** and backtrack along Boston's poshest shopping district, browsing all the way. At Dartmouth Street, turn right and head into **Copley**

Square, where the **Old South Church ❽**, the **Boston Public Library ❾**, **Trinity Church ❿**, and the **John Hancock Tower ⓫** all stand. For more shopping, head for the upscale **Copley Place ⓬** complex, reached through the Westin Hotel at the corner of Dartmouth and Huntington Avenue. A walkway takes you over Stuart Street into the shopping galleries. Continue through to the Marriott Hotel, and take another walkway over Huntington to the **Prudential Center ⓭** for more shopping and viewing the city at the Prudential Center Skywalk. Exit onto Boylston Street and turn left walking past the Berklee College of Music, turning left again onto Mass Ave. Walk several blocks to the reflecting pool and expansive plaza of the **Mary Baker Eddy Library ⓮** and the **First Church of Christ, Scientist ⓯**. Just across Mass Ave. at Huntington Avenue is **Symphony Hall ⓰**.

ber the north–south streets are arranged in alphabetical order, from Arlington to Hereford.

Numbers correspond to the Back Bay, the South End & the Fens map.

TOP ATTRACTIONS

❶ **Boston Public Garden.** Although the Boston Public Garden is often lumped together with Boston Common, the two are separate entities with different histories and purposes and a distinct boundary between them at Charles Street. The Common has been public land since Boston was founded in 1630, whereas the Public Garden belongs to a newer Boston, occupying what had been salt marshes on the edge of the Common. By 1837 the tract was covered with an abundance of ornamental plantings donated by a group of private citizens. The area was defined in 1856 by the building of Arlington Street, and in 1860 the architect George Meacham was commissioned to plan the park.

The central feature of the Public Garden is its irregularly shaped pond, intended to appear, from any vantage point along its banks, much larger than its nearly 4 acres. The pond has been famous since 1877 for its foot-pedal-powered (by a captain) **Swan Boats** (☎ *617/522–1966*

Fodor's Choice
★

⊕ *www.swanboats.com* ✉ *Swan Boats $2.75* ⊘ *Swan Boats mid-Apr.–June 20, daily 10–4; June 21–Labor Day, daily 10–5; Day afterLabor Day–mid-Sept., weekdays noon–4, weekends 10–4*), which make leisurely cruises during warm months. They were invented by one Robert Paget, who was inspired by the swan-drawn boat that carries Lohengrin in the Wagner opera of the same name. (Paget descendants still run the boats.) The pond is favored by ducks and swans, and for the modest price of a few boat rides you can amuse children here for an hour or more. Near the Swan Boat dock is what has been described as the world's smallest suspension bridge, designed in 1867 to cross the pond at its narrowest point.

The Public Garden is America's oldest botanical garden and has the finest formal plantings in central Boston. The beds along the main walkways are replanted for spring and summer. The tulips during the first two weeks of May are especially colorful, and there's a sampling of native and European tree species.

The dominant work among the park's statuary is Thomas Ball's equestrian **George Washington** (1869), which faces the head of Commonwealth Avenue at the Arlington Street gate. This is Washington in a triumphant pose as liberator, surveying a scene that, from where he stood with his cannons at Dorchester Heights, would have included an immense stretch of blue water. Several dozen yards to the north of Washington (to the right if you're facing Commonwealth Avenue) is the granite-and-red-marble **Ether Monument,** donated in 1866 by Thomas Lee to commemorate the advent of anesthesia 20 years earlier at nearby Massachusetts General Hospital. Other Public Garden monuments include statues of the Unitarian preacher and transcendentalist William Ellery Channing, at the corner opposite his Arlington Street Church; Edward Everett Hale, the author (*The Man Without a Country*) and philanthropist, at the Charles Street Gate; and the abolitionist senator Charles Sumner and the Civil War hero Colonel Thomas Cass, along Boylston Street.

The park contains a special delight for the young at heart; follow the children quack-quacking along the pathway between the pond and the park entrance at Charles and Beacon streets to the *Make Way for Ducklings* bronzes sculpted by Nancy Schön, a tribute to the 1941 classic children's story by Robert McCloskey. ✉ *Bounded by Arlington, Boylston, Charles, and Beacon Sts., Back Bay.*

❾ Boston Public Library. This venerable institution is a handsome temple
★ to literature and a valuable research library. When the building was opened in 1895, it confirmed the status of architects McKim, Mead & White as apostles of the Renaissance Revival style while reinforcing Boston's commitment to an enlightened citizenry that goes back 350 years, to the founding of the Public Latin School. Philip Johnson's 1972 addition emulates the mass and proportion of the original, though not its extraordinary detail; this skylighted annex houses the library's circulating collections.

You don't need a library card to enjoy the magnificent art. Charles McKim saw to it that the interior of his building was ornamented by several of the finest painters of the day. The murals at the head of the staircase, depicting the nine muses, are the work of the French artist Puvis de Chavannes; those in the book-request processing room to the right are Edwin Abbey's interpretations of the Holy Grail legend. Upstairs, in the public areas leading to the fine-arts, music, and rare-books collections, is John Singer Sargent's mural series on the *Triumph of Religion,* shining with renewed color after its cleaning and restoration in 2003.

You enter the older part of the library from the Dartmouth Street side, passing under the motto *"Omni lux civium"* (Light of all citizens) through the enormous bronze doors by Daniel Chester French, the sculptor of the Lincoln Memorial. Or you can walk around Boylston Street to enter through the addition. The corridor leading from the annex opens onto the Renaissance-style **courtyard**—an exact copy of the one in Rome's Palazzo della Cancelleria—around which the original library is built. A covered arcade furnished with chairs rings a fountain; you can bring books or lunch into the courtyard, which is open all the hours the library is open, and escape the bustle of the city. Beyond the courtyard is the main entrance hall of the 1895 building, with its immense stone lions by Louis Saint-Gaudens (brother of the more-celebrated Augustus), vaulted ceiling, and marble staircase. The corridor at the top of the stairs leads to **Bates Hall,** one of Boston's most sumptuous interior spaces. This is the main reference reading room, 218 feet long with a barrel-arch ceiling 50 feet high. ⊠ *700 Boylston St., at Copley Sq., Back Bay* ☎ *617/536–5400* ⊕ *www.bpl.org* ☉ *Mon.– Thurs. 9–9, Fri. and Sat. 9–5; Oct.–May, also Sun. 1–5. Free guided art and architecture tours Mon. at 2:30, Tues. and Thurs. at 6, Fri. and Sat. at 11, Sun. (Oct.–May) at 2* ⓣ *Copley.*

NEED A BREAK?

You can take a lunch break at **Novel** or **Sebastians Map Room Café** (⊠ *700 Boylston St., at Copley Sq., Back Bay* ☎ *617/859–2251*), adjoining restaurants in the Boston Public Library. The café serves breakfast and lunch in the 1895 map room, and the main restaurant, which overlooks the courtyard, is open for lunch and afternoon tea. Enter through the Dartmouth entrance and turn right; the restaurants are at the end of the corridor. Novel is open weekdays 11:30–4:30, and Sebastians Map Room Café is open Monday–Saturday 9–5.

⑩ ★ Trinity Church. In his 1877 masterpiece, architect Henry Hobson Richardson brought his Romanesque Revival style to maturity; all the aesthetic elements for which he was famous come together magnificently—bold polychromatic masonry, careful arrangement of masses, sumptuously carved interior woodwork. The Episcopal church remains the crowning centerpiece of Copley Square. A full appreciation of its architecture requires an understanding of the logistical problems of building it here. The Back Bay is a reclaimed wetland with a high water table. Bedrock, or at least stable glacial till, lies far beneath wet clay. Like all older Back Bay buildings, Trinity Church sits on submerged wooden pilings. But its central tower weighs 9,500 tons, and most of the 4,500 pilings beneath

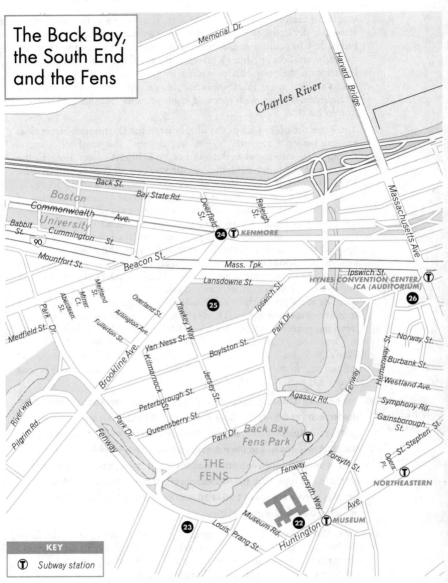

The Back Bay,
the South End
and the Fens

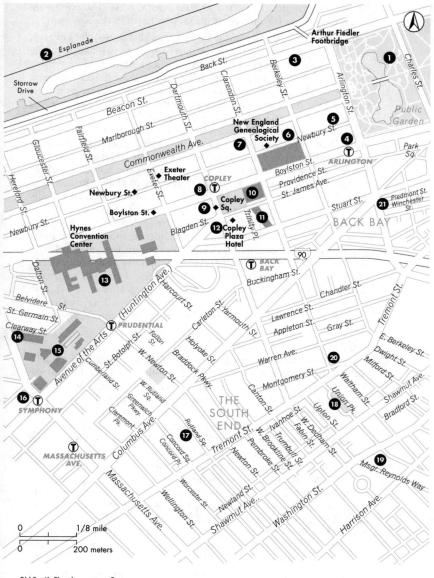

the building are under that tremendous central mass. The pilings are checked regularly for sinkage by means of a hatch in the basement.

Richardson engaged some of the best artists of his day—John LaFarge, William Morris, and Edward Burne-Jones among them—to execute the paintings and stained glass that make this a monument to everything that was right about the pre-Raphaelite spirit and the nascent aesthetic of Morris's Arts and Crafts movement. LaFarge's brilliant paintings, including the intricate ornamentation of the vaulted ceilings, received a much-needed overhaul during the extensive renovations that have recently wrapped up. It was a mammoth job, but the brilliant LaFarge murals have now been returned to their colorful glory, while his spectacular stained-glass windows (restored to full sparkle) are justly considered among the finest in the country. Along the north side of the church, note the Augustus Saint-Gaudens statue of Phillips Brooks—the most charismatic rector in New England, who almost single-handedly got Trinity built and furnished. Shining light of Harvard's religious community and lyricist of "O Little Town of Bethlehem," Brooks is shown here with Christ touching his shoulder in approval. For a nice respite, try to catch one of the Friday organ concerts beginning at 12:15. ■TIP→ **The 11:15 Sunday service is followed by a free guided tour.** ✉ *206 Clarendon St., Back Bay* ☎ *617/536–0944* ✆ *www.trinityboston.org* ✉ *Church free, guided and self-guided tours $6* ⊙ *Mon.–Sat. 9–5, Sun. 1–5; services Sun. at 7:45, 9, and 11:15 AM, and 6 PM; Tues. and Thurs. at 6 PM; Wed. at 12:10 PM. Tours take place several times daily; call to confirm times* Ⓣ *Copley.*

WORTH NOTING

❹ **Arlington Street Church.** Opposite the Park Square corner of the Public Garden, this church was erected in 1861—the first to be built in the Back Bay. Following suit, many of the old Downtown congregations relocated to the district's newly filled land and applied their considerable resources to building churches. Often designed in Gothic and Romanesque Revival styles, these churches have aged well and blend harmoniously with the residential blocks, making the Back Bay a great neighborhood for ecclesiastical architecture. Though a classical portico is a keynote and its model was London's St. Martin-in-the-Fields, Arlington Street Church is less picturesque and more Georgian in character. Note the Tiffany stained-glass windows. During the year preceding the Civil War, the church was a hotbed of abolitionist fervor. Later, during the Vietnam War, this Unitarian-Universalist congregation became famous as a center of peace activism. ✉ *351 Boylston St., Back Bay* ☎ *617/536–7050* ✆ *www.ascboston.org* ⊙ *Call to arrange sanctuary tours. Services Sun. at 11* Ⓣ *Arlington.*

Back Bay Mansions. If you like nothing better than to imagine how the other half lives, you'll suffer no shortage of old homes to sigh over in Boston's Back Bay. Most, unfortunately, are off-limits to visitors, but there's no law against gawking from the outside.

Among the grander Back Bay houses is the **Gamble Mansion** (✉ *5 Commonwealth Ave., Back Bay*) of 1904, which is privately owned. The **Burrage Mansion** (✉ *314 Commonwealth Ave., Back Bay*) is a gem,

The Houses of the Back Bay

The Back Bay remains a living museum of urban Victorian–residential architecture. The earliest specimens are nearest to the Public Garden (there are exceptions where showier turn-of-the-20th-century mansions replaced 1860s town houses), and the newer examples are out around the Massachusetts Avenue and Fenway extremes of the district. The height of Back Bay residences and their distance from the street are essentially uniform, as are the interior layouts, chosen to accord with lot width. Yet there's a distinct progression of facades, beginning with French academic and Italianate designs and moving through the various "revivals" of the 19th century. By the time of World War I, when development of the Back Bay was virtually complete, architects and their patrons had come full circle to a revival of the Federal period, which had been out of fashion for only 30 years when the building began. If the Back Bay architects had not run out of land, they might have gotten around to a Greek Revival revival.

The Great Depression brought an end to the Back Bay style of living, and today only a few of the houses are single-family residences. Most have been cut up into apartments, then expensive condominiums; during the boom years of the late 1990s some were returned to their original town-house status. Interior details have experienced a mixed fate: they suffered during the years when Victorian fashions were held in low regard, and are undergoing careful restoration now that the aesthetic pendulum has reversed itself and moneyed condo buyers are demanding period authenticity. The original facades have survived on all but Newbury and Boylston streets, so the public face of the Back Bay retains much of the original charm and grandeur.

An outstanding guide to the architecture and history of the Back Bay is Bainbridge Bunting's *Houses of Boston's Back Bay* (Harvard, 1967). A few homes are open to the public.

built in 1899 in an extravagant French-château style, complete with turrets and gargoyles, that reflects a cost-be-damned attitude uncommon even among the wealthiest Back Bay families. It now houses privately owned condominiums. The **Cushing-Endicott House** (✉*163 Marlborough St., Back Bay*) was built in 1871 and later served as the home of William C. Endicott, secretary of war under President Grover Cleveland; this was dubbed "the handsomest house in the whole Back Bay" by the author Bainbridge Bunting. The opulent **Oliver Ames Mansion** (✉*355 Commonwealth Ave., corner of Massachusetts Ave., Back Bay*) was built in 1882 for a railroad baron and Massachusetts governor; it's now an office building. The **Ames-Webster House** (✉*306 Dartmouth St., Back Bay*), built in 1872 and remodeled in 1882 and 1969, is one of the city's finest houses; it's still a private home. Two Back Bay mansions are now used by organizations that promote foreign language and culture: the **French Library and Cultural Center** (✉*53 Marlborough St., Back Bay* ✹*frenchlib.org*) and the German-oriented **Goethe Institute** (✉*170 Beacon St., Back Bay* ✹*www.goethe.de/uk/bos*). See the free, biweekly Improper Bostonian, or the *Boston Globe*'s "Calendar" section on Thursday or the weekly listings in the *Boston Phoenix* for details on lectures, films, and other events held in these respected institutions.

Fisher College (⊠ *118 Beacon St., Back Bay* ☎ *617/236–8800* ⊕ *www.fisher.edu*) is housed in a 1903 bowfront whose Classical Revival style epitomizes turn-of-the-20th-century elegance. Step inside to see such genteel touches as the marble stairway with its gold-plated balustrade, the Circassian walnut–panel dining room, and the library's hand-carved rosewood doors with sterling silver knobs. Admission is free, and it's open on weekdays from 8 to 4.

Boylston Street. Less posh than Newbury Street, this broad thoroughfare is the southern commercial spine of the Back Bay, lined with interesting restaurants and shops.

❻ Church of the Covenant. This 1867 Gothic Revival church at the corner of Newbury and Berkeley streets has one of the largest collections of liturgical windows by Louis Comfort Tiffany in the country. It's crowned by a 236-foot-tall steeple—the tallest in Boston—that Oliver Wendell Holmes called "absolutely perfect." Inside, a 14-foot-high Tiffany lantern hangs from a breathtaking 100-foot ceiling. The church is now Presbyterian and United Church of Christ. ⊠ *67 Newbury St., enter at church office, Back Bay* ☎ *617/266–7480* ⊕ *www.churchofthecovenant.org* ⊙ *Call for hrs; Sun. service at 10:30* Ⓣ *Arlington.*

Commonwealth Avenue Mall. The mall that extends down the middle of the Back Bay's Commonwealth Avenue is studded with statuary. One of the most interesting memorials, at the Exeter Street intersection, is a portrayal of naval historian and author Samuel Eliot Morison seated on a rock as if he were peering out to sea. The most recent addition was the **Boston Women's Memorial** in 2003 by Meredith Bergmann, between Fairfield and Gloucester streets. Statues of Abigail Adams, Lucy Stone, and Phillis Wheatley celebrate the progressive ideas of these three women and their contributions to Boston's history. The other figures have only tenuous connections to Boston—Viking explorer Leif Eriksson; Domingo F. Sarmiento, president of Argentina; and even Alexander Hamilton, who tried to block Quincy-born John Adams from the presidency.

A dramatic and personal memorial was added to the mall in 1997 near Dartmouth Street: the **Vendome Monument,** dedicated to the nine firemen who died in a 1972 blaze at the Back Bay's Vendome Hotel. Designed by Ted Clausen and Peter White, the curved black-granite block, 29 feet long and waist high, is etched with the names of the dead. A bronze cast of a fireman's coat and hat are draped over the granite as if to say, "The fire is out; we can rest now." Just across the street from the monument, at 160 Commonwealth Avenue, is the **Vendome Hotel** itself, which first opened in 1872 and is now used as office space. ⊠ *Commonwealth Ave. between Arlington St. and Massachusetts Ave.* Ⓣ *Arlington, Copley.*

⓬ Copley Place. Two bold intruders dominate Copley Square—the **John Hancock Tower** off the southeast corner and the even more assertive Copley Place skyscraper on the southwest. An upscale, glass-and-brass urban mall built between 1980 and 1984, Copley Place includes two major hotels: the high-rise Westin and the Marriott Copley Place. Dozens of shops, restaurants, and offices are attractively grouped on several levels, surrounding bright, open indoor spaces. During the long winter months, locals use the mall to escape the elements and take a shortcut between Back Bay Station and points west. ✉ *100 Huntington Ave., Back Bay* ☎*617/369–5000* ⊕*www.simon.com/findamall* ☉*Shopping galleries Mon.–Sat. 10–9, Sun. noon–6* Ⓣ*Copley.*

Copley Square. Every April thousands find a glimpse of Copley Square the most wonderful sight in the world: this is where the runners of the Boston Marathon end their 26-mi race. A square now favored by skateboarders (much to the chagrin of city officials), the civic space is defined by three monumental older buildings. One is the stately, bow-front 1912 **Fairmont Copley Plaza Hotel,** which faces the square on St. James Avenue and serves as a dignified foil to its companions, two of the most important works of architecture in the United States: Trinity Church—Henry Hobson Richardson's masterwork of 1877—and the Boston Public Library, by McKim, Mead & White. The John Hancock Tower looms in the background. To honor the runners who stagger over the marathon's finish line, bronze statues of the Tortoise and the Hare engaged in their mythical race were cast by Nancy Schön, who also did the much-loved *Make Way for Ducklings* group in the Boston Public Garden. ✉*Bounded by Dartmouth, Boylston, and Clarendon Sts. and St. James Ave., Back Bay* Ⓣ*Copley.*

❺ **Emmanuel Church.** Built in 1860, this Back Bay brownstone Gothic Episcopal church is popular among classical music–loving worshippers—every Sunday at 10 AM from September to May, as part of the liturgy, a Bach cantata is performed; guest conductors have included Christopher Hogwood and Seiji Ozawa. Inside the church is the Leslie Lindsey Chapel—a neo-Gothic memorial created by parents in memory of their daughter, a young bride who perished with her husband during their 1915 honeymoon voyage on the *Lusitania.* ✉*15 Newbury St., Back Bay* ☎*617/536–3355* ⊕*www.emmanuel-boston.org* ☉*Services Sun. at 10 AM* Ⓣ*Arlington.*

❷ **Esplanade.** Near the corner of Beacon and Arlington streets, the Arthur Fiedler Footbridge crosses Storrow Drive to the Esplanade and the **Hatch Memorial Shell.** The free concerts here in summer include the Boston Pops' immensely popular televised Fourth of July performance. For shows like this, Bostonians haul lawn chairs and blankets to the lawn in front of the shell; bring a take-out lunch from a nearby restaurant, find an empty spot—no mean feat, so come early—and you'll feel right at home. An impressive stone bust of the late maestro Arthur Fiedler watches over the walkers, joggers, picnickers, and sunbathers who fill the Esplanade's paths on pleasant days. The green is home port for the fleet of small sailboats that dot the Charles River basin; they belong to Community Boating. Here, too, is the turn-of-the-20th-century **Union Boat Club Boathouse,** headquarters for the country's oldest private rowing club.

Exeter Street Theater. This massive Romanesque structure was built in 1884 as a temple for the Working Union of Progressive Spiritualists. Beginning in 1914, it enjoyed a long run as a movie theater; as the *AIA Guide to Boston* points out, "it was the only movie theater a proper Boston woman would enter, probably because of its spiritual overtones." ⊠*26 Exeter St., at Newbury St., Back Bay* Ⓣ*Copley.*

❼ First Baptist Church. This 1872 structure, at the corner of Clarendon Street and Commonwealth Avenue, was architect Henry Hobson Richardson's first foray into Romanesque Revival. It was originally erected for the Brattle Square Unitarian Society, but Richardson ran over budget and the church went bankrupt and dissolved; in 1882 the building was bought by the Baptists. The figures on each side of its soaring tower were sculpted by Frédéric Auguste Bartholdi, the sculptor who designed the Statue of Liberty. The friezes represent four points at which God enters an individual's life: baptism, communion, marriage, and death. The trumpeting angels at each corner have earned First Baptist its nickname, "Church of the Holy Bean Blowers." If you phone ahead for an appointment on a weekday, you may be surprised by an informal tour. ⊠*110 Commonwealth Ave., Back Bay* ☎*617/267–3148* ⊕*www.firstbaptistchurchofboston.org* ✆*Free* ◷*Mon., Tues., Thurs., and Fri. 11–3; services Sun. at 11* AM Ⓣ*Copley.*

NEED A BREAK?

Espresso Royale Caffe (⊠ *286 Newbury St., Back Bay* ☎ *617/859–9515* Ⓣ*Hynes*) is a basement spot with solid coffee and espresso drinks, snacks, and Wi-Fi access. If you want to try the creations of some of the best local chefs but don't want to pay four-star restaurant prices, stop by **Parish Café** (⊠ *361 Boylston St., Back Bay* ☎ *617/247–4777* ⊕ *www.parishcafe.com* Ⓣ*Arlington*). For about $10, you can get a sandwich designed by the top culinary minds in Boston. The bar is open until 2 AM daily, with food service until 1 AM.

⓯ First Church of Christ, Scientist. The world headquarters of the Christian Science faith mixes the traditional with the modern—marrying Bernini to Le Corbusier by combining an old-world basilica with a sleek office complex designed by I. M. Pei. Mary Baker Eddy's original granite First Church of Christ, Scientist (1894) has since been enveloped by a domed Renaissance Revival basilica, added to the site in 1906, and both church buildings are now surrounded by the offices of the Christian Science Publishing Society, where the *Christian Science Monitor* is produced, and by Pei's complex of church-administration structures completed in 1973. You can hear all 13,290 pipes of the church's famed Aeolian-Skinner organ during services. ⊠*175 Huntington Ave., Back Bay* ☎*617/450–3790* ⊕*www.tfccs.com* ✆*Free* ◷*Services Sept.–June, Sun. at 10* AM *and 7* PM; *July and Aug., Sun. at 10* AM, *Wed. at noon and 7:30* PM Ⓣ*Hynes/ICA, Symphony.*

❸ Gibson House. Through the foresight of an eccentric bon vivant, this house provides an authentic glimpse into daily life in Boston's Victorian era. One of the first Back Bay residences (1859), the Gibson House is relatively modest in comparison with some of the grand mansions built during the decades that followed; yet its furnishings, from its circa-1790

1

Willard clock to the raised and gilded wallpaper to the multipiece faux-bamboo bedroom set, seem sumptuous to modern eyes. Unlike other Back Bay houses, the Gibson family home has been preserved with all its Victorian fixtures and furniture intact. That's the legacy of Charles Gibson Jr., a poet, travel writer, and horticulturist who continued to appear in formal attire—morning coat, spats, and a walking stick—well into the 1940s when he dined daily at the Ritz nearby. As early as 1936, Gibson was roping off furniture and envisioning a museum for the house his grandmother built. His dream was realized in 1957, three years after he died. You can see a full-course setting with a China-trade dinner service in the ornate dining room and discover the elaborate system of servants' bells in the 19th-century basement kitchen. The house serves as the meeting place for the New England chapter of the Victorian Society in America; it was also used as an interior for the 1984 Merchant-Ivory film *The Bostonians*. ■TIP➡ **Though the sign out front instructs visitors not to ring the bell until the stroke of the hour, you will have better luck catching the beginning of the tour if you arrive a few minutes early and ring forcefully.** ✉*137 Beacon St., Back Bay* ☎*617/267–6338* ⊕*www.thegibsonhouse.org* ✉*$7* ☉*Tours Wed.–Sun. at 1, 2, and 3 and by appointment* Ⓣ*Arlington.*

🄀 **John Hancock Tower.** In the early 1970s, the tallest building in New England became notorious as the monolith that rained glass from time to time. Windows were improperly seated in the sills of the stark and graceful reflective blue rhomboid tower, designed by I. M. Pei. Once the building's 13 acres of glass were replaced and the central core stiffened, the problem was corrected. Bostonians originally feared the Hancock's stark modernism would overwhelm nearby Trinity Church, but its shimmering sides reflect the older structure's image, actually enlarging its presence. The Tower is closed to the public. ✉*200 Clarendon St., Back Bay* Ⓣ*Copley.*

🄎 **Mary Baker Eddy Library for the Betterment of Humanity.** One of the largest single collections by and about an American woman is housed at this library within Christian Science Plaza, along with two floors of exhibits celebrating the power of ideas and highlighting the link between spirituality and health. The library is home to the fascinating **Mapparium,** a huge stained-glass globe whose 30-foot interior can be traversed on a footbridge. You can experience a sound-and-light show in the Mapparium and learn about the production of the *Christian Science Monitor* in the Monitor Gallery. The Quest Gallery explores Mary Baker Eddy's life and encourages others to think about their own personal quests, and the Hall of Ideas showcases the ideas of the world's greatest thinkers in a virtual fountain. ✉*200 Massachusetts Ave., Back Bay* ☎*888/222–3711* ⊕*www.marybakereddylibrary.org* ✉*Hall of Ideas and 3rd-fl. library free, exhibits $6* ☉*Tues.–Sun. 10–4.* Ⓣ*Prudential.*

🄂 **Massachusetts Historical Society.** The oldest historical society in the United States (founded in 1791) has paintings, a library, and a 10-million-piece manuscript collection from 17th-century New England to the present. Among these manuscripts are the Adams Papers, which comprise more than 300,000 pages from the letters and diaries of generations of the Adams family, including papers from John Adams and John Quincy

Adams (the second and sixth American presidents, respectively). Casual visitors are welcome, but if you'd like to examine the papers in depth, call ahead. ✉*1154 Boylston St., Back Bay* ☎*617/536–1608* ⊕*www. masshist.org* ✉*Free* ⊘*Weekdays 9–4:45 (Thurs. until 7:45 pm), Sat. 9–4* Ⓣ*Hynes/ICA.*

Newbury Street. Eight-block-long Newbury Street has been compared to New York's 5th Avenue, and certainly this is the city's poshest shopping area, with branches of Chanel, Brooks Brothers, Armani, Burberry, and other top names in fashion. But here the pricey boutiques are more intimate than grand, and people live above the trendy restaurants and hair salons, giving the place a neighborhood feel. Toward the Mass Ave. end, cafés proliferate and the stores get funkier, ending with Newbury Comics, Urban Outfitters, and now, in a nod to the times, Best Buy. Ⓣ *Hynes Convention Center, Copley.*

New England Historic Genealogical Society. Are you related to Miles Standish or Priscilla Alden? The answer may lie here. If your ancestors were pedigreed New Englanders—or if you're just interested in genealogical research of any kind—you can trace your family tree with the help of the society's collections, which stretch back to the 17th century. An introductory lecture on how to perform your own genealogical study is given every first Wednesday of the month at noon and 6 (the evening lecture is canceled from December through March). The society itself dates from 1845 and is the oldest genealogical organization in the country. ✉*99 Newbury St., Back Bay* ☎*888/296–3447* ⊕*www.new englandancestors.org* ✉*$15 fee to use facility* ⊘*Tues. and Thurs.–Sat. 9–5, Wed. 9–9* Ⓣ*Copley.*

▮ NEED A
BREAK?

Care for a read with your caffe latte? Folks gather at the Trident Booksellers & Café (✉*338 Newbury St., Back Bay* ☎*617/267–8688* Ⓣ*Hynes/ICA*) **to review literary best sellers, thumb through the superb magazine selection, and munch on homemade desserts, sandwiches, and soups. It's open until midnight daily.**

❽ **Old South Church.** Members of the Old South Meeting House, of Tea Party fame, decamped to this new parish in 1875, a move not without controversy for the congregation. In an Italian Gothic style inspired by the sociologist John Ruskin and an interior decorated with Venetian mosaics and stained-glass windows, the "new" structure could hardly be more different from the original plain meetinghouse. Old South's congregation is now part of the United Church of Christ. ✉*645 Boylston St., Back Bay* ☎*617/536–1970* ⊕*www.oldsouth.org* ⊘*Services Sun. at 9 and 11 AM, jazz services Thurs. at 6* Ⓣ*Copley.*

⓭ **Prudential Center.** The only rival to the John Hancock's claim on Boston's upper skyline is the 52-story Prudential Tower, built in the early 1960s when the scale of monumental urban redevelopment projects had yet to be challenged. The Prudential Center, which replaced the railway yards that blocked off the South End, now dominates the acreage between Boylston Street and Huntington Avenue two blocks west of the library, and adds considerably to the area's overabundance of mall-style shops and food courts. Its enclosed shopping mall is connected by a glass bridge to the more-upscale Copley Place. As for the Prudential Tower itself, the architectural historian Bainbridge Bunting made an acute observation when he called it "an apparition so vast in size that it appears to float above the surrounding district without being related to it." Later modifications to the Boylston Street frontage of the Prudential Center effected a better union of the complex with the urban space around it, but the tower itself floats on, vast as ever. The **Hynes Convention Center** (☎617/954–2000) is connected to the Prudential Center; there's also a branch of the Greater Boston Visitors Bureau here, in the center court of the mall. **Prudential Center Skywalk**, a 50th-floor observatory atop the Prudential Tower, offers panoramic vistas of Boston, Cambridge, and the suburbs to the west and south—on clear days, you can even see Cape Cod. You can see sailboats skimming the Charles River, the redbrick expanse of the Back Bay, and a glimpse of the precise abstract geometry of the nearby Christian Science Church's reflecting pool. There are also interactive exhibits on Boston's history; the Skywalk is one of the attractions on the Boston CityPass. ✉*800 Boylston St., Back Bay* ☎*617/236–3100, 617/859–0648 for Skywalk* ⊕*www. prudentialcenter.com* ✉*Skywalk $12* ☉*Mon.–Sat. 10–9, Sun. 11–6; Skywalk Nov.–Feb. daily 10–8, Mar.–Oct. daily 10–10* Ⓣ*Hynes/ICA.*

❿ **Symphony Hall.** With commerce and religion accounted for in the Back Bay by such monuments as the Prudential Center and the Christian Science headquarters, the neighborhood still has room for a temple to music: Symphony Hall, home of the Boston Symphony Orchestra and the Boston Pops, and frequent host to guest performers. Built in 1900, Symphony Hall was another contribution of McKim, Mead & White to the Boston landscape. But acoustics rather than aesthetics make this hall special for performers and concertgoers. Although acoustical science was a brand-new field of research when Professor Wallace Sabine planned the interior, not one of the 2,500 seats is a bad one—the secret is the box-within-a-box design. ✉*301 Massachusetts Ave., Back Bay* ☎*888/266–1200 box office, 617/638–9392 tours* ⊕*www.bso.org* ☉*Free walk-up tours Oct.–May, Wed. at 4 and 2nd Sat. of month at 2* Ⓣ*Symphony.*

THE SOUTH END

A fashionable neighborhood created with landfill in the mid-1800s, the South End was deserted by the well-to-do for the Back Bay toward the end of the 19th century. Solidly back in fashion today, its redbrick row houses in various states of refurbished splendor now house a mix of ethnic groups, the city's largest gay community, and some excellent shops.

The South End neither rose haphazardly among cow paths and village lanes, like the older sections of the city, nor followed the strict, uniform grid typical of the Back Bay. It's certainly more a sum of random blocks and park-center squares than of bold boulevards and long vistas. An observation often made is that the Back Bay is French-inspired, whereas the South End is English. The houses, too, are noticeably different from those in Back Bay; although they continue the bowfront style, they aspire to a more-florid standard of decoration.

When the Bay Back was established, the South End was relegated to the status of a social backwater, which may have been due to fickle tastes but likely had something to do with the South End's location. Railroad tracks separated it from the Back Bay, and differences in planning styles and grid patterns never allowed the two districts to comfortably mesh. Even so, in the late 1970s, middle-class professionals began snapping up town houses at bargain prices and restoring them.

Today, a large African-American community resides along Columbus Avenue and Mass Ave., which marks the beginning of the predominantly black neighborhood of Roxbury. Boston's gay community also has a strong presence in the South End, with most of the gay-oriented restaurants and businesses on Columbus Avenue and Tremont Street between East Berkeley Street and Mass Ave. If you like to shop, you'll have a blast in this area, which focuses on home furnishings and accessories, with a heavy accent on the unique and handmade. At the northern tip of the South End, where Harrison Avenue and Washington Street lead to Chinatown, are several Chinese supermarkets, and south of Washington Street is the burgeoning "SoWa" District, home to a growing number of art galleries, many of which have relocated here from pricey Newbury Street.

Numbers correspond to the Back Bay, the South End & the Fens map.

TOP ATTRACTIONS

17 **Rutland Square.** Reflecting a time in which the South End was the most prestigious Boston address, this slice of a park is framed by lovely Italianate bowfront houses. ⊠ *Rutland Sq. between Columbus Ave. and Tremont St.*

18 **Union Park.** Cast-iron fences, Victorian-era town houses, and a grassy area all add up to one of Boston's most charming mini-escapes. ⊠ *Union Park St. between Shawmut Ave. and Tremont St.*

WORTH NOTING

21 **Bay Village.** It seems improbable that such a fine, mellow neighborhood (Edgar Allan Poe was born here) could remain that way, close as the Village is to the busy Theater District and the Massachusetts Turnpike. Yet here it is, another Boston surprise. This pocket of early-19th-century brick row houses is near Arlington and Piedmont streets. Its window boxes and short, narrow streets make the area seem a toylike reproduction of Beacon Hill. Note that, owing to the street pattern, it's nearly impossible to drive to Bay Village, and it's easy to miss on foot. ⊠ *Bounded (roughly) by Arlington, Stuart, Charles, and Marginal Sts.*

20 **Boston Center for the Arts.** Of Boston's multiple arts organizations, this city-sponsored arts-and-culture complex is the one that is closest to "the people." Here you can see the work of budding playwrights, view exhibits on Haitian folk art, or walk through an installation commemorating World AIDS Day. The BCA houses four theaters, a community music

1

center, the Mills Art Gallery, and studio space for some 40 Boston-based contemporary artists. It's a bit of a leap from the original purpose of the **Cyclorama Building,** which was built by William Blackall in 1884 to house a 400- by 50-foot circular painting of the Battle of Gettysburg. After the painting was sent to Pennsylvania, the building was used as a boxing ring, a roller-skating rink, and a mechanics garage (Alfred Champion invented the spark plug here). It now is host to frequent antiques shows and fund-raisers. The **Calderwood Pavilion** next door, created when the old National Theater was razed, houses new theaters, along with condos, restaurants, and a furniture store. ✉*539 Tremont St., South End* ☎*617/426–5000* ⊕*www.bcaonline.org* ✉*Free* ☉ *Weekdays 9–5; Mills Gallery Wed. and Sun. noon–5, Thurs.–Sat. noon–9* Ⓣ*Back Bay/South End.*

⓳ **Cathedral of the Holy Cross.** This enormous 1875 Gothic cathedral dominates the corner of Washington and Union Park streets. The main church of the Archdiocese of Boston and therefore the seat of Archbishop Sean Patrick O'Malley, Holy Cross is also New England's largest Catholic church. ✉*1400 Washington St., South End* ☎*617/542–5682* ⊕*www.angelfire.com/ma4/cathedral/home.html* ☉*Mass Sun. at 7:30* AM *and 11:30* AM, *Mon.–Sat. at 9* AM; *in Spanish Sun. at 9:30* AM, *Tues. and Thurs. at 7* PM Ⓣ*Chinatown, then Bus 49 to Cathedral.*

NEED A BREAK? **Although many South End restaurants are horribly pricey, a good spot to refuel on a budget is Flour Bakery and Café (** ✉*1595 Washington St., South End* ☎*617/267–4300* Ⓣ*Back Bay/South End*)**, a perennial candidate for Boston's best sandwiches and stuffed bread. Also superb are the fresh pizzas, dinner specials, and shockingly delicious pastries.**

THE FENWAY AND KENMORE SQUARE

The marshland known as the Back Bay Fens gave this section of Boston its name, but two quirky institutions give it its character: Fenway Park, which in 2004 saw the triumphant reversal of an 86-year drought for Boston's beloved Red Sox, and the Isabella Stewart Gardner Museum, the legacy of a high-living Brahmin who attended a concert at Symphony Hall in 1912 wearing a headband that read, OH, YOU RED SOX. Not far from the Gardner is another major cultural magnet: the Museum of Fine Arts. Kenmore Square, a favorite haunt for Boston University students, adds a bit of funky flavor to the mix.

After the outsize job of filling in the bay had been completed, it would have been small trouble to obliterate the Fens with gravel and march row houses straight through to Brookline. But the planners, deciding that enough pavement had been laid between here and the Public Garden, hired vaunted landscape architect Frederick Law Olmsted to turn the Fens into a park. Olmsted applied his genius for heightening natural effects while subtly manicuring their surroundings; today the Fens park consists of irregularly shaped reed-bound pools surrounded by broad meadows, trees, and flower gardens.

Prestige Lost

Not long after its conception in the mid-1800s, the South End, somewhat unfairly, lost its elite status to the Back Bay. The literature of the time documents this exodus: the title character in William Dean Howells's *The Rise of Silas Lapham* abandoned the South End to build a house on the waterside of Beacon as material proof of his arrival in Boston society. In *The Late George Apley,* John P. Marquand's Brahmin hero tells how his father decided, in the early 1870s, to move the family from his South End bowfront to the Back Bay—a consequence of his walking out on the front steps one morning and seeing a man in his shirtsleeves on the porch opposite. Regardless of whether Marquand exaggerated Victorian notions of propriety (if that was possible), the fact is that people such as the Apleys did decamp for the Back Bay, leaving the South End to become what a 1913 guidebook called a "faded quarter."

The Fens marks the beginning of Boston's Emerald Necklace, a loosely connected chain of parks designed by Olmsted that extends along the Fenway, Riverway, and Jamaicaway to Jamaica Pond, the Arnold Arboretum, and Franklin Park. Farther off, at the Boston–Milton line, the Blue Hills Reservation offers some of the Boston area's best hiking, scenic views, and even a ski lift.

Numbers correspond to the Back Bay, the South End & the Fens map.

TIMING   Although this area can be walked through in a couple of hours, art lovers could spend a week here, thanks to the glories of the MFA and the Isabella Stewart Gardner Museum. (If you want to do a museum blowout, avoid Monday, when the Gardner is closed.) To cap off a day of culture, plan for an area dinner, then a concert at nearby Symphony Hall. Another option, if you're visiting between spring and early fall, is to take a tour of Fenway Park—or better yet, catch a game. This district is most easily traveled via branches of the MBTA's Green Line; trains operate aboveground on Commonwealth and Huntington avenues. ■ TIP→ **Avoid walking inside the Fens at night, when the marshy areas are poorly lighted.**

TOP ATTRACTIONS

㉕ **Fenway Park.** For 86 years, the Boston Red Sox suffered a World Series dry spell, a streak of bad luck that fans attributed to the "Curse of the Bambino," which, stories have it, struck the team in 1920 when they sold Babe Ruth (the "Bambino") to the New York Yankees. All that changed in 2004, when a maverick squad—including local heroes Jason Varitek, Kevin Youkilis, and particular favorite David Ortiz—broke the curse in a thrilling seven-game series against the team's nemesis in the Series semifinals. This win against the Yankees was followed by a four-game sweep of St. Louis in the finals. Boston, and its citizens' ingrained sense of pessimism, hasn't been the same since. The repeat World Series win in 2007 has just cemented Bostonians' sense that the universe is finally working correctly. There's a palpable sense of justice

Fodor'sChoice ★

A GOOD WALK

With Boston's two major art museums on this itinerary, a case of museum fatigue could set in. Happily, both the Museum of Fine Arts and the Isabella Stewart Gardner Museum are surrounded by the sylvan glades of the Fenway—a perfect oasis and time-out location when you're suffering from gallery gout. From the intersection of Massachusetts and Huntington avenues, with the front entrance of Symphony Hall on your right, walk down Huntington Avenue. On your left is the New England Conservatory of Music and, on Gainsborough Street, its recital center, Jordan Hall. Between Huntington Avenue and the Fenway is the **Museum of Fine Arts (MFA)** ㉒ and, just around the corner, the **Isabella Stewart Gardner Museum** ㉓. If you prefer to pay homage to the Red Sox: from Symphony Hall, go north on Mass Ave., turn left on Commonwealth Avenue, and continue until you reach **Kenmore Square** ㉔; from here it's a 10-minute walk down Brookline Avenue to Yawkey Way and **Fenway Park** ㉕.

being served, and more than a little pride in the way Red Sox caps have become residents' semiofficial uniform.

Fenway may be one of the smallest parks in the major leagues (capacity almost 39,000), but it's one of the most beloved, despite its oddball dimensions and the looming left-field wall, otherwise known as the Green Monster. Parking is expensive and the seats are a bit cramped, but the air is thick with legend. Ruth pitched here when the stadium was new; Ted Williams and Carl Yastrzemski slugged out their entire careers here. ⊠ *4 Yawkey Way, between Van Ness and Lansdowne Sts., The Fenway* ☎ *877/733–7699 box office, 617/226–6666 tours* ⊕ *www. boston.redsox.mlb.com* ⊠ *Tours $12* ☉ *Tours Mon.–Sat. 9–4, Sun. 9–3; on game days, last tour is 3 hrs before game time* Ⓣ*Kenmore.*

DID YOU KNOW?

Yawkey Way is named for the late Tom Yawkey, who bought the team in 1933 as a 30th-birthday present for himself and spent the next 43 years pursuing his elusive grail.

㉓ **Isabella Stewart Gardner Museum.** A spirited young society woman, Isabella Stewart had come in 1860 from New York—where ladies were more commonly seen *and* heard than in Boston—to marry John Lowell Gardner, one of Boston's leading citizens. Through her flamboyance and energetic acquisition of art, "Mrs. Jack" promptly set about becoming the most un-Bostonian of the Proper Bostonians. When it came time finally to settle down with the old master paintings and Medici treasures she and her husband had acquired in Europe—with *her* money (she was heir to the Stewart mining fortune)—she decided to build the Venetian palazzo of her dreams in an isolated corner of Boston's newest neighborhood. She built her palace to center on a spacious inner courtyard. On New Year's Day 1903, she threw open the entrance to Fenway Court (to use the museum's original name)—then as now, a monument to one woman's individuality and taste. Today, it's probably America's most idiosyncratic treasure house.

Fodor$Choice ★

In a city where expensive simplicity was the norm, Gardner's palazzo was amazing: a trove of paintings—including such masterpieces as Titian's *Europa,* Giotto's *Presentation of Christ in the Temple,* Piero della Francesca's *Hercules,* and John Singer Sargent's *El Jaleo*—overflows rooms bought outright from great European houses. Spanish leather panels, Renaissance hooded fireplaces, and Gothic tapestries accent salons; eight balconies adorn the majestic Venetian courtyard. There's a Raphael Room, a Spanish Cloister, a Gothic Room, a Chinese Loggia, and a magnificent Tapestry Room for concerts, where Gardner entertained Henry James and Edith Wharton. Throughout the two decades of her residence, Mrs. Jack continued to build her collection under the tutelage of the young Bernard Berenson, who became one of the most respected art connoisseurs and critics of the 20th century.

> **THE GARDNER HEIST**
>
> On March 18, 1990, the Gardner was the target of one of the world's most sensational heists. Thieves disguised as police officers stole 12 works of art with an estimated value of $200–$300 million. Vermeer's *The Concert* was taken, along with works by Rembrandt, Manet, and Degas. To date, none of the art has been recovered, despite a $5 million reward. Because Mrs. Gardner's will prohibited substituting other works for any stolen art, empty expanses of wall identify spots where the paintings once hung.

At one time Gardner lived on the fourth floor of Fenway Court. When she died, the terms of her will stipulated that the building remain exactly as she left it—paintings, furniture, everything, down to the smallest object in a hall cabinet. Mrs. Jack never believed in insurance, putting her faith in her mansion's entry portal, which carries Renaissance-period figures of both St. George and St. Florian, the patron saints protecting believers from theft and fire. Today, with more than 2,500 works in the collection and rates dramatically lower because of increasing recoveries of stolen art, the Gardner indeed does carry insurance. An intimate restaurant overlooks the garden, and in spring and summer tables and chairs spill outside. To fully conjure up the spirit of days past, try to attend one of the concerts still held from September to May (with a break for the holidays) in the Tapestry Room. A first-floor gallery has revolving exhibits of historic and contemporary art. ■ **TIP→ If you've visited the MFA in the past two days, there's a $2 discount to the admission fee. Also note that a charming quirk of the museum's admission policy waives entrance fees to anyone named Isabella, forever.** ⊠*280 The Fenway, The Fenway* ☎*617/566–1401, 617/566–1088 café* ⊕*www.gardnermuseum.org* ⊠*$12* ⊙*Museum Tues.–Sun. 11–5, open some holidays; café Tues.–Fri. 11:30–4, weekends 11–4. Weekend concerts at 1:30* Ⓣ*Museum.*

㉒ Ⓒ Fodor\$Choice ★ **Museum of Fine Arts.** Count on staying awhile if you have any hope of even beginning to see what's here. Eclecticism and thoroughness, often an incompatible pair, have coexisted agreeably at the MFA since its earliest days. From Renaissance and baroque masters to impressionist marvels to African masks to sublime samples of Native American pottery and contemporary crafts, the collections are happily shorn of both cultural snobbery and shortsighted trendiness.

Founded in 1870, the MFA first resided on the upper floors of the Boston Athenaeum, then a Gothic structure on the site where the Copley Plaza Hotel now stands. As the museum was beginning to outgrow that space, the Fenway area was becoming fashionable, and in 1909 the move was made to Guy Lowell's somewhat severe beaux arts building, to which the West Wing, designed by I. M. Pei, was added in 1981. The move helped cap the half century of expansion of the Back Bay area.

The MFA's collection of approximately 450,000 objects was built from a core of paintings and sculpture from the Boston Athenaeum, historical portraits from the city of Boston, and donations by area universities. The early MFA connoisseurs were as enamored as any cultured Victorians with the great art of European civilizations. Nevertheless, they sought out American works as well; today, the museum's holdings of American art—supplemented by intensive acquisitions in the early 1990s—surpass those of all but two or three U.S. museums. The MFA has more than 60 works by John Singleton Copley; major paintings by Winslow Homer, John Singer Sargent, Fitz Hugh Lane, and Edward Hopper; and a wealth of American works ranging from native New England folk art and colonial portraiture to New York abstract expressionism of the 1950s and 1960s. Also of particular note are the John Singer Sargent paintings adorning the Rotunda. They were specially commissioned for the museum in 1921 and make for a dazzling first impression on visitors coming through the Huntington Street entrance.

American decorative arts are also liberally represented, particularly those of New England in the years before the Civil War. Rooms of period furniture show the progression of taste from the earliest Pilgrim pieces through the 18th-century triumphs of the Queen Anne, Hepplewhite, Sheraton, and Empire styles. Native son Paul Revere, much more than a sounder of alarms, is amply represented as well, with superb silver teapots, sauceboats, and other tableware.

The museum also owns one of the world's most extensive collections of Asian art under one roof. Its Japanese art collection is the finest outside Japan, and Chinese porcelains of the Tang Dynasty are especially well represented. The Egyptian rooms display statuary, furniture, and exquisite gold jewelry; a special funerary-arts gallery exhibits coffins, mummies, and burial treasures. The gathering of classical treasures, including marble busts, jewelry, and glassware, proceeds chronologically from the Cycladic period through the Roman era.

French impressionists abound and are perhaps more comprehensively displayed here than at any other new-world museum outside the Art Institute of Chicago; many of the 38 Monets (the largest collection of his work outside France) vibrate with color. There are canvases by Renoir, Pissarro, Manet, and the American painters Mary Cassatt and Childe Hassam.

Three important galleries explore the art of Africa, Oceania, and the Ancient Americas, expanding the MFA's emphasis on civilizations outside the Western tradition. Highlights include rare examples of the earliest-known figurative sculpture from sub-Saharan Africa, expressive Melanesian works in wood and stone, delicate Olmec jade sculptures, and extraordinary Maya painted ceramics.

The museum has strong collections of textiles, costumes, and prints dating from the 15th century, including many works by Dürer and Goya, and its collection of antique musical instruments is among the finest in the world.

Fifteen second-floor galleries contain the MFA's European painting and sculpture collection, dating from the 11th century to the 20th. Among the standouts are Donatello's marble relief *The Madonna of the Clouds* and J. M. W. Turner's powerful work *The Slave Ship*. Most striking, however, is the **William I. Koch Gallery,** a former tapestry room whose 40-foot-high marble walls are now hung, nearly floor to ceiling, with 53 dramatic Renaissance and baroque paintings by El Greco, Claude Lorraine, Poussin, Rubens, Tintoretto, Titian, Van Dyck, Velázquez, Veronese, and other masters.

The **West Wing,** an airy, well-lighted space, is used primarily to mount special exhibitions, temporary shows drawn from the museum's holdings, and lively contemporary-art and photography exhibits. It also has the Bravo Restaurant, a cafeteria, and a café serving light snacks. From October to April, tea is served from 2:30 to 4 in the second-floor Upper Rotunda, and the year-round cocktail party "MFA Fridays," from 5:30 to 9:30—held weekly in summer and monthly at other times—has become quite the social event. The MFA's Film Program brings new and classic art-house cinema to the museum's theater, often in conjunction with talks with filmmakers. Annual events such as the Boston French Film Festival and the Boston Jewish Film Festival are also held here. Kids can keep busy with workshops (Tuesday–Sunday) and special programs.

In 2005, the museum broke ground on a massive construction project that the trustees hope will keep it in America's cultural vanguard for the next 100 years. In its first phase, a new **East Wing** will be built to house the Art of the Americas collection, expanding the current gallery space by 50%. The contemporary and 20th-century art collections will move to the Gund Gallery, currently housing temporary exhibitions, and a new special-exhibition space will be built beneath the East Courtyard. Other aspects of the 133-year-old building's enormous face-lift will include a new glass-enclosed courtyard, the reopening of the Fenway entrance, and a "crystal spine" to run the full length of the museum. The new American Wing is expected to open in November 2010; the museum will remain open during construction. ⊠ *465 Huntington Ave., The Fenway* ☎ *617/267–9300* ⊕ *www.mfa.org* ⊠ *$17; by donation Wed. 4–9:45* ☉ *Sat.–Tues. 10–4:45, Wed.–Fri. 10–9:45. 1-hr tours daily; call for scheduled times* Ⓣ *Museum.*

WORTH NOTING

㉔ Kenmore Square. Two blocks north of Fenway Park is Kenmore Square, where you'll find fast-food joints, record stores, and an enormous sign advertising Citgo gasoline. The red, white, and blue neon sign from 1965 is so thoroughly identified with the area that historic preservationists fought, successfully, to save it—proof that Bostonians are an open-minded lot who don't insist that their landmarks be identified with the American Revolution. The old Kenmore Square punk clubs have recently given way to a block-long development of chain stores and pricey restaurants, as well as brick sidewalks, gaslight-style street lamps, and tree plantings. The Hotel Commonwealth, a six-story luxury European-style hotel, sits smack in the middle of Kenmore Square.

In the shadow of Fenway Park between Brookline and Ipswich is **Lansdowne Street,** a nightlife magnet for the young and trendy who have their pick of can't-hear-yourself-think dance clubs such as Avalon and Axis. The urban campus of Boston University begins farther west on Commonwealth Avenue, in blocks thick with dorms, shops, and restaurants. ✉ *Convergence of Beacon St., Commonwealth Ave., and Brookline Ave.* Ⓣ *Kenmore.*

THE "STREETCAR SUBURBS"

The expansion of Boston in the 1800s was not confined to the Back Bay and the South End. Toward the close of the century, as the working population of the Downtown District swelled and public transportation (first horsecars, then electric trolleys) linked outlying suburbs with the city, development of the "streetcar suburbs" began. These areas answered the housing needs of the rising native-born middle class as well as the second-generation immigrant families already outgrowing the narrow streets of the North and West ends.

The landfill project that became South Boston—known as "Southie" and not to be confused with the South End—isn't a true streetcar suburb; its expansion predates the era of commuting. Some of the brick bowfront residences along East Broadway in City Point date from the 1840s and 1850s, but the neighborhood really came into its own with the influx of Irish around 1900, and Irish-Americans still hold sway here. Southie is a Celtic enclave, as the raucous annual St. Patrick's Day parade attests.

Among the other streetcar suburbs are Dorchester and Jamaica Plain—rural retreats barely more than a century ago that are now thick with tenements and Boston's distinctive three- and six-family triple-decker apartment houses. Dorchester is almost exclusively residential, tricky to navigate by car, and accessible by the T only if you know exactly where you're going. Jamaica Plain is a hip, young neighborhood with a strong lesbian and ecofriendly population; brunch and a wander through the neighborhood's quirky stores or through the Arnold Arboretum makes for a relaxing weekend excursion. Both towns border Franklin Park, an Olmsted creation of more than 500 acres, noted for its zoo. Farther west, Brookline is composed of a mixture of the affluent and students.

SOUTH BOSTON

Castle Island Park. South Boston projects farther into the harbor than any other part of Boston except Logan Airport, and the views of the Harbor Islands from along Day Boulevard or Castle Island are expansive. At

L Street and Day Boulevard is the L Street Beach, where an intrepid group called the L Street Brownies swims year-round, including a celebratory dip in the icy Atlantic every New Year's Day. Castle Island Park is no longer on an island, but **Fort Independence,** when it was built here in 1801, was separated from the mainland by water. The circular walk from the fort around Pleasure Bay, delightful on a warm summer day, has a stunning view of the city's skyline late at night (South Boston is considered one of the city's safest neighborhoods). The statue near the fort is of Donald McKay, whose clipper ships once sped past this point on their way to California and the Orient. To get here by the T, take the Red Line to Broadway Station. Just outside the station, catch Bus 9 or 11 going east on Broadway, which takes you to within a block of the waterfront. From the waterfront park you can walk the loop, via piers, around the island. ⊠ *Off William J. Day Blvd., South Boston* ☎ *617/727–5290* ⊕ *www.mass.gov/dcr/parks/metroboston/castle.htm* ⊗ *Tours Memorial Day–Labor Day, call for specific tour times.*

Fodor'sChoice
★   **Institute of Contemporary Art.** Housed in a breathtaking cantilevered edifice that juts out over the Boston waterfront, the ICA moved to this site in 2006 as part of a massive reinvention that's seeing the museum grow into one of Boston's most exciting attractions. Since its foundation in 1936, the institute has cultivated its cutting-edge status: it's played host to works by Edvard Munch, Egon Schiele, and Oskar Kokoschka. Andy Warhol, Robert Rauschenberg, and Roy Lichtenstein each mounted pivotal exhibitions here early in their careers. Now the ICA is building a major permanent collection for the first time in its history while continuing to showcase innovative paintings, videos, installations, and multimedia shows. The performing arts get their due in the museum's new theater, and the Water Café features cuisine from Wolfgang Puck. ⊠ *100 Northern Ave., South Boston* ☎ *617/478–3100* ⊕ *www.icaboston. org* ▭ *$12, free Thurs. 5–9, free for families last Sat. of every month* ⊗ *Tues. and Wed. 10–5, Thurs. and Fri. 10–9, weekends 10–5. Tours on select weekends at 2 and select Thurs. at 6* Ⓣ *Courthouse.*

DORCHESTER

Dorchester Heights Monument and National Historic Site. In 1776 Dorchester Heights hill commanded a clear view of central Boston, where the British had been under siege since the preceding year. Here George Washington set up the cannons that Henry Knox, a Boston bookseller turned soldier, and later secretary of war, had hauled through the wilderness after their capture at Fort Ticonderoga. The artillery did its job of intimidation, and the British troops left Boston, never to return. The view of Boston from the site is magnificent, particularly if you go during the hours the graceful white tower is staffed. Climb its 93 steps and you'll be rewarded with vistas from the Blue Hills to the Harbor Islands, although the lovely park grounds are a destination on their own on a warm day. ⊠ *Thomas Park off Telegraph St., near G St., Dorchester* ☎ *617/242–5642* ▭ *Free* ⊗ *Grounds daily. Monument call for schedule* Ⓣ *Broadway, then City Point Bus (9 or 11) to G St.*

1

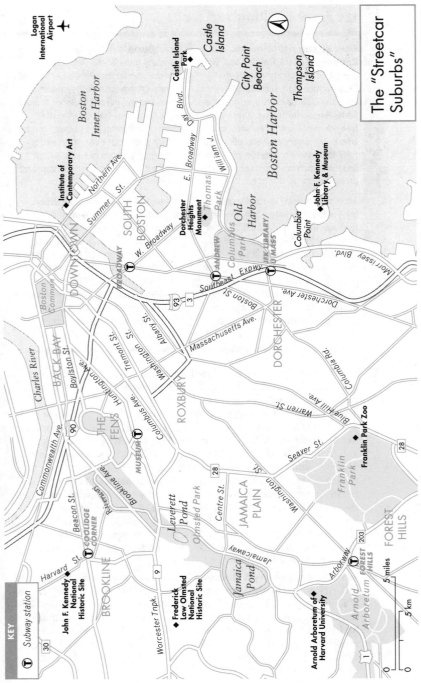

The "Streetcar Suburbs"

Ⓣ Subway station

Let Freebies Ring

Freedom may not be free, but Boston's Freedom Trail is—and so are 13 of the 16 attractions that lie along its path, including Faneuil Hall, the USS *Constitution*, and the State House. Better yet, there are free 90-minute tours for visitors who'd like a guided walk, plus free MP3 tours (downloadable at ⊕ *www. boston.com/travel/boston*) for those preferring to go it alone.

Additional themed routes—most notably the Black Heritage Trail, the Irish Heritage Trail, and HarborWalk—can also be enjoyed at no charge. Ditto for outdoor attractions like the city's major monuments, memorials, parks and public gardens. Boston's to-die-for cemeteries (such as the Granary Burying Ground, a preferred resting place for patriots) also have no price tag attached.

Frugal souls can even take complimentary tours of the Boston Athenaeum, the Boston Public Library, and Trinity Church (one of the country's "architectural gems"). October through May, Symphony Hall offers guided tours, too: Boston Pops tickets can be pretty pricey, but every Wednesday afternoon you can see inside their sublime home base without spending a cent.

Other major sites waive admission at set times: among them, the Institute of Contemporary Art (Thursday evening); the Museum of Fine Arts (Wednesday evening); and the Harvard Art Museums (Saturday morning and every day after 4:30). The Isabella Stewart Gardner Museum, meanwhile, is always free for art lovers under 18—as well as for anyone who happens to be named Isabella!

☺ **Franklin Park Zoo.** Lion and tiger habitats, the Giraffe Savannah, and a 4-acre mixed-species area called the Serengeti Crossing that showcases zebras, ostriches, ibex, and wildebeests keep this zoo roaring. The Tropical Forest, with its renovated Western Lowland Gorilla environment, is a big draw, and wallabies, emus, and kangaroos populate the Australian Outback Trail. From May to September, butterflies flit and flutter at Butterfly Landing, where docents are on hand to answer questions and give advice on attracting the colorful insects to your own garden. The Children's Zoo entices with sheep, goats, and other pet-able beasts. In winter, call in advance to find out which animals are braving the cold. The park, 4 mi from Downtown, is reached by Bus 16 from the Forest Hills (Orange Line) or Andrew (Red Line) T stops; there's plenty of parking. ⊠ *1 Franklin Park Rd., Dorchester* ☎*617/541–5466* ⊕*www.zoonewengland.com* 🖃☉*$12 Oct.–Mar., daily 10–4; Apr.– Sept., weekdays 10–5, weekends 10–6.*

★ **John F. Kennedy Library & Museum.** Chronicling a time now passing from memory to history, the library-museum is both a center for serious scholarship and a focus for Boston's nostalgia for her native son. The stark, white, prowlike building (another modernist monument designed by I. M. Pei) at this harbor-enclosed site pays homage to the life and presidency of John F. Kennedy, an Irish-American blessed with charisma, intellect, and passion, and to members of his family, including his wife, Jacqueline, and brother Robert.

The Kennedy Library is the official repository of his presidential papers; the museum displays a trove of Kennedy memorabilia, including re-creations of his desk in the Oval Office and of the television studio in which he debated Richard M. Nixon in the 1960 election. At the entrance, high and dry during the summer months, is the president's 26-foot sailboat; inside, two theaters show a film about his life. The museum exhibits, ranging from the Cuban missile crisis to his assassination, include 20 video presentations. There's also a permanent display on the late Jacqueline Kennedy Onassis, including some samples of her distinctive wardrobe and such personal mementos as a first edition of *One Special Summer,* the book she and her sister wrote and illustrated shortly after a 1951 trip to Paris. A re-creation of the office Robert Kennedy occupied as attorney general from 1961 to 1964 complements "legacy" videos of John's idealistic younger brother. As a somber note in an otherwise gung-ho museum, continuous videos of the first news bulletin of the assassination and the funeral are shown in a darkened hall. Fourth-floor research facilities are open only to serious researchers. The Steven M. Smith Wing provides space for meetings and events; the facility also includes a store and a small café. ⊠ *Columbia Point, Dorchester* ☎ *617/514–1600* ⊕ *www.jfklibrary.org* 🎟 *$12* ⊙ *Daily 9–5* Ⓣ *JFK/UMass, then free shuttle bus every 20 mins.*

> **BEER HERE**
>
> Before Prohibition, Jamaica Plain was home to a thriving beer industry, the remnants of which today can be seen in the neighborhood's many 19th-century brick breweries, long since converted to offices and lofts. The **Samuel Adams Brewery** (⊠ *30 Germania St., Jamaica Plain* ☎ *617/368–5080*) is the only hint that the area was once awash in hops, malt, and happy tipplers. Complimentary tastings are the highlight of the brewery's tours.

JAMAICA PLAIN

Fodor$Choice ★ **Arnold Arboretum of Harvard University.** This 265-acre living laboratory is incongruously set in a dense urban area. Established in 1872 in accordance with the terms of a bequest from New Bedford merchant James Arnold, it contains more than 4,000 kinds of woody plants, most from the hardy north temperate zone. The rhododendrons, azaleas, lilacs, magnolias, and fruit trees are eye-popping when in bloom, and something is always in season from early April through September. In October the park puts on a display in blazing colors. Peters Hill has a grand view of the Boston skyline and local surroundings. The Larz Anderson bonsai collection, with individual specimens imported from Japan that are more than 200 years old, includes a 3½-acre Leventritt Shrub and Vine Collection. In the visitor center is a 40-to-1 scale model of the arboretum (with 4,000 tiny trees), plus an exhibit on "Science in the Pleasure Ground," a kind of "green" history of the landscape. If you visit during May, Lilac Sunday is an annual celebration of blooming trees, Morris dancing, and picnicking. The arboretum, 6 mi from downtown Boston, is accessible by the MBTA Orange Line or Bus 39 from Copley Square to Forest Hills; then follow the signs at the T station. ⊠ *125 Arborway, at*

Centre St., Jamaica Plain ☎*617/524–1718* ⊕*www.arboretum.harvard. edu* ✉*Free* ☉*Grounds daily dawn–dusk; visitor center weekdays 9–4, Sat. 10–4, Sun. noon–4. Tours Sat. at 10:30, Sun. at 1, Wed. at 12:15, and Fri. at 6; call to confirm* Ⓣ*Forest Hills.*

BROOKLINE

★ **Frederick Law Olmsted National Historic Site.** *At this writing, the site was closed for renovation, but it's expected to reopen in 2010.* Frederick Law Olmsted (1822–1903) is considered the nation's preeminent creator of parks. In 1883 at age 61, while immersed in planning Boston's Emerald Necklace of parks, Olmsted set up his first permanent office at Fairsted, an 18-room farmhouse dating from 1810, to which he added another 18 rooms for his design offices. Plans and drawings on display include projects as the U.S. Capitol grounds, Stanford University, and Mount Royal Park in Montréal. You can also tour the design rooms (some still in use for preservation projects) where Olmsted and staff drew up their plans; highlights include a 1904 "electric blueprint machine," a kind of primitive photocopier. The 1¾-acre site incorporates many trademark Olmstedian designs, including areas of meadow, wild garden, and woodland; Olmsted believed body and spirit could be healed through close association with nature. The site became part of the National Park Service in 1979; Olmsted's office played an influential role in the creation of this federal agency. In 1916 Olmsted's son, who carried on his father's work here, wrote the words that were to serve as a statement of purpose for legislation establishing the Park Service that same year: "To conserve the scenery and the natural and historic objects and the wildlife therein and to provide for the enjoyment of the same in such manner and by such means as will leave them unimpaired for the enjoyment of future generations." ✉*99 Warren St., Brookline* ☎*617/566–1689* ⊕*www.nps.gov/frla/index.htm* ✉*Free* ☉*Call for hrs once site reopens in 2010* Ⓣ*Brookline Hills.*

John F. Kennedy National Historic Site. This was the home of the 35th president from his birth on May 29, 1917, until 1921, when the family moved to nearby Naples and Abbottsford streets. Rose Kennedy provided the furnishings for the restored 2½-story, wood-frame structure. You can pick up a brochure for a walking tour of young Kennedy's school, church, and neighborhood. To get here, take the MBTA Green Line to Coolidge Corner and walk north on Harvard Street four blocks. ✉*83 Beals St., Brookline* ☎*617/566–7937* ⊕*www.nps.gov/jofi* ✉*$3, tours free* ☉*Mid-May–Nov., Wed.–Sun. 10–4:30, call to confirm; tours every ½ hr 10–3:30, with open house 3:30–4:30* Ⓣ*Coolidge Corner.*

Exploring
Cambridge

WORD OF MOUTH

"On our second day we took the T out to Harvard and started off walking down Brattle Street to see some of the homes. We veered into Harvard Yard going into the Law School Library. It's funny to see that only tourists were wearing Harvard t-shirts or sweatshirts."

—Myer

Updated
by Bethany
Cassin
Beckerlegge

The city of Cambridge takes a lot of hits, most of them thrown across the Charles River by jealous Bostonians. But Boston's Left Bank—an überliberal academic enclave where the city council spends more energy arguing about the regulation of nanotechnologies than on fixing potholes and funding preschools—is arguably a must-visit if you're spending even just three days in the Boston area.

The city is punctuated at one end by the funky tech-noids of MIT, and at the other by the soaring—and occasionally seething—rhetoric of the Harvard University community. Civic life connects the two camps into an urban stew of 100,000 residents who represent nearly every nationality in the world, work at every kind of job from tenured professor to taxi driver, and are passionate about living on this side of the river.

The Charles River is Cantabrigians' backyard, running track, and festival ground, and there's virtually no place in Cambridge more than a 10-minute walk from its banks. No visit to Cambridge would be complete without an afternoon (at least) in Harvard Square. It's a hub, a hot spot, and home to every variation of the human condition. A walk down Brattle Street past Henry Wadsworth Longfellow's house is a joy in spring, summer, and fall (you have to be hard core to love Harvard Square in the dead of winter). Farther along Massachusetts Avenue is Central Square, an ethnic melting pot of people and restaurants. Ten minutes more brings you to MIT, with its eclectic architecture, from postwar pedestrian to Frank Gehry's futuristic fantasyland.

In addition to providing a stellar view, the Mass Ave. Bridge, spanning the Charles from Cambridge to Boston, is also notorious in MIT lore for its Smoot measurements see "Campus Pranksters" under Massachusetts Institute of Technology). Cambridge dates from 1630, when the Puritan leader John Winthrop chose this meadowland as the site of a carefully planned village he named Newtowne. The Massachusetts Bay Colony chose Newtowne as the site for the country's first college in 1636. Two years later, John Harvard bequeathed half his estate and his private library to the fledgling school, and the college was named in his honor. The town elders changed the name to Cambridge, emulating the university in England where most of the Puritan leaders had been educated.

When Cambridge was incorporated as a city in 1846, the boundaries were drawn to include the university area (today's Harvard Square and Tory Row), and the more-industrial communities of Cambridgeport and East Cambridge. By 1900 the population of these urban industrial and working-class communities, made up of Irish, Polish, Italian, Portuguese, and French Canadian residents, dwarfed the Harvard end of town. Today's city is much more a multiethnic urban community than an academic village. Visitors in search of any kind of ethnic food

TOP REASONS TO GO

■ Do the Harvard Museum circuit: The Sackler for art; the Semitic Museum; the Peabody and the Natural History Museum for artifacts and culture.

■ Visit MIT to wander the halls, visit its museum, and see Frank Gehry's Seuss-like Stata Center.

■ Browse the new- and used-book stores, and trawl the artsy boutiques in Harvard Square. Take a break with a hot chocolate at Burdick's (near the Dexter Pratt House or grab an espresso at the ultracute Café Pamplona on Bowe Street.

■ Breathe the rarefied air of Harvard on an official tour, then return to real life with an ice-cream cone from Herrell's or a burger from Mr. Bartley's Burger Cottage.

■ Amble down Brattle Street, visiting the 1700s era homes of Tory Row (Washington really did sleep here.), and have a treat at Hi-Rise bakery in the original Blacksmith House of Longfellow's poem.

or music will find it in Cambridge—the local high school educates students who speak more than 40 different languages at home. When MIT, originally Boston Tech, moved to Cambridge in 1916, it was the first educational institution that aimed to be more than a trade school, training engineers but also grounding them in humanities and liberal arts. Many of MIT's postwar graduates remained in the area, and went on to form hundreds of technology-based firms engaged in camera manufacturing, electronics, and space research. By the 1990s, manufacturing had moved to the burbs and software developers, venture capitalists, and robotics and biotech companies claimed the former industrial spaces. This area around Kendall Square is now nicknamed "Intelligence Alley."

GETTING ORIENTED

Just minutes from Boston, Cambridge is easily reached by taking the Red Line train (otherwise known as the "T") outbound to any stop past Charles Street. In Cambridge any commercial area where three or more streets meet in a jumble of traffic and noise has been dubbed a "square." Harvard Square draws the most visitors, but other neighborhood squares exude their own charms. Inman Square, at the intersection of Cambridge and Hampshire streets, has a fine cluster of restaurants and cafés. Central Square, at Massachusetts Avenue (known by locals as "Mass Ave.") and Prospect Street, has Irish pubs, music clubs, and a row of furniture stores. Porter Square, about a mile northwest of Harvard Square on Mass Ave., has several shopping centers and, within the nearby Porter Exchange, a mall filled with Japanese noodle and food shops. Somerville's Davis Square, just over the border of northwest Cambridge and easily accessible on the Red Line, is a hip neighborhood with great eateries, lively bars, and candlepin bowling. At Kendall Square, near the Massachusetts Institute of Technology (MIT) and the heart of the city's thriving biotech industry, an art-house multiplex shows first-run films. The Cambridge Multicultural Arts Center, an intriguing gallery and performance space, is in East Cambridge, near the Cambridgeside Galleria mall and numerous Portuguese cafés and restaurants.

Harvard Square is the best place to begin any visit to Cambridge. The area is notorious for its aggressive drivers, lack of parking, and flood of pedestrians who can make driving in the area downright frightening. Do yourself a favor and take the T. If you insist on driving, avoid endlessly circling the block by pulling into a garage. Two good ones: the Harvard Square garage is at JFK and Eliot streets, and the University Place garage is behind the Charles Hotel, on University Road at Bennett Street. Some offer validation from specific retailers—ask about it when you park. There's also a small public lot on Church Street between Brattle Street and Mass Ave. Those who like to gamble for meters can find a large concentration of the coin-operated gizmos underneath the Harvard Square Hotel on Mt. Auburn Street. Take note, though: even if you're lucky enough to snag one, the one-hour limits will probably impede your visit.

HARVARD SQUARE

In Cambridge, all streets point toward Harvard Square. In addition to being the gateway to Harvard University and its various attractions, Harvard Square is home to the tiny yet venerable folk-music club Passim (Bob Dylan played here, and Bonnie Raitt was a regular during her time at Harvard), first-run and vintage movie theaters, concert and lecture venues, and a tempting collection of shops. But real estate is expensive in Harvard Square, and if you're returning after a lapse, you'll notice a shift in the neighborhood's persona. Beloved mom-and-pop shops continue to succumb to proliferating chain-store competitors. The Gap has an outpost in Harvard Square, alongside four Starbucks outlets and three mobile-phone stores. Even the Harvard Coop bookstore is now operated by Barnes & Noble. The good news is that the independent one-of-a-kind shops have migrated north and now line the stretch of Mass Ave. between Harvard and Porter Square.

Harvard Square is a multicultural microcosm. On a warm day, street musicians coax exotic tones from their Andean pan flutes and Chinese erhus, while cranks and local pessimists pass out pamphlets warning against all sorts of end-of-the-world scenarios. Everyone is on a cell phone, speaking in dozens of languages. In the small plaza atop the main entrance to the Harvard T station known as "the Pit," skaters and punks strut and pose while fresh-faced students impress each other and/or their dates, and quiet clusters study the moves and strategy of the chess players seated outside Au Bon Pain.

TIMING Harvard Square is worth an afternoon, at least—more if you plan to explore Harvard's natural-history or art museums.

A good place to start is the **Cambridge Visitor Information Booth.** Volunteers at this kiosk outside the MBTA station entrance hand out free maps, brochures, and guides about the city. Material available includes a walking tour of historic places, an excellent list of bookstores in the area, and a guide to seasonal events. If you plan ahead you can check

A GOOD WALK

Begin your tour at the **Cambridge Visitor Information Booth** in **Harvard Square** ❶ near the MBTA station entrance, where you can find maps and information about the entire city, a guide to local bookstores, and brochures that cover walking tours of old Cambridge and seasonal events. Be sure to pick up the Harvard Square Business Association's excellent 25¢ map of the area. If you want to revisit Cambridge's Tory beginnings, walk past the **Wadsworth House** ❷, a clapboard house on Mass Ave. that dates from 1726, and enter the dignified hush of the Yard at **Harvard University** ❸. Admire the exterior of **Widener Library** ❹ (only students and their guests are allowed inside); it houses one of the largest collections of books, historical materials, and journals in the academic world. Then circle back through the yard, crossing Mass Ave. to view the **First Parish in Cambridge and the Old Burying Ground** ❺ on the corner of Church Street. Through the iron railing of the cemetery, you can make out a number of tombstones. Buried here are the remains of 17th- and 18th-century Tory landowners, slaves, and soldiers. Continue up Garden Street to **Christ Church** ❻, designed in 1761 and still an active parish. The Cambridge Common, across Garden Street, has a terrific playground, and is a good spot to take a rest.

Retrace your steps along Mass Ave. and cross the street near the First Parish Church. Cut through Harvard Yard, bearing to your left, pass the modern Science Center, and look for the striking Victorian architecture of Memorial Hall. If you want to understand what makes Harvard a cultural epicenter, a visit to its museums is advised. It's not just that Harvard has everything, it has the best of everything—from Picassos and Pollacks to Egyptian mummies and Moghul miniatures. Just past Memorial Hall, at the intersection of Quincy and Kirkland streets, turn right onto Kirkland Street and then take a quick left onto Divinity Avenue. At 6 Divinity Avenue is Harvard's **Semitic Museum** ❼. At 11 Divinity Avenue is the entrance to the extensive **Peabody Museum of Archaeology & Ethnology** ❾ and the **Harvard Museum of Natural History** ❽ (in the same building).

If you're inclined toward art, the **Arthur M. Sackler Museum** ❿, across Broadway, will show you visions of the ancient world, while the **Carpenter Center for the Visual Arts** ⓫ on Quincy Street offers a strictly contemporary perspective on film and graphic arts. Alas, those coming to ogle the fine wares of the Fogg and Busch-Reisinger museums will have to wait. At this writing, both are shut down for a lengthy renovation that will span at least five years. Happily, some of the collections will be displayed during this time at the Sackler. ∎TIP➡ **Film lovers: visit the film archive section on the Harvard Web site to find film screenings that coincide with your visit.** When you've had your fill of culture, head back to one of the Harvard Square cafés for a snack and serious people-watching.

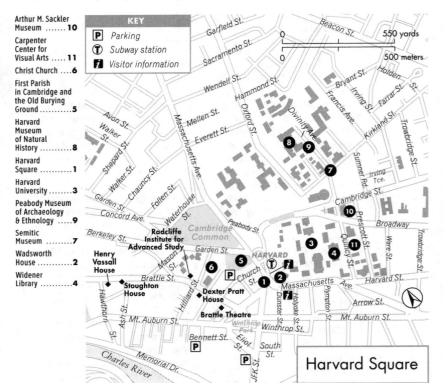

Harvard Square

the organization's Web site for a walking tour available for download to your iPod. The tours are currently free but may in the future charge a fee. The booth is supervised by the Cambridge Tourism office at 4 Brattle Street. ⊠*Harvard Sq., near the MBTA station entrance* ☎*617/497–1630* ⊕*www.cambridge-usa.org* ☉ *Weekdays 9–5, weekends 9–1* Ⓣ*Harvard.*

Numbers correspond to numbers on the Harvard Square map.

TOP ATTRACTIONS

⑩ Arthur M. Sackler Museum. The artistic treasures of the ancient Greeks, Egyptians, and Romans are a major draw here. Make a beeline for the Ancient and Asian art galleries, the permanent installations on the fourth floor, which include Chinese bronzes, Buddhist sculptures, Greek friezes, and Roman marbles. Currently, the Sackler is the only of the University's art museums open to the public. As of June 2008 the Busch-Reisinger and Fogg museums are closed, in the throes of major renovations spanning about five years, At present, visitors to the Sackler will enjoy a sampling of works culled from its art museum siblings. Eventually, the combined collections of all three museums will be represented under one roof under the umbrella name, Harvard Art Museum. Works include Picasso, Klee, Toulouse-Lautrec, and Manet. ⊠*485 Broadway* ☎*617/495–9400* ⊕*www.artmuseums.harvard.edu/*

sackler ✉$9; free Sat. 10–noon and every day after 4:30 ⊙ Mon.–Sat. 10–5, Sun. 1–5 ⊤ Harvard.

NEED A BREAK? The **Broadway Gourmet** (✉ 468 Broadway ☎ 617/547-2334) is just around the corner from the now-defunct Fogg Art Museum. Besides the excellent fresh produce, there's a selection of sandwiches and prepared meals; choose one to be heated up and then grab a seat for a quick bite.

❽ **Harvard Museum of Natural History.** Many museums promise something ☾ for every member of the family; the vast Harvard Museum complex FodorśChoice actually delivers. Swiss naturalist Louis Agassiz, who founded the zool-★ ogy museum, envisioned a museum that would bring under one roof the study of all kinds of life: plants, animals, and humankind. The result is three distinct museums, all accessible for one admission fee.

The **Museum of Comparative Zoology** traces the evolution of animals and humans. You literally can't miss the 42-foot-long skeleton of the underwater *Kronosaurus*. Dinosaur fossils and a zoo of stuffed exotic animals can occupy young minds for hours. The museum is old-fashioned. You can almost feel the brush of the whiskers of the ardent explorers and the naturalists who combed the world for these treasures. It's also the right size for kids—not jazzy and busy, a good place to ask and answer quiet questions.

Oversize garnets and crystals sparkle at the **Mineralogical and Geological Museum,** founded in 1784. The museum also contains an extensive collection of meteorites.

Perhaps the most famous exhibits of the museum complex are the glass flowers in the **Botanical Museum,** created as teaching tools that would never wither and die. This unique collection holds 3,000 models of 847 plant species. Each one is a masterpiece, meticulously created in glass by a father and son in Dresden, Germany, who worked continuously from 1887 to 1936. Even more amazing than the colorful flower petals are the delicate roots of some plants; numerous signs assure the viewer that everything is, indeed, of glass. ✉26 Oxford St. ☎617/495–3045 ⊕www.hmnh.harvard.edu ✉$9, includes admission to Peabody Museum of Archaeology & Ethnology; free for Massachusetts residents Sun. 9–noon year-round and Wed. 3–5 Sept.–May ⊙Daily 9–5 ⊤Harvard.

❶ **Harvard Square.** Tides of students, tourists, political-cause proponents, ☾ and bizarre street creatures are all part of the nonstop pedestrian flow FodorśChoice at this most celebrated of Cambridge crossroads.
★ Harvard Square is where Mass Ave., coming from Boston, turns and widens into a triangle broad enough to accommodate a brick peninsula (above the T station). The restored 1928 kiosk in the center of the square once served as the entrance to the MBTA station (it's now a newsstand). Harvard Yard, with its lecture halls, residential houses, libraries, and museums, is one long border of the square; the other three are comprised of clusters of banks and a wide variety of restaurants and shops.

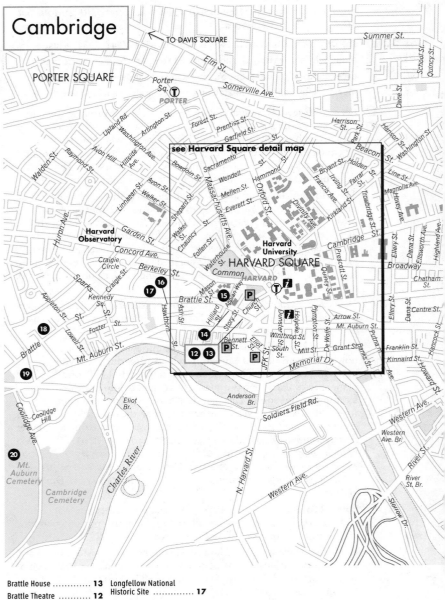

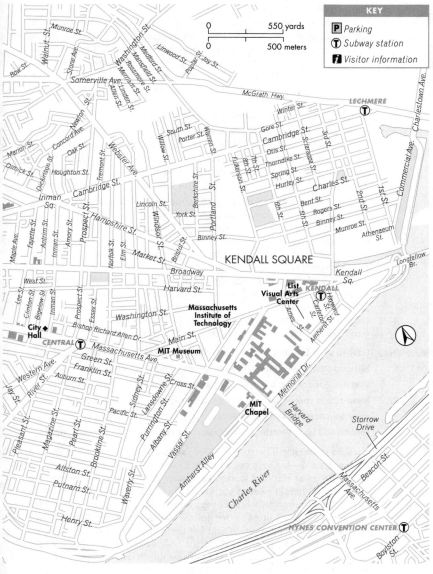

KEY

P Parking

T Subway station

i Visitor information

0   550 yards

0   500 meters

Munroe St.

Walnut St.

Bow St.

Washington St.

Weedford St.

Mansfield St.

Linwood St.

Poplar St.

Joy St.

Somerville Ave.

Stone Ave.

Rossmore St.

Merriam St.

Linden St.

Allen St.

Marion St.

Newton St.

Concord Ave.

Oak St.

South St.

Willow St.

Porter St.

Waverly St.

McGrath Hwy.

LECHMERE

Winter St.

Gore St.

Cambridge St.

Otis St.

Thorndike St.

Scirappa St.

3rd St.

Charlestown Ave.

Commercial Ave.

Dimick St.

Dickinson St.

Houghton St.

Tremont St.

Webster Ave.

Cambridge St.

Inman Sq.

Prospect St.

Hampshire St.

Lincoln St.

York St.

Berkshire St.

Portland St.

Binney St.

7th St.

8th St.

Fulkerson St.

Spring St.

Hurley St.

Charles St.

Bent St.

Rogers St.

Binney St.

6th St.

5th St.

1st St.

2nd St.

Munroe St.

Athenaeum St.

Maple Ave.

Fayette St.

Antrim St.

Amory St.

Inman St.

Windsor St.

Norfolk St.

Elm St.

Market St.

Bristol St.

KENDALL SQUARE

Longfellow Br.

West St.

Lee St.

Clinton St.

Bigelow St.

Prospect St.

Essex St.

Broadway

Harvard St.

Kendall Sq.

T KENDALL

Howard St.

Washington St.

Massachusetts Institute of Technology

List Visual Arts Center

Carletonst.

Ames St.

Amherst St.

Western Ave.

River St.

Auburn St.

Franklin St.

Green St.

CENTRAL **T**

Bishop Richard Allen Dr.

Massachusetts Ave.

Main St.

MIT Museum

Memorial Dr.

City Hall

Jay St.

Pleasant St.

Magazine St.

Pearl St.

Brookline St.

Sidney St.

Pacific St.

Purrington St.

Albany St.

Vassar St.

Lansdowne St.

Cross St.

MIT Chapel

Harvard Bridge

Storrow Drive

Allston St.

Putnam St.

Waverly St.

Amherst Alley

Henry St.

Charles River

Massachusetts Ave.

Beacon St.

HYNES CONVENTION CENTER **T**

Boylston St.

On an average afternoon, you'll hear earnest conversations in dozens of foreign languages; see every kind of youthful uniform from Goth to impeccable prep; wander by street musicians playing Andean flutes, singing opera, and doing excellent Stevie Wonder or Edith Piaf imitations; and lean in on a tense outdoor game of pickup chess between a street-tough kid and an older gent wearing a beard and a beret, while you slurp a cappuccino or an ice-cream cone (the two major food groups here). An afternoon in the square is people-watching raised to a high art; the parade of quirkiness never quits.

As entertaining as the locals are, Harvard Square has fine inanimate attractions, too. The historic buildings are worth noting and, even if you're only a visitor (as opposed to a prospective student genius), it's still a thrill to walk though the big brick-and-wrought-iron gates to Harvard Yard, past the residence halls and statues, on up to Widener Library.

Across Garden Street, through an ornamental arch, is **Cambridge Common,** decreed a public pasture in 1631. It's said that under a large tree that once stood in this meadow George Washington took command of the Continental Army on July 3, 1775. A stone memorial now marks the site of the "Washington Elm." Also on the Common is the Irish Famine Memorial by Derry artist Maurice Herron, unveiled in 1997 to coincide with the 150th anniversary of "Black '47," the deadliest year of the potato famine. It depicts a desperate Irish mother sending her child off to America. At the center of the Common, a large memorial commemorates the Union soldiers and sailors who lost their lives in the Civil War. ⊕ *www.harvardsquare.com* Ⓣ *Harvard.*

NEED A BREAK?

Herrell's Ice Cream (✉ *15 Dunster St., Harvard Sq.* ☎ *617/497–2179*) is a Harvard Square institution. Mix-ins (those yummy bits of candy and cookie that make ice cream a full-fledged decadence) were born here. Add the hand-rolled cones and nine flavors of chocolate, and you've got a don't-miss delicacy. The friendly scoopers are young, punk Cambridge-ites—their tattoos and body piercings make odd counterpoints to the sweet sundaes.

❸ ★ **Harvard University.** The tree-studded, shady, and redbrick expanse of Harvard Yard—the very center of Harvard University—has weathered the footsteps of Harvard students for more than 300 years. In 1636 the Great and General Court of the Massachusetts Bay Colony voted funds to establish the colony's first college and a year later chose Cambridge as the site. Named in 1639 for John Harvard, a young Charlestown clergyman who died in 1638 and left the college his entire library and half his estate, Harvard remained the only college in the New World until 1693, by which time it was firmly established as a respected center of learning. Local wags refer to Harvard as WGU—World's Greatest University—and it's certainly the oldest and most famous American university. It boasts numerous schools or "faculties," including the Faculty of Arts and Sciences, the Medical School, the Law School, the Business School, and the John F. Kennedy School of Government.

Although the college dates from the 17th century, the oldest buildings in Harvard Yard are of the 18th century; together the buildings chronicle American architecture from the colonial era to the present. **Holden**

Chapel, completed in 1744, is a Georgian gem. The graceful **University Hall** was designed in 1815 by Charles Bulfinch. An 1884 statue of John Harvard by Daniel Chester French stands outside; ironically for a school with the motto of "Veritas" ("Truth"), the model for the statue was a member of the class of 1882, as there is no known contemporary likeness of Harvard himself. **Sever Hall,** completed in 1880 and designed by Henry Hobson Richardson, represents the Romanesque revival that was followed by the neoclassical (note the pillared facade of Widener Library) and the neo-Georgian, represented by the sumptuous brick houses along the Charles River, many of which are now undergraduate residences. **Memorial Church,** a graceful steepled edifice of modified Colonial revival design, was dedicated in 1932. Just north of the Yard is **Memorial Hall,** completed in 1878 as a memorial to Harvard men who died in the Union cause; it's High Victorian both inside and out. It also contains the 1,166-seat Sanders Theatre, site of year-round concerts—student and professional—and the venue for the festive Christmas Revels.

Many of Harvard's cultural and scholarly facilities are important sights in themselves, including the **Harvard Museum of Natural History,** the **Peabody Museum of Archaeology & Ethnology,** and the **Widener Library.** Of the three much-loved art museums (the Fogg, the Busch-Reisinger, and the Arthur M. Sackler) only the latter remains. The two former are currently closed for extensive renovations. Collections of all three will eventually open under one roof with the singular umbrella title of Harvard Art Museum. Be aware that most campus buildings, other than museums and concert halls, are off-limits to the general public.

Harvard University Events & Information Center (✉ *Holyoke Center, 1350 Massachusetts Ave.* ☎ *617/495–1573* ⊕ *www.harvard.edu*), run by students, includes a small library, a video-viewing area, computer terminals, and an exhibit space. It also distributes maps of the university area and has free student-led tours of Harvard Yard. The tour doesn't include visits to museums, and it doesn't take you into campus buildings, but it provides a fine orientation. The information center is open year-round (except for during spring recess and other semester breaks), Monday through Saturday 9–5. Tours are offered September–May, Monday–Friday at 10 and 2 and Saturday at 2. From the end of June through August, guides offer four tours: Monday–Saturday at 10, 11:15, 2, and 3:15. Groups of 20 or more can schedule their tours ahead. ✉ *Bounded by Massachusetts Ave., Mt. Auburn St., Holyoke St., and Dunster St.* ☎ *617/495–1573 for Harvard directory assistance* ⊕ *www.harvard. edu* Ⓣ *Harvard.*

DID YOU KNOW? One perk of being a University Professor (holding an endowed chair)— a title awarded to about a dozen preeminent members of the Harvard faculty—is the official right to graze cattle in Harvard Yard. Not surprisingly, few, if any, ever do.

 Peabody Museum of Archaeology & Ethnology. With one of the world's outstanding anthropological collections, the Peabody focuses on Native American and Central and South American cultures; there are also interesting displays on Africa. The Hall of the North American Indian is particularly outstanding, with art, textiles, and models of traditional dwellings from across the continent. The Mesoamerican room juxtaposes ancient relief carvings and weavings with contemporary works from the Maya and other peoples. ⊠*11 Divinity Ave.* ☎*617/496–1027* ⊕*www.peabody.harvard.edu* ✉*$9, includes admission to Harvard Museum of Natural History, accessible through the museum; free for Massachusetts residents only Sun. 9–noon year-round and Wed. 3–5 Sept.–May* ⊙*Daily 9–5* Ⓣ*Harvard.*

WORTH NOTING

⓫ **Carpenter Center for the Visual Arts.** This gravity-defying mass of concrete and glass, built in 1963 to contrast with the now-defunct and more-traditional Fogg Art Museum next door, is the only building in North America designed by the French architect Le Corbusier. The open floor plan provides students with five stories of flexible workspace, and the ramp penetrating the building ensures that the creative process is always visible and public. The center regularly holds free lectures and receptions with artists on Thursday evenings. At the top of the ramp, the **Sert Gallery** plays host to changing exhibits of contemporary works and has a café. The Main Gallery on the ground floor often showcases work by students and faculty. The **Harvard Film Archive** downstairs screens films nightly, often accompanied by discussions with the filmmakers. ⊠*24 Quincy St.* ☎*617/495–3251* ⊕*www.ves.fas.harvard.edu/ccva.html* ✉*Galleries free, film screenings $8* ⊙*Main Gallery Mon.–Sat. 9 AM– 11 PM, Sun. noon–11 PM; Sert Gallery Tues.–Sun. 1–5* Ⓣ*Harvard.*

❻ **Christ Church.** This modest, yet beautiful gray clapboard structure was designed in 1761 by Peter Harrison, the first architect of note in the Colonies. During the Revolution, members of its mostly Tory congregation fled for their lives. The organ was melted down for bullets and the building was used as a barracks during the Siege of Boston. (Step into the vestibule to look for the bullet hole left during the skirmish.) Martha Washington requested that the church reopen for services on New Year's Eve in 1775. The church's historical significance extends to the 20th century: Teddy Roosevelt was a Sunday school teacher here, and Martin Luther King Jr. spoke from the pulpit to announce his opposition to the Vietnam War. ⊠*Zero Garden St.* ☎*617/876–0200* ⊕*www.cccambridge.org* ⊙*Visit building any day 8–4. Sun. services at 7:45 and 10:15, with choral evensong at 4; Tues. and Wed. services at 12:10* Ⓣ*Harvard.*

NEED A BREAK?

Need a news fix? Out of Town News (⊠ *Harvard Sq.* ☎*617/354–7777*) **has got you covered. Browse the world at this fascinating international news seller. Peruse the racks at this fabled landmark for international publications in languages from around the world. Definitely worth a browse.**

❺ ★ **First Parish in Cambridge and the Old Burying Ground.** Next to the imposing church on the corner of Church Street and Mass Ave., a spooky-looking colonial graveyard houses 17th- and 18th-century tombstones of ministers, early Harvard presidents, and Revolutionary War soldiers. The wooden Gothic Revival church, known locally as "First Church" or

"First Parish," was built in 1833 by Isaiah Rogers. The congregation dates to two centuries earlier, and has been linked to Harvard since the founding of the college. The church sponsors the popular lecture series **"Forum"** (☎617/495–2727 ⊕*www.cambridgeforum.org*), featuring well-known authors and academics. ✉*3 Church St.* ☎*617/876–7772* ⊕*www.firstparishcambridge.org* ☉*Church weekdays 8–4, Sun. 8–1, service at 10:30. Burying ground daily dawn–dusk* Ⓣ*Harvard.*

❼ Semitic Museum. An almost unknown gem, this Harvard institution serves as an exhibit space for Egyptian, Mesopotamian, and ancient Near East artifacts and as a center for archaeological exploration. Who knew that the Sphinx may have had curls? The museum's extensive collection rotates among temporary exhibits. The building also houses the Department of Near Eastern Languages and Civilization, with offices tucked among the artifacts. Note that there are no elevators. ✉*6 Divinity Ave.* ☎*617/495–4631* ⊕*www.fas.harvard.edu/~semitic* ✇*Free* ☉*Weekdays 10–4, Sun. 1–4* Ⓣ*Harvard.*

❷ Wadsworth House. On the Harvard University side of Harvard Square stands the Wadsworth House, a yellow clapboard structure built in 1726 as a home for Harvard presidents. It served as the first headquarters for George Washington, who arrived on July 2, 1775, to take command of the Continental Army, which he did the following day. The house, closed to the public, now houses general Harvard offices. ✉*1341 Massachusetts Ave.* Ⓣ*Harvard.*

❹ Widener Library. Harvard University's Harry Elkins Widener Library was named for a young book lover who went down with the *Titanic*. Holding more than 15 million volumes in more than 90 libraries around the world, the Harvard University Library system is second in size in the United States only to the Library of Congress, and Widener Library itself is one of the world's largest individual book repositories. Sixty-five miles of bookshelves snake around six stories above and four stories below ground. Two additional levels are attached by underground tunnel. The imposing neoclassical structure was designed by one of the nation's first major African-American architects, Julian Abele. In the center of the building stands the private collection of Mr. Widener himself (including his Gutenberg Bible and Shakespeare First Folio) in a circular room featuring his original desk. It was his mother's express wish that fresh flowers be placed on the desk each day, a tradition that continues to this day. The library isn't open to the public; people with a "scholarly need" can apply for admission at the privileges office inside. ✉*Harvard Yard* ☎*617/495–2411* ⊕*hcl.harvard.edu/widener* Ⓣ*Harvard.*

BRATTLE STREET/TORY ROW

Brattle Street remains one of New England's most elegant thoroughfares. Elaborate mansions line both sides from where it meets JFK Street to Fresh Pond Parkway. Brattle Street was once dubbed Tory Row because during the 1770s its seven mansions, on lands that stretched to the river, were owned by staunch supporters of King George. These properties were appropriated by the patriots when they took over Cambridge in the summer of 1775. Many of the historic houses are marked with blue signs, and although only two (the Hooper-Lee-Nichols House and the Longfellow National Historic Site) are fully open to the public, it's easy to imagine yourself back in the days of Ralph Waldo Emerson and Henry David Thoreau as you stroll the brick sidewalks. Less than 2 mi down Brattle Street from Harvard Square stretches Mt. Auburn Cemetery, an exquisitely landscaped garden cemetery.

> **WORD OF MOUTH**
>
> "You should definitely try to visit the Longfellow House the next time you get to Cambridge. It is a beautiful place full of original furnishings from the Longfellow family. The park service is so committed to maintaining it that visitors are asked to check bags and purses during the tour so that they don't brush against anything in the house!"   —Vttraveler

TIMING If you opt to walk all the way to Mt. Auburn Cemetery (it's about 1½ mi from Longfellow National Historic Site), allot two to three hours for a leisurely stroll. In good weather, it's a joy, a kind of country paradise within the borders of the city.

Numbers in the box and margin correspond to the Cambridge map.

TOP ATTRACTIONS

17 ★ **Longfellow National Historic Site.** Henry Wadsworth Longfellow, the poet whose stirring tales of the Village Blacksmith, Evangeline, Hiawatha, and Paul Revere's midnight ride thrilled 19th-century America, once lived in this elegant mansion. If there's one historic house to visit in Cambridge, this is it. The house was built in 1759 by John Vassall Jr., and is one of several original Tory Row homes on Brattle Street; George Washington lived here during the Siege of Boston from July 1775 to April 1776. Longfellow first boarded here in 1837, and later received the house as a gift from his father-in-law on his marriage to Frances Appleton, who burned to death here in an accident in 1861. For 45 years Longfellow wrote his famous verses here and filled the house with the exuberant spirit of his own work and that of his literary circle, which included Ralph Waldo Emerson, Nathaniel Hawthorne, and Charles Sumner, an abolitionist senator. Longfellow died in 1882; but the splendor of the house remains—from the Longfellow family furniture to the wallpaper to the books on the shelves (many the poet's own)—all preserved for future generations by the National Park Service that currently runs it. ■TIP➔**Longfellow Park, across the street, is the place to stand to take photos of the house.** The park was created to preserve the view immortalized in the poet's "To the River Charles." ✉*105 Brattle St.* ☎*617/876–4491* ⊕*www.nps.gov/long* ✉*$3* ☉*Check Web site for seasonal tour schedules* ⓣ*Harvard.*

13 **Brattle House.** This 18th-century, gambrel-roof Colonial once belonged to the Loyalist William Brattle. He moved to Boston in 1774 to escape the patriots' anger, then left in 1776 with the British troops. From 1831 to 1833 the house was the residence of Margaret Fuller, feminist author and editor of *The Dial.* Today it's the office of the Cambridge Center for Adult Education and is listed on the National Register of

A GOOD WALK

Begin your walk in Harvard Square at Winthrop Park, a small open space surrounded by bookstores, music shops, clothing outlets, and restaurants, near the juncture of Mt. Auburn and JFK streets. (Note the sign, a favorite of locals, on the American Express Travel Service office: PLEASE GO AWAY OFTEN.) Walk one block along Mt. Auburn as it curves to your right to reach Brattle Street. Proceeding on Brattle Street past a shopping complex, you pass on your left the **Brattle Theatre** ⑫, followed by the **Brattle House** ⑬, an 18th-century Colonial that now serves as headquarters of the Cambridge Center for Adult Education. Another block farther, past the Crate & Barrel store and two historic apothecaries, you pass on the left the yellow **Dexter Pratt House** ⑭, also known as the Blacksmith House, immortalized in Longfellow's "The Village Blacksmith." (Look on the opposite corner from Crate & Barrel for a large granite market indicating the original location of the Blacksmith Shop.) Continue up Brattle just past Hilliard Street. On your left is the Loeb Drama Center, at 64 Brattle Street, where the American Repertory Theatre is based. Across Brattle Street on your right is the **Radcliffe Institute for Advanced Study** ⑮, formerly Radcliffe College.

Continue on Brattle to the next corner with Ash Street to **Henry**

Vassall House ⑯ at the intersection of Hawthorn Street. Across Brattle Street to your right is **Longfellow National Historic Site** ⑰, a mansion built in 1759 by John Vassall Jr. Continuing along Brattle, you reach No. 159, the **Hooper-Lee-Nichols House** ⑱, one of the few Tory homes open to the public. At No. 175 Brattle stands the Ruggles-Fayerweather House, a white Georgian structure built in 1764 that was taken over by revolutionaries in August 1775 and served as a hospital after the Battle of Bunker Hill. At the next corner turn left onto Elmwood Avenue. At the intersection of Fresh Pond Parkway is **Elmwood** ⑲, another Georgian home and now the official residence of Harvard's president.

Continue west and cross Fresh Pond Parkway and Mt. Auburn Street. Continue slightly uphill and west on Mt. Auburn to **Mt. Auburn Cemetery** ⑳. After exploring the cemetery (maps are provided) you can retrace your steps or catch Bus 71 or 73 just outside the cemetery to get back to the square. Or you can follow Mt. Auburn east, cross over to Memorial Drive on your right, and walk back along the Charles River to JFK Street. This is especially pleasant on summer Sundays, when this section of Memorial Drive is closed to car traffic.

Historic Places. ✉*42 Brattle St.* ☎*617/547–6789* ⊕*www.ccae.org* ⊘*Mon.–Thurs. 9–9, Fri. 9–7, Sat. 9–2. Summer hrs vary* Ⓣ*Harvard.*

NEED A BREAK?

Algiers Coffee House (✉*40 Brattle St.* ☎*617/492–1557*), upstairs from the Brattle Theatre, is a favorite evening hangout for young actors and artists. Linger over your mint tea or plate of hummus, and don't expect rapid service.

⑫ Brattle Theatre. Occupying a squat, barnlike building from 1890, the Brattle Theatre is set improbably between a modern shopping center and a Colonial mansion. The resident repertory company gained notoriety in the 1950s when it made a practice of hiring actors blacklisted as Communists by the U.S. government. For the last half century it has served as the square's independent movie house, screening indie, foreign, obscure, and classic films, from nouveau to noir. ⊠ *40 Brattle St.* ☎ *617/876–6837* ⊕ *www.brattlefilm.org* Ⓣ *Harvard.*

⑳ Mt. Auburn Cemetery. A cemetery might not strike you as a first choice for a visit, but this one is a pleasure. Opened in 1831, it was the country's first garden cemetery, and more than 90,000 people have been buried here—among them Henry Wadsworth Longfellow, Mary Baker Eddy, Winslow Homer, Amy Lowell, Isabella Stewart Gardiner, and architect Charles Bullfinch. The grave of engineer Buckminster Fuller bears an engraved geodesic dome. In spring, local nature lovers and bird-watchers come out of the woodwork to see the warbler migrations and the glorious blossoms. Brochures, maps, and audio tours are at the entrance. Picnicking, jogging, and bicycling are not permitted. ⊠ *580 Mt. Auburn St.* ☎ *617/547–7105* ⊕ *www.mountauburn.org* ⊗ *May–Sept., daily 8–7; Oct.–Apr., daily 8–5* Ⓣ *Harvard; then Watertown (71) or Waverly (73) bus to cemetery.*

⑮ Radcliffe Institute for Advanced Study. The famed women's college, situated around a serene yard, was founded in 1879 and wedded to Harvard University in 1977. It was subsumed under Harvard in 1999, when its name officially changed from Radcliffe College. ⊠ *10 Garden St.* ☎ *617/495–8601* ⊕ *www.radcliffe.edu* Ⓣ *Harvard.*

> **NEED A BREAK?**
>
> Once beyond the vicinity of Harvard Square, Brattle Street lacks eateries, so before your walk consider stocking up at **Darwin's Ltd.** (⊠ *148 Mt. Auburn St.* ☎ *617/354–5233*), which carries delectable, Cambridge-inspired sandwiches and other "comestibles and spirituous provisions."

WORTH NOTING

⑭ Dexter Pratt House. Also known as the "Blacksmith House," this yellow Colonial is now owned by the Cambridge Center for Adult Education. The tree itself is long gone, but this spot inspired Longfellow's lines: "Under a spreading chestnut tree, the village smithy stands." The blacksmith's shop, today commemorated by a granite marker, was next door, at the corner of Story Street. ⊠ *56 Brattle St.* Ⓣ *Harvard.*

> **NEED A BREAK?**
>
> The **Hi-Rise Bread Company in the Blacksmith House** (☎ *617/492–3003*), on the first floor of the Dexter Pratt House, is the perfect stop for a pick-me-up coffee and fresh-baked treat or fantastic sandwich on their homemade bread. Snag a table at the outdoor café; it's a choice spot for people-watching. Chocolate lovers may be seduced by the aromas emanating from **L. A. Burdick Chocolates** (⊠ *52 Brattle St.02138* ☎ *617/491–4340* ⊕ *www. burdickchocolate.com*); rich confections or elegant hot cocoa may be just the things to restore flagging spirits.

ALL IN GOOD FUN

Harvard's Hasty Pudding Club is well known for its theatricals—its pun-filled burlesque shows (particularly the annual Man and Woman of the Year spectacles) have elicited groans from audiences for more than a century. The similarly irreverent Harvard Lampoon has been influencing American comedy since the club's inception; early members wrote for the *New Yorker*, while more recently it has proven fertile ground for television comics and writers: the *National Lampoon*, *Saturday Night Live*, and *The Simpsons* were all spawned by its alumni. The *Lampoon Castle* (simultaneously located at 44 Bow Street, 14 Linden Street, 17 Plympton Street, and 57 Mt. Auburn Street), replete with hidden doors and secret passages, was built for the club in 1909 by William Randolph Hearst and Boston socialite Isabella Stewart Gardner. The copper ibis on top is reputedly electrified to ward off pranksters from the daily *Harvard Crimson* newspaper, who at the height of the Cold War cut it down and formally presented it to the Soviet Union as a "gift from the students of America." Connections at the State Department had to be called in to retrieve the purloined bird.

⑲ Elmwood. Shortly after its construction in 1767, this three-story Georgian house was abandoned by its owner, colonial governor Thomas Oliver. Elmwood House was home to the accomplished Lowell family for two centuries. Elmwood is now the Harvard University president's residence ever since student riots in the 1960s drove President Nathan Pusey from his house in Harvard Yard. ✉*33 Elmwood Ave.* Ⓣ*Harvard.*

⑯ Henry Vassall House. One of Brattle Street's seven Tory houses occupied by wealthy families linked by friendship, if not blood, the house may have been built as early as 1636. In 1737 it was purchased by John Vassall Sr.; four years later he sold it to his younger brother, Henry. It was used as a hospital during the Revolution, and the traitor Dr. Benjamin Church was held here as a prisoner. The house was remodeled during the 19th century. It's now a private residence. ✉*94 Brattle St.* Ⓣ*Harvard.*

⑱ Hooper-Lee-Nichols House. Now headquarters of the Cambridge Historical Society, this is one of two Tory-era homes on Brattle Street fully open to the public. (The Emerson family gave it to the society in 1957.) Built between 1685 and 1690, the house has been remodeled at least six times but has maintained much of the original structure. The downstairs is elegantly, although sparsely, appointed with period books, portraits, and wallpaper. An upstairs bedroom has been furnished with period antiques, some belonging to the original residents. Visits are by tour only; tours run about one hour. ✉*159 Brattle St.* ☎*617/547–4252* 🖃*$5* ⊙*Call for tour schedule* Ⓣ*Harvard.*

KENDALL SQUARE/MIT

Harvard Square may be the center of the "People's Republic of Cambridge," but the Kendall Square neighborhood is the city's hard-driving capitalist core. Gritty industrial buildings share space with sleek office blocks and the sprawling Massachusetts Institute of Technology. Although the MIT campus may lack the ivied elegance of Harvard Yard, major modern architects, including Alvar Aalto, Frank Gehry, I. M. Pei, and Eero Saarinen, created signature buildings here. To reach MIT, take the Red Line T to Kendall station; if you're headed for the MIT Museum on the western edge of the campus, the Central Square station is more convenient.

TOP ATTRACTIONS

List Visual Arts Center. Local Boston-area artists and art students consider the List Gallery to be the most interesting gallery in town. Founded by Albert and Vera List, pioneer collectors of modern art, this MIT center has three galleries showcasing exhibitions of cutting-edge art and mixed media. Works from the center's collection of contemporary art, such as Thomas Hart Benton's painting *Fluid Catalytic Crackers* and Harry Bertoia's altarpiece for the MIT Chapel, are on view here and around campus. The center's Web site includes a map indicating the locations of more than 25 of these works. ⊠*20 Ames St.Bldg. E 15* ☎*617/253–4680* ⊕*web.mit.edu/lvac* ⊠*Free* ⊙*Tues., Wed., and Fri.–Sun. noon–6, Thurs. noon–8* Ⓣ*Kendall/MIT.*

Massachusetts Institute of Technology. Celebrated for both its brains and its cerebral sense of humor, this once-tidy engineering school at right angles to the Charles River is growing like a sprawling adolescent, consuming old industrial buildings and city blocks with every passing year. Once dissed as "the factory," particularly by its Ivy League neighbor, MIT mints graduates that are the sharp blades on the edge of the information revolution.

Founded in 1861, MIT moved to Cambridge from Copley Square in the Back Bay in 1916. It has long since fulfilled the predictions of its founder, the geologist William Barton Rogers, that it would surpass "the universities of the land in the accuracy and the extent of its teachings in all branches of positive science." Its emphasis shifted in the 1930s from practical engineering and mechanics to the outer limits of scientific fields.

Architecture is important at MIT. Although the original buildings were obviously designed by and for scientists, many represent pioneering designs of their times. The **Kresge Auditorium,** designed by Eero Saarinen, with a curving roof and unusual thrust, rests on three, instead of four, points. The nondenominational **MIT Chapel,** a circular Saarinen design, is lighted primarily by a roof oculus that focuses natural light on the altar and by reflections from the water in a small surrounding moat; it's topped by an aluminum sculpture by Theodore Roszak. The serpentine **Baker House,** now a dormitory, was designed in 1947 by the Finnish architect Alvar Aalto in such a way as to provide every room with a view of the Charles River. Sculptures by Henry

Moore and other notable artists dot the campus. The latest addition is the newly minted Green Center, punctuated by the splash of color that is Sol Lewitt's 5,500-square-foot mosaic floor mural.

The East Campus, which has grown around the university's original neoclassical buildings of 1916, also has outstanding modern architecture and sculpture, including the stark high-rise **Green Building** by I. M. Pei, housing the Earth Science Center. Just outside is Alexander Calder's giant stabile (a stationary mobile) *The Big Sail.* Another Pei work on the East Campus is the **Wiesner Building,** designed in 1985, which houses the **List Visual Arts Center.** Architect Frank Gehry made his mark on the campus with the cockeyed, improbable **Ray & Maria Stata Center,** a complex of

CAMPUS PRANKSTERS

A popular recurring exhibit at the MIT Museum is the "Hall of Hacks," a look at the pranks MIT students have played over the years. Most notable here is a rare photo of Oliver Reed Smoot Jr., a 1958 MIT Lambda Chi Alpha pledge. Smoot's future fraternity brothers used the diminutive freshman to measure the distance of the nearby Harvard Bridge. Every 5 feet and 6 inches became "one Smoot." The markings on the bridge are repainted by the frat every two years, and Boston police actually use them to indicate location when filing accident reports. All told, the bridge is "364.4 Smoots plus 1 ear" long.

buildings on Vassar Street. The center houses computer, artificial intelligence, and information systems laboratories, and is reputedly as confusing to navigate on the inside as it is to follow on the outside. East Campus's **Great Dome,** which looms over neoclassical Killian Court, has often been the target of student "hacks," and has at various times supported a telephone booth with a ringing phone, a life-size statue of a cow, and a campus police cruiser. Nearby, the domed **Rogers Building** has earned unusual notoriety as the center of a series of hallways and tunnels dubbed "the infinite corridor." Twice each winter, the sun's path lines up perfectly with the corridor's axis, and at dusk students line the third-floor hallway to watch the sun set through the westernmost window. The phenomenon is known as "MIT-henge."

MIT maintains an information center in the Rogers Building and offers free tours of the campus weekdays at 11 and 3. Check holiday schedule as the tours are often suspended during school holidays. General hours for the information center are weekdays 9–5. ✉ *77 Massachusetts Ave.* ☎ *617/253–4795* ⊕ *web.mit.edu* Ⓣ *Kendall/MIT.*

NEED A BREAK?

Toscanini's Ice Cream (✉ *899 Main St.* ☎ *617/491–5877*) is a well-loved local spot, specializing in all sorts of creative flavors. Also a good place for coffee, the shop frequently has small art exhibits. From the MIT Museum it's two blocks up Mass Ave. toward Central Square; look for it on the right.

WORTH NOTING

☪ **MIT Museum.** A place where art and science meet, the MIT Museum displays photos, paintings, and scientific instruments and memorabilia in a dynamic, hands-on setting. The world's largest collection of holograms is downright eye-popping, though young kids may prefer the moving gestural sculptures of Arthur Ganson. The robot room shows off inventions of MIT's renowned robotics lab and an extensive exhibit on artificial intelligence. ⊠ *265 Massachusetts Ave.* ☎ *617/253–5927* ⊕ *web.mit.edu/museum* ✉ *$7.50* ۞ *Daily 10–5* Ⓣ *Kendall/MIT.*

Where to Eat

WORD OF MOUTH

"Forced to choose between these three North End bakeries, I'd likely rank them Modern Pastries, Maria's, and Mike's. But they're all really good. Heck, you're on vacation, so why not toss caution to the winds and sample from all three? That's one of the things vacations are for, after all. It's only a cannoli, and you can walk it off continuing along the Freedom Trail."

—bachslunch

Updated
by Susan
MacCallum-
Whitcomb

When it comes to food, in Boston the Revolution never ended. While Bostonians have proudly clung to their traditional eats (chowders, baked beans, and cream pies can still be found) most diners now choose innovative food without excessive formality. There are still palaces of grand cuisine, but Boston and Cambridge now favor the kind of restaurant overseen by a creative mastermind, often locally born, concocting inspired food served in human surroundings.

Bostonians have caught the passion for artisanal breads, cafés with homemade pastries, and all manner of exquisite and unique specialties. As an example, many high-end restaurants have added uncommon flavors of ice cream—central to Boston living for more than 150 years—to their menus. A young generation of highly trained and well-traveled chefs is reclaiming the regional cuisine. It turns out that the area's wild mushrooms work in a ragout, the cheddar makes a fine quiche, the clambake can be miniaturized, and rabbit fits into a savory ravioli.

A rule of thumb is to seek out what the locals most enjoy—the fish and shellfish abundant from the nearby shores. Although the city has many notable seafood restaurants, almost anyplace you eat will likely have two or three offerings from the sea. Treatments used to be limited to lobsters boiled or baked and fish broiled or fried, but nowadays chefs are more inventive. You may be offered a wood-roasted lobster with vanilla sauce or, in a Chinese restaurant, lobster stir-fried with ginger and scallion. Others are pushing scallops sliced thin and served raw under a dab of olive oil and chickpea puree.

Anything spicy and different has long been popular in the university culture of Cambridge, and the high rate of immigration in recent decades has fueled Bostonians' appetite for foreign cuisines. Variety abounds, evoking the bygone aristocracies of Russia, Persia, Thailand, Ethiopia, or Cambodia, or serving large immigrant communities from Latin America, Asia, Europe, and Africa. In the last few years an influx of Italian restaurants, both traditional and contemporary, have landed on city corners outside the North End.

The dominant trend today, however, is homegrown—both on the plate and in the kitchen. Because most of Boston's talented chefs have worked their way up the ranks in local kitchens, they prefer to sponsor and cultivate their sous-chefs rather than hire anonymous talent. And while a handful of local chefs have garnered celebrity status, the city has yet to draw (some might say invite) big-name, nationally known chefs into its tight-knit circle.

Eating-Out Strategy

To find the best around Boston follow the roads that radiate out from Downtown like the spokes of a giant wheel. Smack inside the hub are the huge, and hugely famous, waterfront seafood restaurants—but go north, west, or south and you're suddenly in the neighborhoods, home to numerous smaller restaurants on the way up. Search "Best Bets" for top recommendations by price, cuisine, and experience. Or find a review quickly in the alphabetical listings for each neighborhood. Delve in and enjoy!

Tipping

Never tip the maître d'. In most restaurants, tip the waiter at least 15%–20%. (To figure the amount quickly, just triple the tax [5%] on the bill and, if you like, add a little more.) Bills for parties of six or more sometimes include service. Tip at least $1 per drink at the bar, and $1 for each coat checked.

Smoking

Smoking is prohibited in all enclosed public spaces in Boston and Cambridge, including restaurants and bars.

What It Costs

Entrée prices fluctuate with the state of the economy. Top-tier restaurants remain impervious to market changes, but more restaurants are accommodating every price range with small or half portions at a lower price. Credit cards are widely accepted, but many restaurants (particularly smaller ones Downtown) accept only cash. Our restaurant reviews indicate which credit cards are accepted (if any) at each establishment, but it's a good idea to double-check.

WHAT IT COSTS AT DINNER				
¢	$	$$	$$$	$$$$
under $8	$8–$14	$15–$24	$25–$32	over $32

Prices are per person for a main course at dinner.

What to Wear

Boston is a notch or two more reserved in its fashion than New York or Los Angeles. Its dining dress code normally hovers at the level of casual chic. Few of the city's most formal restaurants require jackets and even at some of the most expensive places jeans are acceptable as long as they're paired with a dressy top and posh shoes. Shorts are appropriate only in the most casual spots. When in doubt, call and ask.

Mealtimes

Boston's restaurants close relatively early; most shut their doors by 10 or 11 PM, and a few have bars that stay open until 1 AM. Restaurants that serve breakfast often do so until 11 AM or noon, at which point they start serving lunch.

Reservations

Reservations generally need to be made at least a few nights in advance, but this is easily done by your concierge or online at www.opentable.com. Tables can be hard to come by if you want to dine between 7 and 9, or on Friday or Saturday night. But most restaurants will get you in if you show up and are willing to wait.

BEST BETS FOR BOSTON DINING

With hundreds of restaurants to choose from, how will you decide where to eat? Fodor's writers and editors have selected their favorite restaurants by price, cuisine, and experience in the Best Bets lists below. Find specific details about a restaurant in the full reviews, listed alphabetically later in the chapter.

Fodor'sChoice★

All Star Sandwich Bar, p. 135
Antico Forno, p. 128
Chez Henri, p. 136
Clio, p. 122
East Coast Grill and Raw Bar, p. 136
Eastern Standard, p. 122
Oleana, p. 138
Pigalle, 123
Radius, p. 127
Toro, p. 133

By Price

$

Hi-Rise Bread Company, p. 137
Matt Murphy's Pub, p. 143
Rubin's, p. 144

$$

The Butcher Shop, p. 132
Pomodoro, p. 130
Silvertone, p. 127
West Side Lounge, p. 139

$$$

Lineage, p. 143
Neptune Oyster, p. 130
Sage, p. 133
Sel de la Terre, p. 134

$$$$

Aujourd'hui, p. 119
Craigie on Main, p. 136
Grill 23 & Bar, p. 122
Harvest, p. 137

By Cuisine

AMERICAN

The Butcher Shop, p. 132
Franklin Café, p. 132
Green Street, p. 137
The Publick House, p. 143

ASIAN

Elephant Walk, p. 137
Ginza, p. 143
Myers + Chang, p. 133
Wagamama, p. 128

FRENCH

Bouchée, p. 119
Craigie on Main, p. 136
Hamersley's Bistro, p. 132
Ten Tables, p. 147

ITALIAN

Carmen, p. 129
Marco, p. 129
Sorellina, p. 124
Via Matta, p. 125

SEAFOOD

B&G Oysters, p. 131
Daily Catch, p. 129
Legal Sea Foods, p. 138
No Name Restaurant, p. 134

STEAK HOUSE

Abe & Louie's, p. 119
Capital Grille, p. 122
Grill 23 & Bar, p. 122

By Experience

BAR MENU

Davio's, p. 122
Sage, p. 133
Via Matta, p. 125

BREAKFAST

Clio, p. 122
Sensing, p. 130
Zaftigs, p. 144

CHILD-FRIENDLY

Full Moon, p. 137
Legal Sea Foods, p. 138
Mr. Bartley's Burger Cottage, p. 138
(⇨ also Best Bets with Kids box below)

HISTORIC INTEREST

Durgin Park Market Dining Room, p. 128
Locke-Ober, p. 127
Union Oyster House, p. 131

HOT SPOTS

Myers + Chang, p. 133
Silvertone, p. 127
Via Matta, p. 125

SPECIAL OCCASION

Craigie on Main, p. 136
Sorellina, p. 124
Ten Tables, p. 147
Upstairs on the Square, p. 139

BOSTON

BACK BAY/BEACON HILL

This high-end area encompasses Newbury Street, Commonwealth Avenue, and a slew of enticing restaurants. Toward Beacon Hill, restaurants and the dining rooms of the large hotels tend to be quite dressy. Things are trendier and looser at the newer bistros and espresso bars that predominate around Kenmore Square, the Back Bay's western border.

$$$–$$$$
STEAK

✕ **Abe & Louie's.** Go ahead: live the fantasy of the robber baron feasting among cavernous fireplaces and deep-textured, plush mahogany booths. Abe & Louie's may be a tad Disney-esque in its decor, but its menu lives up to the promise with gorgeous, two-tiered raw platters and juicy rib-eye steaks under velvety hollandaise. Even the linen napkins have little buttonholes for the perfect collar hold. ⊠*793 Boylston St., Back Bay* ☎*617/536–6300* ⊟*AE, D, DC, MC, V* Ⓣ*Copley.*

$$$$
FRENCH

✕ **Aujourd'hui.** This culinary landmark is elaborate and formal—one of a few remaining palaces of elegance in town. There are New England touches, but the entire space sports a Continental (and specifically French) vibe. Discreetly located on the second floor of the Four Seasons hotel, Aujourd'hui is a magnet for the city's power brokers and well-heeled travelers who cozy up to the renovated bar and lounge, which serves tasty martinis year-round. The food reflects an inventive approach to regional ingredients and New American cuisine. Some entrées, such as beef strip loin with foie gras or roasted striped bass over crispy veal sweetbreads can be extremely rich, but the menu also offers several solid vegetarian options. Window tables overlook the Public Garden. ⊠*Four Seasons, 200 Boylston St., Back Bay* ☎*617/351–2037* ⊟*AE, D, DC, MC, V* ⊘*Closed Mon. No lunch. Brunch only Sun.* Ⓣ*Arlington.*

¢
ECLECTIC

✕ **Boloco.** This unassuming eatery near the Berklee College of Music started a chain reaction when it opened in 1997. Today Boloco (short for Boston Local Company) has more than a dozen area outposts. All offer "inspired burritos" that extend far beyond the standard Mexican variety. Fillings, for instance, can include Buffalo chicken with blue cheese, braised pork in Thai peanut sauce, or organic tofu topped with hummus and feta. The resulting wraps are easy on both your wallet and the environment. Thanks to ecofriendly initiatives—like using naturally raised meats and biodegradable cups—Boloco is certified by the Green Restaurant Association. ⊠*137 Massachusetts Ave., Back Bay* ☎*617/369–9087* ⊠*71 Mt. Auburn St., Harvard Square* ☎*617/354–5838* ⊕*www.bocolo.com* ⚠*Reservations not accepted* ⊟*AE, D, DC, MC, V* Ⓣ*Hynes/ICA.*

$$–$$$
FRENCH

✕ **Bouchée.** With its sunken patio and two-story dining room, Bouchée is a warm, noisy, and lovable neighborhood bistro. There's a wide variety of brasserie-style French cuisine such as raw bar items, salade Niçoise, cassoulet, and steak frites, plus easy-to-eat flatbread pizzas. Shiny tiles and brass fixtures gleam in the first floor bar while the second floor is more spacious and filled with well-to-do Back Bay residents. ⊠*159 Newbury St., Back Bay* ☎*617/450–4343* ⊟*AE, D, DC, MC, V* Ⓣ*Copley.*

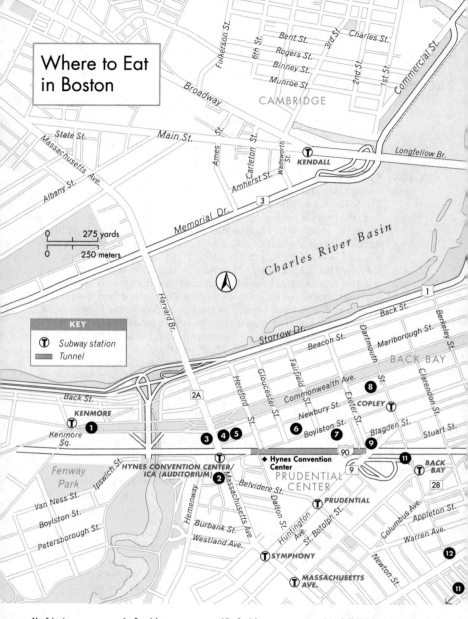

Where to Eat in Boston

CAMBRIDGE

Charles River Basin

BACK BAY

KEY

🅃 Subway station
⬛ Tunnel

KENMORE

Fenway Park

Hynes Convention Center

PRUDENTIAL CENTER

BACK BAY

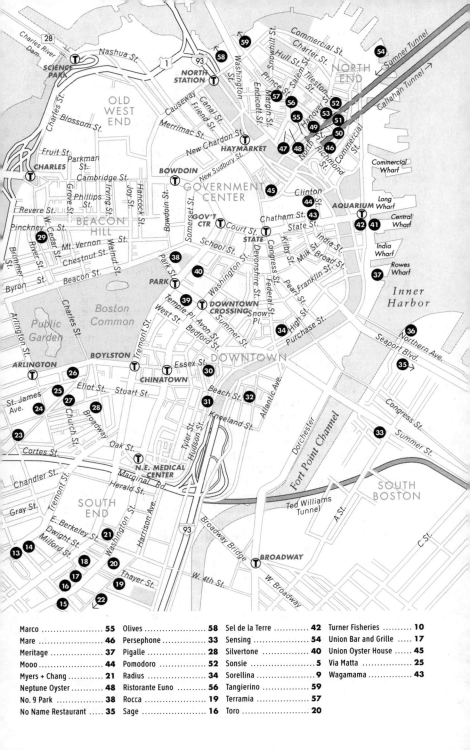

$$$$
STEAK

✕**Capital Grille.** A carnivore's utopia awaits within these clubby, dark-wood walls. Steak-house staples such as lobster and crab cakes and a massive shellfish platter start things nicely, followed by succulent meats such as the 24-ounce dry-aged porterhouse. The crowd-watching is as tasty as the food: VIPs in striped suits make deals over dessert, and wives in Manolo Blahnik heels sip martinis. ⊠*359 Newbury St., Back Bay* ☎*617/262–8900* ▤*AE, D, DC, MC, V* ⊘*No lunch* Ⓣ*Hynes/ICA.*

$$$$
FRENCH
Fodor'sChoice
★

✕**Clio.** Years ago when Ken Oringer opened his snazzy leopard skin–lined hot spot in the tasteful boutique Eliot Hotel, the hordes were fighting over reservations. Things have quieted down since then, but the food hasn't. Luxury ingredients pack the menu, from foie gras and tiny eels called elvers to the Kobe beef Oringer serves at Uni, the small but adventurous sashimi bar set up in a side room off the main dining room. A magnet for romantics and foodies alike, the place continues to serve some of the city's most decadent and well-crafted meals. ⊠*Eliot Hotel, 370 Commonwealth Ave., Back Bay* ☎*617/536–7200* ⚑*Reservations essential* ▤*AE, D, MC, V* ⊘*No lunch* Ⓣ*Hynes/ICA.*

$$$–$$$$
ITALIAN

✕**Davio's.** Eating here is like sitting at the grown-ups' table for the first time. Comfy armchairs and a grand, high-ceilinged dining room give diners a sense of self-importance. Come at lunch, like the rest of the city's power elite, for great pastas (half portions are available) and over-size salads. For dinner, those rushing off to the theater grab a quick bite at the bar—others are in for a lengthy meal, since the kitchen's focus on sophisticated Italian cuisine makes every meal a special occasion. ⊠*75 Arlington St., Back Bay* ☎*617/357–4810* ▤*AE, DC, MC, V* ⊘*No lunch weekends* Ⓣ*Arlington.*

$$
AMERICAN
Fodor'sChoice
★

✕**Eastern Standard Kitchen and Drinks.** A vivid red awning beckons those entering this spacious brasserie-style restaurant. The bar area and red banquettes are filled most nights with Boston's power players (members of the Red Sox management are known to stop in), thirtysomethings, and students from the nearby universities all noshing on raw-bar specialties and comfort dishes such as veal schnitzel, rib eye, and burgers. The cocktail list is one of the best in town, filled with old classics and new concoctions. A covered, heated patio offers alfresco dining much of the year. ⊠*528 Commonwealth Ave., Kenmore Sq.* ☎*617/532–9100* ▤*AE, D, DC, MC, V* Ⓣ*Kenmore.*

$$$–$$$$
STEAK
★

✕**Grill 23 & Bar.** Pinstriped suits, dark paneling, Persian rugs, and waiters in white jackets give this steak house a posh demeanor. The food is anything but predictable, with dishes such as prime steak tartar with a shallot marmalade and weekly cuts of beef like the flat-iron steak or the Berkeley, a 16-ounce rib eye. Seafood specialties such as spice-crusted salmon give beef sales a run for their money. Chef Jay Murray exclusively uses prime, all-natural Brandt beef. Desserts, such as the wonderful warm pear cobbler, are far above those of the average steak house. ⊠*161 Berkeley St., Back Bay* ☎*617/542–2255* ▤*AE, D, DC, MC, V* ⊘*No lunch* Ⓣ*Back Bay/South End.*

$$
MIDDLE EASTERN
★

✕**Lala Rokh.** Persian miniatures and medieval maps cover the walls of this beautifully detailed fantasy of food and art. The focus is on the Azerbaijanian corner of what is now northwest Iran, including exotically flavored specialties and dishes such as familiar (and superb here) eggplant puree, pilaf, kebabs, *fesanjoon* (the classic pomegranate-walnut sauce), and lamb stews. The staff obviously enjoys explaining the menu, and the wine list is well selected for foods that often defy wine matches. ⊠*97 Mt. Vernon St., Beacon Hill* ☎*617/720–5511* ⊟*AE, DC, MC, V* ⊘*No lunch weekends* Ⓣ*Charles/MGH.*

$$–$$$$
SEAFOOD

✕**Legal Sea Foods.** What began as a tiny restaurant upstairs over a Cambridge fish market has grown to important regional status, with more than 20 East Coast locations, plus a handful of national ones. The hallmark is the freshest possible seafood, whether you have it wood grilled, in New England chowder, or doused with an Asia-inspired sauce. The smoked-bluefish pâté is delectable, and the clam chowder is so good it has become a menu staple at presidential inaugurations. This location has private dining inside its beautiful, bottle-lined wine cellar. ⊠*26 Park Sq., Theater District* ☎*617/426–4444* ⊟*AE, D, DC, MC, V* Ⓣ*Arlington.*

$$$$
FRENCH

✕**L'Espalier.** In late 2008 L'Espalier left its longtime home in a Back Bay town house, reopening in the Mandarin Oriental Hotel complex. The new locale, with its floor-to-ceiling windows and modern decor, looks decidedly different. But chef-owner Frank McClelland's dishes—from caviar and roasted foie gras to venison with escargot de Bourgogne—are as elegant as ever. In the evening, three-course prix fixe and seasonal degustation menus tempt discriminating diners. À la carte options are available for weekday power lunches; finger sandwiches and sublime sweets are served for weekend tea. ⊠*774 Boylston St., 2nd fl., Back Bay* ☎*617/262–3023* ⊕*www.lespalier.com* ⚖*Reservations essential* ⊟*AE, D, DC, MC, V* ⊘*Closed Sun. No lunch weekends* Ⓣ*Copley.*

$$$–$$$$
CONTINENTAL

✕**Mooo.** Inside the swanky Fifteen Beacon hotel, Mooo opened in 2007 offering a luxurious, refined dining space that remains civilized despite the restaurant's somewhat goofy name. Chef David Hutton's menu strays toward steak-house fare (hence the title) with dishes driven by local ingredients; look for a well-rounded list of raw-bar items, iceberg lettuce salads, dry-aged sirloins, and a smattering of seafood selections. Portions are as exaggerated as the prices, so it's a worthwhile visit and the wine list, with more than 1,000 entries, including a few century-old bottles, is an impressive but expensive proposition. ⊠*15 Beacon Hotel, 15 Beacon St., Beacon Hill* ☎*617/670–2515* ⊟*AE, D, DC, MC, V* Ⓣ*Park St.*

$$$$
CONTINENTAL
Fodor'sChoice
★

✕**No. 9 Park.** Chef Barbara Lynch's stellar cuisine draws plenty of well-deserved attention from its place in the shadow of the State House's golden dome. Settle into the plush but unpretentious dining room and indulge in pumpkin risotto with rare lamb or the memorably rich prune-stuffed gnocchi drizzled with bits of foie gras. The wine list bobs and weaves into new territory but is always well chosen and the savvy bartenders are of the classic ilk, so you'll find plenty of classics and very few cloying, dessertlike sips here. ⊠*9 Park St., Beacon Hill* ☎*617/742–9991* ⊟*AE, D, DC, MC, V* Ⓣ*Park St.*

$$$$
FRENCH
Fodor'sChoice
★

✕**Pigalle.** A quaint, 20-table spot, Pigalle is a romantic destination to hit before taking in a show in the neighboring Theater District. Chef Marc Orfaly spices up basic French fare (steak frites, cassoulet) by throwing in the occasional Asian-inspired special. He plays around with global

DINING DEALS

In years past, frugal gourmets could often save big by dining out at lunch rather than dinner. But today many fine restaurants, in an effort to pare back, have stopped serving midday meals. The good news is that budget-friendly prix-fixes and "bail out" specials are showing up increasingly on evening menus. Scope out the offerings at individual restaurant Web sites or click ⊕ *www.bostonchefs.com* for the latest promotions.

Ready to eat your heart out? More deals are dished up during Boston's annual Restaurant Weeks. Spread over 12 days in March and again in August, this culinary extravaganza features fab food at recession-proof prices (think two-course lunches for only $15.09 or three-course dinners for $33.09). More than 185 area establishments participate. For details, visit ⊕ *www.bostonusa.com/ restaurantweek.*

flavors so don't be alarmed to find spicy Szechuan pork on the nightly specials. For a delicious, cozy meal, this spot consistently has some of the best service in town. A jazz pianist adds a musical note Friday evenings. ⊠ *75 Charles St. S, Theater District* ☎ *617/423–4944* ⚑ *Reservations essential* ▭ *AE, D, DC, MC, V* ◷ *No lunch* Ⓣ *Boylston.*

$$–$$$
AMERICAN
✕ **Sonsie.** Café society blossoms along Newbury Street, particularly at Sonsie, where a well-heeled crowd sips coffee up front or angles for places at the bar. Lunch and dinner dishes, such as charcoal duck breast and leg with brown rice and five-spice turnips, are basic bistro with an American twist. The restaurant is a terrific place for weekend brunch, when the light pours through the long windows, and is at its most vibrant in warm weather, when the open doors make for colorful people-watching. A downstairs wine room meanwhile offers more intimacy. ⊠ *327 Newbury St., Back Bay* ☎ *617/351–2500* ▭ *AE, D, MC, V* Ⓣ *Hynes/ICA.*

$$$–$$$$
ITALIAN
✕ **Sorellina.** A roar of approval went up when this cavernous Back Bay space opened. It's faded into a loving hum but the noise remains. This is a sexy space filled with well-heeled locals (some live in the gorgeous apartment building above it) who come for the modern twist on basic Italian dishes. Crudo, carpaccio, and arancini dot the list of starters while handmade ravioli with toasted chestnuts and maccheroncelli (fat, tubular noodles) with wagyu meatballs take the spotlight. Just save room for dessert: it's always a highlight here. ⊠ *1 Huntington Ave., Back Bay* ☎ *617/412–4600* ▭ *AE, DC, MC, V* ◷ *No lunch* Ⓣ *Copley, Back Bay.*

$$$–$$$$
SEAFOOD
✕ **Turner Fisheries.** On the first floor of the Westin hotel in Copley Square, Turner Fisheries is second only to Legal Sea Foods in its traditional appeal. Turner broils, grills, bakes, fries, and steams everything in the ocean but also prepares classic and modern sauces, vegetables, and pasta with panache. Any meal should begin with the creamy chowder—the restaurant has won Boston's yearly Chowderfest competition too many times to contend any more. Round it out with one of the city's best-looking lobster rolls. ⊠ *Westin Copley Place Boston,*

10 *Huntington Ave., Back Bay*
☎*617/424–7425* ⚐*Reservations*
essential ▤*AE, D, DC, MC, V*
☺*No lunch* Ⓣ*Copley.*

$$$–$$$$ ✕ **Via Matta.** Abuzz with well-heeled
ITALIAN   locals every night, the city's most
stylish Italian spot is paradoxically
one of its simplest on the culinary
front. The kitchen's emphasis is on
fresh, intensely flavored ingredients in traditional dishes like pappardelle with rabbit, chestnuts, dates, and olives and Sicilian tuna salad mixed with white beans and grilled zucchini. The abutting *enoteca* (café)—all mosaic tile and dim lighting—serves daily pizzas and is the perfect spot for a rendezvous or a nightcap. ⊠*79 Park Plaza, Back Bay* ☎*617/422–0008* ⚐*Reservations essential* ▤*AE, DC, MC, V* Ⓣ*Arlington.*

CHARLESTOWN

This little neighborhood across Boston Harbor contains the Bunker Hill Monument, the USS *Constitution,* and one culinary landmark, the famous Olives, a standout among the local taverns.

$$$ ✕ **Olives.** You may not see chef Todd English tending the wood-fire brick
MEDITERRANEAN   oven here—these days he's splitting his time between his many restau-
★   rants in New York and elsewhere. But don't worry, English's recipes are in good hands. Witness smart offerings such as the signature Olives tart with caramelized onions and goat cheese, or a number of wood-grilled fish and meat dishes. A view into the open kitchen and noisy dining room only add to the excitement. If you can't secure a reservation, come early or late or be prepared for an extended wait. ⊠*10 City Sq., Charlestown* ☎*617/242–1999* ▤*AE, D, DC, MC, V* ☺*No lunch* Ⓣ*Community College.*

$$–$$$ ✕ **Tangierino.** Chef Samad Naamad draws visitors into his enchanting—
MOROCCAN   and recently expanded—Moroccan fantasy with hearty, spice-driven food, fragrant cocktails, nightly belly-dancing shows, and one of the city's few hookah bars. Indulge in small plates like calamari rubbed with *ras al hanout*; then enjoy a drawn-out meal of entrées cooked in a tagine (a clay pot used for slow cooking). ⊠*83 Main St, Charlestown* ☎*617/242–6009* ▤*AE, D, DC, MC, V* Ⓣ*Community College.*

CHINATOWN

Boston's Chinatown is the focal point for Asian cuisines of all types, from authentic Cantonese and Vietnamese to Malaysian, Japanese, and Mandarin. Many places are open after midnight, while the rest of the city sleeps or lurks. It's definitely worth the trek, especially if you're tracking down live-tank seafood prepared in Hong Kong or Chiu Chow style.

$$–$$$ ✕ **Chau Chow City.** Spread across three floors, this is the largest, glitziest,
CHINESE   and most versatile production yet of the Chau Chow dynasty, with dim

On the Menu

Not for nothing did Boston become known as the home of the bean and the cod: simple Yankee specialties—many of them of English origin—and traditional seafood abound.

Boston baked beans are a thick, syrupy mixture of navy beans, salt pork, and molasses cooked for hours. They were originally made by Puritan women on Saturday so that the leftovers could be eaten on Sunday without breaking the Sabbath by cooking.

You may also want to keep an eye out for Parker House rolls, yeast-bread dinner rolls first concocted at the Parker House Hotel in the 1870s.

Boston cream pie is an addictive simple yellow vanilla cake filled with a creamy custard and iced with chocolate frosting. Many traditional New England eateries (and some steak houses and hotel restaurants) serve a house version. Occasionally you'll find a modernized version, with some creative new element added at trendier restaurants.

The city's beer-drinking enthusiasm is older than the Declaration of Independence—which, incidentally, was signed by Samuel Adams, an instigator of the Boston Tea Party and the man whose name graces the bottles of the country's best-selling craft-brew beer.

sum by day and live-tank seafood by night. Overwhelmed? At lunch, head to the third floor for dim sum. Or sit on the main floor and order the clams in black-bean sauce, the sautéed pea-pod stems with garlic, or the honey-glazed shrimp with walnuts. ⊠ *83 Essex St., Chinatown* 🕿 *617/338–8158* ▤ *AE, D, MC, V* Ⓣ *Chinatown.*

$-$$
JAPANESE
★

✕**Ginza.** One of Chinatown's best restaurants turns out a remarkably fresh and creative raw-fish menu. The *kmeeks* maki is a roll of crab-stick tempura, grilled eel, cucumber, avocado, and roe. For something equally fresh but much simpler, opt for the sashimi appetizer—small, gleaming slabs of maguro (bluefin) tuna, salmon, and yellowtail. Cooked foods are also available, but sushi is the real star. Late night, the room feels even more like Tokyo: waitresses in kimonos flit from the sushi bar to tables at top speed, and Japanese-American club kids table-hop and flirt. There's another location in Brookline (⇨ *below*). ⊠ *16 Hudson St., Chinatown* 🕿 *617/338–2261* ▤ *AE, MC, V* Ⓣ *Chinatown.*

DOWNTOWN

Boston's downtown scene revs up at lunchtime, but the streets get quiet after 5 PM, when everyone goes back to the suburbs. The city center is great for after-hours dining, though, especially in the hideaway restaurants around the former Leather District.

$$-$$$
FRENCH
★

✕**Les Zygomates.** *Les zygomates* is the French expression for the muscles on the human face that make you smile—and this combination wine bar–bistro inarguably lives up to its name, with quintessential French bistro fare that is both simple (made with a number of New England sourced ingredients) and simply delicious. The lunch and dinner prix-fixe menus beautifully match the ever-changing wine list, with all wines served by the 2-ounce taste, 6-ounce glass, or bottle. An oyster bar has recently been added and there is live jazz six nights a week. ✉*129 South St., Downtown* ☎*617/542–5108* ⧖*Reservations essential* ▭*AE, D, DC, MC, V* ⊘*Closed Sun. No lunch Sat.* Ⓣ*South Station.*

$$$–$$$$
CONTINENTAL
✕**Locke-Ober.** Chef-owner Lydia Shire gave this old Boston spot a much-needed update when she took the reins in 2001. The ornate woodwork gleams again, and the once-stodgy kitchen is turning out classics with flair—and a slightly lighter touch. Traditionalists needn't worry, though; many favorites remain on the menu, including Shire's signature JFK lobster stew, Indian pudding, which has never been better, and clams casino. There is valet parking after 6 PM. ✉*3 Winter Pl., Downtown* ☎*617/542–1340* ⧖*Reservations essential* ▭*AE, D, MC, V* ⊘*Closed Sun. No lunch* Ⓣ*Downtown Crossing.*

$$
MODERN
AMERICAN
✕**Persephone.** Set inside fashion boutique Achilles Project, this eco-friendly Fort Point restaurant attracts a mix of neighborhood artists and young office workers. Diners first converge in the lounge, which separates the boutique from the restaurant, to play Guitar Hero and munch on bar snacks such as baked-to-order pretzels. The main dining room, once you get there, has exposed-brick walls and aluminum accents, giving it an industrial feel that provides a simple backdrop to match chef Michael Leviton's sustainable, locally sourced food. Listed from small to extra-large on the menu, dishes include a veal shoulder that's big enough to share and tub-trawled Maine halibut that's panfried to produce a crispy skin. For drinks, there's a rotating cocktail list, a sake list, and a small but unique wine list. ✉*283 Summer St., Fort Point Channel, South Boston* ☎*617/695–2257* ⊕*www.achilles-project.com* ▭*AE, D, MC, V* ⊘*Closed Sun. and Mon. No lunch Sat.* Ⓣ*South Station.*

$$$–$$$$
FRENCH
Fodor's Choice
★
✕**Radius.** Acclaimed chef Michael Schlow's notable contemporary French cooking lures scores of designer-and-suit clad diners to the Financial District. The decor and menu are minimalist at first glance, but closer inspection reveals equal shares of luxury, complexity, and whimsy. Peruse the menu in the dining room for such choices as roasted beet salad, a selection of ceviches, buttery Scottish salmon, or huckleberry-and-goat-cheese cheesecake for dessert. At the bar they serve a phenomenal (and award-winning) burger. Either way, it's a meal made for special occasions and business dinners alike. ✉*8 High St., Downtown* ☎*617/426–1234* ⧖*Reservations essential* ▭*AE, DC, MC, V* ⊘*Closed Sun. No lunch Sat.* Ⓣ*South Station.*

$–$$
AMERICAN
✕**Silvertone.** Devotees of this hip basement restaurant swear by the no-fuss options such as a truly addictive macaroni and cheese, meat loaf, and steak tips. Among the more-interesting offerings are the appetizers, such as the spicy Caesar salad, and the fish of the day, which might be trout amandine or locally caught bluefish. The wine list is compact but varied and retains one of the lowest mark-ups in the city. ✉*69 Bromfield St., Downtown* ☎*617/338–7887* ⧖*Reservations not accepted* ▭*AE, D, DC, MC, V* ⊘*Closed Sun. No lunch Sat.* Ⓣ*Park St.*

FANEUIL HALL

A perfect refueling stop before hitting the Freedom Trail, Faneuil Hall is a tourist magnet, packed with fast-food concessions as well as some more-serious alternatives. If you're not on a schedule, and if you've seen enough of Faneuil Hall and want a change of scene, you shouldn't rule out a walk to the North End.

$$
AMERICAN
✕**Durgin Park Market Dining Room.** You should be hungry enough to cope with enormous portions, yet not so hungry you can't tolerate a long wait (or sharing a table with others). Durgin Park was serving its same hearty New England fare (Indian pudding, baked beans, corned beef and cabbage, and a prime rib that hangs over the edge of the plate) back when Faneuil Hall was a working market instead of a tourist attraction. The service is as brusque as it was when fishmongers and boat captains dined here. ✉*340 Faneuil Hall Market Pl., North Market Bldg.* ☎*617/227–2038* ▤*AE, D, DC, MC, V* Ⓣ*Government Center.*

$
JAPANESE
✕**Wagamama.** Students and young families give this popular London-based noodle chain high marks for its cheap bowls of noodles and broth. Customers rotate quickly through the airy, communal-style dining room as spiky-haired servers take orders on handheld electronic devices. The easy-to-read menu includes a glossary of terms and dish names. Vegetarian curry arrives with hearty fried slices of sweet potato, eggplant, and squash while the teriyaki steak soba is a flavorful combo of beef, pan-fried soba noodles, and bok choi. A short selection of domestic wines and Japanese and American beers rounds out the list. ✉*250 Quincy Market Bldg., Faneuil Hall Market Pl.* ☎*617/742–9242* ▤*AE, D, DC, MC, V* Ⓣ*Government Center.*

NORTH END

The North End is Boston's oldest immigrant neighborhood. At the end of the 19th century, Paul Revere's house was a crowded tenement, and at the beginning of this one, black-clad Italian grandmothers continue to push past suburban foodies to get the best of the local groceries. Since the late 1990s, small storefront restaurants have been converting from red-sauce tourist traps to innovative trattorias. And some of Boston's most authentic old-country restaurants are still here (as you might guess, the smaller the place, the better the kitchen), along with charming cafés serving to-die-for espresso and cannoli. Many of the restaurants don't take credit cards or reservations, but because they're so close to each other, it's easy to scout among them for a table.

$–$$
ITALIAN
Fodor's Choice
★
✕**Antico Forno.** Many of the menu choices come from the eponymous wood-burning brick oven, which turns out surprisingly delicate pizzas simply topped with tomato and fresh mozzarella. Don't overlook the hearty baked dishes and handmade pastas; the specialty, gnocchi, is rich and creamy but light. The room is cramped and noisy, but the hubbub is part of the fun. ✉*93 Salem St., North End* ☎*617/723–6733* ▤*MC, V* Ⓣ*Haymarket.*

$$$
ITALIAN
★
✕**Bricco.** A sophisticated but unpretentious enclave of nouveau Italian, Bricco has carved out quite a following. And no wonder: the hand-made pastas alone are argument for a reservation. Simple but well-balanced

main courses such as roast chicken marinated in seven spices and a brimming brodetto (fish stew) with half a lobster and a pile of seafood may linger in your memory. You're likely to want to linger in the warm room, too, gazing through the floor-to-ceiling windows while sipping a glass of Sangiovese from the all-Italian wine list. ⊠*241 Hanover St., North End* ☎*617/248–6800* ⌲*Reservations essential* ▤*AE, D, MC, V* ☾*No lunch* Ⓣ*Haymarket.*

\$\$–\$\$\$
ITALIAN
✕**Carmen.** Here's the kind of undeniably friendly, downright cute hole-in-the-wall that keeps the neighborhood real. With seating for 40, Carmen keeps its capacity crowds happy with glasses of wine and small tapas-style plates of roasted red pepper and olives at the up-front bar. At tables, meanwhile, diners tuck into clean-flavored specials such as creamy homemade pappardelle with lamb ragu. Desserts and coffee, however, aren't on the menu. ⊠*33 North Sq., North End* ☎*617/742–6421* ▤*AE, MC, V* ☾*Closed Mon. No lunch Sun.–Thurs.* Ⓣ*Haymarket.*

\$–\$\$
SEAFOOD
✕**Daily Catch.** You've just got to love this place—for the noise, the intimacy, and, above all, the food. Shoulder-crowdingly small and always brightly lighted, the storefront restaurant specializes in calamari dishes, black-squid-ink pastas, and linguine with clam sauce. There's something about a big skillet of linguine and calamari that would seem less perfect if served on fine white china. ⊠*323 Hanover St., North End* ☎*617/523–8567* ⌲*Reservations not accepted* ▤*No credit cards* Ⓣ*Haymarket.*

\$\$\$–\$\$\$\$
ITALIAN
✕**Mamma Maria.** Don't let the clichéd name fool you: Mamma Maria is far from a typical red-sauce joint, although some locals think it can feel stuffy. From the handmade wild-mushroom ravioli to the authentic sauces and entrées to some of the best desserts in the North End, you can't go wrong here. The view, meanwhile, is lovely; gaze out onto cobblestone-lined North Square as you finish your pappardelle layered with braised rabbit and a finale of *limoncello* (an Italian lemon-flavored liquor). ⊠*3 North Sq., North End* ☎*617/523–0077* ▤*AE, D, DC, MC, V* ☾*No lunch* Ⓣ*Haymarket.*

\$–\$\$\$
ITALIAN
✕**Marco.** The second-story dining room is meant to evoke a charming Italian bistro and succeeds with its warm tones and decorative fireplace. Your best bet here is to go for a family-style selection of antipasti, pastas (handmade tagliatelle with Bolognese is a must), and grilled meats. Plates are meant to be shared and grazed over while enjoying a bottle or two from the all-Italian wine list. This is an unpretentious spot where candlelight and laughter usually fill the room. ⊠*253 Hanover St., 2nd fl., North End* ☎*617/742–1276* ▤*AE, D, MC, V* ☾*Closed Mon.* Ⓣ*Haymarket.*

\$\$–\$\$\$\$
ITALIAN
✕**Mare.** Anchoring a tucked-away corner on Richmond Street, this organic Italian seafood restaurant has stepped out of tradition and moved into nouveau Italian. Ignore the distraction of the color-changing walls, lighted by fluorescent neon, and scope out the menu: the chefs here prefer the simplicity of grilling and poaching seafood and meat dishes rather than dousing them in seasonings, which presents a simple but delicious option among its red-sauce-heavy neighbors. Go for a plate of wild boar pappardelle. And don't miss the mixed grill—a

selection of fresh-caught fish prepared with a touch of seasoning. ⊠*135 Richmond St., North End* ☎*617/723–6273* ⊟*AE, D, MC, V.* ☉*Closed Sun. and Mon. in winter. No lunch* Ⓣ*Haymarket.*

$$–$$$
SEAFOOD
★
✕**Neptune Oyster.** This tiny oyster bar, the first of its kind in the neighborhood, has only 20 chairs, but the long marble bar has extra seating for about 20 more patrons and mirrors hang over the bar with handwritten menus. From there, watch the oyster shuckers as they deftly undo handfuls of bivalves. The *plateau di frutti di mare* is a gleaming tower of oysters and other raw-bar items piled over ice that you can order from the slip of paper they pass out listing each day's crustacean options. And the lobster roll, hot or cold, overflows with meat. Service is prompt even when it gets busy (as it is most of the time). Go early to avoid a long wait. ⊠*63 Salem St., North End* ☎*617/742–3474* ⌦*Reservations not accepted* ⊟*AE, DC, MC, V* Ⓣ*Haymarket.*

$$
ITALIAN
✕**Pomodoro.** This teeny trattoria—just eight tables—is worth the wait, with excellent country Italian favorites such as rigatoni with white beans and arugula, and a sweet veal scaloppini with balsamic glaze, light-but-filling zuppa di pesce. The best choice could well be the clam-and-tomato stew with herbed flat bread, accompanied by a bottle of Vernaccia. Pomodoro doesn't serve dessert, but it's easy to find great espresso and pastries in the cafés on Hanover Street. ⊠*319 Hanover St., North End* ☎*617/367–4348* ⌦*Reservations essential* ⊟*No credit cards* ☉*No lunch weekdays* Ⓣ*Haymarket.*

$$
ITALIAN
✕**Ristorante Euno.** Tiny and friendly, Euno is the North End's culinary mouse that roars. The rustic room used to be a butcher shop, and meat hooks still stud the wall, doubling as coat hangers. Everything from start (a bowl of the buttery olives) to middle (handmade pastas and risottos) to finish (porcini-dusted tuna with roasted vegetables) explains why this postage-stamp gem is a neighborhood favorite. It's usually full on weekends but weeknights, try for a table in the romantic downstairs dining room. ⊠*119 Salem St., North End* ☎*617/573–9406* ⊟*AE, DC, MC, V* ☉*No lunch* Ⓣ*Haymarket.*

$$$–$$$$
CONTEMPO-
RARY FRENCH
✕**Sensing.** Though it is a younger sister to Michelin Chef Guy Martin's Sensing in Paris, the Fairmont Battery Wharf restaurant retains a distinct New England flavor. That's hardly surprising since it prides itself on using locally sourced seasonal ingredients. From artful appetizers (the six-item Sensing Snacking Platter is ideal for indecisive types) through to the generously portioned desserts, the food is elegant without being fussy. Ditto for the decor in the minimalist main dining room. An open kitchen area with counter seating means foodies can watch as entrées like nori-wrapped salmon or rib eye with eggplant fries are being prepared. Re-envisioned breakfast classics (such as eggs Benedict with truffle salsa) also make this an excellent choice for a morning meal. ⊠*Fairmont Battery Wharf, 3 Battery Wharf, North End*

☎*617/994–9000* ⊕*www.sensing restaurant.com* ▤*AE, D, DC, MC, V* Ⓣ*Haymarket.*

$$–$$$ ✕**Terramia.** Nearly everything this
ITALIAN little autumnal-color restaurant
kicks out tastes home-cooked
and authentic. The simple, largely
southern Italian cuisine is full of
game (look for boar, venison, and
quail specials) and rich, fresh pas-

> **TO MARKET, TO MARKET**
>
> A tasteful market tour such as **Michele Torpor's North End Market Tours** (☎*617/523–6032* ⊕*www.micheletopor.com*) can teach you the finer points of local cuisine.

tas tossed with equally fresh ingredients. The risottos come perfectly
cooked and powerfully flavored. Dessert and coffee aren't on the menu,
though. Lines can get long on weekends. ✉*98 Salem St., North End*
☎*617/523–3112* ▤*AE, DC, MC, V* ◷*No lunch* Ⓣ*Haymarket.*

$$–$$$ ✕**Union Oyster House.** Established in 1826, this is Boston's oldest con-
SEAFOOD tinuing restaurant, and almost every tourist considers it a must-see. If
you like, you can have what Daniel Webster had—oysters on the half
shell at the ground-floor raw bar, which is the oldest part of the restaurant and still the best. The rooms at the top of the narrow staircase are
dark and have low ceilings—very Ye Olde New England—and plenty of
nonrestaurant history. The small tables and chairs (as well as the endless
lines and kitschy nostalgia) are as much a part of the charm as the simple and decent (albeit pricey) food. One cautionary note: locals hardly
ever eat here. There is valet parking after 5:30 PM Monday through Saturday. ✉*41 Union St., Government Center* ☎*617/227–2750* ▤*AE,
D, DC, MC, V* Ⓣ*Haymarket.*

SOUTH END

Boston's South End is a highly diverse neighborhood, these days home
to many of the city's gay professionals, hip straight couples, and young
families. Barely a month seems to go by when a hot restaurant doesn't
open—either at the restaurant row at the bend of Tremont Street or up
and down the length of Washington Street.

$$$ ✕**B&G Oysters, Ltd.** Chef Barbara Lynch (of No. 9 Park fame) has made
SEAFOOD yet another fabulous mark on Boston with a style-conscious seafood
Fodor'sChoice restaurant that updates New England's traditional bounty with flair.
★ Designed to imitate the inside of an oyster shell, the iridescent bar glows
with silvery, candlelit tiles and a sophisticated crowd. They're in for
the lobster roll, no doubt—an expensive proposition at $25, but worth
every cent for its decadent chunks of meat in a perfectly textured dress-
ing. If you're sans reservation, be prepared to wait: the line for a seat
can be epic. ✉*550 Tremont St., South End* ☎*617/423–0550* ▤*AE,
D, MC, V* Ⓣ*Back Bay/South End.*

$$–$$$ ✕**banQ.** Casually chic patrons sit at candlelit tables at this former South
ASIAN FUSION End bank. Its wood-strip ceiling looks like the canopy of a stylized Ban-
yan Tree, while a frosted-glass wine cellar "trunk" holds the restaurant's
250-bottle wine list. Aside from the stylish setting, the pièce de résis-
tance is Chef Ranveer Brar's Southeast-Asian-inspired French cuisine.
Appetizers such as the juicy pan-seared scallops with guava sauce and

wasabi-cured cantaloupe are a masterful union of tropical and Continental flavors. Your friendly server will help you decide on an entrée, with options ranging from the buttery, boneless côtes-du-Rhone braised short ribs to sesame swordfish. Brunch is served Sunday. ⊠ *1375 Washington St., South End* ☎ *617/451–0077* ⊕ *www.banqrestaurant.com* ⊟ *AE, D, DC, MC, V* ⊘ *No lunch* Ⓣ *Back Bay/South End.*

$$
AMERICAN
✕ **The Butcher Shop.** Chef Barbara Lynch has remade the classic meat market as a polished wine bar–cum–hangout, and it's just the kind of high-quality, low-pretense spot every neighborhood could use. Stop in for a glass of wine, chat with any of the friendly but cosmopolitan clientele, and grab a casual, quick snack of homemade prosciutto and salami, daily pasta and sandwich specials, or a plate of artisanal cheeses. Reservations are accepted for parties of six or more. ⊠ *552 Tremont St., South End* ☎ *617/423–4800* ⊟ *AE, D, DC, MC, V* Ⓣ *Back Bay/ South End.*

$$
SPANISH
✕ **Estragon.** The urbane 1930s decor makes this South End Spanish restaurant feel high-class, but the tapas plates and easy-to-share *raciones* (entrées) make dining here an entirely casual experience. A selection of traditional tapas, such as blistered padron peppers and sizzling shrimp in garlic and oil, can easily fill up two people when coupled with entrées like paella or the grilled rib eye. Adventurous diners might go for the whole roasted suckling pig head instead. Look for a seat on the couches in the back lounge for a more social dining experience. A semiprivate dining area in the front is candlelighted and more intimate. ⊠ *700 Harrison Ave., South End* ☎ *617/266–0443* ⊕ *www.estragontapas.com* ⊟ *AE, D, DC, MC, V* ⊘ *No lunch* Ⓣ *East Newton.*

¢–$
AMERICAN
✕ **Flour Bakery + Café.** When the neighbors need coffee, or a sandwich, or a muffin, or just a place to sit and chat, they come here. A communal table in the middle acts as a gathering spot around which diners enjoy classic sandwiches and a few specialties, like the grilled chicken with Brie and arugula or the BLT with applewood-smoked bacon. Take-out dinner specials range from pecan-encrusted chicken to home-style meat loaf. ⊠ *1595 Washington St., South End* ☎ *617/267–4300* ⚐ *Reservations not accepted* ⊟ *D, MC, V* Ⓣ *Massachusetts Ave.*

$–$$
AMERICAN
✕ **Franklin Café.** This place has jumped to the head of the class by keeping things simple yet effective. (The litmus: local chefs gather here to wind down after work.) Try anything with the great chive mashed potatoes and don't miss the double-thick buttermilk fried pork loin. The vibe is generally more bar than restaurant, so be forewarned: it can get loud. Waits for tables can be downright impossible on weekend nights, and desserts are not served. ⊠ *278 Shawmut Ave., South End* ☎ *617/350–0010* ⚐ *Reservations not accepted* ⊟ *AE, D, DC, MC, V* Ⓣ *Back Bay/South End.*

$$$–$$$$
FRENCH
✕ **Hamersley's Bistro.** Gordon Hamersley has earned a national reputation, thanks to such signature dishes as a grilled mushroom-and-garlic sandwich, roast chicken, and souffléed lemon custard. He's one of Boston's great chefs and is famous for sporting a Red Sox cap instead of his white chef's hat. His place has a full bar, a café area with 10 tables for walk-ins, and a larger dining room that's a little more formal and decorative than the bar and café, though nowhere near as stuffy as

it looks. Brunch is served Sunday. ✉ *553 Tremont St., South End* ☎ *617/423–2700* ▤ *AE, D, DC, MC, V* ⊘ *No lunch* Ⓣ *Back Bay/South End.*

$–$$ ✕ **Myers + Chang.** Pink and orange
CHINESE dragon decals cover the windows of this all-day Chinese café where Joanne Chang (of Flour fame) has returned to her familial cooking roots. Sharable platters of dumplings, wok-charred udon noodles, and stir fries are packed with fresh ingredients and flavors. The staff is young and hip, and the crowd generally follows suit. ✉ *1145 Washington St., South End* ☎ *617/542–5200* ▤ *AE, MC, V* Ⓣ *Back Bay/South End.*

$$$ ✕ **Rocca.** Long-time local restaurateur Michela Larson and partner Gary
ITALIAN Sullivan designed this colorful, spacious South End spot based on inspirations from Liguria, Italy. The food—simple with a focus on seafood and fresh pasta—carries that same theme with highlights like handmade pesto and whole-roasted fish. The patio, one of only a few in the neighborhood, is shaded with bright yellow umbrellas and gets crowded in the summer. ✉ *500 Harrison Ave, South End* ☎ *617/451–5151* ▤ *AE, MC, V* ⊘ *No lunch* Ⓣ *Back Bay/South End.*

$$–$$$ ✕ **Sage.** Intensely fragrant Italian specialties and a pretty dining room
ITALIAN are the draws here. Local chef Anthony Susi has a steady hand with pastas and gnocchis, and he can also render fine "secondi" courses, such as rabbit Milanese with saffron risotto. Sit at the bar and graze through the menu of small bites like Kobe bruschetta or crispy duck leg. Brunch is served Sunday. ✉ *1395 Washington St., South End* ☎ *617/248–8814* ▤ *AE, MC, V* Ⓣ *Back Bay/South End.*

$$–$$$ ✕ **Toro.** The buzz from chef Ken Oringer's tapas joint still hasn't qui-
SPANISH eted down—for good reason. Small plates of garlic shrimp and crusty
Fodor's Choice bread smothered in tomato paste are hefty enough to make a meal out
★ of many, or share the regular or vegetarian paella with a group. An all-Spanish wine list complements the plates. Crowds have been known to wait it out for more than an hour. ✉ *1704 Washington St., South End* ☎ *617/536–4300* ⚠ *Reservations not accepted* ▤ *AE, MC, V* Ⓣ *Massachusetts Ave.*

$$–$$$ ✕ **Union Bar and Grille.** There's rarely a quiet night at Union, where the bar
AMERICAN buzzes with the neighborhood's coolest residents and couples on dates fill the darkly lighted dining room's leather banquettes. Despite all the show, the menu keeps things relatively down-to-earth with tender-as-can-be burgers, spice-rubbed grilled steak, and thick, crispy fries. Brunch is served weekends. ✉ *1357 Washington St., South End* ☎ *617/423–0555* ▤ *AE, MC, V* ⊘ *No lunch* Ⓣ *Back Bay/South End.*

3

WATERFRONT

Tourists flock to Faneuil Hall and the Marketplace almost year-round, so tried-and-true cuisine tends to dominate there. However, some of Boston's most famous seafood restaurants are on the waterfront.

$–$$
SEAFOOD

╳**Barking Crab Restaurant.** It is, believe it or not, a seaside clam shack plunk in the middle of Boston, with a stunning view of the downtown skyscrapers. An outdoor lobster tent in summer, in winter it retreats indoors to a warmhearted version of a waterfront dive, with chestnuts roasting on a cozy woodstove. Look for the classic New England clambake—chowder, lobster, steamed clams, corn on the cob—or the spicier crab boil. ✉ *88 Sleeper St., Northern Ave. Bridge, Waterfront* ☎*617/426–2722* ▤*AE, DC, MC, V* Ⓣ*South Station.*

GREET THE CHEF

Eating out is considered an event in Beantown, and—true to their natures—Bostonians have strong opinions on the subject, which they like to share with their restaurateurs. Everything from menus to mood lighting is open to debate. So if you've had a particularly satisfying gastronomic experience, ask to meet the chef. Chances are that he or she will gladly visit your table for a victory lap.

$$–$$$
SEAFOOD

╳**Legal Sea Foods.** What better place than the waterfront to build one of the snazziest branches of the local Legal Sea Foods chain? The classic and contemporary seafood preparations mirror those of the other locations, but this one's dining room is full of colorful tiles and sea-inspired sculpture. ✉*255 State St., Waterfront* ☎*617/227–3115* ▤*AE, D, DC, MC, V* Ⓣ*Aquarium.*

$$–$$$
CONTINENTAL

╳**Meritage.** Set inside the stately Boston Harbor Hotel, Meritage stays focused with its astounding wine list. Chef Daniel Bruce creates scintillating menus to match the cellar's treasures (listed, appropriately, like a wine list with headings like "full bodied" and "sparklers"). All menu items are available as small or large plates, and priced at $16 or $32 respectively. With the stunning Rowes Wharf as its backdrop, Meritage has, perhaps, the city's finest waterfront view. ✉*Boston Harbor Hotel at Rowes Wharf, 70 Rowes Wharf, Waterfront* ☎*617/439–3995* ▤*AE, D, DC, MC, V* ☉*Closed Mon. No lunch. Brunch only Sun.* Ⓣ*Aquarium.*

$–$$
SEAFOOD
★

╳**No Name Restaurant.** Famous for not being famous, the No Name has been serving fresh seafood, simply broiled or fried, since 1917. Once you find it, tucked off New Northern Avenue (as opposed to Old Northern Avenue) between the World Trade Center and the Bank of America Pavilion, you can close your eyes and pretend you're in a little fishing village—it's not much of a stretch. ✉*15½ Fish Pier, off New Northern Ave., Waterfront* ☎*617/338–7539* ▤*AE, D, MC, V* Ⓣ*Courthouse.*

$$$
FRENCH
★

╳**Sel de la Terre.** Sitting between the waterfront and what used to be the Central Artery, this is a hot spot to hit before the theater, after sightseeing, or for a simple lunch Downtown. The rustic, country-French menu features items like steak frites with red-wine-shallot reduction. Stop by the *boulangerie* (bread shop) to take home fresh, homemade loaves, which are some of the best in the city. ✉*255 State St., Waterfront* ☎*617/720–1300* ⚑*Reservations essential* ▤*AE, D, DC, MC, V* Ⓣ*Aquarium.*

Refueling

If you're on the go, you might want to try a local chain restaurant where you can stop for a quick bite or get some takeout. The ones listed below are fairly priced, committed to quality, and use decent, fresh ingredients.

Au Bon Pain. The locally based chain whips up quick salads and sandwiches, fresh-daily croissants, and muffins, and has plenty of fruit and juices.

Bertucci's. Thin-crust pizzas fly fast from the brick ovens here, along with pastas and a decent tiramisu.

BoLoCo. For quick, cheap, healthful, and high-quality wraps and burritos, this is easily the city's most dependable (and also locally based) chain.

Finagle A Bagel. Find fresh, doughy bagels in flavors from jalapeño cheddar to triple chocolate, plus sandwiches and salads. Service is swift and efficient.

CAMBRIDGE

Among other collegiate enthusiasms, Cambridge has a long-standing fascination with ethnic restaurants. A certain kind of great restaurant has also evolved here, mixing world-class cooking with a studied informality. Famous chefs, attired in flannel shirts, cook with wood fires and borrow flavors from every continent. For more posh tastes and the annual celebrations that come with college life (or the end of it), Cambridge also has its share of linen-cloth tables.

¢–$
AMERICAN
Fodor'sChoice
★

✕**All Star Sandwich Bar.** This place has a strict definition of what makes a sandwich: no wraps. It has put together a list of classics, like crispy, overstuffed Reubens and beef on weck, which are served quickly from an open kitchen. The only nonsandwich item on the board is a hot dog. Bathed in primary colors, the space has about a dozen tables that fill up at lunchtime. At dinner burgers are also served, along with a small selection of beer and wine. ✉*1245 Cambridge St., Cambridge* ☎*617/868–3065* ⚭*Reservations not accepted* ⊟*MC, V* Ⓣ*Central/Inman.*

$–$$
MEDITERRANEAN

✕**Baraka Café.** Tiny Baraka may be atmospherically challenged, but after a few bites you won't care. Chef-owner Alia Rejeb was born in France and raised in Tunisia—a fact reflected sharply in her menu. Imagine a smoky, creamy dish of peppers awakened with mint, oregano, and cheese (*mechouia*) or a spice-laden deep-chocolate cake, redolent of star anise. Make a meal from the selection of small plates or try an entrée of couscous or marinated vegetables. No alcohol is served. ✉*80½ Pearl St., Cambridge* ☎*617/868–3951* ⚭*Reservations essential* ⊟*No credit cards* ⊘*Closed Mon. No lunch Sun.* Ⓣ*Central.*

$$–$$$
AMERICAN

✕**The Blue Room.** Totally hip, funky, and Cambridge, The Blue Room blends a host of cuisines from Moroccan to Mediterranean with fresh, local ingredients. Brightly colored furnishings, counters where you can meet others while you eat, and a friendly staff add up to a good-time place that's serious about food. Try the braised lamb shank with couscous, or perhaps the grilled Portobello with ricotta gnocchi. An extraordinary buffet brunch with grilled meats and vegetables, as well as regular breakfast fare and a gorgeous array of desserts, is served on Sunday. ⊠*1 Kendall Sq., Cambridge* ☎*617/494–9034* ⊟*AE, D, DC, MC, V* ⊘*No lunch* ⊤*Kendall/MIT.*

$$$
MEDITERRANEAN
★
✕**Casablanca.** Long before *The Rocky Horror Picture Show,* Harvard and Radcliffe types would put on trench coats and head to the Brattle Theatre to see *Casablanca,* rising to recite the Bogart and Bergman lines in unison. Then it was on to this restaurant, where the walls are painted with scenes from the film, for more of the same. The path to this local institution is still well worn, thanks to deep-flavored wild mushroom tart and slow-roasted leg of lamb with charred tomatoes. The bar still attracts a worldly graduate-student crowd with its range of local beers and classic cocktails. ⊠*40 Brattle St., Cambridge* ☎*617/876–0999* ⊟*AE, D, DC, MC, V* ⊤*Harvard.*

$$$
ECLECTIC
Fodor'sChoice
★
✕**Chez Henri.** French with a Cuban twist—odd bedfellows, but it works for this sexy, confident restaurant. The dinner menu gets serious with cassoulet with braised lamb and white beans, tuna au poivre, and sinfully sweet double-decker chocolate cake. At the cozy bar you can sample spiced fries, clam fritters, and the best grilled three-pork Cuban sandwich in Boston. The place fills quickly with Cantabrigian locals—an interesting mix of students, professors, and sundry intelligentsia. ⊠*1 Shepard St., Cambridge* ☎*617/354–8980* ⊟*AE, DC, MC, V* ⊘*No lunch* ⊤*Harvard.*

$$$–$$$$
FRENCH
✕**Craigie on Main.** Late in 2008 Chef Tony Maws shuttered the popular Craigie Street Bistrot, reopening in this new eatery a few blocks away in Central Square. Though the premises are larger (with room for a full bar!), Maws's passion for all things fresh, local, and organic hasn't wavered. He is in the kitchen every morning, prepping ingredients which most likely came from the Harvard Square farmers' market or another local purveyor. The menu changes daily, so options can range from a Spanish-style octopus to tender beef short ribs to pork done three ways. Sunday and Wednesday are Chef's Whim Night, meaning that after 9 PM you'll eat (and likely love) whatever Maws feels like cooking for a discounted price. Brunch is served Sunday. ⊠*833 Main. St., Cambridge* ☎*617/497–5511* ⊕*www.craigieonmain.com* ⊟*AE, MC, V* ⊘*Closed Mon.* ⊤*Central.*

$$–$$$$
MEDITERRANEAN
✕**Dante.** With one of the best patio views of the Charles River, Dante almost resembles a seaside café on the Amalfi coast. Almost. Chef-owner Dante DeMagistris culls flavors from that region, and a few others, to present a seafood- and pasta-heavy menu with entrées that focus on hearty portions of protein like porcini-basted scallops and basil-roasted guinea hen. Try the chef's tasting menu for seven to nine courses that might include a number of specialties not on the daily menu. ⊠*Royal Sonesta Hotel, 40 Edwin H. Land Blvd., Cambridge* ☎*617/497–4200* ⊟*AE, D, MC, V* ⊘*Closed Sun.* ⊤*Lechmere.*

$–$$$
AMERICAN
Fodor'sChoice
★
✕**East Coast Grill and Raw Bar.** Owner-chef-author Chris Schlesinger built his national reputation on grilled foods and red-hot condiments. The Jamaican jerk, North Carolina pulled pork, and habañero-laced "pasta from Hell" are still here, but this restaurant has made an extraordinary play to establish itself in the front ranks of fish restaurants. Spices and

condiments are more restrained, and Schlesinger has compiled a wine list bold and flavorful enough to match the highly spiced food. The dining space is completely informal. A killer brunch (complete with a do-it-your-self Bloody Mary bar) is served on Sunday. ⊠*1271 Cambridge St., Cambridge* ☎*617/491–6568* ▤*AE, D, MC, V* ⊘*No lunch* Ⓣ*Central.*

$–$$
ECLECTIC
★
✕**Elephant Walk.** The chef of this popular Cambodian-French fusion house, Longtaine de Monteiro, learned to manage a Cambodian kitchen as the wife of a diplomat and for a time ran a restaurant in Provence. Her daughter, Nadsa, now runs the kitchen. The common element in both cuisines (which are listed separately on the menu) is garlic, from appetizers such as *moules* (mussels) swimming in butter infused with the stuff to superb Cambodian spring rolls, delicate salads, and a red curry of surpassingly fresh flavor. Vegetarians and diners suffering food allergies are easily accommodated. ⊠*2067 Massachusetts Ave., Cambridge* ☎*617/492–6900* ▤*AE, D, DC, MC, V* Ⓣ*Porter.*

$–$$
AMERICAN
☾
✕**Full Moon.** Here's a happy reminder that dinner with children doesn't have to mean hamburgers. Choices include child pleasers such as home-made mac and cheese as well as grown-up entrées that include grilled sirloin with blue-cheese butter. Youngsters can spread out with plenty of designated play space and juice-filled sippy cups while adults weigh the substantial menu and a well-paired wine list. ⊠*344 Huron Ave., Cambridge* ☎*617/354–6699* ⚠*Reservations not accepted* ▤*MC, V* Ⓣ*Harvard.*

$$–$$$
AMERICAN
★
✕**Green Street.** The tables are small and the service is casual, but the relatively inexpensive New England menu speaks to the young, artistic community that now claims the neighborhood. Locally caught bluefish with a tomato basil vinaigrette is a highlight from the menu, which mostly features modern comfort fare. An emphasis on microbrews and cocktails (the latest owner is a wiz of a bartender) gives this restaurant a relaxed and neighborly bar scene. ⊠*280 Green St., Cambridge* ☎*617/876–1655* ▤*AE, MC, V* ⊘*No lunch* Ⓣ*Central.*

$$$–$$$$
AMERICAN
✕**Harvest.** The New England–inspired menu of up-to-date dishes is hedged with traditional regional favorites made with locally sourced ingredients. Starters at the newly renovated restaurant include mussel soup laced with saffron; Long Island duck breast and George's Bank cod are among the recommended main plates. The open kitchen makes some noise, but customers at the ever-popular bar don't seem to mind. Warm weather brings the opening of a lush outdoor patio. Brunch is served Sunday. ⊠*44 Brattle St., on the walkway, Cambridge* ☎*617/868–2255* ▤*AE, D, DC, MC, V* Ⓣ*Harvard.*

$–$$
AFGHAN
✕**The Helmand.** The area's first Afghan restaurant is named after a province of Afghanistan south of Kabul. Try either their white or brown rice, terrific *aushak* (ravioli stuffed with leeks), the various kebabs you might expect, and an excellent vegetarian menu you might not, with a number of choices grilled and stewed in novel ways. ⊠*143 1st St., Cambridge* ☎*617/492–4646* ⚠*Reservations essential* ▤*AE, MC, V* ⊘*No lunch* Ⓣ*Lechmere.*

$
AMERICAN
☾
✕**Hi-Rise Bread Company.** The best sandwiches start with stellar bread. Here, a range of breads are made on-site and sandwiches are given odd names like Bill's Seoul Show (chicken, bacon, and tarragon mayo

on corn bread). The service matches the noontime rush: brusque and slightly harried. But once you get through the line with your daily soup and a Mahatma Gloves (curried-chicken salad with cashews), you can join the neighborhood regulars at wooden, communal tables and take in a noisy but comforting slice of Cambridge life. ⊠ *208 Concord Ave., Cambridge* ☎ *617/876–8766* ⚹ *Reservations not accepted* ⊟ *MC, V* Ⓣ *Harvard.*

$$$
SEAFOOD

✕ **Legal Sea Foods.** All the regional seafood classics, from famed New England chowder to a sumptuous raw bar, can be found here, in the Cambridge outpost of the Legal chain. Just as worthwhile are the more-modern takes: seafood stew with Indian spices, for example, and grilled swordfish with mango salsa. ⊠ *5 Cambridge Center, Kendall Sq.* ☎ *617/864–3400* ⊟ *AE, D, DC, MC, V* Ⓣ *Kendall/MIT.*

¢–$
VIETNAMESE
★

✕ **Le's.** Vietnamese noodle soup called *pho* is the name of the game in this quick-and-casual eatery (it's set inside a mall in Harvard Square). At less than $10, it's a meal unto itself. Get it filled with chicken, shrimp, or beef, steaming hot in a big bowl. Fresh salads and stir-fries are offered as well. It's all notably fresh fare, and, even better, it's healthy, without gloppy sauces, and many of the dishes are steamed. ⊠ *36 JFK St., Cambridge* ☎ *617/864–4100* ⊟ *AE, MC, V* Ⓣ *Harvard.*

¢–$
AMERICAN

✕ **Mr. Bartley's Burger Cottage.** It may be perfect cuisine for the student metabolism: a huge variety of variously garnished thick burgers, deliciously crispy French fries (regular and sweet potato), and onion rings. There's also a competent veggie burger. The nonalcoholic "raspberry lime rickey," made with fresh limes, raspberry juice, sweetener, and soda water, is the must-try classic drink. Tiny tables in a crowded space make eavesdropping unavoidable. ⊠ *1246 Massachusetts Ave., Cambridge* ☎ *617/354–6559* ⚹ *Reservations not accepted* ⊟ *No credit cards* ⊘ *Closed Sun.* Ⓣ *Harvard.*

$$–$$$
MEDITERRANEAN
Fodor's Choice
★

✕ **Oleana.** Chef-owner Ana Sortun is one of the city's culinary treasures—and so is Oleana. Here, flavors from all over the Middle Eastern Mediterranean sing loud and clear, in the hot, crispy fried mussels starter, and in the smoky eggplant puree beside tamarind-glazed beef. Fish gets jacked up with Turkish spices, then grilled until it just barely caramelizes. In warm weather, the back patio is a hidden piece of utopia—a homey garden that hits the perfect note of casual refinement. ⊠ *134 Hampshire St., Cambridge* ☎ *617/661–0505* ⚹ *Reservations essential* ⊟ *AE, MC, V* ⊘ *No lunch* Ⓣ *Central.*

$$$–$$$$
ITALIAN

✕ **Rialto.** The ultraposh dining room and its bar have drifted back to their Italian beginnings with a few signature New England favorites, such as grilled local clams and Macomber turnips (a local, sweet, white turnip), still among items to order. An updated menu encourages ordering the salads, pastas, and meats as appetizer, midcourse, and entrée with each dish layered with deeper and richer flavors. Or try the no-fail favorites like Tuscan-style sirloin steak with portobello-and-arugula salad, from chef Jody Adams, one of Boston's most admired kitchen wizards. ⊠ *Charles Hotel, 1 Bennett St., Harvard Sq., Cambridge* ☎ *617/661–5050* ⊟ *AE, DC, MC, V* ⊘ *No lunch* Ⓣ *Harvard.*

$-$$ ✕**Tamarind Bay.** This tiny, subterranean space is brick lined and warm—
INDIAN a cozy place to try dishes from all over India. The owners, longtime
residents, decided to open a restaurant that truly represented their
homeland cuisine, hence the *chat* (warm vegetarian or chicken salads)
dishes aren't filled with creamy yogurt, but marinated lightly with fresh
ingredients, and all of the dishes are made to order. Lamb chops *bhunna*
masala are a sweet, spicy trio of chops served on a crescent-shape plate.
A small selection of Indian wines is also available. ✉*75 Winthrop St.,
Cambridge* ☎*617/491–4552* ⊟*AE, MC, V* Ⓣ*Harvard.*

$-$$ ✕**Tanjore.** The menu at this fully regional restaurant reaches from Sindh
INDIAN to Bengal, with some strength in the western provincial foods (Gujarat,
★ Bombay) and their interesting sweet-hot flavors. The *Baigan Bhurta* is a
platter of grilled, mashed eggplant; the rice dishes, chais, and breads are
all excellent and the lunchtime buffet is usually a quick in-and-out affair.
The spicing starts mild, so don't be afraid to order "medium." ✉*18
Eliot St., Cambridge* ☎*617/868–1900* ⊟*AE, D, MC, V* Ⓣ*Harvard.*

$$$-$$$$ ✕**Upstairs on the Square.** In the middle of Harvard Square, this restaurant
CONTINENTAL strikes just the right balance between funky and urbane, with pink lin-
ens and fringes tempering the dining room's old-boy look. The Monday
Club Bar offers a more casual, yet still chic, spot to nosh. Entrées aren't
too straitlaced either; you might try a crispy skate wing with seared
foie gras or a charcoaled lamb sirloin with Japanese eggplant on the
side. Finish with an apple custard tart. ✉*91 Winthrop St., Cambridge*
☎*617/864–1933* ⊟*AE, DC, MC, V* Ⓣ*Harvard.*

$$ ✕**West Side Lounge.** *Understated* is the buzzword at this relaxed but
AMERICAN suave bistro, where the food is as comfortable as the setting. A homey,
★ rotating menu complements the room's earthy tones and cushy ban-
quette seating. The crispy seasoned fries are a justified hit—they all but
fly out of the kitchen—and the black-pepper mussels release an aromatic
cloud of steam when they arrive. Couples on first dates and groups of
regulars gather nightly for the well-priced specials and signature cocktails that change with the seasons. Brunch is served Sunday. ✉*1680
Massachusetts Ave., Cambridge* ☎*617/441–5566* ⊟*AE, D, DC, MC,
V* ☺*No lunch* Ⓣ*Porter or Harvard.*

BROOKLINE

Going to Brookline is a nice way to get out of the city without really
leaving town. Although it's surrounded by Boston on three sides,
Brookline has its own suburban flavor, seasoned with a multitude of
historic—and expensive—houses and garnished with a diverse ethnic
population that supports a string of sushi bars and a small list of kosher
restaurants. Most Brookline eateries are clustered in the town's commercial centers: Brookline Village, Washington Square, Longwood, and
bustling Coolidge Corner.

$-$$ ✕**Elephant Walk.** Technically this outpost of Elephant Walk (the other
ECLECTIC is in Cambridge) is in Boston, but psychologically it's the gateway to
★ Brookline. The French-Cambodian menu is separated by region, so you
get the best of both worlds. Tease your palate with an exotic assortment of dumpling appetizers, spring rolls that you wrap in fresh lettuce

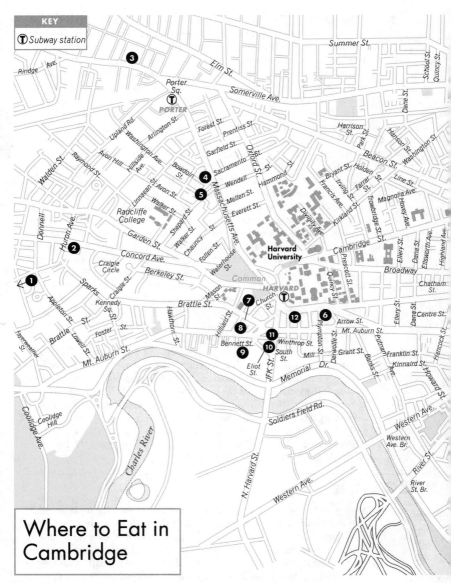

KEY

ⓣ Subway station

Where to Eat in Cambridge

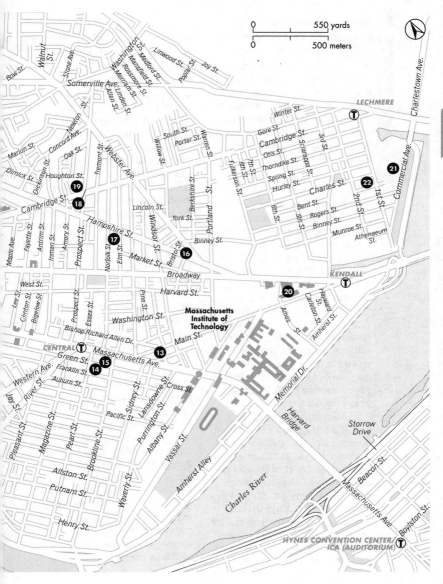

CLOSE UP

Best Bets with Kids

Though it's unusual to see children in Boston's most elite restaurants, eating out with youngsters does not have to mean culinary exile. The vast majority of restaurants are happy to accommodate kids with simplified dishes and an out-of-the-way booth. Here are some particularly family-friendly options.

Charley's Saloon. Saloons may be no place for kids, but this is no real saloon. Charley's doles out American classics (cheeseburgers, steaks, and apple pies) in a fun retro setting. Kids can color and people-watch. ✉ *284 Newbury St., Back Bay* ☎ *617/266–3000.* **Full Moon.** Kids will delight in the play kitchen and dollhouse, and parents can cheer that they get to tuck into lovelies such as grilled salmon with sautéed spinach. Meanwhile there's plenty of macaroni and cheese or quesadillas for the young ones. ✉ *344 Huron Ave., Cambridge* ☎ *617/354–6699.* **Joe's American Bar & Grille.** So what if the restaurant looks as if it has been decorated by a raving mob at a July 4 parade? Next to an oversize burger and a slice of apple pie, the red, white, and blue overload is kind of fun. The clam chowder is almost always a hit with all generations. ✉ *279 Dartmouth St., Back Bay* ☎ *617/536–4200.* **Kingfish Hall.** Parents can dig into the fresh raw bar and junior can sup on clam chowder while watching the grill in the open kitchen. ✉ *188 Faneuil Hall Market Pl., South Market Bldg.* ☎ *617/523–8860.* **Legal Sea Foods.** Smack between Faneuil Hall and the New England Aquarium, Legal is a great break after a long day on your feet. The children's meals, extra rolls, and playful menus don't hurt matters either. ✉ *255 State*

St., Waterfront ☎ *617/227–3115.* **Mr. Bartley's Burger Cottage.** Maybe it's the frappés (thick milk shakes), silly cartoons all over the walls, or just the fun, high-energy vibe. Whatever it is, Bartley's is a hit with kids. ✉ *1246 Massachusetts Ave., Cambridge* ☎ *617/354–6559.* **P. F. Chang's China Bistro.** Straightforward, Americanized, and inexpensive Chinese food makes the rounds in this theatrically decorated spot. Kids love the lemon chicken and the fake Imperial sculptures and screens; parents love the prices and the accommodating staff. ✉ *8 Park Plaza, Back Bay* ☎ *617/573–0821.* **Stephanie's on Newbury.** Here's comfort food at its best—sophisticated enough for parents, simple enough for kids. The place is pretty but homey, and has plenty of booths for spreading out. ✉ *190 Newbury St., Back Bay* ☎ *617/236–0990.* **Summer Shack.** Boston überchef Jasper White has given New England seafood an urban tweak in his laid-back, loud, and fun spot next to the Prudential Center. The colors are bright, and the entire affair is like one big indoor clambake. ✉ *10 Scotia St., Back Bay* ☎ *617/867–9955.* **Zaftigs.** Fill up on huge plates of deli fixings such as matzo-ball soup, first-rate knishes, and heaping plates of grilled chicken, thick-cut onion rings, and three-cheese macaroni. Families cram the place regularly, so servers are used to kids' requests. ✉ *335 Harvard St., Brookline* ☎ *617/975–0075.*

leaves, and mouthwatering coq au vin. The airy atmosphere evokes a British Colonial hotel; the food reminds you of why Phnom Penh was "the Paris of Asia." The desserts, though, are pure Paris. ⊠ *900 Beacon St., Boston* ☎ *617/247–1500* ⊟ *AE, D, DC, MC, V* Ⓣ *St. Mary's.*

$$–$$$
JAPANESE
✕ **Fugakyu.** The name sounds vaguely offensive in English, but in Japanese it means "house of elegance." The interior hits the mark, with tatami mats, rice-paper partitions, and wooden ships circling a moat around the sushi bar. The menu is both elegant and novel, with Boston's first live-tank sashimi, the rare Japanese *matsutake* mushrooms in a vegetarian stir-fry, and appetizers such as marinated scallops served in a martini glass. Bento boxes are available at lunch only. ⊠ *1280 Beacon St., Brookline* ☎ *617/734–1268* ⊟ *AE, D, DC, MC, V* Ⓣ *Coolidge Corner.*

$$
JAPANESE
★
✕ **Ginza.** The two Ginzas (there's one in Chinatown) are both popular with sushi lovers, but this spot gains extra points for its broad selection of sake. Avant-sushi these days includes hot spices, fried morsels, boozy marinades, and presentations with such props as a martini glass. There are lots of good appetizers and hot dinners as well, including teriyaki, tempura, and *nabemono* (one-pot meals). ⊠ *1002 Beacon St., Brookline* ☎ *617/566–9688* ⊟ *AE, MC, V* Ⓣ *Brookline.*

$$–$$$
SEAFOOD
★
✕ **Lineage.** Downtown is saturated with decent seafood options but few hit the mark on inventive fare quite like Lineage. Chef-owner Jeremy Sewall puts the restaurant's central wood-burning stove to good use and roasts everything from halibut to pork chops. His cousin Mark is a lobsterman and provides a fresh catch now and then. A number of seats at the bar, along with ample dining room space, allow diners the option of a casual meal or a comfortable fine-dining experience. ⊠ *242 Harvard St., Brookline* ☎ *617/232–0065* ⊟ *AE, MC, V* ⊘ *Closed Mon. No lunch* Ⓣ *Coolidge Corner.*

$–$$
IRISH
✕ **Matt Murphy's Pub.** Boston has dozens of Irish pubs, but very few are notable for food—this being a welcome exception. Matt Murphy's makes real poetry out of thick slabs of bread and butter served on wooden boards, giant servings of soup, fish-and-chips presented in a twist of newspaper, shepherd's pie, and hot rabbit pie. Don't miss the house-made ketchup with your French fries or the nightly jam sessions with local rock bands who crowd into one tiny corner of the bar after 11 PM. ⊠ *14 Harvard St., Brookline* ☎ *617/232–0188* ⊟ *No credit cards* Ⓣ *Brookline Village.*

$–$$
AMERICAN
✕ **The Publick House.** What started as a simple neighborhood beer bar has reached cultlike status for Brookline-ites and beyond. Serving more than 175 out-of-the-ordinary and artisanal beers, the bar also offers tasty sandwiches, smaller entrées, and main dishes, many of which have beer incorporated into them. A Smuttynose grilled chicken sandwich, for example, is marinated in IPA, and fried shrimp are battered with Japanese bread crumbs and Whale's Tale pale ale, and there are beer recommendations to match. An adjacent taproom—the Monk's Cell—specializes in Belgian brews. Weekend nights find long lines, but one taste of the city's only "cuisine à la bier" is absolutely worth it. ⊠ *1648 Beacon St., Brookline* ☎ *617/277–2880* ⊟ *MC, V* ⊘ *No lunch* Ⓣ *Washington Square.*

$–$$
INDIAN

✕**Rani.** One of Brookline's more-unusual restaurants serves excellent Indian cuisine in the Hyderabadi style, which incorporates northern and southern flavors. Dishes are complex, rich, and layered with sweet and salty. *Murg musalam,* a roasted chicken in a fragrant brown sauce, is tender and juicy, and any of the tandoori dishes (meats cooked in a clay oven) are designed for beginners. The variety of specialty breads is impressive, and the sleek interior fills up nightly with locals looking for a change of pace from Downtown's more-casual Indian buffet. ✉*1353 Beacon St., Brookline* ☎*617/734–0400* ▭*AE, D, MC, V* Ⓣ*Coolidge Corner.*

> **BEST BANG FOR YOUR BUCK**
>
> **Ginza** (Chinatown, Brookline) for sushi
>
> **Matt Murphy's Pub** (Brookline) for hearty, heartwarming Irish food
>
> **Silvertone** (Downtown) for burgers and beer
>
> **Rubin's** (Brookline) for deli sandwiches which are piled with almost a full pound of meat
>
> *See also "By Price" in Best Bets chart at the beginning of this chapter.*

$
DELI

✕**Rubin's.** The last kosher Jewish delicatessen in the Boston area is award-winning and serves a hand-cut pastrami sandwich a New Yorker can respect. There are *kasha varnishkes* (buckwheat with bow-tie noodles), hot brisket, and many other high-cholesterol classics but, of course, no real cream for your coffee or dairy desserts. ✉*500 Harvard St., Brookline* ☎*617/731–8787* ▭*AE, DC, MC, V* ⊘*Closed Sat. No dinner Fri.* Ⓣ*Coolidge Corner.*

$–$$
SPANISH
★

✕**Taberna de Haro.** Although Bostonians have already fallen for tapas, this is the first tapas bar to fully capture authentic Spanish cuisine. At dinner, along with a few entrées, you have a choice of about 40 tapas, including classics such as a tortilla Espanola, jamon Serrano, and garlic shrimp. A well-planned and inexpensive all-Spanish wine list is hand-selected by the owners, and an outdoor patio fills up throughout the summer. Call ahead for a shorter wait. ✉*999 Beacon St., Brookline* ☎*617/277–8272* ⌲*Reservations not accepted* ▭*DC, MC, V* ⊘*Closed Sun. No lunch* Ⓣ*Coolidge Corner.*

$
AMERICAN

✕**Zaftigs.** Here's something different: a contemporary version of a Jewish delicatessen. How refreshing to have genuinely lean corned beef, a modest slice of cheesecake, low-sugar homemade borscht, and a lovely whitefish-salad sandwich. Believe breakfast is the most important meal? It's served all day. Weekend brunch time can bring hour-long waits for a plate of the area's best pancakes, though. ✉*335 Harvard St., Brookline* ☎*617/975–0075* ▭*AE, D, MC, V* Ⓣ*Coolidge Corner.*

ALLSTON

More or less northwest of Downtown, this densely packed little enclave of grunge mixes twentysomething college students with immigrants from four continents. In general, the restaurants are homey and cheap, but the best offer a culinary world tour. A number of places allow low-key BYOB (Blanchard's and Marty's on Harvard Avenue are both great wine stores). For cheap eats and a young vibe, the neighborhood can't be beat.

$-$$
BRAZILIAN

✕**Café Brazil.** Terrific meaty entrées from Brazil's Minas Gerais region fill the menu, including a fine mixed grill and a couple of fish stews from the neighboring province of Bahia. This little place also turns out a great version of the fried yucca appetizer called *mandioca*. The decor is basic travel posters, but the down-home cooking itself could almost transport you to Brazil. Live Brazilian music adds further ambience on weekends. ⊠*421 Cambridge St., Allston* ☎*617/789–5980* ⊟*AE, D, MC, V* ⊤*Harvard.*

¢–$
SOUTHERN

✕**Soul Fire Barbecue.** What this neighborhood needed most took a long time to get here, but there's finally a quick stop for barbecue, complete with a range of sauces and styles. The pit resides in the kitchen but the enticing, smoky aroma fills the whole high-ceiling space. Everything from pulled pork to spare- and baby back ribs to hickory-roasted chicken can be smothered in the sauce of your choice. There is also a bar to sit at that's covered with old soul and blues album covers. ⊠*182 Harvard Ave., Allston* ☎*617/787–3003* ⊟*AE, MC, V* ⊤*Harvard.*

JAMAICA PLAIN

This neighborhood is a kind of mini-Cambridge: multiethnic and filled with cutting-edge artists, graduate students, political idealists, and yuppie families. Recently, the area, known for its affordable and unusual ethnic spots, has seen a swell of a more gentrified—but no less creative—sort.

$-$$
ITALIAN

✕**Bella Luna.** Sci-fi jokes are sprinkled across this spot's spaced-out menu of eccentric pizzas, calzones, and Italian standards. The "Pizza Menino" (named for the city's mayor) is topped with pepperoni, sausage, mushrooms, and peppers, and the "Diedre Delux" mixes dried cranberries, caramelized onions, and Gorgonzola cheese. Work by local artists lines the walls, and local musicians provide the music in its lounge, the Milky Way. (The weekly schedule ranges from jazz to salsa.) ⊠*284 Armory St., Sam Adams Brewery complex, Jamaica Plain* ☎*617/524–6060* ⊟*AE, MC, V* ⊤*Stony Brook.*

$-$$
INDIAN

✕**Bukhara.** The menu here covers the cuisines of several Indian regions so the daily midday buffet essentially lets you eat your way around the country. The condiments alone could keep you satiated, but check out the dosas, curries, and anything from the tandoor oven. The spice quotient varies from mild to incendiary. ⊠*701 Centre St., Jamaica Plain* ☎*617/522–2195* ⊟*AE, D, DC, MC, V* ⊤*Forest Hills.*

$-$$
AMERICAN
★

✕**Centre Street Café.** It's impossible not to love J.P.'s funky and fun hangout, where neighborhood residents pack the limited number of tables and local artwork fills the walls. The eclectic menu veers from ethnic inspirations like spicy cream-sauced shrimp and rice to superfresh salads brimming with local produce. Lines snake around the block every Sunday for the spectacular (and spectacularly filling) brunch. ⊠*669A Centre St., Jamaica Plain* ☎*617/524–9217* ⌕*Reservations not accepted* ⊟*MC, V* ⊤*Green St.*

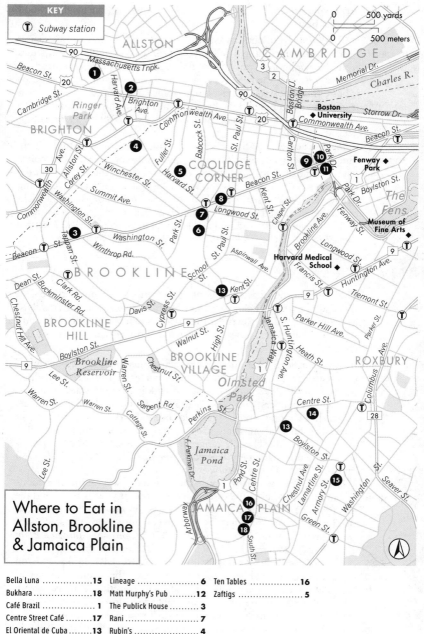

Where to Eat in Allston, Brookline & Jamaica Plain

I Scream, You Scream

Come snow, sleet, or horrendous humidity, Boston's appetite for ice cream remains undiminished. Flavors far exceed basic vanilla with burnt caramel, honey-anise, or cinnamon that could bring tears to your eyes (and not due to an "ice-cream headache").

Christina's (⊠ *1255 Cambridge St., Cambridge* ☎ *617/492–7021*), Inman Square's dessert mecca, serves such creatively flavored scoops as Wild Turkey–walnut and an amazingly addictive chocolate mousse. Dieting meets decadence at **Emack & Bolio's** (⊠ *290 Newbury St., Back Bay* ☎ *617/536–7127*), a pint-size parlor that's half juice bar, half ice-cream counter. You can lap up the delicious handiwork of ice-cream maestro Steve Herrell, pioneer of the "smoosh-in" (candy and nuts mixed into the cold stuff), at **Herrell's** (⊠ *15 Dunster St., Cambridge* ☎ *617/497–2179*). Simple

but sublime cones have addicted many a Bostonian to the fun and funky likes of **J. P. Licks** (⊠ *659 Centre St., Jamaica Plain* ☎ *617/524–6740*). Don't miss J. P. Licks' ice-cream floats—equal parts cream and fizz. If you're looking for serious ice cream, look no farther than **Toscanini's** (⊠ *899 Main St., Cambridge* ☎ *617/491–5877*) . With such exotic flavors as cardamom and burnt caramel, and textures that range from refreshing to truly rich, Toscanini's has few (if any) equals. If it's quantity or a good cause that you're after, nothing beats the **Scooper Bowl** (☎ *800/525–4669* ⊕ *www.scooper bowl.org*), an annual all-you-can-eat extravaganza held in early June at City Hall Plaza. Organizers serve up 10 tons of brand-name ice-cream (including Baskin-Robbins, Ben & Jerry's, and Häagen-Dazs). Proceeds benefit the Dana-Farber Cancer Institute.

$
CARIBBEAN
✕**El Oriental de Cuba.** This small haven, which was refurbished into a bigger, better space after a fire, serves a large variety of excellent Cuban food, including a restorative chicken soup, a classic Cuban sub, superb rice and beans (opt for the red beans over the black), and sweet "tropical shakes." The *tostones* (twice-fried plantains) are beloved during cold New England winters by the city's many Cuban transplants. *Breakfast also served.* ⊠ *416 Centre St., Jamaica Plain* ☎ *617/524–6464* ⊟ *AE, D, MC, V* Ⓣ *Stony Brook.*

$-$$
MEXICAN
★
✕**Tacos El Charro.** Drag naysayers who claim that "Boston has no *real* Mexican restaurants" to this authentic hole-in-the-wall. Order them one of the delectable soft tacos crammed with chicken or pineapple-flavored pork, or tempt them with a rich enchilada or savory goat stew. Wash it all down with a thickly blended *horchata* (a cold, frappélike drink made with rice, milk, and ground almonds). Soon the guilty offenders will be thanking you while eating their words—along with everything else. Odds are they won't even comment on the perfunctory decor. ⊠ *349 Centre St., Jamaica Plain* ☎ *617/983–9275* ⌨ *Reservations not accepted* ⊟ *AE, D, DC, MC, V* ◷ *Closed Tues.* Ⓣ *Jackson Sq.*

$$
FRENCH
★
✕**Ten Tables.** Jamaica Plain's postage-stamp-size, candlelighted boîte is an enchanting mix of Gallic elegance and chummy neighborhood revelry. So, too, the food. Simple but high-quality dishes such as saffron-scented

potato leek velouté and Sicilian style fish stew—followed by a carefully chosen "one perfect cheese" plate—seamlessly seal the deal. A $29 prix-fixe menu available every night but Wednesday makes ordering easy. Just be prepared to wait it out for one of tables, or make a reservation weeks in advance. ✉ *597 Centre St., Jamaica Plain* ☎*617/524–8810* ▭*MC, V* ⊘*No lunch* Ⓣ*Stony Brook.*

WORTH A SPECIAL TRIP

$$–$$$ ✕**Blue Ginger.** Chef Ming Tsai's nimble maneuvers in the kitchen have
ASIAN   caught the nation's eye via a public TV cooking program, *Simply Ming,*
★   and his many cookbooks, including the first, *Blue Ginger: East Meets West Cooking with Ming Tsai (1999)*. Plan ahead (and make sure Tsai is there) to savor his Occident-meets-Asian cuisine. Top choices include his mother's recipe for three-vinegar roasted shrimp and the flavor-packed garlic and black pepper lobster served with the shell as part of the presentation. Thanks to a recent expansion, small plates are also now available in a walk-in lounge. The nearest T stops (Riverside or Woodland on Green Line D) are a 10-minute cab ride away, but Blue Ginger is next to the Wellesley Commuter Rail stop. If you're driving, the 15-mi trip from downtown Boston is an easy jaunt west on the Massachusetts Turnpike to Route 16/Washington Street. ✉ *583 Washington St., Wellesley* ☎*781/283–5790* ▭*AE, MC, V* ⊘*No lunch weekends.*

Where to Stay

WORD OF MOUTH

"For a splurge, we stayed once in a harbor view room at the Boston Harbor Hotel and it was fantastic. Just gorgeous. For slightly less, I like the Fairmont Copley and the Colonnade. Both are convenient locations and nice hotels. For slightly outside the city, I've always liked the Royal Sonesta in Cambridge. It's not as convenient to mass transit as it could be, though they do have shuttle. But the river view rooms are lovely. The Charles Hotel in Harvard square is another really nice, though pricey, option."

—china_cat

Updated by
Diane Bair
and Pamela
Wright

Coming to Boston? Pack a hard hat. In spite of a flat-lining economy, new names like Mandarin Oriental, InterContinental, and Renaissance have joined the old guard and upped the stakes for local hoteliers. To compete you've gotta have flat-screen TVs, MP3 decks, Wi-Fi. Even hotels that haven't changed so much as a pair of drapes for decades ("old" equals "good" in Boston, yes?) suddenly took notice, and started collecting swatches of zebra-print leather.

In short, Boston hotels spent a bazillion dollars on extreme makeovers in the past couple of years, and the dust hasn't quite settled. So you may want to ask, "Is the renovation completed yet?" before you book.

If your fondest Boston memories include tea at the Ritz-Carlton, get over it. Boston's grande dame, built in 1927 and host to Winston Churchill, British royalty, and rooftop soirees for the city's high society, has gone the way of Jordan Marsh and the Bailey's sundae. The Taj chain now owns the hotel (though the Ritz flag still flies over the nearby Ritz-Carlton Boston Common). More proof that times are a-changing: the InterContinental hotel is offering a "mancation" package for two, including manly spa treatments and fly-fishing lessons. Design-wise, minimal is the new glitzy. The gilt ceilings, Colonial-style furnishings and massive chandeliers that have always equalled luxury in this town seem positively quaint compared to the stylish newcomers all done up in fiber optics, art-glass, even Texas limestone. For every gilded old historic hotel, there's a brash newcomer in red leather and black lacquer.

Many luxury hotels have been plumping up their amenities, giving you more perks for the price. They're also offering deals like "Stay three nights, get a fourth night free," in a nod to the rough economy. Even less-expensive establishments are adding pillow-top mattresses, down duvets, high-speed Internet access, and wireless connections. ■ TIP→ **Be sure to check out promotional packages.** Weekend rates at some of the city's best hotels, especially those that cater to a business crowd on weekdays, can be far below standard "rack" rates and often include free perks such as parking, breakfast, or cocktails to entice leisure travelers. More competition translates to more beds to fill, so the deals are out there if you're willing to spend some time sleuthing them out on the Web.

If you're looking for a clean place to sleep and don't need all the fancy-schmancy stuff, consider one of the city's moderately priced chain hotels, or, even better, a bed-and-breakfast or guest house. Cheaper than most hotels, B&Bs are homey bases from which to experience Boston's famous neighborhoods, from the hip and gastronomically diverse South End to the hallowed, gas-lighted streets of Beacon Hill or slightly out-of-town enclaves such as Brookline and Cambridge.

Choosing a Neighborhood

Some of the most luxurious hotels are clustered near the Boston Common and Public Garden in **Beacon Hill**, **Back Bay**, and **Downtown**. These prime locations offer access to the Theater District, Chinatown, the shopping meccas of Newbury and Boylston streets, and the Downtown Crossing shopping district. Stay close to the theaters at the **Boston Park Plaza** or the **Radisson**, or near the water at the **Boston Harbor Hotel, Fairmont Battery Wharf,** or **Marriott Long Wharf**. The **Hyatt Regency** and the **Omni** give you easy access to the shops of Downtown Crossing (although, sadly, Filene's Basement is still closed for renovation) and the seasonal perks of the Common. The **Kenmore Square** area has a distinct student vibe. Adjacent to Fenway Park is Lansdowne Street, a strip of college bars and nightclubs for young adults. The Fenway offers beautiful parks and community gardens. A short trolley ride east will bring you to the heart of Boston, and a short ride west will bring you to the suburbs of Brookline, Brighton, and Newton. Consider the **Hotel Commonwealth** in this area. Cozy B&Bs are your best bet in the **South End**, well known as a gay-friendly area strewn with boutiques, excellent restaurants, and cafés. Inns such as the stylish **Clarendon Square** and the bargain **82 Chandler Street B&B** blend perfectly with the neighborhood's brownstone- and tree-lined streets. For an active vacation, stay at a riverside property in **Cambridge**. Several larger hotels here give you easy access to Memorial Drive and the Charles. Closed to traffic on Sunday in summer Memorial Drive becomes an excellent venue for biking, running, and in-line skating. Hot spots in Harvard and Central squares are minutes away.

The suburb of **Brookline** is largely residential with lovely homes and parks, but there are still several bustling areas such as Coolidge Corner and Washington Square that give you plenty of shopping, dining, and recreation options. Most of the lodging selections in this area are B&Bs. The subway offers quick access to downtown Boston.

WHAT IT COSTS FOR HOTELS				
¢	$	$$	$$$	$$$$
under $75	$75–$149	$150–$224	$225–$325	over $325

Prices are for two people in a standard double room in high season, excluding 12.45% tax and service charges.

Booking Tips

Commencement weekends in May and June book months in advance; prices can be triple the off-season rate, with minimum stays of two to four nights. Leaf-peepers arrive in early October, and fall conventions bring waves of business travelers, especially in the Seaport District. Events such as the Boston Marathon in April and the Head of the Charles in October are busy times for large hotels and small inns alike.

How to Save

Scirubg a great rate at the property of your choice is much easier than it used to be. A luxury hotel in Back Bay for less than $200 per night, once the stuff of urban myth, can be had with a bit of luck, patience, and Web savvy. (▪ TIP➔ **Steer clear of any listing in a neighborhood called "Boston/X." You'll end up in "X.")**

Book a new hotel right after it opens. There might be a glitch or two, but you'll luck into low introductory rates—they hope you'll love 'em and come back. In winter, large Back Bay hotels lure travelers with competitive packages and rates, especially on weekends. Keep in mind that children often stay free (or at a discounted rate) in their parents' room. The cutoff age ranges from 12 to 18.

4

BEST BETS FOR BOSTON LODGING

Fodor's offers a selective listing of quality lodging experiences in every price range, from the city's best budget beds to its most sophisticated luxury hotels. Here, we've compiled our top recommendations by price and experience. The very best properties—in other words, those that provide a particularly remarkable experience in their price range—are designated in the listings with the Fodor's Choice logo.

Fodor'sChoice★

Back Bay Hotel, p. 153
Boston Harbor Hotel, p. 165
Charles Hotel, p. 181
Charlesmark Hotel, p. 154
Fairmont Copley Plaza, p. 156
Gryphon House, p. 174
InterContinental, p. 168
Lenox Hotel, p. 158
Nine Zero, p. 171
Royal Sonesta Hotel, p. 186

By Price

$

463 Beacon Street Guest House, p. 153
John Jeffries House, p. 164

$$

Clarendon Square Inn, p. 177

Courtyard by Marriott Boston Copley Square, p. 155
Encore, p. 177
Inn @ St. Botolph, p. 158

$$$

Colonnade Hotel, p. 154
Gryphon House, p. 174

$$$$

Hotel Commonwealth, p. 175
Liberty Hotel, p. 164
Mandarin Oriental Boston, p. 159

By Experience

BEST GYM

Four Seasons, p. 157
InterContinental, p. 168
Ritz-Carlton Boston Common, p. 173
Seaport Hotel, p. 173

BEST HOTEL BAR

Back Bay Hotel, p. 153
Copley Square Hotel, p. 155
Hotel Commonwealth, p. 175
Liberty Hotel, p. 164

BEST FOR KIDS

Fairmont Copley Plaza, p. 156
Marriott Long Wharf, p. 170
Royal Sonesta, p. 186
(⇨ also Bring the Kids box below)

BEST LOCATION

Courtyard by Marriott Boston Copley Square, p. 155
Four Seasons, p. 157
Lenox Hotel, p. 158
Taj Boston Hotel, p. 160
Westin Copley Place, p. 161

BEST POOL

Colonnade Hotel, p. 154
InterContinental, p. 168
Marriott Long Wharf, p. 170
Seaport Hotel, p. 173

BEST FOR ROMANCE

Boston Harbor Hotel, p. 165
Fairmont Copley Plaza, p. 156
InterContinental, p. 168

BEST SERVICE

Back Bay Hotel, p. 153
Boston Harbor Hotel, p. 165
Boston Park Plaza Hotel, p. 153
Charles Hotel, p. 181

BEST VIEWS

Four Seasons, p. 157
Liberty Hotel, p. 164
Marriott Custom House, p. 170
Taj Boston Hotel, p. 160
Westin Boston Waterfront, p. 174

HIPSTER HOTELS

Charlesmark Hotel, p. 154
Copley Square Hotel, p. 155
Eliot Hotel, p. 156
Hotel Marlowe, p. 184
Mandarin Oriental Boston, p. 159

BOSTON

BACK BAY

$–$$ **463 Beacon Street Guest House.** There's not even a sign on the door of this handsome brownstone—that's how much it blends in with its residential neighbors. International visitors and college students have discovered this rooming house, warming to its slightly quirky, visiting-an-old-auntie charm. Check out the old black-and-white photos of Boston in the hallways as you head to your guest room (each is slightly different, as befits an old house). The antiques-filled sitting room functions as a guest room in summertime, and it's the best room in the house. Digs are tidy but basic, with hardwood floors; those on the fifth floor are loft-style. Some rooms are small and share a bath. No meals are served, but some of the rooms have kitchenettes. **Pros:** the restaurants along Newbury Street (three blocks away) and Boylston Street are within walking distance. **Cons:** some rooms have a two-person occupancy limit, and because of the layout, the house isn't appropriate for children. ✉*463 Beacon St., Back Bay* ☎*617/536–1302* ⊕*www.463beacon.com* ⇱*20 rooms, 17 with bath* ⌂*In-room: No a/c (some), kitchen, Wi-Fi. In-hotel: Public Wi-Fi, no elevator, laundry facilities, parking (fee), no kids under 7* ▤*D, MC, V* Ⓣ*Kenmore.*

$$$–$$$$ **The Back Bay Hotel.** "Great staff." "Great bar." "Great vibe." See a
Fodor'sChoice   pattern yet? Travelers rave about this hotel, formerly Jurys Boston, one
★   of the few in the city where you can nip into the bar for a beverage and actually chat with a friendly local or two. There's something about this place that thaws even the frostiest Bostonian—and it's not just the Irish coffee talking. Part of a Dublin-based hotel chain, the Back Bay Hotel may remind you more of Iceland than Ireland, design-wise. There's a fire-and-ice thing going on, from the bed of icy glass shards in the igloolike gas fireplace on the lower level to the puffs of steam coming from the staircase waterfall. Eye-catching blown-glass chandeliers add to the cool appeal. The hotel gets the small touches right, such as free bottled water in the fridge, toasty down comforters, and heated towel racks. Readers praise the pub grub at on-site Cuff's Bar, but the noisy bar scene isn't for everyone. **Pros:** lively, friendly bar, great amenities, friendly staff. **Cons:** no pool, very small gym. ✉*350 Stuart St., Back Bay* ☎*617/266–7200* ⊕*www.doylecollection.com* ⇱*222 rooms, 3 suites* ⌂*In-room: Refrigerator, DVD (some), Wi-Fi. In-hotel: Restaurant, room service, bar, laundry service, concierge, public Wi-Fi, parking (fee)* ▤*AE, D, DC, MC, V* Ⓣ*Back Bay/South End.*

$$–$$$$ **Boston Park Plaza Hotel & Towers.** Adore antiques? Check out this historic grand hotel, created in 1927 by renowned hotelier E. M. Statler. One traveler's "return to a more elegant time" is another's "faded glory," and so it is with the Park Plaza. This Boston classic is the antithesis of the ultracool, ultramodern hotels cropping up in the city. The lobby, with its original plaster moldings and massive chandelier, is quite grand. Tiny though they are, guest rooms are comfy, with beds topped by puffy down comforters and lush linens. The less said about the miniscule bathrooms, however, the better. On the 15th floor, the concierge level, rooms are slightly larger and have access to a private lounge. Todd English's Bonfire is a Latin American–style steak house, and Whiskey Park is a staple in the chic bar scene; don't miss Finale, the go-to place for decadent desserts. Elaborate afternoon tea is offered in the lobby café, and room service is available around the clock. Overall, consider this one if "character" ranks high on your list—or if you can nab a room for a great rate. **Pros:** pretty lobby, great restaurants on the Park Plaza block, helpful concierge. **Cons:** rooms are cramped, bathrooms are small, some complain about noisy guests and "paper-thin" walls. ⊠*64 Arlington St., Back Bay* ☎*617/426–2000 or 800/225–2008* ⊕*www. bostonparkplaza.com* ⮰*941 rooms, 39 suites* ⌂*In-room: Refrigerator (some), Ethernet, Wi-Fi. In-hotel: 9 restaurants, room service, bars, gym, laundry service, concierge, executive floor, public Wi-Fi, parking (fee), some pets allowed* ⊟*AE, D, DC, MC, V* Ⓣ*Arlington.*

$–$$$

Fodor's Choice
★

🛏**Charlesmark Hotel.** Hipsters and romantics who'd rather spend their cash on a great meal than a hotel bill have put this skinny little boutique hotel on the map. You can typically grab a room for around $139 ($119 in winter), an amazing value considering the Copley Square location: the shops and restaurants of Boylston and Newbury streets are at the doorstep. An outdoor patio is a great place to watch the passing parade (or the Boston Marathon—this hotel is right on the finish line). Smallish guest rooms have contemporary custom-made oak furnishings (yacht-like, with lots of nooks and crannies to stash belongings) plus surround-sound stereo and wireless throughout. Free continental breakfast and Wi-Fi are examples of how the hotel provides cost-saving incidentals. You can order Thai food in the cocktail lounge, but if that doesn't suit you, walk to one of 40-some restaurants in the 'hood. The Charlesmark doubles as a gallery, with the work of local artists lining the winding brick corridors. **Pros:** great price point for what you get; great location near T, shopping, and dining; free Wi-Fi and water bottles. **Cons:** hot-air heating system is noisy, not much storage space, rooms at the front of the house can be noisy due to lounge and traffic. ⊠*655 Boylston St., Back Bay* ☎*617/247–1212* ⊕*www.thecharlesmarkhotel.com* ⮰*40 rooms* ⌂*In-room: DVD, VCR, Wi-Fi. In-hotel: Bar, laundry service, public Wi-Fi* ⊟*AE, D, DC, MC, V* ⦿❙*CP* Ⓣ*Copley.*

$$$–$$$$
★

🛏**Colonnade Hotel.** The recent makeover at this dependent luxury hotel was a hit. The hotel has gone from so-*over* '80s brass-and-mahogany to a clean, modern look with tones of espresso, khaki, chocolate, and chrome. All this would be mere window dressing if it weren't for new, guest-friendly touches like flat-panel TVs, DVD players, and alarm clock/MP3 players, plus extendable reading lights and fab high-tech coffeemakers. The look is slightly masculine but quite comfy, with pillow-top mattresses, high-thread-count sheets, and a round worktable (replacing the typical desk) so guests can eat or work comfortably. Floor-to-ceiling windows (these actually open) are triple glazed to keep out the traffic noise of Huntington Avenue. In summer the roof deck pool is a huge draw. Open to hotel guests only, the pool area has great views of the neighborhood and live music. Some transportation around the area is available using the hotel's Smart cars—a nice green touch. For your gustatory needs, Brasserie Jo is an authentic French brasserie.

■TIP➜ **Sign up for their "I Prefer" program and Internet use is free. Pros:** roof deck pool, across the street from Prudential Center for shopping and restaurants, good Red Sox packages. **Cons:** pool is seasonal only. ✉*120 Huntington Ave., Back Bay* ☎*617/424–7000 or 800/962–3030* ⊕*www.colonnadehotel.com* ✎*276 rooms, 9 suites* ♿*In-room: Safe, Wi-Fi. In-hotel: Restaurant, room service, bar, pool, gym, laundry service, concierge, public Wi-Fi, parking (fee), some pets allowed* ▭*AE, D, DC, MC, V* Ⓣ*Prudential Center.*

$$$ ▦**Copley Square Hotel.** Thanks to a $17 million renovation, the Copley Square Hotel has hurtled into the present with high-tech registration pods, fully stocked workstations, cushy mattresses, and the like. Pretty good for a hotel that can also claim to have been the first in the Back Bay, opening in 1891 and having provided classic Boston-style respite for over a century to a caliber of celebrity that includes Babe Ruth, Ella Fitzgerald, and Billie Holiday. The rooms are so pleasingly contemporary you might overlook the fact that they're teeny. But the old-meets-new vibe is fun, and the neighborhood couldn't be livelier; the hotel itself is home to minibar, Boston's social spot of the moment. If minibar's banquette seating is filled or reserved, order some Kobe sliders and chill until Saint (the downstairs nightclub) starts throbbing. To maximize your z's, get a room in the back of the house, high up, where traffic noise—and the rowdy partying—isn't so audible. **Pros:** free Wi-Fi throughout, free wine tasting nightly, cool bars on-site, above-par bar food at minibar. **Cons:** small rooms, rooms facing Huntington Avenue can be very noisy. ✉*47 Huntington Ave., Back Bay* ☎*617/536–9000* ⊕*www.copleysquarehotel.com* ✎*143 rooms* ♿*In-room: Safe, Wi-Fi. In-hotel: 2 restaurants, room service, bars, gym, laundry service, public Internet, public Wi-Fi, parking (fee), some pets allowed* ▭*AE, D, DC, MC, V* ❏❘ *EP* Ⓣ*Copley.*

$$–$$$ ▦**Courtyard by Marriott Boston Copley Square.** Some consider this site to be the best Courtyard by Marriott they've ever seen, praising its modern, upscale, and large-for-Boston rooms. They don't mind that the lobby isn't grand, there's no doorman, and room service consists of a handful of menus to nearby eateries. The privations end, however, once you see your room, decked out in colorful, contemporary furnishings, and glammed up with cherry cabinets, granite countertops, and 37-inch flat-screen TVs. Small niceties include cookies and fruit in the lobby (4 PM) and make-up mirrors in the bathrooms. You can't beat the location: walk to Prudential Center and Copley Place shops and Back Bay restaurants, galleries, and boutiques, plus there's a big grocery store right around the corner. Packages are worth checking out, and include a Sam Adams pub-crawl deal. **Pros:** good-size modern rooms (nicer than the "big" Marriott, some say), great location, free Internet. **Cons:** restaurant is fairly lame (reader tip: get the cheapest room available and eat elsewhere), no room service. ✉*88 Exeter St., Back Bay* ☎*617/437–9300 or 800/321–2211* ⊕*www.courtyardboston.com* ✎*77 rooms, 4 suites* ♿*In-room: Refrigerator (some), Ethernet. In-hotel: Restaurant, gym, laundry service, public Wi-Fi* ▭*AE, D, DC, MC, V* Ⓣ*Copley.*

$$$–$$$$
★

Eliot Hotel. Step off the posh boulevard of Commonwealth Avenue into this luxurious den, where zebra-print rugs meet crystal chandeliers and well-heeled Sox fans rub elbows with visiting parents of local college students. Befitting a high-end boutique hotel, rooms are done up in sumptuous silks, with poufy mattresses and Italian marble bathrooms. The majority of the rooms are one- or two-bedroom suites; all have marble-topped bar areas (with sink) and flat-panel TVs. ■TIP→**Rooms ending in 02 have views of Commonwealth Avenue; those ending in 04 and 08 are larger corner rooms.** The award-winning Clio restaurant, helmed by star-chef Ken Oringer, garners raves for its contemporary French-American cuisine. Or you can dine at the Uni Sashimi Bar, a less-expensive option. The Eliot is close to Newbury Street and a short walk from Kenmore Square. Fenway Park is two blocks away, making this property a hit with sports fans. Parents of college kids happily hole up here during parent's weekends and graduations. A sweet perk for fitness buffs: free passes to the nearby Boston Sports Club. This property has popped up on several "best" lists, but there are a couple of caveats. Readers warn that rooms near elevators are noisy and complain of lapses in service. **Pros:** good location, great restaurants, pet-friendly. **Cons:** very small bathrooms, elevator noise, lapses in service by young staff. ⊠ *370 Commonwealth Ave., Back Bay* ☎ *617/267–1607 or 800/443–5468* ⊕ *www.eliothotel.com* ⇆ *16 rooms, 79 suites* ⌂ *In-room: Refrigerator, Wi-Fi. In-hotel: 2 restaurants, room service, bar, laundry service, concierge, public Wi-Fi, parking (fee), some pets allowed* ⊟ *AE, DC, MC, V* Ⓣ *Hynes.*

$$$$
Fodor's Choice
★

Fairmont Copley Plaza. Back in the day, Judy Garland slept here, and made rowdy guest appearances at the piano bar, according to a waiter at the Fairmont's Oak Room. For those who, like Judy, believe that too much of a good thing is just about right, the deliciously decadent, unabashedly romantic Fairmont lures. Richly decorated, and very ornate—we're talking clouds on the ceiling here—this 1912 landmark favors romance and tradition over sleek and modern. Really love pampering? Stay on the Fairmont Gold floor (worth the extra cost, readers say), an ultradeluxe club level offering a dedicated staff, free breakfast and tea-time snacks (mini-crab cakes and other delectables), and library. Shopping fanatics adore the close proximity to Newbury Street, the Prudential Center, and Copley Place. The Oak Room restaurant matches its mahogany-panel twin in New York's Plaza Hotel; the equally stately—and tryst-worthy—Oak Bar has live music and one of the longest martini menus in town. If you're missing your dog, take Catie Copley, the in-house Labrador retriever, for a walk around the 'hood, a "green" touch we like. If you drive a hybrid, you can park it for free. **Pros:** very elegant, great Copley Square location, cozy bar. **Cons:** tiny bathrooms with scratchy towels, charge for Internet access (no charge on Fairmont Gold level), small fitness center is busy at peak times. ⊠ *138 St. James Ave., Back Bay* 🕾*617/267–5300 or 800/441–1414* 🖷*617/375–9648* ⊕*www.fairmont.com/copleyplaza* 📲*366 rooms, 17 suites* ⚒*In-room: Safe, refrigerator, Ethernet, Wi-Fi (fee). In-hotel: Restaurant, room service, bar, gym, laundry service, concierge, executive floor, public Wi-Fi, parking (fee), some pets allowed* ▤*AE, D, DC, MC, V* ⊤*Copley, Back Bay/South End.*

$$$$
★ 🔲 **Four Seasons.** Jeans-clad millionaires and assorted business types cluster in the glossy lobby of the Four Seasons, while TV anchor folk dis the competition over 'tinis and Bristol Burgers in the Bristol Lounge. (Visiting celebs are whisked to the 3,000-square-foot, $6,900-per-night Presidential Suite—no waiting in the lobby for them!) In spite of competition from trendy newcomers like the Mandarin Oriental, the Four Seasons remains the gold standard of Boston's ultra-posh hotels. Designers resisted the trend of soothing taupe for bright shots of citron and apricot in public spaces; guest rooms sport black-and-cream toile with gold and lemon accents, large bay windows, and oversize work areas. Luxury amenities include DVD players, 42-inch plasma TVs, and L'Occitane toiletries. (Even celebrities steal the soaps, we're told.) If you spring for the basic city-view room, you can enjoy fab views of the Public Garden from the pool and whirlpool on the eighth floor, or from Aujourd'hui, the hotel's top-rated contemporary French restaurant, or the Bristol Lounge. ▀TIP➜ **Check the Web for fantastic winter-weekend deals.** **Pros:** great location, overlooking the Public Garden and a short walk to Newbury Street shops and the Theater District, Mercedes courtesy car makes drop-offs (within a 2-mi radius) around town. **Cons:** front entrance can get busy (valet parking service can be slow); restaurants are pricey. ⊠*200 Boylston St., Back Bay* 🕾*617/338–4400 or 800/819–5053* ⊕*www.fourseasons.com/boston* 📲*197 rooms, 76 suites* ⚒*In-room: Safe, refrigerator, Ethernet, Wi-Fi. In-hotel: 2 restaurants, room service, bar, pool, gym, laundry service, concierge, public Wi-Fi, parking (fee), some pets allowed* ▤*AE, D, DC, MC, V* ⊤*Arlington.*

$$$
🔲 **Hilton Boston Back Bay.** It's perfect, if you like the anonymity of a large hotel and a location that's convenient to everything. And you can't beat the oversize rooms, the big, comfy beds, and the availability of a pool and hot tub. (You'll really love all this if you snagged a super-cheap deal on line.) This 26-story hotel occupies a corner pocket between the Prudential Center (shopping, restaurants) and the Christian Science Church complex. Readers describe the guest rooms as "pleasant," and "fine," if a bit "old school"; wall-to-wall windows overlook the Back Bay and Fenway Park. (Views vary from room to room. You might have a great view of Boston's iconic neon Citgo sign! Bostonians would consider this a *good* thing, as the Citgo sign is a beloved—if odd—landmark.) Generally, rooms above the ninth floor have the best views. Bathrooms have oversize showers. Try one of the older rooms, which have windows that open (some even have balconies). **Pros:** large rooms and bathrooms, good roof-level fitness center, free Wi-Fi in

the lobby. **Cons:** fee for Internet in guest rooms, expensive breakfast buffet ("go elsewhere," readers advise). ⊠ *40 Dalton St., Back Bay* ☎*617/236–1100 or 800/874–0663* ⊕*www.hilton.com* ✆*385 rooms, 5 suites* ☖ *In-room: Refrigerator, Ethernet. In-hotel: Restaurant, room service, bar, pool, gym, laundry service, concierge, public Wi-Fi, parking (fee)* ⊟*AE, D, DC, MC, V* ⦿*CP* ⊤*Hynes.*

$$ 🖼 **Inn@St. Botolph.** Nip into the 7/11 for a snack, then cross the street to your lovely brownstone. Enter your key code to get in, and presto! You're home. The Inn@St. Botolph feels more like a friend's sleek city apartment than a hotel, complete with a kitchen, fireplace, and big flat-screen TV. There's no check-in desk, no restaurant, no valet (you have to park at a public garage and walk "home"), and you may not see another soul during your stay, making this place a minimalist's delight. Like its sister property, XV Beacon, the 16-room inn delivers plenty of style. It's done up in chic shades of chocolate and cinnamon by local designer Celeste Cooper; luxurious touches include leather chairs, Frette towels and robes, and a rainfall shower. Set on a quiet residential street lined with brownstones, the inn is a short walk to Prudential Center and bustling Back Bay. It's a great value for the 'hood—just be sure to factor in parking ($26–$38 or so per night at a nearby garage) or the whammy of a hefty parking ticket if you don't. This may not be the best place to be if you're a newbie to Boston and need some hand-holding, but great for independent types and longer stays (there's a 24-hour supermarket nearby to facilitate fridge-stocking). **Pros:** affordable style, great location, posh yet homey, good espresso machine in lounge. **Cons:** skimpy breakfast (skip it), DIY parking, no front desk (but there's a manager on call from 7 AM to 10 PM). ⊠ *99 St. Botolph St., Back Bay* ☎*617/236–8099* ⊕*innatstbotolph.com* ✆*16 rooms* ☖ *In-room: Safe, kitchen, refrigerator, DVD, Internet, Wi-Fi. In-hotel: Gym, laundry facilities, public Internet, public Wi-Fi* ⊟*AE, D, DC, MC, V* ⦿ *CP.*

$$$–$$$$ 🖼 **Lenox Hotel.** Family-owned and graced with period (circa 1901)

Fodor's Choice details, this boutique-ish Back Bay property is a pleasing alternative

★ to the nearby big-box hotels. It's also a dandy option if you need more services—like room service, a business center, and a fitness room— than the more-basic Charlesmark Hotel (across the street) can deliver. The Copley Square location means you're steps away from a slew of restaurants and shops, and a T stop is right across the street. No car needed—a good thing, since overnight parking costs a bundle. (Skip the hotel's garage and use a city parking facility to save some cash.) Readers appreciate the sweet, small touches (like the cookies and bottled water at turndown service) and give kudos to the friendly staff. Standard guest rooms have custom-made furnishings, marble baths and flat-screen TVs (suites have mirror TVs in bathrooms). Of the 24 more-spacious corner rooms, 12 have working fireplaces. The sophisticated City Bar is a popular evening destination for its infused vodka martinis. Sólás pub is a more-casual option. Skip the pricey hotel breakfast and hit the bagel shop across the street. ■TIP→ **Book your reservation from the hotel's Web site; they guarantee the best price. Pros:** fantastic Copley Square location, historic/architectural charm. **Cons:** bathrooms are small; no minibar/mini-refrigerator, safe, or coffeemaker (though available upon request). ⊠*61 Exeter St., Back Bay* ☎*617/536–5300 or 800/225–7676* 🖷*617/267–1237* ⊕*www.lenoxhotel.com* ⇨*187 rooms, 27 suites* ♿*In-room: Wi-Fi. In-hotel: 3 restaurants, room service, bars, gym, laundry service, concierge, public Wi-Fi, parking (fee)* ▤*AE, D, DC, MC, V* Ⓣ*Copley.*

$$$$ ▥**Mandarin Oriental Boston.** From the welcome pot of green tea to the guest basket that includes rubber duckies for the tub, the new Mandarin Oriental offers a level of service that many guests are calling "out of this world." Need your pants hemmed in 30 minutes? No problem— it's that kind of place. So what if the Asian esthetic seems a tad out of place in Boston? Overlooking Boylston Street's shops and restaurants, this limestone and marble hotel offers direct access to Prudential Center and Copley Place. Public areas are gallery-like, and adorned with Asian art on loan from the Peabody Essex Museum, while guest rooms—large for a city hotel—are outfitted in contemporary Asian style with pale woods and silk in gold or jade green, with soaking tubs, rain shower heads, and 400-thread-count Frette linens. Even if you don't drink, pop into M Bar for a look at the cool glass-topped, illuminated bar. You may have to elbow your way in; M Bar is on the hot list among local singles. Boston's best dining and shopping is at your doorstep: settle in with a gooey sampling from the Cheese Cave, or a plate of caramelized miso black cod at Asana restaurant, perhaps the hotel's best example of East-meets-West. Don't miss a visit to the quartz crystal steam room at the spa, especially if you've overindulged on mandarin martinis. **Pros:** amazing level of service, very quiet, good-size rooms. **Cons:** small fitness center, some complain design is sterile, no pretty views. ⊠*776 Boylston St., Back Bay* ☎*617/535–8888* ⊕*www.mandarinoriental.com/boston* ⇨*136 rooms, 12 suites* ♿*In-room: Safe, refrigerator (some), DVD (upon request), Internet, Wi-Fi. In-hotel: 2 restaurants, room service, bar, pool, gym, spa, laundry service, public Internet, public Wi-Fi, parking (fee), some pets allowed* ▤*AE, D, DC, MC, V* ⊷❙ *EP.*

$$$–$$$$ ▥**Marriott Hotel at Copley Place.** It's busy-busy, with throngs of tourists and their offspring, but you can't beat the location and the amenities of this 38-story "megahotel." To give you a sense of the size of this one, you can enter three ways: from the street-level lobby, a glass sky bridge from the Prudential Center–Hynes Auditorium complex, or the Copley Place shopping mall. (The Westin hotel also connects to Copley Place.) It's great in bad weather; you barely need to go outside. Rooms are generic Marriott with flat-screen TVs; the best ones overlook Boston Harbor or the Charles River. Readers praise the spacious guest rooms as "above average for the price," and give the hotel high marks its friendly staff, great sports bar, and awesome location, while others complain about long waits at the elevators, "factory-like" feel, and a kiddie-crowded swimming pool. One person's "lively buzz" is another one's "too crowded," something to keep in mind as you weigh the merits of this one against the Westin Copley Place (753 rooms) and others in the neighborhood. **Pros:** exceptional service, plush beds, great location between two shopping malls. **Cons:** crowded pool area, chaotic lobby, housekeeping not always up to par. ⊠*110 Huntington Ave., Back Bay* ☎*617/236–5800 or 800/228–9290* ⊕*www.marriott.*

com 📎1,100 *rooms, 47 suites* ⚐*In-room: Safe, refrigerator, Ethernet. In-hotel: Restaurant, room service, bar, gym, laundry service, concierge, executive floor, public Wi-Fi, parking (fee)* ▤*AE, D, DC, MC, V* Ⓣ*Copley, Back Bay/South End.*

$-$$ 🖼️**Newbury Guest House.** Shopping enthusiasts have designated this elegant redbrick-and-brownstone property the "center of the universe." Located on Boston's most fashionable shopping street, the 1882 rowhouse inn looks the part, with natural pine flooring, Victorian furnishings, and prints from the Museum of Fine Arts. A recent re-do has expanded and prettied-up the lobby, but some complain that guest rooms are looking worn. On the plus side, guests can order room service from the tiny French bistro, La Voile, located downstairs. Some rooms have bay windows; others have decorative fireplaces. Room 209 is the prettiest, with its lovely but nonworking fireplace. Limited parking is available. **Pros:** cozy, homey, great location. **Cons:** some say that rooms don't look as nice as the Web site indicates, small bathrooms, street noise. ✉*261 Newbury St., Back Bay* 🕿*617/670–6100 or 800/437–7668* ⊕*www.newburyguesthouse.com* 📎*32 rooms* ⚐*In-room: Wi-Fi. In-hotel: No elevator, concierge, public Wi-Fi, parking (fee)* ▤*AE, D, DC, MC, V* ❘⦿❘*BP* Ⓣ*Hynes, Copley.*

$$$ 🖼️**Radisson Hotel Boston.** Boxy and unsexy on the outside, this circa-1970s high-rise hotel, at the edge of the Theater District, suits price-sensitive students and families just fine. The abundant oversize rooms with queen-size beds sleep four comfortably and get extra points for private balconies and luxurious beds with adjustable-firmness mattresses, goose-down quilts, and 250-thread-count sheets. Readers praise the clean, crisp rooms and central location, while others deem the decor "tired" and bemoan the tiny swimming pool. You don't have to leave the property for entertainment: the Radisson's restaurant, Rustic Kitchen, hosts a live cooking show on Friday nights, and the hotel is home to a small off-Broadway theater, the Stuart Street Playhouse. **Pros:** excellent value for the money; free Wi-Fi throughout the property; corner rooms, such as 24 and 25, have great city views. **Cons:** neighborhood is less safe at night, some say restaurant is overpriced. ✉*200 Stuart St., Back Bay* 🕿*617/482–1800 or 800/333–3333* ⊕*www.radisson.com/ bostonma* 📎*326 rooms, 30 suites* ⚐*In-room: Safe, Wi-Fi. In-hotel: 2 restaurants, room service, pool, gym, laundry service, concierge, public Wi-Fi, parking (fee)* ▤*AE, D, DC, MC, V* Ⓣ*Arlington, Boylston.*

$$$$ 🖼️**Taj Boston Hotel.** Old-school elegance reigns at the Taj, formerly the Ritz-Carlton Boston. Standing guard at the corner of fashionable Newbury Street and the Public Garden, the Taj is doing its best to win over the old Ritz fans, as well as woo new ones, with discounted weekend rates and a bit of freshening up. Small changes include plush new robes and towels in guest rooms, and Molton Brown bath amenities. The Taj has added vibrant floral displays in the lobby, and offers three meals daily in the Café, although the restaurant has been pretty empty of late. Happily, some of the best features of the old Ritz remain, including wood-burning fireplaces (and fireplace butlers), Boston's best afternoon tea, and glorious views. If these features make your heart beat a little faster, you'll be as happy as one of the swans in the Public Garden's lagoon at the Taj.

Readers warn: Avoid rooms on the 16th floor, under the roof-deck party space. **Pros:** great location on the corner of Newbury and Arlington streets, white-glove service, great views. **Cons:** some readers complain of "snootier than thou" attitude of some staffers. ⊠ *15 Arlington St., Back Bay* ☎*617/536–5700* ⊕*www.tajhotels.com* ⇗*228 rooms, 45 suites* △*In-room: Safe, refrigerator, Ethernet. In-hotel: Restaurant, room service, bar, gym, laundry service, concierge, executive floor, parking (fee), some pets allowed* ▤*AE, D, DC, MC, V* ⓣ*Arlington.*

$$$–$$$$ 🖼**Westin Copley Place Boston.** If the idea of sleeping in an upscale shopping mall appeals to you, meet your new favorite hotel. The Westin has its own pod of retail shops, including the top-notch Grettacole Spa, plus it's connected by a covered skywalk to Copley Place (high-end shopping) and the Hynes Convention Center—a real treat in the winter. They've just launched the Westin Unwind program here, so you can see cooking demos and the like from Tuesday to Saturday. The top-floor rooms of this contemporary 36-story hotel have some of the best views in Boston—of the Charles River, Copley Square, the South End, Back Bay, and Boston skylines (especially gorgeous when a-twinkle at night). No surprise that business travelers and visiting families love this place, especially when you factor in the pool, fitness center, and the fabulous Copley Square location. Guest rooms are awash in beiges, dark greens, and blues, with wildly comfortable beds and plush linens. For dining, you can't go wrong with a meal at Turner Fisheries Bar and Restaurant (don't miss the award-winning clam chowder). ■**TIP**➔ **Check the Starwood Web site for promotional rates. Also stay on July 4 and get amazing views of the fireworks over the Charles River.** **Pros:** great location, great views, clean, spacious rooms. **Cons:** big and busy-feeling, pool area is nothing special, some say it's overpriced. ⊠*10 Huntington Ave., Back Bay* ☎*617/262–9600 or 800/937–8461* ⊕*www.westin.com/copleyplace* ⇗*753 rooms, 50 suites* △*In-room: Safe, refrigerator, Wi-Fi. In-hotel: 5 restaurants, room service, bar, pool, gym, spa, laundry service, concierge, executive floor, public Wi-Fi, airport shuttle, some pets allowed (fee)* ▤*AE, D, DC, MC, V* ⓣ*Copley, Back Bay/South End.*

BEACON HILL

$$$ 🖼**Beacon Hill Hotel & Bistro.** Two 19th-century town houses have been ★ meticulously renovated to house this intimate boutique hotel on Beacon Hill. You can't beat the location on Charles Street, one of the city's premier addresses, within walking distance of the Public Garden, Back Bay, and Government Center. Minimalist-style rooms are individually decorated with soft neutral colors and plush bed linens. Rooms have plenty of natural light filtering through the large windows overlooking city streets. There's a rooftop deck for lounging and a popular street-side bistro with fireplace and bar that's open for breakfast, lunch, and dinner. **Pros:** Beacon Hill location, with boutiques and restaurants within walking distance, parking available at nearby Boston Common garage. **Cons:** rooms are small. ⊠*25 Charles St., Beacon Hill* ☎*617/723–7575 or 888/959–2442* ⊕*www.beaconhillhotel.com* ⇗*12 rooms, 1 suite* △*In-room: Wi-Fi. In-hotel: Restaurant, laundry service, public Wi-Fi* ▤*AE, D, DC, MC, V* ��ⓞⓘ*BP* ⓣ*Arlington, Charles/MGH.*

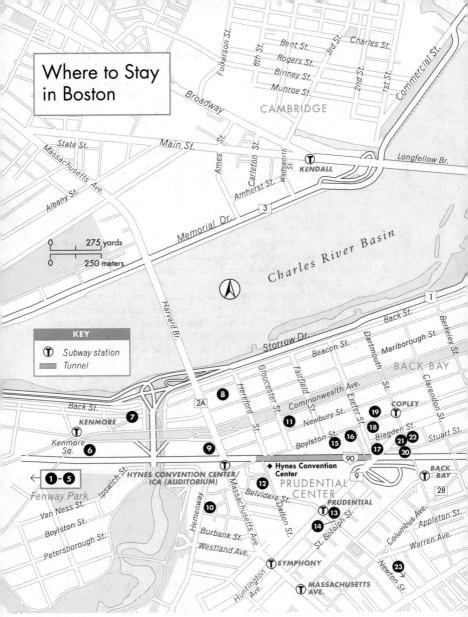

Where to Stay in Boston

CAMBRIDGE

Fulkerson St. · 6th St. · 5th St. · Bent St. · Rogers St. · Binney St. · Munroe St. · 3rd St. · 2nd St. · 1st St. · Charles St. · Commercial St.

Broadway

State St. · Main St. · Ames St. · Carleton St. · Wadsworth St. · Amherst St.

T KENDALL

Longfellow Br.

Massachusetts Ave.

Albany St.

Memorial Dr.

3

Charles River Basin

Harvard Br.

1

Back St. · Berkeley St.

Storrow Dr.

Beacon St. · Dartmouth St. · Marlborough St.

BACK BAY

2A

Back St.

KENMORE ⑦

Gloucester St. · Hereford St. · Fairfield St. · Exeter St. · Clarendon St.

Commonwealth Ave.

⑧

⑪ Newbury St.

COPLEY

⑲ **T**

⑱

T KENMORE

Kenmore Sq. ⑥

Boylston St.

⑮ ⑯

Blagden St.

⑰ ㉑ ㉒

Stuart St.

⑨

90

⑳

① - ⑤

Ipswich St.

T HYNES CONVENTION CENTER/ ICA (AUDITORIUM)

◆ Hynes Convention Center

9

T BACK BAY

Fenway Park

Van Ness St.

Boylston St.

Petersborough St.

Hemenway St.

⑩

Burbank St.

Westland Ave.

Belvidere St. · Dalton St. · Massachusetts Ave.

⑫

PRUDENTIAL CENTER

PRUDENTIAL

T ⑬

⑭

St. Botolph St.

28

Columbus Ave. · Appleton St. · Warren Ave.

Newton St.

㉓

T SYMPHONY

Huntington Ave.

T MASSACHUSETTS AVE.

KEY

T Subway station

▦ Tunnel

0 — 275 yards
0 — 250 meters

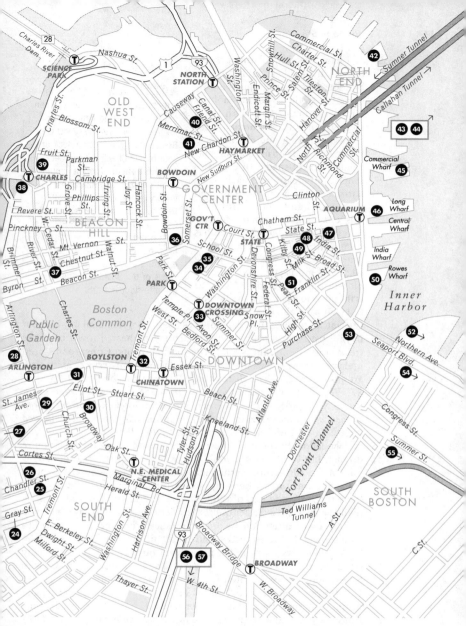

$$$–$$$$ 🏨 **Fifteen Beacon.** Although it's housed in an old (1903) beaux arts building, this boutique hotel is anything but stodgy. The tiny lobby is all black mahogany with bold splashes of red, brightened with recessed lighting and abstract art. Rooms are done up in soothing-but-gender-neutral shades of espresso, taupe, and cream, and each has a flat-screen TV, a gas fireplace, and surround-sound stereo. However, this once highly touted property is resting on its laurels. Little has been done to update the hotel in years, and what was once cutting edge and hip is starting to look a bit worn and tattered. ■TIP→**This is the place to be for Boston's Harborfest (July 4) celebration, when guests can watch fireworks from the roof deck (open from Memorial Day to Labor Day). Pros:** bathrooms have huge mirrors and heated towel bars, the steak-house restaurant is a favorite for fine dining. **Cons:** rooms need updating, some rooms are very small, inconsistent service, mattresses are just average. ⊠*15 Beacon St., Beacon Hill* ☎*617/670–1500 or 877/982–3226* ⊕*www.xvbeacon.com* ⇱*58 rooms, 2 suites* ♿*In-room: Safe, refrigerator, Ethernet, Wi-Fi. In-hotel: Restaurant, room service, bar, laundry service, concierge, public Wi-Fi, some pets allowed* ▭*AE, D, DC, MC, V* Ⓣ*Government Center, Park St.*

> **DECKED OUT**
>
> Psst . . . why pay extra bucks for a room with a view when you can get those stunning panoramas for free by enjoying lofty vistas of Boston from the rooftop deck of your hotel? Check out the deck at **Fifteen Beacon**, a great vantage point for watching Harborfest fireworks; **Beacon Hill Hotel & Bistro**, a cozy perch overlooking Charles Street on Beacon Hill; **the Colonnade**, home of Boston's best roof-deck pool; and **Clarendon Square Inn**, for stunning views of the Boston skyline from the fifth-floor hot tub.

$ 🏨 **John Jeffries House.** It's devilishly tricky to locate, especially if you're
★ driving, but once you do, you'll discover the JJH is a real find. This turn-of-the-20th-century building, across from Massachusetts General Hospital, was once a housing facility for nurses. Now, it's a sedate four-story inn, and one of the best values in town. The Federal-style double parlor has a cluster of floral-pattern chairs and sofas where you can relax with afternoon tea or coffee. Guest rooms are furnished with handsome upholstered pieces, and nearly all have kitchenettes. Triple-glazed windows block much noise from busy Charles Circle; many rooms have views of the Charles River. The inn is adjacent to Charles Street, home to lovely cafés, specialty boutiques, and antiques shops. Guests are a well-mannered mix of business travelers, Europeans, and hospital visitors. **Pros:** close to Beacon Hill, free Wi-Fi, good value. **Cons:** located near a hospital so you might hear ambulance sirens. ⊠*14 David G. Mugar Way, Beacon Hill* ☎*617/367–1866* ⊕*www.john jeffrieshouse.com* ⇱*23 rooms, 23 suites* ♿*In-room: Kitchen (some), DVD (some), Wi-Fi. In-hotel: Public Wi-Fi, parking (fee)* ▭*AE, D, DC, MC, V* �𝄙*CP* Ⓣ*Charles/MGH.*

$$$$ 🏨 **Liberty Hotel Boston.** Boston's most buzz-worthy hotel, bar none, is the Liberty, set in the old (19th century) Charles Street Jail. The jail puns eventually wear thin—the bar is called "Alibi," a restaurant is

"Clink," and so on—but you can't deny the cool factor of this unique luxury hotel. Recent guests have included Lindsay Lohan (whose DUI mug shot hangs in the bar) and Bruce Willis. Jailhouse rock (vis-à-vis granite) meets modern style here, where they've incorporated some of the jail's features into the $150 million re-do, including the trademark windows, catwalks, and even jail cells. This circa 1851 National Historic Landmark building sits at the foot of Beacon Hill, close to boutiques and restaurants. A soaring lobby of exposed brick leads to 18 guest rooms (in the main building), while an adjacent 16-story tower houses 280 more rooms with expansive views of the city. Aside from the SOLITARY sign you hang from your door when you wish to be alone, there's nothing about the rooms that suggest confinement. Small but freshly modern, they provide luxe linens, flat-panel TVs and Wi-Fi. Some offer cool views of the Charles River. Don't expect a quiet getaway here—the Alibi bar (the former drunk tank) draws lines to get in—so just go with it, and join the party. (Don't miss the fried mac-and-cheese balls at **Clink**.) **Pros:** great in-house restaurant, Scampo; lively nightlife; Beacon Hill location. **Cons:** some say HVAC system is noisy, lively nightlife, service has a few bugs to work out. ⊠*215 Charles St., Beacon Hill* ☎ *617/224–4000 or 860/507–5245* ⊕*www.libertyhotel. com* ⇌*298 rooms* ♿*In-room: Safe, refrigerator (some), DVD, Ethernet, Wi-Fi (fee). In-hotel: 2 restaurants, room service, bars, gym, water sports, bicycles, laundry service, concierge, public Wi-Fi, parking (fee), some pets allowed (fee)* ▭ *AE, D, DC, MC, V* Ⓣ*Charles.*

DOWNTOWN

$$$$ Ⓗ**Boston Harbor Hotel at Rowes Wharf.** One of the most splurge-worthy
Fodor'sChoice   places to stay in Boston, this waterfront hotel's dramatic entryway is
★   an 80-foot archway topped by a rotunda, so eye-catching that it qualifies as a local landmark. The lobby, too, is stunningly elegant, with marble arches, antique maps, and a huge tumble of fresh flowers. Guest rooms sport marble bathrooms, custom-made desks, Frette linens, high-end radio/CD players, flat-panel TVs and laptop-size safes. Amenities abound—there's even complimentary daily shoe shines. The older, well-heeled clientele appreciates these niceties, along with the fabulous views of the city and Boston harbor. Meritage restaurant has a unique, wine-inspired menu that pairs small plates with appropriate vintages, under light fixtures that mimic a starry sky. At the health club you can request workout clothes if you forgot yours. **Pros:** readers praise the impeccable service, beautiful rooms and views, easy walk to Faneuil Hall, water shuttle runs from Logan Airport to the back door of the hotel. **Cons:** gym equipment somewhat outdated, spa gets booked, so may not have availability. ⊠*70 Rowes Wharf, Downtown/Waterfront* ☎*617/439–7000 or 800/752–7077* ⊕*www.bhh.com* ⇌*204 rooms, 26 suites* ♿*In-room: Safe, refrigerator, Wi-Fi. In-hotel: 2 restaurants, room service, bar, pool, gym, spa, laundry service, concierge, public Wi-Fi, airport shuttle, parking (fee), some pets allowed* ▭*AE, D, DC, MC, V* Ⓣ*Aquarium, South Station.*

$$–$$$ Ⓗ**Bulfinch Hotel.** The clean, crisp, contemporary look of this boutique
★   hotel is simplicity at its best. Steps from TD Banknorth Garden (forever

known as Boston Garden) and an easy walk to Government Center, Faneuil Hall, and the North End, this unique nine-floor flat-iron (triangular) property offers one of the best values in town, if you don't mind tiny digs. The minimalist rooms have honey-hue walnut furnishings, gunmetal light fixtures, marble-tiled baths, and high-end mattresses, plus flat-screen TVs, CD players, and work desks. The neutral and white-on-white color scheme adds additional serenity—a welcome oasis from the maddening Garden crowds just outside the door, though some guests complain of spotty cleaning. **Pros:** great prices, free Internet, lots of restaurants and bars nearby (including an on-site lounge and tapas restaurant), close to North Station commuter rail and the T. **Cons:** small guest rooms and lobby, staff can be indifferent, lots of party-hearty clientele. ⊠*107 Merrimac St., Downtown* ☎*617/624–0202 or 877/267–1776* ⊕*www.bulfinchhotel.com* ⤷*79 rooms* ⌂*In-room: Ethernet. In-hotel: Restaurant, bar, gym, laundry service, concierge, parking (fee), some pets allowed* ▤*AE, D, DC, MC, V* Ⓣ*North Station.*

$$$$ ⬚**Fairmont Battery Wharf.** Of the (surprisingly) few hotels clustered along Boston's waterfront, this new one feels like it plays the part better than the others. That could be because it's situated along the recently expanded Boston Harborwalk, the walkway of paths and parks that runs from Charlestown to Dorchester. It could also be due to the presence of the Coast Guard Station next door, and the constant coming and going of vessels big and small. You can even get here by boat, since the water taxi ($10) runs between the airport and the hotel. Inside, they've resisted the obvious nautical theme and gone for a "manly modern" look—lots of polished nickel, maple, and granite, with contemporary glass sculpture by artist Nikolas Weinstein sparkling overhead. Guest rooms sport all the good stuff you'd expect at this price point, including marble baths, flat-screen TVs, work desks with ergonomic chairs, and high-tech coffeemakers. A couple of unexpected things we love: real clocks and, in most king rooms, comfy leather recliners. The hotel has made much ado of its signature restaurant, Sensing, created by Michelin-starred chef Guy Martin, but the place hasn't yet been embraced by Boston foodies. That may change as residents move into private apartments in the Fairmont's four-building colony, and when/if the dining public finds its way to Sensing (we think its worth the trip). The restaurant's outdoor patio should morph into a rocking hot spot in summertime—there are very few chic waterfront dining spots in the city. **Pros:** great water views from lobby, access to Harborwalk, close to the North End (Boston's Italian district). **Cons:** fairly new development lacks neighborhood feel, some "unobstructed" water views are in fact partially obstructed. ⊠*3 Battery Wharf, Downtown* ☎*617/994–9000* ⊕*www.fairmont.com/batterywharf* ⤷*120 rooms, 30 suites* ⌂*In-room: Safe, Internet, Wi-Fi. In-hotel: 2 restaurants, room service, bar, gym, spa, laundry service, concierge, executive floor, public Internet, public Wi-Fi, parking (fee), some pets allowed (fee)* ▤*AE, D, DC, MC, V* ❙⦿❙ *EP.*

$$–$$$ ⬚**Harborside Inn.** "We're not a pampering hotel like the Four Seasons," ★   owner Mark Hagopian warns. Then again, the Harborside Inn won't charge you for incidentals, and room rates are commonly 20% less

than those of neighboring properties. The independent-minded travelers who discover this place, a mix of youngish business travelers and weekenders, don't feel that they're missing out. The former 14th-century mercantile look is sort of modern-marine minimalist, with shipwreck prints and scenes of Boston Harbor, exposed brick walls, hardwood floors, Federal-style furnishings and teak accents. Amenities include flat-screen TVs and complimentary Wi-Fi. Walk to lively Faneuil Hall, Quincy Market, and the North End, and then return to the homey vibe of the inn. Many of the snug, variously shaped rooms (no two are alike) have windows overlooking the small, open lobby, which extends eight stories up to the roof. ■TIP➡**For a great view request a room overlooking the city; for a quieter stay book a room that faces the interior atrium.** Pros: good value for the area, close to Quincy Market, North End, New England Aquarium, water taxi, historic setting. **Cons:** nearby nightclubs can be noisy; atrium-view rooms feel closed-in, some say. ✉*185 State St., Downtown/Waterfront* ☎*617/723–7500 or 888/723–7565* ⊕*www.harborsideinnboston.com* ⌁*98 rooms, 2 suites* ☖*In-room: Safe (some), refrigerator (some), DVD, Wi-Fi. In-hotel: Laundry service, concierge, public Wi-Fi* ▭*AE, D, DC, MC, V* Ⓣ*Aquarium.*

$$$–$$$$
★
▦**Hilton Boston Financial District.** If you're looking for sleek, comfortable, and business-like, you'll find it at this luxury hotel. The 1928 building, the first art deco building and first skyscraper in the city, sports stylish teal and taupe carpeting. The lobby's mahogany paneling and soft gold lighting complement the restored bronze elevators and original letterbox. Guest rooms are spacious, with high ceilings and crown moldings; some overlook the waterfront. (For extra space, ask for a room at the end of the hallway.) Comforting touches include terry robes, feather pillows, and nightly turndown service. Night owls can take advantage of the 24-hour health club and business center. Readers praise the efficient, professional staff. **Pros:** well-maintained, clean, and quiet; friendly, helpful staff. **Cons:** poor-quality breakfast buffet (try the nearby Bean Leaf Café, instead), expensive food in general (lots of options in the neighborhood, though), daily fee for Wi-Fi, hard to find. ✉*89 Broad St., Downtown* ☎*617/556–0006* ⊕*www.hilton.com* ⌁*362 rooms, 66 suites* ☖*In-room: Safe, refrigerator, Wi-Fi. In-hotel: Restaurant, room service, bar, gym, laundry service, concierge, public Wi-Fi, parking (fee), some pets allowed* ▭*AE, D, DC, MC, V* Ⓣ*State.*

$$–$$$$
▦**Hyatt Regency Boston.** Business travelers who frequent this 22-story Downtown Crossing hotel enjoy the consistent top-notch service and high-end amenities that come standard in guest rooms, including Sony Dream Machines, pillow-top mattresses and featherbeds (with foam beds upon request), granite baths, plush bathrobes, and high-end bath products. Another plus for road warriors: the hotel is a short walk from the Financial District, not to mention Boston Common and Chinatown,

HOTELS TO DINE FOR

Hotel dining has come a long way since the clam-strip plate at HoJo's (great though it was!).

■ **Boston Harbor Hotel.** The wine-pairing dinner at Meritage is seriously wow-worthy.

■ **Eliot Hotel.** Clio dishes up fab French food with a contemporary tilt.

■ **Four Seasons.** Splurge-worthy neo-French cuisine is paired with stunning views of the Public Garden at Aujourd'hui. Great vegetarian choices, too.

■ **Mandarin Oriental.** Asana offers an Asian twist on American favorites. Try chef Nicolas Boutin's daily bento box or hang with other foodies at the chef's table.

■ **Nine Zero.** Dedicated carnivores love Ken Oringer's creative take on steakhouse fare, KO Prime. (Runner-up in this category: Jamie Mammano's Mooo, at Fifteen Beacon.)

■ **Westin Copley Place Boston.** Pop downstairs to Turner Fisheries for (at least) a quick bowl of award-winning clam chowder and some oysters.

and the fitness center is open 24/7. Savvy vacationers find weekend bargains and good package deals with theater tickets and shopping discounts. The sleek lobby has marble floors and columns, dark woods, and bold, geometric rugs. Spacious guest rooms, set around four atriums, are decorated with mahogany furnishings, taupe linen walls, and soothing earth tones. We like the fact that this property is fairly green— among other things, they compost leftover food and use energy-efficient lighting, including motion-detector light switches in guest rooms. **Pros:** high-end amenities in a moderately priced hotel, good package deals, saunas and whirlpools. **Cons:** views of neighboring office buildings from guest rooms, few chairs around indoor pool, small gym, thin walls. ⊠ *1 Ave. de Lafayette, Chinatown* ☎*617/912–1234 or 800/233–1234* ⊕*www.regencyboston.hyatt.com* ➦*474 rooms, 26 suites* ⌂*In-room: Safe, refrigerator, Ethernet, Wi-Fi (fee). In-hotel: Restaurant, room service, bar, pool, gym, laundry service, concierge, executive floors, public Wi-Fi (fee), parking (fee), some pets allowed* ⊟*AE, D, DC, MC, V* Ⓣ*Chinatown, Downtown Crossing.*

$$$$ **InterContinental Boston.** Call it the anti-boutique hotel. Boston's
Fodor'sChoice 424-room InterContinental Hotel, facing the harbor and the Rose Ken-
★ nedy Greenway—is housed in two opulent, 22-story towers wrapped in blue glass. In a nod to the city's history, the towers equal the height of the masts of the old tall ships, and the pewter bar in RumBa, the hotel's rum bar, would surely delight metalsmith Paul Revere. (It also harks back to Boston's connection with the rum trade.) Miel, the hotel's organic Provencal brasserie, is open 24/7. Hallways are lined with Texan limestone, and lobbies are gleaming with Italian marble and leather—there's not a red brick in the place. Guest rooms are oversize, wired with the latest technology, and have flat-screen TVs, and readers rave about the spalike bathrooms ("the best bathroom I have ever seen"), done in mosaic tile and granite, with separate tubs and showers. Another drawing card here is the 6,600-square-foot spa and health

PET-FRIENDLY PADS

Some Boston hotels roll out the red carpet for their VIPs (Very Important Pets).

It's Fido's birthday? **Hotel Marlowe** will order a special cake from Polka Dog Bakery. And, the pet ambassadors at the **Fairmont Copley** will be happy to take your pets out for a scenic stroll around the city. At the **Onyx Hotel,** Lassie can have her own bed, fleece blanket, and gourmet dog biscuits; fine felines get a scratching post, too. There are also pet-sitting and pet-walking services. The **Ritz-Carlton Boston Common** Pampered Pet package includes a welcome fruit-and-cheese platter, dog biscuits, a ceramic water bowl, customized dog tag, and a purr-fect one-hour pampering session for you and your pet—one of you gets a massage and the other gets groomed.

club, and a pool that overlooks Atlantic Avenue and the Greenway. Sushi-Teq, the hotel's sushi-tequila restaurant, draws crowds, while movers and shakers from local financial, real estate, and law firms of the Financial District make merry after work in the bars. **Pros:** rooms have great views and great bathrooms, close to Financial District and South Station, brasserie open 24 hours. **Cons:** huge function rooms mean lots of conventioneers, far from Newbury Street and museums, guests say that soundproofing could be better. ⊠ *510 Atlantic Ave., Downtown/Waterfront* ☎ *617/747–1000* ⊕ *www.intercontinentalboston. com* ⤴ *424 rooms, 38 suites* ⚷ *In-room: Safe, refrigerator, DVD, Wi-Fi. In-hotel: 2 restaurants, room service, bar, pool, gym, spa, laundry service, concierge, executive floor, public Wi-Fi, parking (fee)* ▤ *AE, D, DC, MC, V* Ⓣ *South Station.*

$$$-$$$$
★
🏨 **Langham Hotel.** The red awnings of this 1922 Renaissance Revival landmark (the former Federal Reserve Building) lead to a gleaming lobby of honeyed gold, deep red, and creamy marble, a stark contrast to the ubiquitous gray suits of Financial District types who gather here. Crystal chandeliers light the hallways, and jewel-tone fabrics swath guest rooms—it's not daring, but it works. While the place is all business during the week (except for the luncheon crowd at Café Fleuri), families and couples drop in on weekends for the dramatically lower room rates and specialty packages. The hotel is racheting up its cool factor with the new Bond restaurant and bar, which has become a hot spot. Plus, Café Fleuri is the site of an all-chocolate buffet Saturday afternoon (September–June) and a wonderful jazz brunch on Sunday. ∎ TIP➜ **Use a public parking lot, where rates are cheaper on weekends.** **Pros:** fabulous Sunday brunch, cool bar, good discounts on weekends. **Cons:** it's a bit of a hike to Newbury Street and Boston museums, pricey during the week, expensive valet parking. ⊠ *250 Franklin St., Downtown* ☎ *617/451–1900 or 800/543–4300* ⊕ *www.boston.langham hotels.com* ⤴ *318 rooms, 17 suites* ⚷ *In-room: Safe, refrigerator, Wi-Fi (fee). In-hotel: 2 restaurants, room service, bar, pool, gym, spa, laundry*

service, concierge, public Wi-Fi (fee), parking (fee), small pets allowed ▭*AE, D, DC, MC, V* Ⓣ*South Station.*

$$$$ 🏨**Marriott Custom House.** While the property is, strictly speaking, a Marriott Vacation Club (read: time shares), the one-bedroom, one-bath suites are available to hotel guests for overnight stays. For visitors even moderately interested in the city's history, this is great news. Built in 1847 and used as Boston's customs office until 1986, this stunning Greek Revival structure—topped with the iconic 495-foot clock tower (as seen in the opening credits of TV's *Boston Legal*)—feels like a museum, especially when historic actor Mike LePage shows up dressed as President John Adams. Even the bar might be considered historic; it's housed in the old Counting Room, where shipping receipts were tallied. A ride up to the 26th-floor observation deck reveals awesome views of Boston and the water—and views from guest rooms aren't too shabby either. That said, this isn't a full-service hotel. There's no room service, no pool, and no restaurant. But the myriad restaurants of Quincy Market are mere steps away, and you can also cook in your room with groceries or charge food (and use the pool) at the Marriott Long Wharf. Rooms are done up in royal blue and gold, accented with nautical prints framed in gilt. In summertime, it's a hot ticket (book three weeks in advance). **Pros:** a must for history buffs, water views, great location near Quincy Market, Aquarium, etc. **Cons:** fee for Internet access, street noise from nearby bars, no pool. ✉*3 McKinley Sq., Downtown* ☎*617/310–6300* ⊕*www.marriott.com/hotels* ⌁*84 suites* ♿*In-room: Kitchen, refrigerator, DVD, VCR, Internet (fee). In-hotel: Bar, gym, laundry facilities, laundry service, concierge, parking (fee)* ▭*AE, D, DC, MC, V* ⧟ *EP.*

$$$–$$$$ 🏨**Marriott Long Wharf.** Families can't resist this waterfront hotel, thanks to its close proximity to New England Aquarium, whale-watch tours, and the shops and restaurants of Quincy Market. Even the Italian-flavored North End isn't far, if you're willing to walk a bit. Cute Christopher Columbus Park is right outside the door, with brick walkways and wisteria-covered archways. And then there's the Marriott's great swimming pool, overlooking the harbor, plus a huge gym and an itty-bitty game room . . . convenience is the name of the game here. Jutting out into the bay, this airy, multi-tiered redbrick hotel resembles a ship. Most of the rooms, pleasantly decorated in cream and gold brocade with pillow-top mattresses, open onto a five-story atrium. Some rooms have views of the park or New England Aquarium. Clean-freak alert: Plush feather duvets on the beds are changed every night. There's no excuse to avoid the gym here—it's open 24 hours a day. ■TIP➡ **Head to Quincy Market instead of eating on-site, even for breakfast. Pros:** waterfront location, good weekend rates (check the Web for deals), convenience store close by. **Cons:** standard guest rooms are small for families, so you'll need adjoining rooms or a suite; restaurant is pricey. ✉*296 State St., Downtown/Waterfront* ☎*617/227–0800 or 800/228–9290* ⊕*www. marriott.com/boslw* ⌁*397 rooms, 15 suites* ♿*In-room: Safe, refrigerator, Ethernet, Wi-Fi (fee). In-hotel: Restaurant, room service, bar, pool, gym, laundry facilities, laundry service, concierge, public Wi-Fi (fee), executive floor, parking (fee)* ▭*AE, D, DC, MC, V* Ⓣ*Aquarium.*

$$–$$$$ ⊡ **Millennium Bostonian Hotel.** The Millennium hotel has finished its $24 million transformation. The low-lighted contemporary lobby with a gas fireplace and small sitting area features polished woods and accents of black and red. Guest rooms got face-lifts, too—the working fireplaces and balconies remain (hooray!)—punched up with stone entryways, wood paneling, crown moldings and earth-tone hues, accented with Boston-theme photography and artwork. Rooms are updated with duvets and 300-thread-count sheets, flat-screen TVs, and safes large enough for laptops, and Wi-Fi is now available in public spaces. As part of the renovation, windows got extra soundproofing—a real plus in a busy area like Quincy Market. **Pros:** location, updated rooms. **Cons:** some rooms still get street noise. ⊠ *Faneuil Hall Marketplace, 26 North St., Downtown* ☎*617/523–3600 or 866/866–8086* ⊕*www. millenniumhotels.com* ⬐*187 rooms, 14 suites* ⟁*In-room: Safe, refrigerator, Wi-Fi (fee). In-hotel: Restaurant, room service, bar, gym, laundry service, concierge, public Wi-Fi, parking (fee)* ▤*AE, D, DC, MC, V* ⊤*Government Center, Haymarket.*

$$$$ ⊡ **Nine Zero.** The little doggie dish outside the entrance is a tip-off—this
Fodor'sChoice   isn't an ordinary hotel. Owned by Kimpton Hotels, this property is styl-
★   ish and swank. The lobby is a knockout, with copper metallic draperies and high-backed leather chairs. Giant suspended glass globes stand in for chandeliers. It all adds up to a spare feel, the better to complement the cool threads of the youngish, style-conscious crowd. Guest rooms sport bold patterns, curvy black armoires, and full martini bars; some have floor-to-ceiling windows. Unexpected features include in-room yoga (turn on their yoga channel, and ask them to bring you a yoga basket) and "guppy love" (they'll lend you a goldfish bowl if you get lonely). Corner rooms (ending in 05) have awesome views of the Long-fellow Bridge and the gold dome of the State House, but you'll pay a premium for them. The gym is really small, so ask for a free pass to a local fitness club. **Pros:** great style, lobby wine-tasting every evening (from 5 to 6), Mario Russo (Newbury Street) bath products, KO Prime, a popular steak house run by überchef Ken Oringer. **Cons:** smallish rooms, overlooks a cemetery, high parking fees. ⊠ *90 Tremont St., Downtown* ☎*617/772–5800 or 866/646–3937* ⊕*www.ninezero.com* ⬐*185 rooms, 5 suites* ⟁*In-room: Safe, refrigerator, Ethernet, Wi-Fi. In-hotel: Restaurant, room service, bar, gym, laundry service, concierge, public Wi-Fi, parking (fee), some pets allowed* ▤*AE, D, DC, MC, V* ⊤*Park St., Government Center.*

$$–$$$$ ⊡ **Omni Parker House.** America's oldest continuously operating hotel
★   got a $30 million face-lift, so you can steep yourself in Boston history but still watch a flat-screen TV, work out with the latest equipment, and stash your stuff in a laptop-size safe. And, happily, you can still get Boston cream pie for breakfast, since they invented it here. If any hotel really says "Boston," it's this one, where JFK proposed to Jackie, and Charles Dickens gave his first reading of *A Christmas Carol*. In fact, you may well see a Dickens impersonator in the lobby, since history tours put the Parker House on their hit list. The downside: guests' rooms are small (furnishings were custom-built to fit). At least they're nicely turned out, with red-and-gold Roman shades, ivory wall coverings and

4

cushy mattress covers. The hotel stands opposite old City Hall, on the Freedom Trail. **Pros:** historic, near Downtown Crossing on Freedom Trail. **Cons:** small rooms, some say thin-walled rooms can be noisy. ✉ *60 School St., Downtown* ☎ *617/227–8600 or 800/843–6664* ⊕ *www.omniparkerhouse.com* ⬢ *551 rooms, 21 suites* ⟁ *In-room: Safe, Wi-Fi. In-hotel: 2 restaurants, room service, bars, gym, laundry service, concierge, public Wi-Fi, parking (fee), some pets allowed* ▭ *AE, D, DC, MC, V* Ⓣ *Government Center, Park St.*

$$$–$$$$ 🔲 **Onyx Hotel.** Sexy, supper-club atmosphere oozes from this contemporary boutique hotel a block from North Station, making it a favorite of hipsters and hoopsters alike (the Celtics and the Bruins play nearby). Sip an ice-cold martini and nibble some tapas in the intimate Ruby Room, with its flashy velvet-padded chairs and black-granite bar lighted with fiber optics. The crowd in the Ruby Room varies. If there's a concert going on at nearby TD Banknorth Garden, you might party with band members and assorted fans. If the Celtics or the Bruins are playing at home in the Garden, you'll get a lively, sports-loving crowd (unless somebody's having a terrible season). Later, head upstairs to slip into your leopard-print bathrobe and cushy socks. Rooms are done in black and taupe with checkerboard carpeting and colorful accents, including red suede chairs. All have plush linens, flat-screen TVs, DVD players, surround-sound, free Wi-Fi, and Aveda bath products. **Pros:** good location for catching a sporting event or concert at the Garden, near North Station commuter rail and T stop, near several inexpensive restaurants and bars. **Cons:** smallish rooms and bathrooms, small gym (but they do offer free passes to the Boston Sports Club). ✉ *155 Portland St., Downtown* ☎ *617/557–9955 or 866/660–6699* ⊕ *www. onyxhotel.com* ⬢ *110 rooms, 2 suites* ⟁ *In-room: Safe, refrigerator, DVD, Wi-Fi. In-hotel: Restaurant, room service, bar, gym, laundry service, concierge, public Wi-Fi, some pets allowed* ▭ *AE, D, DC, MC, V* ⦿*CP* Ⓣ *North Station.*

$$$–$$$$ 🔲 **Renaissance Boston Hotel.** Set along the working wharves of Boston Harbor, near the BCEC and the Institute of Contemporary Art, the Renaissance plays to a watery theme that you'll notice the moment you enter the lobby. Glass orbs are filled with blue or green liquid, while a lighting fixture and staircase are spiral-shaped like a nautilus shell. The building is flooded with light, and nearly all guest rooms have water views. It all adds up to a clean, cool, modern ambience, completely different than the dark woods and comfy Colonial look you encounter at the city's older hotels. The pool is a lap pool, not designed for lingering. If it all feels a bit no-nonsense, that's just fine to the business-folk who make up much of the hotel's clientele. A nice touch for female solo travelers: the restaurant has an open kitchen with a chef's table, so you can dine here without the dreaded "All by yourself?" treatment. The mood changes on weekends, when package deals lure weekenders and family travelers. **Pros:** inviting lobby bar and lounge area, close proximity to Silver Line (take the T to the airport), restaurant is comfortable for solo guests. **Cons:** some guest-room views of Boston Harbor are more industrial than scenic, hordes of conventioneers, a bit away from major city attrractions. ✉ *606 Congress St., Downtown/Seaport*

District ☎*617/338–4111 or 888–796–4664* ⊕*www.marriott.com/*
hotels/travel/boswf-renaissance-boston-waterfront-hotel ⬍*471 guest*
rooms ♿*In-room: Safe, DVD, Ethernet, Wi-Fi (fee). In-hotel: 2 res-*
taurants, room service, bar, pool, gym, spa, laundry service, concierge,
public Wi-FI, parking (fee) 🚻*AE, D, DC MC, V* Ⓣ*Silver Line Way.*

$$$$ 🏨 **Ritz-Carlton Boston Common.** The LA Sports Club, the Ritz's mega–
★   fitness center, is the go-to gym for pop stars who are performing in
Boston, so you might feel a bit more fabulous—or a whole lot fatter—
simply by hanging out here. While traditionalists often compare this
hotel unfavorably to the other Ritz-Carltons, it's only fair to judge it
for what it is: a sleek, contemporary hotel that speaks more to rock
stars than royalty. Warm wood walls and trim complement an extensive art collection in the lobby lounge, where furnishings are draped
in velvet and silk, and lamps are made of hand-blown Venetian glass.
Guest rooms are dressed in apricot, yellow, and blue, with hardwood
armoires, separate marble showers and deep tubs and the all-important
flat-screen HDTV. Some rooms have spectacular views of Boston Common. A short walk will get you to Downtown Crossing's shopping zone,
the Theater District, and Newbury Street. Besides the fitness center,
the hotel complex houses a movie theater. **Pros:** killer gym, central
location. **Cons:** readers complain that guest rooms are too dark and
lack "wow" factor, food service is "brutally expensive." (Lots of other
options in Downtown Crossing, though.) ✉*10 Avery St., Downtown*
☎*617/574–7100 or 800/241–3333* ⊕*www.ritzcarlton.com* ⬍*150*
rooms, 43 suites ♿*In-room: Safe, refrigerator, Ethernet, Wi-Fi. In-*
hotel: Restaurant, room service, bar, pool, gym, laundry service, con-
cierge, executive floor, public Wi-Fi, parking (fee), some pets allowed
🚻*AE, D, DC, MC, V* Ⓣ*Boylston St.*

$$$$ 🏨 **Seaport Hotel.** Wearing a badge on your lapel? You'll be among your
★   own tribe here, where the hotel is part of the Seaport World Trade Center, a mammoth conference complex. If you need to keep your mind on
business, you won't mind at all that your hotel is a bit distant from the
heart of the city. (You'll have a hard time resisting the great pool and
fitness center, though.) Inside this gleaming waterfront property is a
crisply elegant lobby and adjacent lobby bar, done up in kicky hues of
kiwi and carrot. The huge rooms have handcrafted cherry furniture and
marble bathrooms as well as Wi-Fi and Seaportal, a touch-screen Web
portal for phone calls, hotel and meeting updates, and Boston tourism
info. Bug out of your meeting early to swim in the heated lap pool or
get a facial at the luxurious Wave Health & Fitness Club. **Pros:** great
pool area and gym, no-tipping policy, water taxi stops across the street
from the hotel. **Cons:** located away from city center, long lines at valet
car pickup, room service is expensive (good, though). ✉*World Trade*
Center, 1 Seaport La., Downtown/Seaport District ☎*617/385–4000*
or 877/732–7678 ⊕*www.seaportboston.com* ⬍*402 rooms, 24 suites*
♿*In-room: Safe, refrigerator (some), Ethernet, Wi-Fi. In-hotel: Restau-*
rant, room service, bar, pool, gym, laundry service, concierge, executive
floor, public Wi-Fi, parking (fee), some pets allowed 🚻*AE, D, DC,*
MC, V Ⓣ*Silver Line.*

$$$–$$$$ ▦ **Westin Boston Waterfront.** A modern 17-story tower of gleaming glass and steel, this South Boston waterfront property is connected to the mammoth Boston Convention & Exhibition Center, a magnet for the men and women wearing suits and badges. Rooms are handsome with a neutral palette of whites, tans, and pastels, punctuated with cherrywood furnishings. Most—some 85%—have water or skyline views. When you're not in meetings, work out the kinks at the state-of-the-art fitness center, with a slew of up-to-date machines, an indoor pool, and steam and sauna rooms. **Pros:** lobby stations with wireless check-in, Silver Line from Logan takes you directly to hotel, the Westin's signature "heavenly" beds. **Cons:** clusters of conventioneers and meeting-goers crowd the

> **JUST OFF ROUTE 128**
>
> In town for business in the high-tech 'hood of Route 128? Avoid rush-hour traffic and stay at the **Doubletree Guest Suites Boston/Waltham** (☎ 781/890–6767 ⊕ www.bostonwalthamsuites.dou bletree.com). It's easily accessible from the highway. Parking is free, and food is served in the lounge day and night. Squeeze in a workout in the fitness center, a swim in the indoor pool, or a soak in the crescent-shape hot tub. When it comes to smoothing the rough edges of business travel, these folks have it down. Runner-up: the **Westin Hotel Waltham-Boston** (☎ 781/290–5601 ⊕ www.star woodhotels.com/westin).

place, too sterile for some tastes, rooms are pricey during top conventions. ✉ *425 Summer St., Downtown/Seaport District* ☎ *617/532–4600* ⊕ *www.starwoodhotels.com* ➴ *761 rooms, 32 suites* ♿ *In-room: Safe, refrigerator, Ethernet, Wi-Fi (fee). In-hotel: Restaurant, room service, bar, pool, gym, laundry service, concierge, public Wi-Fi (fee), parking (fee)* ☰ *AE, D, DC, MC, V* Ⓣ *South Station.*

KENMORE SQUARE

$$$ ▦ **Gryphon House.** Many of the suites in this four-story, 19th-century
Fodor'sChoice brownstone are thematically decorated: one evokes rustic Italy; another
★ is inspired by neo-Gothic art. Among the many amenities—including gas fireplaces, wet bars, DVD and CD players, and private voice mail—the enormous bathrooms with oversize tubs and separate showers are the most appealing. Even the staircase (there is no elevator) is extraordinary: a 19th-century wallpaper mural, *El Dorado*, wraps along the walls. Trompe-l'oeil paintings and murals by local artist Michael Ernest Kirk decorate the common spaces. Another nice touch: free passes to the Museum of Fine Arts and Isabella Stewart Gardner Museum. **Pros:** elegant suites are lush and spacious, gas fireplaces are in all the rooms, helpful, friendly staff. **Cons:** may be too fussy for some, there's no elevator or handicapped access. ✉ *9 Bay State Rd., Kenmore Sq.* ☎ *617/375–9003 or 877/375–9003* ⊕ *www.innboston.com* ➴ *8 suites* ♿ *In-room: Refrigerator, DVD, Wi-Fi. In-hotel: No elevator, public Wi-Fi, parking (fee)* ☰ *AE, D, MC, V* ⦿*CP* Ⓣ *Kenmore.*

¢ ▦ **Hostelling International Boston.** The bare-bones, low-cost option near the Museum of Fine Arts is ideal if you don't mind sharing one of the six-person dormitories with a slew of backpacking, college-age travelers. (Private rooms are available for a higher price.) Bright purple paint enlivens the rather drab decor, but everything is ultraclean. Linens are provided (no sleeping bags allowed), and there's a full kitchen and TV room for guests to use. Discounted tickets are often available to cultural events, and continental breakfast is included. Run by American Youth Hostels, the lodging does not require membership but does suggest reservations. Travelers under 18 must be accompanied by parent or guardian. **Pros:** facilities are clean and up to date, it's open 24 hours a day, you can't beat the price. **Cons:** you'll feel like you're back in the college dorm, don't expect a lot of privacy, it gets noisy during busy times. ⊠ *12 Hemenway St., Kenmore Sq.* ☎ *617/536–1027* ⊕ *www. bostonhostel.org* ⤴ *10 rooms without bath* ⧌ *In-room: No a/c, no phone, no TV. In-hotel: Restaurant, laundry facilities, public Wi-Fi* ▤ *MC, V* Ⓣ *ICA.*

¢–$ ▦ **Hostelling International Fenway.** Dying to see the boys of summer play in legendary Fenway Park but don't want to pay big bucks for lodging? (And who has money left over after dishing it out for the hard-to-come-by Red Sox tickets?) This clean and convenient hostel, popular with young baseball fans and groups, offers low-cost dormitory rooms ($39–$48 per person) and private rooms for one to three people ($96–$129 per night) in the Fenway 'hood. You'll have use of kitchen and laundry facilities, too. Open June through mid-August only. **Pros:** cheap digs in the Fenway 'hood; laundry facilities add to the convenience; discounts on tickets to shows and cultural events (not the Red Sox, alas), tours, and area restaurants available to guests. **Cons:** rooms are small and basic, not a lot of privacy. Expect some party-hardy b-ball crowds. ⊠ *575 Commonwealth Ave., Kenmore Sq.* ☎ *617/267–8599* ⊕ *www.bostonhostel.org* ⤴ *10 rooms without bath* ⧌ *In-room: No a/c, no phone, no TV. In-hotel: Laundry facilities, public Wi-Fi* ▤ *MC, V* Ⓣ *Kenmore.*

$$$$ ▦ **Hotel Commonwealth.** Luxury and service without pretense makes this
★   hip hotel anything but common, blending old-world charm with modern conveniences for a sophisticated, boutiquey feel. Rich color schemes enhance the elegant rooms, and king- or queen-size beds are piled with down pillows and Italian linens. Choose rooms with views of bustling Commonwealth Avenue or Fenway Park. All rooms have marble baths and floor-to-ceiling windows, separate work areas (divided by a curtain) and flat-screen TVs. The wildy accommodating staff and car and driver available to guests are added bonuses. Extra niceties include complimentary newspapers at the front desk. The much-acclaimed seafood restaurant, Great Bay (be sure to make reservations upon arrival) and the Eastern Standard Bar & Restaurant are also on-site. **Pros:** luscious bedding and bath products, great service, Red Sox fans will love the views of Fenway Park from some of the rooms (request these when booking), on-site restaurant is one of the best in the city for fresh fish. **Cons:** hotel and surroundings can be mobbed during a Red Sox game, small gym. ⊠ *500 Commonwealth Ave., Kenmore Sq.* ☎ *617/933–5000 or 866/784–4000* ⊕ *www.hotelcommonwealth.com* ⤴ *149 rooms, 1 suite* ⧌ *In-room: Safe, refrigerator, DVD, Ethernet, Wi-Fi. In-hotel: 3*

CLOSE UP

Bring the Kids

Most Boston hotels allow kids, but a few go out of their way to make them feel welcome with a slew of special features and packages. **Fairmont Copley Plaza** offers a Just Ducky package that includes tickets for the Boston Duck Boat tour, a copy of Robert McCloskey's *Make Way for Ducklings,* and a free plush duck. The **Royal Sonesta** family fun package includes four free tickets to the Boston Science Museum and bedtime cookies and milk. **Park Plaza** has a family package that includes free parking, in-room movies with popcorn and candy, and four tickets to the New England Aquarium. **Langham Hotel** offers a Very Important Baby package, including unlimited diapers during your stay, baby bedding, stroller, and nursery items, preordered baby food, valet parking, and more.

If you're looking for a place for kids to splash around, **the Seaport Hotel** and the **Sheraton Boston Hotel** have two of the largest pools in the city. Many city hotels allow children under a certain age to stay in their parents' room at no extra charge. Request a "Kids Love Boston" brochure from the **Greater Boston Convention & Visitors Bureau** (☎ *617/536–4100 or 888/733–2678* ⊕ *www.bostonusa. com*). The Web site lists a variety of family-friendly packages that include such extras as complimentary use of strollers and discounts to city attractions.

restaurants, room service, bar, gym, laundry service, concierge, public Wi-Fi, parking (fee) ⊟ *AE, D, DC, MC, V* Ⓣ *Kenmore.*

SOUTH END

$$ ⊞ **82 Chandler Street Bed & Breakfast.** Location and price are the sell-
★ ing points of this 1863 redbrick row house, a five-minute walk from Copley Square and Amtrak's Back Bay station. Each room is individu-ally decorated in shades of green, red, blue, or yellow and is accessible via the four-story main staircase; all are no-frills but are white-glove clean. Standard rooms have a discreetly placed kitchen area. The best room, with wide bay windows overlooking downtown, is on the top floor and has a working fireplace and a skylight. **Pros:** lots of his-toric charm, good price point, recently repainted and refreshed. **Cons:** minimum two-night stays in summer, rooms are tiny, paper-thin walls. ⊠ *82 Chandler St., South End* ☎ *617/482–0408* ⊕ *www.82chandler. com* ⇆ *3 rooms, 2 studios* ⅋ *In-room: Kitchen (some), refrigerator (some), Wi-Fi. In-hotel: No elevator, no kids under 12* ⊟ *No credit cards* ℺| *CP* Ⓣ *Back Bay/South End.*

$ ⊞ **Berkeley Residence YWCA Boston.** This bare-bones facility offers single ($62) and double ($94) rooms within walking distance of Back Bay and South End restaurants and shops. A dining room serves inexpen-sive meals. The Back Bay T station (which also serves Amtrak) is three blocks away. Apply in advance if you wish to stay longer than two months. Long-term stays are $923 per month, which includes breakfast and dinner. Men, housed on a male-only floor or a mixed-gender floor, can stay up to 13 nights; women can stay longer. **Pros:** cheapest stay in town, economical long-term option for women traveling alone. **Cons:** not a lot of privacy, rooms can be hot and stuffy in dog days of summer. ⊠*40 Berkeley St., South End* ☎*617/375–2524* ⊕*www.ywcaboston. org* ⬅*200 rooms without bath* ⚭*In-room: No a/c, no phone, no TV. In-hotel: Restaurant, laundry service, public Wi-Fi* ▤*MC, V* ⦿|*BP* Ⓣ*Back Bay/South End.*

$–$$ 🏨 **Chandler Inn.** At the end of one of the South End's prettiest streets, this gay-friendly lodging is an easy walk to the T, the Amtrak station, or any of Tremont Street's trendy restaurants. This formerly plain-Jane inn boosted its fab quotient with a major room redesign. Forty rooms got a face-lift from two of Boston's hottest designers. (The other 15 rooms are now "economy" rooms whose rates dip as low as $79.) On the downside, rooms are dorm-room small; the bathrooms are minuscule, and the in-window air conditioners can be noisy. But if money is an object, this hotel is a contender. ■ TIP➜ **Try to snag a room whose number ends in 08, as these are sun-lighted corner rooms with views of the Back Bay.** Fritz, a popular sports bar, moonlights as a brunch spot on weekends. The inn is a lively scene during June's Gay Pride celebrations. **Pros:** can't beat the price, friendly staff, deluxe rooms are stylish. **Cons:** parking is tough in this area and expensive, rooms can be noisy, expect more hostel than hotel in economy rooms. ⊠*26 Chandler St., South End* ☎*617/482–3450 or 800/842–3450* ⊕*www.chandlerinn. com* ⬅*55 rooms* ⚭*In-room: Wi-Fi. In-hotel: Restaurant, bar, public Wi-Fi, some pets allowed* ▤*AE, D, DC, MC, V* Ⓣ*Back Bay.*

$$–$$$$ 🏨 **Clarendon Square Inn.** Tucked into a quiet South End neighborhood, ★ this hip property is popular with travelers who appreciate the intimacy of a B&B and the style and sophistication of an upscale hotel. A massive renovation blended original 1860 Victorian touches, including hardwood floors, marble fireplaces, and decorative moldings, with modern art and up-to-date amenities. All rooms have queen-size beds and baths with limestone floors, tile walls, and whirlpools or two-person showers; some even have skylights. The fifth floor has a roof deck and hot tub with a view of the Boston skyline. **Pros:** stylish decor, more boutique than B&B. **Cons:** only three rooms means reservations are often tough to come by; families or party-hearty visitors may find it too refined, once-free parking now costs $25. ⊠*198 W. Brookline St., South End* ☎*617/536–2229* ⊕*www.clarendonsquare.com* ⬅*3 rooms* ⚭*In-room: DVD, Wi-Fi. In-hotel: No elevator, public Wi-Fi, parking (fee)* ▤*AE, D, MC, V* ⦿|*CP* Ⓣ*Back Bay/South End.*

$$–$$$ 🏨 **Encore.** What happens when talented architect Reinhold Mahler and creative set designer David Miller pool their energies and talents? You get this stylish, sophisticated converted 19th-century town house, within easy walking distance to trendy South End shops and restaurants, and the Prudential Center. Sun-filled rooms, each named after a famous playwright (Sondheim, Albee, Bernstein), are spacious and spotless, decked out with modern Italian furnishings, contemporary rugs, brushed-steel and chrome touches, and brick accent walls. The Albee room has a private deck (the playwright has stayed in the room); all rooms have ultramodern baths with glossy tiles, steel sinks and deluxe amenities. All this for a value-packed price. **Pros:** trendy South End location, high-end amenities, lush linens, David and Reinhold are gracious hosts. **Cons:** small breakfast nook; two-night minimum on weekends in season, you'll haul luggage up two or three flights of stairs. ⊠*116 W. Newton St., South End* ☎*617/247–3425* ⊕*www.encorebandb. com* ⌨*3 rooms* &*In-room: DVD, Wi-Fi. In-hotel: No elevator, public Wi-Fi, parking (fee), children under age 10 are discouraged* ⊟*AE, D, DC, MC, V* ⦿*CP* ⓣ*Back Bay.*

BOSTON OUTSKIRTS

BRIGHTON

$$$ ⊡**Best Western Terrace Inn.** In a residential neighborhood between Boston University and Boston College, on the line that divides Boston from Brookline, this motel is well priced, if unremarkable. Thanks to a recent renovation, guest rooms are spiffed up in a modern taupe palette. All rooms have refrigerators and microwave ovens; suites have kitchenettes. There's a Whole Foods supermarket just a block away. The T is nearby but the ride to downtown Boston and major attractions can take up to an hour due to traffic. **Pros:** economical option for parents visiting BU or BC students, free parking. **Cons:** slow T ride to downtown. ⊠*1650 Commonwealth Ave., Brighton* ☎*617/566–6260 or 866/764–3603* ⊕*www.bostonbw.com* ⌨*68 rooms, 6 suites* &*In-room: Kitchen (some), refrigerator, Wi-Fi. In-hotel: No elevator, public Wi-Fi, parking (no fee)* ⊟*AE, D, DC, MC, V* ⦿*CP* ⓣ*Washington St.*

BROOKLINE

$$ ⊡**Bertram Inn.** If you prefer quiet and old-fashioned, you'll feel right at home in this historic, antiques-laden inn, within walking distance to lively Cleveland Circle. Built in 1907 as a wedding present for a wealthy Boston merchant's daughter, the Victorian-style building retains some original elements, like wood floors, paneled walls, and marble fireplaces. Each room is unique; one has hummingbird wallpaper, another a high canopy bed with steps. The room off the large living room is a favorite, with a four-poster bed, Oriental rug, cherry paneling, and working fireplace. Mix and match your favorite features. Some rooms have ultradeluxe (and superexpensive) Duxiana mattresses; some have workstations. **Pros:** fresh fruit, pastries, snacks, and drinks are available all day; large living room with fireplace and leather couches and porch with wicker cushioned rockers are nice places to relax. **Cons:** dust balls in the corners and ashes in the fireplaces, it's a walk and a T ride to downtown Boston. ⊠*92 Sewall Ave., Brookline* ☎*617/566–2234 or 800/295–3822* ⊕*www.bertraminn.com* ⌨*14 rooms* &*In-room: DVD, Ethernet, Wi-Fi. In-hotel: No elevator, public Wi-Fi, parking (fee), some pets allowed, no kids under 7* ⊟*AE, D, DC, MC, V* ⦿*BP* ⓣ*St. Paul St.*

$$$ ⊡**Brookline Courtyard by Marriott.** If you enjoy the anonymity and predictability of a chain hotel and don't mind an outside of Boston location,

this is a decent choice. The hotel is popular with families of students at nearby colleges—there are about a dozen schools within 5 mi of here, including Boston University and Boston College—who like the fact that they can treat the kids to dinner at one of several funky Coolidge Corner eateries, then unwind in the indoor pool and hot tub or hit the small gym. The T is right outside the door, as are 15 or so restaurants. (An on-site eatery is open for breakfast only.) And in the Stuff You Won't Find Everywhere Department: rooms with Sabbath locks on the door for Jewish guests. This property is also more child-friendly than some; ask for the two-room suite or one of the seven "extended king" rooms. **Pros:** indoor pool, close to T station, 1 mi from Fenway Park, roomy bathrooms. **Cons:** staff can be indifferent. ✉ *40 Webster St., Brookline* ☎ *617/734–1393 or 866/296–2296* ⊕ *www.marriott.com/ bosbl* ⇆ *188 rooms* ⚹ *In-room: Ethernet, Wi-Fi. In-hotel: Restaurant, pool, gym, laundry facilities, public Internet, public Wi-Fi, parking (fee)* ▤ *AE, D, DC, MC, V* Ⓣ *Beacon St.*

$$–$$$ ▦ **Inn at Longwood Medical.** Within walking distance of Fenway Park and the Museum of Fine Arts, this modern Best Western affiliate is also near six hospitals. Many hotel guests are patients or relatives of patients (there's a discounted medical rate, even on the busiest weekends). In summer expect baseball fans to crowd the halls and lobby. Rooms are Best Western cookie-cutter, but nicely appointed with desks and updated linens and bed coverings. **Pros:** friendly, helpful staff, medical rate packages, attached to Longwood Galleria Mall and food court, museum package deals. **Cons:** many guests are here for medical treatments or visiting family members in nearby hospitals so the vibe can be a tad subdued. ✉ *342 Longwood Ave., Brookline* ☎ *617/731–4700 or 800/468–2378* ⊕ *www.innatlongwood.com* ⇆ *140 rooms, 15 suites* ⚹ *In-room: Kitchen (some), Wi-Fi. In-hotel: Restaurant, room service, bar, laundry service, public Internet, public Wi-Fi, parking (fee)* ▤ *AE, D, DC, MC, V* Ⓣ *Longwood.*

DORCHESTER

$$–$$$ ▦ **Courtyard by Marriott South Boston.** Tucked behind the Fortress, a behemoth storage facility, this property is a higher-end option to the neighboring Holiday Inn Express (⇨ *below*). What this hotel has going for it will hit you in the face, figuratively speaking, as soon as you enter. Standing in front of the crescent-shape cherry reception desk (topped by a big flat-screen TV), you can easily take it all in. There's the 24-hour grocery store, the business center (with a neat two-sided fireplace), the lobby lounge, and the breakfast bar, all done up in coral and green, with leather chairs and cherry pillars. Guest rooms are pleasant enough, with two queen beds in a standard room. It's all brighter than the drab surroundings. The T station is two blocks away, and shuttles ($5 one way) will get you to Boston Medical Center, UMass Boston, the John Hancock building, the BCEC, and the Andrews Square T-station. Fun feature: the Beantown Trolley shows up regularly, especially in season; join 'em for a day of sightseeing 'round town. **Pros:** free parking, airport shuttle, family-friendly with weekend package deals. **Cons:** not much going on in this area, small pool. ✉ *63R Boston St., Dorchester*

☎617/436–8200 or 800/642–0303 ⊕www.marriott.com/bosso ⇱161
rooms, 5 suites ♿In-room: Refrigerator, Ethernet, Wi-Fi. In-hotel: Bar,
pool, gym, laundry service, public Internet, airport shuttle, parking (no
fee) ▤AE, D, DC, MC, V ⼌CP ⓉAndrews Sq.

$ ⊡**Holiday Inn Express.** Just off the Southeast Expressway, this may be
a convenient option if you're in town for business and don't need the
ambience (or price tag) of downtown digs. Lower floors overlook a
car wash and Dorchester's triple-deckers, but sixth-floor suites have
views of the Boston skyline. Guest rooms are decorated in navy and
taupe with Danish maple furnishings and cool chrome lamps. It's a five-
minute walk to public transportation into the city; shuttles to the airport, BCEC, Black Falcon Pier, and Andrews Square T-stop are $5 each
way. **Pros:** price is right, lobby is comfy place to hang out, free breakfast (and cookies anytime). **Cons:** some rooms have crummy industrial
views, not the best area in town, have to reserve the shuttle to Downtown or walk to the T. ✉69 Boston St., Dorchester ☎617/288–3030
or 800/315–2621 ⊕www.hiexperience.com/boston ⇱112 rooms, 6
suites ♿In-room: Refrigerator, Ethernet, Wi-Fi. In-hotel: Gym, laundry
service, concierge, executive floor, public Internet, airport shuttle, parking (no fee) ▤AE, D, DC, MC, V ⼌CP ⓉAndrews Sq.

LOGAN AIRPORT (EAST BOSTON)

$$–$$$ ⊡**Hilton Boston Logan Airport.** Quiet rooms, competitive prices, and an
on-airport location make this modern Hilton a popular choice with
in-and-out visitors to Boston. There's a skywalk to terminals A and
E and a free shuttle bus to the airport. Rooms have been recently
updated with granite countertops in the baths and desks with ergo-
nomic chairs. There's an unremarkable restaurant, Berkshires, and a
casual, publike eatery on the premises, and a health club with a steam
room. **Pros:** easy access to Logan Airport, competitive prices. **Cons:**
extras like Internet access and parking can add up, skimpy Continental
breakfast. ✉1 Hotel Dr., East Boston ☎617/568–6700 ⊕www.hilton
familyboston.com ⇱595 rooms, 5 suites ♿In-room: Refrigerator,
Ethernet, Wi-Fi. In-hotel: Restaurant, room service, bar, pool, gym,
executive floor, public Internet, public Wi-Fi, parking (fee) ▤AE, D,
DC, MC, V ⓉSilver Line.

$$$–$$$$ ⊡**Hyatt Harborside at Boston Logan International Airport.** A 15-story glass
structure punctuates this luxury hotel, on a point of land separating
the inner and outer sections of Boston Harbor. Half of the rooms have
sweeping views of either the city skyline or the ocean; the others over-
look planes taking off and landing at the airport. The Hyatt operates
its own 24-hour shuttle to all Logan Airport terminals and the airport
T stop. Rooms, all decorated in soothing taupes and beiges, are sound-
proof. **Pros:** convenient base for early flights out of Boston, pool area
has skyline views, competent, can-do staff. **Cons:** overpriced restaurant
(skip it), airport shuttle service can be frustratingly slow. ✉101 Har-
borside Dr., East Boston ☎617/568–1234 or 800/233–1234 ⊕www.
harborside.hyatt.com ⇱273 rooms, 6 suites ♿In-room: Ethernet,
Wi-Fi (fee). In-hotel: Restaurant, room service, bar, pool, gym, laundry

service, concierge, public Wi-Fi, airport shuttle, parking (fee) ▭*AE, D, DC, MC, V* ⊤*Airport.*

CAMBRIDGE

$$-$$$ 🛏 **A Cambridge House Bed & Breakfast.** A gracious 1892 Greek Revival home listed on the National Register of Historic Places, A Cambridge House has richly carved cherry paneling, a grand fireplace, elegant Victorian antiques, and polished wood floors overlaid with Oriental rugs. One of the antiques-filled guest rooms has fabric-covered walls, and many have four-poster canopy beds. Rooms in the adjacent carriage house are smaller, but all have working fireplaces. Harvard Square isn't terribly close, but public transportation is available nearby. The owner also has a town house with 18 hotel-style, prosaic rooms next door; be sure you know what you're getting when you book the room. **Pros:** the pretty public sitting areas with fireplaces are cozy places to relax, free parking, complimentary coffee, tea, and hot chocolate served all day. **Cons:** not a lot happening in the area, the removed-from-it-all setting is not for everyone. ✉*2218 Massachusetts Ave., Cambridge* ☎*617/491–6300 or 800/232–9989* ⊕*www.acambridgehouse.com* ➥*15 rooms* ♨*In-room: Wi-Fi. In-hotel: No elevator, public Wi-Fi, parking (no fee)* ▭*AE, MC, V* ⦿❘*CP* ⊤*Davis Sq.*

$$$-$$$$ 🛏 **Boston Marriott Cambridge.** Businesspeople and vacationing families like the sleek, modern look and efficiency of this 26-story, high-rise hotel in Kendall Square, Cambridge's high-tech district, just steps from the subway and MIT. It's also a prime location for viewing July 4 fireworks. Rooms, recently redone, are decorated in the Marriott chain's signature greens, with floral spreads and drapes. A room on one of the two concierge floors nets you complimentary breakfast, hors d'oeuvres, and desserts in the lounge. **Pros:** top-floor rooms have stunning skyline and river views, luxe bed linens, family-friendly, decent cost-saving packages on weekends. **Cons:** high-rise chain doesn't have a lot of charm, tiny pool. ✉*2 Cambridge Center, Cambridge* ☎*617/494–6600 or 800/228–9290* ⊕*www.marriotthotels.com/boscb* ➥*433 rooms, 11 suites* ♨*In-room: Ethernet, Wi-Fi. In-hotel: 2 restaurants, room service, bar, pool, gym, laundry service, concierge, executive floor, public Wi-Fi, parking (fee)* ▭*AE, D, DC, MC, V* ⊤*Kendall/MIT.*

$$$$ 🛏 **Charles Hotel.** Gracious service, top-notch amenities, and a great location on Harvard Square keep this first-class hotel in high demand. The
Fodor's Choice
★ New England Shaker interior is contemporary yet homey; antique quilts and art by nationally recognized artists hang throughout. Relax in the lobby library, chock-full of titles, some autographed by authors who frequent the hotel. Also sign up for a guided art tour of the hotel or pick up a self-guided map. Guest rooms come with lots of nice touches, like terry robes, handcrafted quilts, flat-screen TVs (plus LCD-mirror TVs in the bathroom), and Bose radios. For a partial river or skyline view, ask for something above the seventh floor. Both of the hotel's restaurants—Rialto and Henrietta's Table—are excellent. ■ TIP➔ **For the best rate, call the hotel directly. Pros:** your wish is their command, on-site spa, health club, premier jazz club, and two of the area's top

KEY

Ⓣ Subway station

Where to Stay in Cambridge

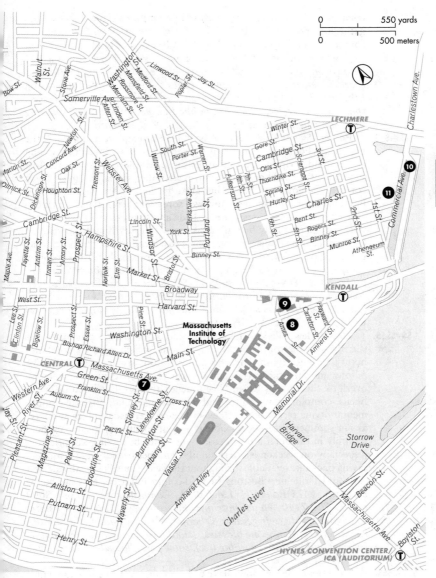

4

restaurants; Harvard Square is close by; outdoor skating rink is a fun gathering spot for families during the winter months. **Cons:** luxury comes with a price, great for visiting Cambridge sites but less convenient to downtown Boston (though Red Line T is two blocks away). ⊠*1 Bennett St., Cambridge* ☏*617/864–1200 or 800/882–1818* ⊕*www. charleshotel.com* ⌑*294 rooms, 45 suites* ⌂*In-room: Safe, refrigerator, Ethernet, Wi-Fi. In-hotel: 2 restaurants, room service, bars, pool, gym, spa, laundry service, concierge, public Internet, public Wi-Fi, parking (fee), some pets allowed* ⊟*AE, DC, MC, V* Ⓣ*Harvard.*

$$–$$$ 🏨**Harvard Square Hotel.** Want to be in Harvard Square and not pay the big bucks? For basic lodgings in a great location, you won't go wrong at this nondescript property that feels more dormitory than hotel. Just steps from the neighborhood's many restaurants, shops, and lively street corners, the hotel has simple but clean rooms, with refrigerators and Internet access. Bathrooms—always a sore point here—have been modernized, and guest rooms got new beds and flat-screen TVs. The desk clerks are particularly helpful, assisting with everything from sending faxes to securing dinner reservations. **Pros:** location can't be beat, some windows open for fresh air. **Cons:** baths are small; Wi-Fi, in-lobby computer use, and parking cost extra. ⊠*110 Mt. Auburn St., Cambridge* ☏*617/864–5200 or 800/458–5886* ⊕*www.harvardsquarehotel. com* ⌑*73 rooms* ⌂*In-room: Refrigerator, Ethernet, Wi-Fi. In-hotel: Laundry service, concierge, public Internet, public Wi-Fi, parking (fee)* ⊟*AE, D, DC, MC, V* Ⓣ*Harvard.*

$$–$$$$ 🏨**Hotel Marlowe.** Vivid stripes, swirls, and other patterns punctuate this
★   slightly over-the-top, lively boutique hotel, which expertly combines luxury, unique stylish flair, and unpretentious service. Leopard-print pillows and fake-fur throws add whimsy to the spacious rooms; many overlook the Charles River. Nice touches abound, like luscious Frette linens, complimentary coffee and tea each morning, popular complimentary wine receptions each evening, and free use of bikes and kayaks in summer. Free book readings and other literary events are held monthly in the hotel lobby. **Pros:** luxury with below-market price tag (especially on weekends), very family- and pet-friendly, great money-saving packages available throughout the year. **Cons:** it's a cab ride or a walk and T ride into Boston; the wild colors and decor may not be for everyone. ⊠*25 Edwin H. Land Blvd., Cambridge* ☏*617/868–8000 or 800/825–7140* ⊕*www.hotelmarlowe.com* ⌑*222 rooms, 14 suites* ⌂*In-room: Safe, refrigerator, Ethernet, Wi-Fi. In-hotel: Restaurant, room service, bar, gym, bicycles, laundry service, concierge, public Internet, public Wi-Fi, parking (fee), some pets allowed* ⊟*AE, D, DC, MC, V* Ⓣ*Lechmere.*

$$$–$$$$ 🏨**Inn at Harvard.** You don't have to be an alumnus to enjoy the handsome, hushed elegance of this hotel, which borders Harvard Yard and has a Georgian-style brick exterior that mirrors many of those on campus. Bathrooms have been spiffed up with new fixtures, tubs, and showers. Guest rooms were also updated. The skylight atrium, used as a lobby, restaurant, and meeting space, is studded with sculptures and fine woodwork, and a comfy, albeit stuffy, hangout for Harvard executives and visiting parents and profs. Rooms have classic furnishings, with

A+ AMENITIES

Beacon Hill Hotel & Bistro. Stroll the shops on Charles Street, wander the Public Garden, and come back to the hotel for a drink on the rooftop deck.

Boston Harbor Hotel. You can park your yacht at the hotel's private marina. There's also a water taxi service.

Charles Hotel. The hotel's lending library is stuffed with titles, many autographed by authors who frequent the hotel. Art experts conduct tours of the hotel's extensive art collection.

The Colonnade. Live concerts are held at the RTP (rooftop pool),

with food, drinks, and sweeping city views.

Fairmont Copley Plaza. Guests of culturally themed suites receive benefits like backstage passes to the Boston Symphony Orchestra.

Ritz-Carlton Boston Common. The Sports Club/LA, on property, offers 100,000 square feet of the latest fitness equipment. The Ritz has a bath butler who will set up a customized aromatherapy bath (think rose petals).

Royal Sonesta. The family-friendly pool has river and city views, and the New England Science Museum is right next door.

understated black, brown, and neutral fabric and wall colors. Oversize windows frame views of Harvard Square or Harvard Yard and help give rooms a bright, cheerful feel. **Pros:** great location in midst of bustling Cambridge/Harvard University, rooms all have flat-screen TVs. **Cons:** smallish rooms and bathrooms, some say not worth the price. ⊠*1201 Massachusetts Ave., Cambridge* ☎*617/491–2222 or 800/458–5886* ⊕*www.theinnatharvard.com* ⇋*109 rooms, 4 suites* ⚐*In-room: Wi-Fi (fee). In-hotel: Restaurant, room service, gym, laundry service, concierge, public Internet, public Wi-Fi, parking (fee)* ▭*AE, D, DC, MC, V* ⓣ*Harvard.*

$–$$$ 🖼️**Irving House.** Tucked away on a residential street three blocks from Harvard Square, this four-story gray clapboard B&B is a bargain. It has two small porches, hardwood floors, and Oriental carpets, making it homier than a hotel; there's a real sense of conviviality among guests, who are mostly European visitors and visiting parents and profs. Rooms are small but super-clean. They're being refurbished room by room, with new paint and furnishings; ask for one of the redone rooms when you book. The limited off-street parking is a real coup in car-clogged Cambridge. **Pros:** location and price, large downstairs sitting area has microwave, ice, and guest refrigerator; coffee, tea, and pastries are available until 10 PM. **Cons:** parking spaces are first-come, first served; small baths, some with only showers; rooms with a shared bath have no TV. ⊠*24 Irving St., Cambridge* ☎*617/547–4600 or 877/547–4600* ⊕*www.cambridgeinns.com/irving* ⇋*44 rooms, 29 with bath* ⚐*In-room: No TV (some), Wi-Fi. In-hotel: No elevator, laundry facilities, concierge, public Internet, public Wi-Fi, parking (no fee)* ▭*AE, D, MC, V* ⫶⊙⫶*CP* ⓣ*Harvard.*

$$$ ⬛Kendall Hotel. You might expect a hotel in a techno-zone such as Kendall Square to be all stainless steel and chrome, but this one is quite homey and ultrafriendly. In the former home of Engine House 7, it is stuffed with firehouse memorabilia. Owner Charlotte Forsythe loves collectibles, so an antique Chinese checkerboard and a ceramic Dalmatian add to the whimsical mix. Rooms are done up in Easter-egg hues. A seven-story addition includes an enclosed rooftop lounge, eight deluxe rooms, and four suites with kitchens, offering lots of space for families or anyone looking for a lot of room and kitchen facilities. Nice touch: the hotel hosts a wine hour from 5 to 6 PM nightly on the seventh floor. **Pros:** accommodating staff make guests feel right at home; hot buffet breakfast is included; quiet rooms. **Cons:** may be too tchotchke-filled for some tastes. ⊠*350 Main St., Cambridge* ☎*617/577–1300 or 866/566–1300* ⊕*www.kendallhotel.com* ⬦*73 room, 4 suites* ⬥*In-room: Ethernet, Wi-Fi. In-hotel: Restaurant, bar, laundry service, public Internet, public Wi-Fi, parking (fee)* ▤*AE, D, DC, MC, V* ❴◐❵*BP* Ⓣ*Kendall/MIT.*

$$$–$$$$ ⬛Le Meridien Cambridge. Witty and stylish, without going overboard,
★   this modern hotel (formerly the Hotel at MIT) riffs on its high-tech Cambridge location. Lobby art on loan from MIT is interactive and high tech, and guests get free access to the MIT museum. Rooms, recently refurbished, are Euro-style residential, with platform beds, flat-screen TVs, and ergonomically designed furniture. In the lobby and the large, open-kitchen restaurant, cool metal highlights are mixed with burnished maple, redwood, and oak. It's a hub for techie business travelers and a real bargain for weekend vacationers. **Pros:** tech-savvy rooms and surroundings, fitness center is open 24 hours, great off-season, Internet rates. **Cons:** a bit out of the way, with a 10-minute or so walk to the T. ⊠*20 Sidney St., Cambridge* ☎*617/577–0200 or 800/222–8733* ⊕*www.lemeridien.com/cambridge* ⬦*196 rooms, 14 suites* ⬥*In-room: Safe, Ethernet, Wi-Fi. In-hotel: Restaurant, room service, bar, gym, laundry service, concierge, public Internet, public Wi-Fi, parking (fee)* ▤*AE, D, DC, MC, V* Ⓣ*Central, Kendall/MIT.*

$$–$$$ ⬛Royal Sonesta Hotel. An impressive collection of modern art, displayed
Fodor'sChoice   throughout the hotel, sleek, updated rooms, and a friendly, professional
★   staff make this Cambridge riverfront property a bit of a surprise. Its location next to the Museum of Science and Galleria shopping center and an attractive indoor–outdoor pool add to its appeal. Some rooms have superb views of Beacon Hill and the Boston skyline. Guest rooms are done in neutral earth tones, with modern amenities such as flat-screen TVs, gaming consoles, Wi-Fi, and CD clock radios. The hotel has family suites and great packages. **Pros:** kids feel welcome here, easy to drive to and parking is on-site (fee), nice pool, certified green hotel. **Cons:** a bit sterile. ⊠*40 Edwin Land Blvd., off Memorial Dr., Cambridge* ☎*617/806–4200 or 800/766–3782* ⊕*www.sonesta.com/boston* ⬦*379 rooms, 21 suites* ⬥*In-room: Safe, refrigerator, Ethernet, Wi-Fi. In-hotel: 2 restaurants, room service, bars, pool, gym, bicycles, laundry service, concierge, public Internet, public Wi-Fi, parking (fee)* ▤*AE, D, DC, MC, V* Ⓣ*Lechmere.*

$$$–$$$$ □ **Sheraton Commander.** The beloved, aging Harvard Square Hotel, with its signature neon light, finally got a face-lift. Most rooms and public areas have been updated with classic furnishings and handsome, jewel colors. It's got great bones and a fab location, minutes from Harvard Square. History buffs will appreciate the lovely arches found throughout the building and elegant touches, such as the bi-level ballroom, with a carved ceiling and gilt mirrors. Guest rooms are comfortably modern, though, with Internet access (free on Club level and in suites) and cushy leather lounge chairs. ■ **TIP→ If you book a standard room, don't pay for Internet access; log on for free at the workstation in the lobby. Pros:** historical landmark with period architecture and detailing; helpful, knowledgeable staff. **Cons:** small bathrooms; some rooms have views of the parking lot. ⊠ *16 Garden St., Cambridge* ☎ *617/547–4800* ⊕ *www. starwoodhotels.com* ⇆ *175 rooms, 24 suites* ♿ *In-room: Ethernet. In-hotel: Restaurant, room service, bar, gym, laundry service, concierge, executive floor, public Internet, public Wi-Fi, parking (fee)* ▭ *AE, D, DC, MC, V* Ⓣ *Harvard.*

Nightlife and the Arts

WORD OF MOUTH

"There are $9 rush tickets available for concerts to the Boston Symphony, a world-class orchestra. Tickets are available at 5pm for Tuesday and Thursday evening concerts and 10am for Friday's matinee concerts."

—yk

Updated
by Bethany
Cassin
Beckerlegge

Boston's classic cultural attractions include the Museum of Fine Arts, the Boston Symphony Orchestra and Pops, and the Isabella Stewart Gardner Museum. Newcomers such as the Institute for Contemporary Art and the revitalized Children's Museum are also a big draw. For those enjoying live shows, the compact Theater District offers traveling Broadway shows, national comedy and music acts, and previews of new plays soon headed to New York.

For those preferring a more casual, less expensive night out, Boston provides plenty of alternatives. Indie rock and jazz clubs abound, dance clubs and lounges cater to all types of night owls, and countless bars blaring local games can be found in any neighborhood. Take in a late-night bite at Miel in the Intercontinental Hotel, scan the crowd at Felt for both local and visiting celebrities, or check out the revitalized club scene on Lansdowne Street. Whether it's cheering on the Sox, Celtics, or Pats at a watering hole, rocking out at an underground club, or chilling out at an elegant lounge, Boston has cultural amusements for all types.

NIGHTLIFE

First and foremost, Boston is a Cinderella city. With public transportation shutting down each night between midnight and 1 AM, most nightspots follow accordingly, with last call typically around 2 AM. While true night owls may be disappointed at the meager late-night options, there are plenty of possibilities for those open to stepping out on the earlier side. The martini crowd may want to stroll Newbury and Boylston streets in the Back Bay, selecting from the neighborhood's swank restaurants, lounges, and clubs. Coffee- and tea-drinkers can find numerous cafés in Cambridge and Somerville, particularly Harvard and Davis squares. And beer swillers—well, there's pretty much an option on every corner. If you're having trouble finding a place to down a pint, you must have wandered out of Boston. For dancing, Lansdowne Street near Fenway Park has a mix of student-oriented clubs, sports bars, techno clubs, and a bar where dueling pianists take requests from the crowd at a fever pitch. There's also a thriving "lounge" scene in Downtown's coolest hybrid bar-restaurant-clubs, providing a mellower, more-mature alternative to the student-focused club scene. Tourists crowd Faneuil Hall for its pubs, comedy club, and dance spots. The South and North ends, as well as Cambridge and Somerville, cater to the "dinner-and-drinks" set, while those seeking great rock clubs should look no further than Allston, Jamaica Plain, and Cambridge.

KNOW-HOW

GETTING INFORMED

The best source of arts and nightlife information is the *Boston Globe's* "Sidekick" section, available Monday through Saturday in the paper and on www.boston.com/ae/sidekick. Also worth checking are the Thursday "Calendar" section of the *Boston Globe;* the Friday "Scene" section of the *Boston Herald;* the free entertainment guide *Stuff@Night,* which is available in drop boxes around town; and the listings in the *Boston Phoenix,* a free weekly that comes out on Thursday, and The *Improper Bostonian,* published biweekly. The Friday and Sunday "Arts" sections in the *Boston Globe* and the Saturday and Sunday "Arts" sections in the *Boston Herald* also contain recommendations for the week's top events. *Boston* magazine's arts section gives a more-selective, but less-detailed, overview. The listings at www.thephoenix. com, www.weeklydig.com, and www. boston.com (a Web site affiliated with the *Boston Globe)* provide up-to-the-minute information online. Comprehensive theater listings can be found at www.theatermirror.com.

GETTING TICKETS

Boston's supporters of the arts are an avid group; tickets often sell out well in advance, particularly for the increasing number of shows making pre-Broadway stops. Buy tickets when you make your hotel reservations if possible. Most theaters take telephone orders and charge them to a major credit card, generally with a small service fee.

BosTix is a full-price Ticketmaster outlet that sells half-price tickets for same-day performances. The "menu board" in front of the booth (corner of Boylston and Dartmouth streets)

and on the Web site (⊕www. bostix.com) announces the available events. Only cash and traveler's checks are accepted. On Friday, Saturday, or Sunday show up at least a half hour early. There's a booth in Quincy Market (◷10–6 Tuesday through Saturday and 11–4 on Sunday) and a booth in Copley Square (◷10–6 Monday through Saturday and 11–4 on Sunday).

Broadway Across America— Boston (☎*866/523–7469* ⊕*www. broadwayacrossamerica.com*) brings Broadway shows to Boston and serves as a pre–New York testing ground for Broadway shows. Productions usually take place at the Colonial and Wilbur theaters, the Charles Playhouse, and the Opera House.

Live Nation/NEXT Ticketing (☎*877/598–8497* ⊕*www.live nation.com*), a Boston-based outlet, handles tickets for shows at the Orpheum Theatre, Paradise Rock Club, and other nightclubs. All transactions are conducted online, but technical assistance is available Monday through Saturday 10–5.

Ticketmaster (☎*617/931–2000 or 617/931–2787* ⊕*www.ticketmaster. com*) allows phone charges, weekdays 9 AM–10 PM and weekends 9–8, with no refunds or exchanges. It also has outlets in local stores; call for locations.

5

THE SKINNY ON . . .

WHAT'S PLAYING

Check the listings in a local weekly such as *The Improper Bostonian* or *The Weekly Dig.*

COVERS

Cover charges for local acts and club bands generally run $5–$15; big-name acts can be double that. Dance clubs usually charge a cover of $5–$10.

LAST CALL

Because Boston retains some vestiges of its puritanical "blue laws," the only places open after the official 2 AM closing time for bars and clubs are a few restaurants in Chinatown (at some you can ask for "cold tea" and still get a beer); a few

all-night diners, which won't serve alcohol; and Miel, a 24-hour brasserie at the InterContinental Hotel. Bars may also close up shop early if business is slow or the weather is bad. Blue laws also prohibit bars from offering happy-hour drink specials, although happy-hour food specials abound.

SMOKING

Boston and Cambridge's tough anti-cigarette laws ban smoking in all bars and restaurants.

PAYING

Nearly all nightlife spots accept major credit cards; cash-only places are noted.

BARS

BOSTON
ALLSTON

The **Sports Depot** has televisions visible from any vantage point, and if there's a game on, you'll be able to see it here. The menu includes a wide variety of greasy favorites, from burgers and wings to chili and fries, quesadillas and tacos to pizza and steak tips. ⊠*353 Cambridge St., Allston* ☎*617/783–2300* ⊕*www.sportsdepotboston.com* Ⓣ*Harvard.*

Sunset Grill & Tap is a bit off the beaten path and looks at first glance like any other unpretentious neighborhood hangout. But venture inside and choose from more than 500 varieties of beer, 112 of which are on tap. Forget about pale domestic brews; try something unpronounceable from a faraway country—and if you're really thirsty, get a yard of it. ⊠*130 Brighton Ave., Allston* ☎*617/254–1331* ⊕*www.allstonsfinest. com* Ⓣ*Harvard.*

BACK BAY/BEACON HILL

★ **The Alley,** just off Boston Common, packs several watering holes onto one cozy street for those wanting a late night without having to crisscross the city. With a mechanical bull and loud music, the **Liquor Store** (⊠*25 Boylston Pl.* ☎*617/357–6800* ⊕*www.liquorstoreboston.com*) is a place to check your inhibitions at the door. **Sweetwater Café** (⊠*3 Boylston Pl.* ☎*617/351–2515* ⊕*www.sweetwatercafeboston.com*) has a booming sound system and plenty of drink options. ⊠*Boylston Pl. off Boylston St., Theater District* Ⓣ*Boylston.*

Bukowski Tavern is a narrow barroom with a literary flair and more than 100 beers on the menu. The burgers are cheap (if you're daring, try the peanut-butter burger), the draught selection is original, and the sound track is loud and very cool. ⊠ *50 Dalton St., Back Bay* ☎ *617/437–9999* ▤ *No credit cards* Ⓣ *Hynes/ICA.*

The Cactus Club is one of the few places in Boston that makes a decent margarita. In summer months, the restaurant's street-side outdoor patio is popular for kicking back, sipping frozen drinks, and watching the stylish Back Bay crowds pass by. ⊠ *939 Boylston St., Back Bay* ☎ *617/236–0200* ⊕ *www.best margaritas.com* Ⓣ *Hynes/ICA.*

Champions Sports Bar welcomes sports fans—the more rabid, the better. And with more than 30 televisions, you'll be sure to get a good view. Visiting-team fans may be welcome, but expect to be drowned out by cheers for the home team. ⊠ *Boston Copley Marriott, Copley Place Mall, 110 Huntington Ave., Back Bay* ☎ *617/279–6996* ⊕ *www.championsboston.com* Ⓣ *Prudential Center.*

Cheers, formerly known as the Bull & Finch Pub, was dismantled in England, shipped to Boston, and reassembled here. Though it was the inspiration for the TV series *Cheers,* it doesn't look anything like the bar in the show. Addressing that complaint, however, a branch in Faneuil Hall that opened in 2001 is an exact reproduction of the TV set. ⊠ *Hampshire House, 84 Beacon St., Beacon Hill* ☎ *617/227–9605* ⊕ *www.cheersboston.com* Ⓣ *Park St., Arlington, Charles/MGH.*

Fodor's Choice ★ **Gypsy Bar** is the place to go if you're on the prowl. Expect scantily clad, well-imbibed club cats here. It's a great option for singles who want to dance the night away. ⊠ *116 Boylston St., Theater District* ☎ *617/482–7799* ⊕ *www.gypsybarboston.com* Ⓣ *Boylston.*

Jacque's Cabaret, an institution for more than 60 years, is anything but traditional. Nightly female-impersonator shows draw everyone from drag queens to bachelorette parties to watch while swilling cocktails from paper cups. Downstairs, Jacque's Underground features indie rock bands and cabaret acts on Friday and Saturday. Because of a long-running licensing dispute, the whole carnival shuts down nightly at midnight. ⊠ *79 Broadway, Theater District* ☎ *617/426–8902* ⊕ *www. jacquescabaret.com* ▤ *No credit cards* Ⓣ *Arlington.*

Oak Bar has an elegant backdrop of whirring ceiling fans, marble, and (of course) oak that evokes cricket matches under the Bombay sun and duels fought over illicit love affairs. The old-world atmosphere is perfect for perusing a generous menu of signature martinis, single malts, and desserts. ⊠ *Fairmont Copley Plaza hotel, 138 St. James Ave., Back Bay* ☎ *617/267–5300* ⊕ *www.fairmont.com/copleyplaza/* Ⓣ *Copley.*

THE REAL CHEERS

TV's *Cheers* may have ended in 1993, but that doesn't stop die-hard fans from paying their respects at the "real" Cheers bar on Beacon Street (or its new second location in Faneuil Hall). So what if there's no Norm or Cliff around, not everyone knows your name, or the place doesn't look quite the same as the TV version? You can find your own kind of notoriety here by devouring the double-decker "Norm burger" and adding your name to the Hall of Fame.

5

POE @ The Rattlesnake lures in Back Bay shoppers and the post-work crowd. A few blocks off the Public Garden, the restaurant–bar has pool tables, televised sports, and (in-season) an open-air rooftop patio. ✉ *384 Boylston St., Back Bay* ☎ *617/859–8555* ⊕ *www.rattle snakebar.com* Ⓣ *Arlington.*

Saint, despite its name, draws patrons who are anything but. The spacious underground lounge consists of two rooms: an airy main space is decorated in blue and silver, with long couches to lounge on over appetizers while making eyes across the room. A more-devilish "bordello room" is all plush red velvet and tasseled light fixtures, and has private alcoves for more-intimate conversation. *90 Exeter St., Back Bay* ☎ *617/236–1134* ⊕ *www.saint nitery.com* Ⓣ *Copley.*

TOP SPORTS BARS
■ **Champions,** Back Bay
■ **The Fours,** Old West End
■ **Fritz Lounge,** South End
■ **Sports Depot,** Allston
■ **Sports Grille Boston,** Old West End

The Sevens is a laid-back alternative to the tony atmosphere of Beacon Hill. There's nothing stuffy or pretentious here, just good pints and old-fashioned mixed drinks, plus darts and the televised game of the night. ✉ *77 Charles St., Beacon Hill* ☎ *617/523–9074* Ⓣ *Charles/MGH.*

Sonsie keeps the stereo volume at a manageable level. The bar crowd, which spills through the French doors onto a sidewalk café in warm weather, is full of young, trendy, cosmopolitan types and professionals. ✉ *327 Newbury St., Back Bay* ☎ *617/351–2500* ⊕ *www.sonsieboston. com* Ⓣ *Hynes/ICA.*

Top of the Hub is a lounge with a wonderful view over the city; that and the hip jazz help to ease the sting of pricey drinks. ✉ *Prudential Tower, 800 Boylston St., 52nd fl., Back Bay* ☎ *617/536–1775* ⊕ *www. topofthehub.net* Ⓣ *Prudential Center, Hynes/ICA.*

21st Amendment, named after the amendment that ended Prohibition, is a convivial pub across from the State House that draws state legislators and lobbyists as well as neighborhood regulars. They all trade gossip (and favors) at notched wooden tables over beer and barbecue chicken salad. Or, come for lively trivia (with discounted wings) on Sunday nights. ✉ *150 Bowdoin St., Beacon Hill* ☎ *617/227–7100* ⊕ *www.21stboston. com* Ⓣ *Park St.*

CHARLESTOWN

Massachusetts' oldest watering hole is Charlestown's **Warren Tavern,** more than 200 years old and once frequented by Paul Revere. Today it caters mostly to tourists and Charlestown professionals. It's an easy stop for a pint en route to the Bunker Hill Monument or historic Navy Yard. Ask for the homemade potato chips with your ale of choice. ✉ *2 Pleasant St., Charlestown* ☎ *617/241–8142* ⊕ *www.warrentavern.com* Ⓣ *Community College.*

DOWNTOWN

Beantown Pub, right on the Freedom Trail, is the only pub in Boston where you can enjoy a Sam Adams lager while overlooking the grave of Adams himself. It's a great place to watch the game or get a snapshot of the throngs of tourists, professionals, and students going by. The menu—also available late-night—includes burgers, sandwiches, and other traditional pub fare. ✉ *100 Tremont St., Downtown* ☎ *617/426–0111* ⊕ *www.beantownpub.com* Ⓣ *Park St., Downtown Crossing.*

Felt is *the* place to see and be seen. Dress to impress; once past the velvet ropes, you may spot a celebrity here at a pool table, on the dance floor, or just enjoying a cocktail. ✉ *533 Washington St., Downtown* ☎ *617/350–5555* ⊕ *feltclubboston.com* Ⓣ *Chinatown, Downtown Crossing, Boylston, Park Street.*

The Good Life is a creative martini bar, with such exotic varieties as cucumber, strawberry-basil, and caramel macchiato. On the basement level is the Afterlife Lounge, with more than 150 frozen vodka options on the menu. ✉ *28 Kingston St., Downtown* ☎ *617/451–2622* ⊕ *www. goodlifebar.com* Ⓣ *Downtown Crossing.*

J.J. Foley's is yet another Irish pub that's worth a visit. Blue-collar workers down their Guinness pints along with neighboring Financial District suits, shoppers from Downtown Crossing take a break with a cider or ale. The atmosphere is no-frills, no-fuss. ✉ *21 Kingston St., Downtown* ☎ *617/338–7713* Ⓣ *Downtown Crossing.*

The Kinsale by day offers lunch and a pint to the business crowds of Government Center. By night, the pub comes alive with revelers from nearby Faneuil Hall. The pub was reassembled here, piece by piece, after being constructed in Ireland, and has live music several nights a week. ✉ *2 Center Plaza, Downtown* ⊕ *www.classicirish.com* ☎ *617/742–5577* Ⓣ *Government Center.*

Last Hurrah, at the Omni Parker House, might make you feel like a Brahmin, even if just for a drink or two. The historic setting and location right on the Freedom Trail make it an easy stop for those hitting the main sites Downtown. ✉ *60 School St., Downtown* ☎ *617/227–8600* ⊕ *www.omnihotels.com* Ⓣ *Downtown Crossing, Park Street.*

Limelight Stage + Studios is a karaoke bar where bold patrons can belt out their favorite tunes to the audience, and more shy types can rent a "studio" room with friends. Linger around the main room to perhaps catch a local celebrity—American Idol contestant Ayla Brown, Mayor Menino, and other familiar faces have graced the stage in the past. Expect theatrics and a lively crowd. ✉ *204 Tremont St., Downtown/Theater District* ☎ *877/557–8271* ⊕ *www.limelightboston.com* 🖃 *Main stage: $5 before 10 PM, $10 after 10 PM; private studios: $10 per person per hr* ⊗ *Thurs. 8 PM–1 AM, Fri. and Sat. 7 PM–1 AM* Ⓣ *Bolston, Park St.*

Fans of rock and roll should head to **Revolution Rock Club:** there's live music three nights per week, and DJs on the other evenings. Expect to hear alternative, classic rock, and punk on the dance floor. There are two floors for mixing and mingling. ✉ *200 High St., Downtown/*

Financial District ☎617/261–4200
⊕*www.revolutionrockbar.com*
◷ *Weekdays 11:30* AM*–2* AM*, Sat.
5* PM*–2* AM Ⓣ*Aquarium*
RumBa, in the InterContinental hotel,
highlights two distinctive spirits:
rum (more than 70 varieties) and
champagne. Vintage rums are available
for sampling; the champagne
lounge area has a more-secluded
atmosphere for quieter celebrations. ✉*510 Atlantic Ave., Downtown* ☎617/217–5152 ⊕*www.
intercontinentalboston.com/dining* Ⓣ*South Station, Aquarium.*

> **MOST HISTORIC PUBS**
>
> ▪ **Bell in Hand Tavern,** Faneuil Hall
>
> ▪ **Doyle's,** Jamaica Plain
>
> ▪ **Green Dragon Tavern,** Faneuil Hall
>
> ▪ **The Last Hurrah,** Downtown
>
> ▪ **Warren Tavern,** Charlestown

Vinalia brings a little bit of Napa Valley to Boston's Downtown Crossing, with a cool wine bar and lounge serving more than 40 vintages by
the glass; there are also wine and cheese tastings every Wednesday night.
✉*34 Summer St., Downtown* ☎617/737–1777 ⊕*www.vinaliaboston.
com* ◷ *Weekdays 11:30* AM*–2* AM*, Sat. 5* PM*–2* AM*.*

FANEUIL HALL

★ **Bell in Hand Tavern** is the country's oldest continuously operating pub.
It's on the perimeter of Faneuil Hall and has live music every night of
the week. If you're brave, you can join the Tuesday-night karaoke.
✉*45-55 Union St., Faneuil Hall* ☎617/227–2098 ⊕*www.bellinhand.
com* Ⓣ*Haymarket.*

The Black Rose is decorated with family crests, pictures of Ireland, and
portraits of the likes of Samuel Beckett, Lady Gregory, and James
Joyce—just like a Dublin pub. Its Faneuil Hall location draws as many
tourists as locals, but nightly performances by traditional Irish and
contemporary performers make it worth braving the crowds. ✉*160
State St., Faneuil Hall* ☎617/742–2286 ⊕*www.irishconnection.com/
index.php?id=41* Ⓣ*Government Center, Haymarket, State.*

Cheers in Faneuil Hall, the city's second location, was created by popular demand. The owners of the former Bull & Finch in Beacon Hill,
which was the inspiration for the show, created an exact reproduction
of the TV set, complete with Sam's Red Sox jacket and the photo of the
Indian chief behind the bar. Despite overpriced burgers and seafood,
tourists and students are frequent customers. ✉*Faneuil Hall Marketplace, Government Center* ☎617/227–0150 ⊕*www.cheersboston.com*
Ⓣ*Government Center, Haymarket.*

Green Dragon Tavern is a less-rowdy pub than its Faneuil Hall neighbors.
It has cover bands a few nights a week, regular lunch specials, and very
friendly waitstaff. ✉*11 Marshall St., Faneuil Hall* ☎617/367–0055
Ⓣ*Haymarket, Government Center.*

Hennessy's claims to be the best Irish pub in town, although it has plenty
of competition in that category, not least from its neighboring watering holes of Faneuil Hall. Expect a rowdy crowd on weekends, and
a quieter scene during the workweek. ✉*25 Union St., Faneuil Hall*
☎617/742–2121 Ⓣ*Haymarket, Government Center.*

The Hong Kong is a contender for Faneuil Hall's rowdiest bar. Packed with bachelorette parties, fraternity boys hungry for a famous Scorpion Bowl, and those ready to hit the dance floor, the Hong Kong is often a first or last stop on a bar crawl. Even if you don't plan to stay, sampling a beef teriyaki stick is worth the trip. ⊠*65 Chatham St., Faneuil Hall* ☎*617/227–2226* ⊕*www.hongkongboston.com* ⊤*Aquarium, State, Government Center.*

Jose McIntyre's, an Irish-Mexican bar, satisfies your double craving for a margarita and a Guinness— each expertly poured. The eclecticism continues with a dance floor,

> **TOP SPOTS**
>
> ■ Rock out at the **Paradise**, the **Middle East, T. T. the Bear's Place**, and **Great Scott.**
>
> ■ Toss back a pint (or two) at an authentic Irish pub such as the **Burren, Doyle's,** or the **Kinsale.**
>
> ■ Indulge your sweet tooth at **Finale** or the **Four Seasons'** dessert buffet.
>
> ■ Check out the hot salsa scene at **Ryles,** the **Havana Club, El Bembe.**

several big-screen TVs, and a pool table. ⊠*160 Milk St., Faneuil Hall* ☎*617/451–9460* ⊕*www.irishconnection.com/index.php?id=42* ⊤*Aquarium.*

Kitty O'Shea's, on the outskirts of Faneuil Hall in the Financial District, is a sister pub to the original in Dublin. The bar, the fireplace, the stained-glass windows, and even some of the staffers have been imported from the Emerald Isle, giving the impression of a dyed-in-the-wool Irish establishment. ⊠*131 State St., Downtown* ☎*617/725–0100* ⊕*www.kittyosheasboston.com* ⊤*Aquarium, State.*

The Living Room, on the outskirts of the North End, has killer martinis and tasty appetizers in an upscale setting modeled after its name—feel free to stretch out on the lounge's many elegant love seats and armchairs, or pull up a seat at the bar. On weeknights, the bar is quieter, with friends meeting for drinks or watching the game; on weekends, expect a packed house, a DJ, and dancing. ⊠*101 Atlantic Ave., Waterfront* ☎*617/723–5101* ⊕*www.thelivingroomboston.com* ⊤*Haymarket, Aquarium.*

The Purple Shamrock is a tourist favorite. Just off Faneuil Hall, the bar has live music (including karaoke some nights), standard pub grub, and a chance to mingle with your fellow travelers. Be prepared to wait in line on weekends. ⊠*1 Union St., Faneuil Hall* ☎*617/227–2060* ⊤*Haymarket, Government Center.*

THE FENS

Boston Beer Works is a "naked brewery," with all the works exposed— the tanks, pipes, and gleaming stainless-steel and copper kettles used in producing beer. Seasonal brews, in addition to a regular selection, are the draw for students, young adults, and tourists. It's too crowded and noisy for intimate chats, and good luck trying to get in when there's a home game. ⊠*61 Brookline Ave., Fens* ☎*617/536–2337* ⊤*Kenmore.*

The Foundation Lounge transplants a West Coast vibe in the sleek Hotel Commonwealth. Wear your best nightclub attire, nosh on choices from the Zensai (Japanese-style appetizers) menu, and groove to what the guest DJs from around the world are spinning. ✉*500 Commonwealth Ave., The Fens* ☎*617/859–9900* ⊕*www.foundationlounge.com* ⊙*Tues.–Sun. 5 PM–2 AM.*

Jake Ivory's, on the always lively Lansdowne Street, is a bar known for its dueling piano players. Each night is a competition as the two pianists attempt to outperform the other. Bring a few extra dollars to put in requests, and expect a raucous crowd. Open Thursday through Saturday only. ✉*9 Lansdowne St., Fens* ☎*617/247–1222* Ⓣ*Kenmore.*

> ### BOSTON'S BEST IRISH PUBS
>
> ■ **The Burren,** Somerville
>
> ■ **Doyle's,** Jamaica Plain
>
> ■ **The Druid,** Cambridge
>
> ■ **The Kinsale,** Downtown
>
> ■ **Kitty O'Shea's,** Downtown

Jillian's, a sprawling nightspot, with multiple bars, pool tables, a bowling alley, and a nightclub is like Chuck E. Cheese for adults. If you're just going for drinks and pool, you can kick back with ease; expect to wait for a lane if you want to bowl. ✉*145 Ipswich St., Fens* ☎*617/437–0300* ⊕*www.jilliansboston.com* Ⓣ*Kenmore.*

JAMAICA PLAIN

Fodor's Choice ★ **Doyle's Café,** truly an institution, is a friendly, crowded, neighborhood Irish pub that opened in 1882 and has been a Boston political landmark ever since. Candidates for everything from Boston City Council to the U.S. Senate drop by to eat corned beef and cabbage, sample one of the 21 brews on tap or 60 single-malt Scotches, and, of course, make speeches and shake hands. ✉*3484 Washington St., Jamaica Plain* ☎*617/524–2345* ⊕*www.doyles-cafe.com* ⊟*No credit cards* Ⓣ*Green St., Forest Hills.*

OLD WEST END

Boston Beer Works near the TD Banknorth Garden is nearly identical to its sister location outside Fenway Park, but this one is naturally frequented by more Celtics and Bruins fans. ✉*112 Canal St., Old West End* ☎*617/896–2337* Ⓣ*North Station.*

Harp is the place for a crowded, rollicking atmosphere, just outside North Station and the TD Banknorth Garden. Although technically an Irish pub, the Harp is a three-story megabar that serves postgame or concert crowds, sports fans, and ticketless night owls wanting to be close to the action. ✉*85 Causeway St., Old West End* ☎*617/742–1010* ⊕*www.harpboston.com* Ⓣ*North Station.*

The Ruby Room, in the Onyx Hotel, is true to its name, with every shade of red imaginable. It's a sexy and comfortable spot to sip a designer cocktail and nosh on appetizers. Try the apricotti martini or the chocolate cinnamon bread pudding. ✉*Onyx Hotel, 155 Portland St., Old West End* ☎*617/557–9950* ⊕*www.rubyroomboston.com* Ⓣ*North Station.*

Sports Grille Boston is a heavyweight sports bar with 140 televisions tuned to every contest in the country and then some. A quick tour of Boston's championship seasons, both past and present, is evident from the memorabilia on the walls. Pack the Pepto for an overstuffed

Blue-Law Blues

Why do Boston bars close so early? Something of the old Puritan ethic of the Massachusetts Bay Colony lingers in the so-called "blue laws" that prohibit sales of alcoholic drinks at bars and restaurants after 1 AM on weekdays and 2 AM on weekends. The state remains of two minds when it comes to social leniency. The first state to legalize gay marriage was also one of the last states to allow liquor sales on Sunday. (Both became legal in 2004.)

Historians surmise that the origin of the blue laws goes back to colonial times when special laws were actually written on blue paper. In 17th-century Boston, it was forbidden to walk on the street on Sunday, or to sing, dance, fiddle, pipe, or use a musical instrument at night. Most

of these laws have been repealed (though it's still technically illegal to sit on the grass on Boston Common without a proclamation from the mayor). But periodic attempts to push back closing time still meet with heavy opposition from conservative neighborhood groups.

Late-night revelers party on in other ways. Asking for "cold tea" at certain Chinatown restaurants might get you a beer, and at certain Irish bars around town, the lights are off but somebody's home. A modern trend has been to form "private clubs" such as Rise, on Stuart Street, where members pay yearly fees for the privilege of partying (although not drinking) all night. Thankfully, it's no longer illegal to dance until dawn.

5

bar menu of burgers and fried foods. ✉*132 Canal St., Old West End* ☎*617/367–9302* Ⓣ*North Station.*

SOUTH BOSTON

Lucky's Lounge is a subterranean spot with live jazz on weekends, perfect martinis, and a mixed yuppie–artist crowd. The Rat Pack vibe is a lot of fun, and the salads, pizzas, and homemade meat loaf are first-rate. ✉*355 Congress St., Fort Point, South Boston* ☎*617/357–5825* ⊕*www.luckyslounge.com* Ⓣ*South Station.*

SOUTH END

★ Depending on the patron's mood, **Clery's** can be a neighborhood bar, an Irish pub, a dance hall, or a karaoke bar, as all are offered here. Lines can get long on weekend nights, so plan ahead. ✉*113 Dartmouth St., Back Bay/South End* ☎*617/262–9874* ⊕*www.irishconnection.com/ clerys.html* ◷*11 AM–1:30 AM.* Ⓣ*Copley*

Club Café is among the smartest spots in town for gay men and lesbians—even when they're dining or partying with their straight friends. Behind stylish restaurant 209, the two-room "video lounge" is a relaxed vibe to dance to current and classic music videos, watch cult movies and TV shows, or bust out with weekly karaoke. There's never a cover charge. ✉*209 Columbus Ave., South End* ☎*617/536–0966* ⊕*www. clubcafe.com* Ⓣ*Back Bay/South End.*

Delux Café & Lounge is a great spot to mix with twentysomething hipsters or to grab creative, affordable comfort food that always includes a grilled-cheese sandwich worth trying. Yellowing posters and postcards on the wall give the place a retro vibe. The quesadillas are generally worth the wait for a table. ⊠ *100 Chandler St., South End* ☎*617/338–5258* Ⓣ*Back Bay/South End.*

The Fours is all about sports. Located just outside the TD Banknorth Garden, it's packed with fans on game and concert nights. Visit during lunch on a weekday for a quieter atmosphere. ⊠*166 Canal St., Old West End* ☎*617/720–4455* ⊕*www.thefours.com* Ⓣ*North Station.*

Franklin Cafe is a neighborhood institution known for great martinis, microbrews on tap, and upscale pub food. There's no placard bearing its name, just look for the martini sign (or the crowd waiting for a dinner table) to know you're there. ⊠*278 Shawmut Ave., South End* ☎*617/350–0010* ⊕*www.franklincafe.com* Ⓣ*Back Bay/South End.*

Fritz Lounge is a gay sports bar popular with the local after-work crowd. Casually dressed patrons sip brew from the large beer list or drop in for steak and eggs during the hopping weekend brunch. ⊠*26 Chandler St., South End* ☎*617/482–4428* ⊕*www.fritzboston.com* ⊟*No credit cards* Ⓣ*Back Bay/South End.*

CAMBRIDGE AND SOMERVILLE

FodorsChoice **The Burren** pulls in a devoted local, mostly student, crowd. It's got all the
★ elements of a great Irish bar—expertly poured Guinness on tap, comfort food such as fish-and-chips, bangers and mash, and shepherd's pie, and live Irish music nightly—all in a warm, friendly environment. ⊠*247 Elm St., Somerville* ☎*617/776–6896* ⊕*www.burren.com* Ⓣ*Davis.*

Cambridge Brewing Company is a cheerful, collegial, cavernous micro-brewery that's a favorite among MIT students and techies. Try a pint of the company's Cambridge Amber or Charles River porter. If you've got a group, order a "tower" (83 ounces). In warm weather you can sit outside on the patio. ⊠*1 Kendall Sq., Bldg. 100, at Hampshire St. and Broadway, Cambridge* ☎*617/494–1994* ⊕*www.cambrew.com* Ⓣ*Kendall/MIT.*

Casablanca has a Moroccan interior replete with wicker chairs and ceiling fans. The bar serves fantastic martinis and rich North African–influenced appetizers. It's the cool place to be, especially with a date: rattan love seats and Bogey's aura make it an ideal spot for two. ⊠*40 Brattle St., Cambridge* ☎*617/876–0999* ⊕*www.casablanca-restaurant.com* Ⓣ*Harvard.*

★ **Chez Henri,** a French-Cuban restaurant equidistant from Harvard and Porter squares, has a hip after-work bar scene. There you'll find the best Cuban sandwiches north of Miami, and mojitos *muy fuertes* with which to wash them down. ⊠*1 Shepard St., midway between Harvard and Porter Sqs., Cambridge* ☎*617/354–8980* ⊕*www.chezhenri.com* Ⓣ*Harvard, Porter.*

Dante, in the Royal Sonesta hotel, offers a sleek bar and lounge for both real and aspiring jet-setters. In addition to creative cocktails and an expertly created wine list, Dante offers a variety of parties, including football tailgating, barbecue get-togethers, and other festive events that also showcase the latest creations from executive chef Dante deMag-istris. In warmer months head outside to the patio for great views of the Boston skyline and sailboats along the Charles River. ⊠*40 Edwin Land Blvd., Royal Sonesta Hotel, East Cambridge* ☎*617/497–4200*

BIG-PICTURE BOSTON

Gone Baby Gone (2007): Ben Affleck's directorial debut follows the case of a missing girl in Dorchester with plenty of South Boston, Dorchester, and Chelsea scenes, as well as the historic Mount Auburn Cemetery in Cambridge.

The Departed (2006): Hometown boys Matt Damon and Mark Wahlberg star in this thriller of lies and betrayal between the Irish mob and state police. Visit Chinatown to see where Matt Damon leads Leonardo DiCaprio on a good chase, mimic Martin Sheen with a ride on the Red Line between South Station and Park Street, or conduct your own clandestine meeting (just like Mark Wahlberg and DiCaprio) under Dorchester's Neponset Bridge.

Fever Pitch (2005): Drew Barrymore falls for Jimmy Fallon, a die-hard Sox fan. Show your team spirit by visiting the North End (where Fallon's character lives), Boston Common (where Fallon confesses his love for the Sox to Barrymore), and (of course) Fenway Park.

Mystic River (2003): Murder mystery set in South Boston, although much of the film was actually filmed in Eastie (East Boston). Take a drive across the Tobin Bridge, which is a prominent backdrop in many scenes, or have a pint at Doyle's, the famous pub in Jamaica Plain, where a despondent Tim Robbins gets drunk.

Legally Blonde (2001): Reese Witherspoon takes on Harvard Law School. See aerial shots of Cambridge and close ups of Harvard Yard.

Next Stop Wonderland (1998): A nurse (Hope Davis) and a plumber (Alan Gelfant) are slowly drawn to one another; great scenes of everyday Boston. Have a pint at the Burren in Davis Square, where Davis hangs with friends; tour the New England Aquarium, where Gelfant volunteers; or take the Blue Line out to Revere Beach, where the lovebirds finally connect.

Good Will Hunting (1997): Matt Damon is a "Southie"-born genius janitor at MIT. Harvard Square features prominently in scenes where Damon woos Minnie Driver's character; relax at the Boston Public Garden, where Damon and Robin Williams have a heart-to-heart. South Boston (particularly the L Street Tavern) is also well represented.

Governor Deval Patrick has been instrumental in bringing film crews to the city, so expect to see more celebrities in Boston than in previous years. For a movie-themed afternoon, consider a guided walking or bus tour with Boston Movie Tours (866/MOVIE45). Movie locations include those from *The Departed*, *Fever Pitch*, *Good Will Hunting*, and more.

⊕*www.restaurantdante.com* ⊘ *Mon.–Thurs. 5:30* PM *–10* PM, *Fri. and Sat. 5:30–11* PM Ⓣ*Lechmere, Kendall Square.*
Druid makes you feel like you're in Dublin with well-poured pints, a dusky atmosphere, and black-and-white pudding on the menu. Its location in residential Inman Square gives you a chance to get to know the locals. ✉*1357 Cambridge St., Cambridge* ☎*617/497–0965* ⊕*www.druidpub.com* Ⓣ*Lechmere, Harvard; then Bus 69.*

★ **Enormous Room,** somewhat whimsically named, is tucked into a tiny space above a restaurant in Central Square. Cambridge hipsters line up on weekends in front of the door, which is coolly unmarked. Inside, they nosh on Middle Eastern appetizers, including the "enormous platter" full of chicken skewers, olives, pita wedges, and other bites perfect for sharing. Instead of tables or booths, you'll find luxurious rugs and oversize throw pillows for stretching out, drinking, and people-watching. ⊠ *569 Massachusetts Ave., Cambridge* ☎ *617/491–5550* ⊕ *www.enormous.tv* ⓣ *Central.*

TOP LOUNGES
■ **The Enormous Room,** Cambridge
■ **The Good Life,** Downtown
■ **The Living Room,** Waterfront
■ **Lucky's Lounge,** South Boston
■ **West Side Lounge,** Cambridge

Grendel's Den is low lighted and brick walled, the quintessential grad-student hangout. During happy hour (5–7:30 daily and 9–11:30 Sunday through Thursday), spinach, artichoke, clam dip, littleneck clams, and other tasty entrées go for half price with a $3-per-person drink purchase. ⊠ *89 Winthrop St., Cambridge* ☎ *617/491–1160* ⊕ *www. grendelsden.com* ⓣ *Harvard.*

The Independent, in Somerville's Union Square, offers a hip place for a pint, a martini, or even a hot toddy. Try the "Moscow Mule," a cocktail featuring organic vodka, fresh limes, and ginger beer. ⊠ *75 Union Sq., Union Sq.* ☎ *617/440–6022* ⊕ *www.theindo.com* ☺ *Sun.–Thurs. 4:30 PM– 1 AM, Fri. and Sat. 4 PM–2 AM* ⓣ *Bus 86, 87, 91, CT2*

John Harvard's Brew House dispenses—from behind its long, dark bar— ales, lagers, pilsners, and stouts brewed on the premises. It even smells like a real English pub. The food is no-frills and hearty. On Monday, college students get selected appetizers at half price. ⊠ *33 Dunster St., Cambridge* ☎ *617/868–3585* ⊕ *www.johnharvards.com* ⓣ *Harvard.*

Middlesex Lounge combines the minimalist design of a New York lounge with the laid-back friendliness of a Cambridge pub to create one of the hottest scenes on this side of the river. Rolling settees lend themselves to a variety of seating configurations, or can be cleared at night for dancing to crowd-pleasing electronic and indie music. ⊠ *315 Massachusetts Ave., Cambridge* ☎ *617/868–6739* ⊕ *www.middlesexlounge. com* ⓣ *Central.*

★ **Noir** is a sexy nightspot in the Charles Hotel where Cary Grant and Katharine Hepburn would feel right at home. Sink into a wraparound black-leather couch, order a martini (try the strawberry-basil), and perfect your best air of mystery. ⊠ *Charles Hotel, 1 Bennett St., Cambridge* ☎ *617/661–8010* ⊕ *www.noir-bar.com* ⓣ *Harvard.*

Orleans brings a cool Back Bay vibe to Somerville's Davis Square. It has live music on Friday nights, a lounge full of comfy couches and settees, and a large-projector screen playing the night's game. Try the bar's mango mojito or peach martini for a sweet buzz. ⊠ *65 Holland St., Somerville* ☎ *617/591–2100* ⊕ *www.orleansrestaurant.com* ⓣ *Davis.*

Recently renovated, the **Plough & Stars,** a traditional Irish pub, has Guinness and Bass on tap and rock, Irish, or country music nightly. Narrow and cozy, it's a comfortable, noisy place popular with students and is a fine place to have lunch alone. The cover charge varies. Fun fact: this is where the literary magazine *Ploughshares* was founded. ✉*912 Massachusetts Ave., Cambridge* ☎*617/576–0032* ⊕*www.ploughandstars.com* Ⓣ*Central, Harvard.*

River Gods, a popular bar outside Central Square, is true to its name, cluttered with frequently changing decorations of the pub's namesake gods on every surface. It's also known for a variety of great meals (Irish, Thai, American, and more) done on the cheap. ✉*125 River St., Cambridge* ☎*617/576–1881* ⊕*www.rivergodsonline.com* Ⓣ*Central.*

Temple Bar is a classy place to enjoy a cocktail after a long day exploring, with signature drinks including espresso and chocolate martinis. If you're hungry, be sure to sample executive chef Tom Berry's latest seasonal creations. ✉*1688 Massachusetts Ave., Cambridge* ☎*617/547–5055* ⊕*www.templebarcambridge.com* Ⓣ*Porter, Harvard.*

West Side Lounge tempts cool cats and hipsters with comfort food, a comprehensive list of martinis and cocktails, and late-night lounging. Try the white ginger cosmo or prickly-pear margarita. ✉*1680 Massachusetts Ave., Cambridge* ☎*617/441–5566* ⊕*www.westsidelounge.com* Ⓣ*Porter, Harvard.*

> ### BEST FOR BEER CONNOISSEURS
>
> ■ **Boston Beer Works,** The Fens
>
> ■ **Bukowski Tavern,** Back Bay
>
> ■ **Cambridge Brewing Company,** Cambridge
>
> ■ **John Harvard's,** Cambridge
>
> ■ **Sunset Grill & Tap,** Allston

BOWLING ALLEYS AND POOL HALLS

Pool halls in Boston make a popular winter refuge for teens and university students. Forget Paul Newman and smoky interiors: Boston likes its billiards halls swanky and well lighted, with plenty of polished brass and dark wood. Many of them do double duty as bowling alleys. Be forewarned, however, that in New England bowling is often "candlepin," with smaller balls and different rules. Some pool halls have age requirements (either over 18 or 21); call for details.

Felt is decked out so stylishly with chrome furnishings, cushy lounge chairs, and space-age light fixtures that it's easy to forget that it's a pool hall. Sports stars and other minor celebrities mingle among young professionals and businesspeople on a night out to impress. Upstairs are 16 billiards tables covered with dark-blue felt, and a fourth-floor dance club. ✉*533 Washington St., Downtown* ☎*617/350–5555* ⊕*www.feltclubboston.com* Ⓣ*Chinatown, Downtown Crossing, Boylston, Park Street.*

Flat Top Johnny's is the hippest billiards hall around. Alternative rock, chosen by the tattooed and pierced staff, blares from behind the bar. Artwork by local painters hangs on the exposed-brick walls; the tables are covered in crimson instead of green. The bartender pours one of the best selections of draft beers in the city. Members of Boston's cooler local bands often hang out here on their nights off. ✉*1 Kendall Sq.,*

CLOSE UP

Candlepin Bowling

It was back in 1880 that Justin White adjusted the size of his pins at his Worcester, Masachusetts bowling hall, giving birth to Candlepin Bowling, a highly popular pint-size version of Ten-Pin Bowling. Now played almost exclusively in northern New England and in the Canadian Maritime Provinces, Candlepin Bowling is a game of power and accuracy.

Paradoxically, Candlepin Bowling is both much easier and far more difficult than regular bowling. The balls are much smaller and weigh less than 3 pounds. There are no finger holes, and players of all ages and abilities can whip the ball down the alley. But because both the ball and the pins are lighter, it is far more difficult to bowl strikes and spares. Players are allowed three throws per frame, and bowlers may hit fallen pins (called wood) to knock down other pins. There has never been a perfect "300" score. The top score is 245. Good players will score around 100 to 110, and novice players should be content with a score of 90.

There are a handful of alleys in and around Boston, and many of the alleys maintain their own quirky charm and history. Needham's **Bowlaway** (⊠ *16 Chestnut St., Needham* ☎ *781/444–9614*), one of the area's oldest bowling alleys, has eight cramped lanes in a tucked-away facility down a flight of stairs. Fans say Bowlaway is like bowling in your own basement. The funky **Milky Way Lounge and Lanes** (⊠ *403–405 Centre St., Jamaica Plain* ☎ *617/524–3740*) turns into a club at night and features seven lanes with the original wooden ball returns. Scoring is done on paper. **Boston Bowl** (⊠ *820 Morrissey Blvd., Dorchester* ☎ *617/825–3800*) attracts a more adult crowd and is open 24 hours a day. It has both Ten-Pin and Candlestick Bowling as well as pool tables and a game room. **Sacco's Bowl Haven** (⊠ *45 Day St., Somerville* ☎ *617/776–0552*) is proud that its '50s decor "makes bowling the way it was, the way it is." Run by the fourth generation of the Sacco family, the alley is decorated with old newspaper clippings and has few modern frills.

Bldg. 200, Cambridge ☎*617/494–9565* ⊕*www.flattopjohnnys.com* Ⓣ*Kendall/MIT*.

Jillian's Boston is often called the city's best playground for grown-ups. The multistory complex on the corner of club-hopping Lansdowne Street has more than 30 pool tables, and each floor has a lively bar. On the third level, Lucky Strike Lanes has 16 bowling lanes and an 80-foot video wall blasting sports and music videos, and the ground floor is home to Tequila Rain, "where it's Spring Break 52 weeks a year." Everything's open until 2 AM. ⊠*145 Ipswich St., Fens* ☎*617/437–0300* ⊕*www.jilliansboston.com* Ⓣ*Kenmore*.

Milky Way Lounge & Lanes has classic New England candlepin bowling souped up with dancing, live music, DJ acts, cabaret shows, or karaoke. Particularly popular is Tuesday night "live karaoke," where you can live out your rock-and-roll fantasies in front of your own backup band. It draws a hip urban crowd of twenty- and thirtysomethings,

SWEET NIGHTSPOTS

The Viennese Dessert Buffet at the Four Seasons' **Bristol Lounge** is a scrumptious array of pastries, dessert crepes, and chocolates, accompanied by live jazz. The drinks menu includes chai tea and a pomegranate martini. ✉ *200 Boylston St., Back Bay* ☎ *617/338–4400* ⊕ *www.fourseasons.com* Ⓣ *Arlington, Boylston.*

Finale is all about desserts, and with creative ingredients and immaculate presentations, it's hard to pick just one. Possibilities include a molten chocolate cake, an updated Boston cream pie, and crème brûlée. Tasting plates for sharing and sampling make decision making easy. ✉ *1 Columbus Ave., Theater District* ☎ *617/423–3184* ⊕ *www.finaledesserts.com* Ⓣ *Arlington* ✉ *30 Dunster St., Cambridge* ☎ *617/441–9797* Ⓣ *Harvard* ✉ *1306 Beacon St., Brookline* ☎ *617/232–3233* Ⓣ *Coolidge Corner.*

as well as families with children. ✉ *284 Armory St., Jamaica Plain* ☎ *617/524–3740* ⊕ *www.milkywayjp.com* Ⓣ *Stony Brook.*

CAFÉS AND COFFEEHOUSES

Boston has a great nighttime coffeehouse scene. If you just want a cup of coffee, you can find plenty of Starbucks cafés and Dunkin' Donuts. But beyond the cookie-cutter establishments, a more-interesting set of independent cafés pump out the espresso. A few of them feel like true old-fashioned coffeehouses, complete with live folk music. Others are perfect to recaffeinate your spirits during a busy day of sightseeing. To eavesdrop on the liveliest conversations—some in Italian—head to one of the many espresso bars on Hanover Street in the North End.

BOSTON

Boston Beanstock Coffee Company, a relative newcomer to the North End's café scene, is an independent that's more Starbucks than Italian café. It has comfy couches, a roaring fireplace in winter, free wireless Internet, and a host of soups, sandwiches, and baked goods for sampling. It's one of the few cafés in the neighborhood where you can get a nonespresso cup of joe. ✉ *97 Salem St., North End* ☎ *617/725–0040* ⊕ *www.bostonbeanstock.com* Ⓣ *Haymarket.*

Fodor'sChoice ★ **Caffé Vittoria** is the biggest of the cafés in the North End, with gleaming espresso machines going nonstop. This is a good place to stop for dessert—think tiramisu, cannoli, and gelati—and coffee after a meal in one of the nearby restaurants. ✉ *296 Hanover St., North End* ☎ *617/227–7606* ⊕ *www.vittoriacaffe.com* Ⓣ *Haymarket.*

Tealuxe is the downtown branch of the popular "tea bar," which serves 70 kinds of tea and not a single type of coffee. Faux-antique Chinese tea bins behind the counter clash with more-modern steel-and-copper decor. In summer Newbury Street window-shoppers fill the outdoor patio, enjoying tea and chai of the iced variety. ✉ *108 Newbury St., Back Bay* ☎ *617/927–0400* ⊕ *www.tealuxe.com* Ⓣ *Copley.*

5

★ **Trident Booksellers & Café** stocks esoteric books and magazines, and serves coffee and teas. This is a nice spot for a light meal with a date, solo journal writing or reading, or surfing the Web with free wireless access. The windows facing Newbury Street are great for people-watching. It's open daily until midnight. ⊠ *338 Newbury St., Back Bay* ☎ *617/267–8688* ⊕ *www.tridentbookscafe.com* Ⓣ *Hynes/ICA.*

CAMBRIDGE AND SOMERVILLE

Café Algiers is a genuine Middle Eastern café serving pita-bread lunches, teas, and strong coffee. Small, tightly clustered tables fill both floors. Upstairs you can peer at the soaring, wood-panel cathedral ceiling. Service is sluggish; visit when in the mood to linger over conversation or a novel. ⊠ *40 Brattle St., Cambridge* ☎ *617/492–1557* Ⓣ *Harvard.*

★ **Club Passim** has seen Joan Baez, Bob Dylan, Suzanne Vega, and many other folkies on their way up. It's one of the country's first and most famous venues for live folk music. In the basement room, where the seating is pressed close together, there's table service and a counter where you can buy prepared food—Middle Eastern vegetarian items are especially good. If you travel with your guitar, call about one of the club's many open-mike nights. ⊠ *47 Palmer St., Cambridge* ☎ *617/492–5300, 617/492–7679 box office* ⊕ *www.clubpassim.org* Ⓣ *Harvard.*

Dado Tea has a new-age feel, with an extensive listing of teas, multigrain meals, and a few sweet options, too. The Harvard Square location is a bit roomier than other cafés in the area, and if it's not too crowded, you can linger without interruption. ⊠ *50 Church St., Cambridge* ☎ *617/547–0950* ⊕ *www.dadotea.com* Ⓣ *Harvard* ⊠ *955 Massachusetts Ave., Cambridge* ☎ *617/497–9061* Ⓣ *Harvard, Central.*

★ **Diesel Cafe** is a bright and sunny spot with bold local artwork and spacious booths. In addition to drawing Davis Square hipsters and Tufts students, it's a favorite hangout for lesbians and their friends, who congregate around the pool tables in back. Wireless is available for $5 an hour. ⊠ *257 Elm St., Somerville* ☎ *617/629–8717* ⊕ *www.diesel-cafe. com* Ⓣ *Davis.*

Tealuxe is a "tea bar" with Bombay flair, more than 70 different herbal and traditional blends, an assortment of teatime snacks—and no coffee. It's a favorite hangout for students, who huddle over textbooks as they savor a cup of Earl Grey or ginseng chai at one of the copper-top tables. ⊠ *0 Brattle St., Cambridge* ☎ *617/441–0077* ⊕ *www.tealuxe. com* Ⓣ *Harvard.*

COMEDY CLUBS

Comedy Connection, which has been voted the best comedy club in the country by *USA Today*, has a mix of local and nationally known acts seven nights a week, with two shows Friday and Saturday. The cover is $15–$29. ⊠ *246 Tremont St., in the Wilbur Theatre* ☎ *617/931–2000* ⊕ *www.comedyconnectionboston.com* Ⓣ *Boylston.*

The Comedy Studio, upstairs at the Hong Kong in Harvard Square, schedules a smorgasbord of silly offerings. A host of local and touring comedians make stops here; there's also a popular magic show every Tuesday night. ⊠ *1238 Massachusetts Ave., Harvard Sq.* ☎ *617/661–6507* ⊕ *www.*

thecomedystudio.com 🖂$8–$10 ⊙ *All shows start at 8* PM, *Tues.– Sun.* Ⓣ*Harvard.*

★ **ImprovAsylum** features comedians who weave audience suggestions into seven weekly shows blending topical sketches with improv in shows such as "Lost in Boston" and "New Kids on the Blog." Tickets are $20; students can get a two-for-one deal for $10 apiece. 🖂*216 Hanover St., North End* ☎*617/263–6887* ⊕*www.improv asylum.com* Ⓣ*Haymarket, North Station.*

ImprovBoston in Central Square turns audience suggestions into a situation comedy, complete with theme song and commercials. Be careful when you go to the restroom; you might be pulled onstage. On some nights, performers face off in improv competitions judged by audiences. Shows, which run Wednesday through Sunday, are $7 to $16. There's a beer and wine bar. 🖂*40 Prospect St., Cambridge* ☎*617/576–1253* ⊕*www.improvboston.com* Ⓣ*Central.*

Nick's Comedy Stop presents local comics Thursday through Saturday night. Well-known comedians occasionally pop in. Local boy Jay Leno reportedly got his start here. Reservations are advised on weekends, and cover charges vary. 🖂*100 Warrenton St., Theater District* ☎*617/482–0930* ⊕*www.nickscomedystop.com* Ⓣ*Boylston.*

> ### SWINGING SINGLES SCENES
>
> ■ **Felt**, Downtown
> ■ **Gypsy Bar**, Theater District
> ■ **The Harp**, Old West End
> ■ **The Hong Kong**, Faneuil Hall
> ■ **Museum of Fine Arts** (first Friday), The Fens

DANCE CLUBS

★ **Aria** fills up with the young, the beautiful, and the chic Thursday through Saturday. Doors at this cozy space below the Wilbur Theatre usually open after 10:30. The DJs spin everything from house to reggae to international, but if the dancing gets too steamy, you can revive by sipping a cocktail on one of the plush, red sofas. This is as exclusive as it gets in Boston. 🖂*246 Tremont St., Theater District* ☎*617/338–7080* Ⓣ*Boylston, Chinatown.*

The Estate, part of the Alley entertainment complex, offers guest DJs from around the globe, the occasional live act, belly dancers, and a celebrity (e.g., Paris Hilton) or two. Suite Boston, the property's "subterranean den," often hosts special events such as fashion shows and parties with guest DJs. 🖂*1 Boylston Pl., Downtown/Theater District* ☎*617/351–7000* ⊕*www.theestateboston.com* 🖂$15–$25 ⊙*Thurs.– Sun.* 9 PM–2 AM.

Gypsy Bar almost calls to mind the decadence of a dark European castle, with rich red velvet and crystal chandeliers. Its rows of video screens broadcasting the Fashion Network, however, add a sexier, more-modern touch. Thirtysomething revelers and European students snack on lime-and-ginger-marinated tiger shrimp and sip "See You in Church" martinis (vodka with fresh marmalade) while the trendy dance floor throbs to Top 40 and house music. 🖂*116 Boylston St., Theater District* ☎*617/482–7799* ⊕*www.gypsybarboston.com* Ⓣ*Boylston.*

★ **The Roxy** has a spacious interior that resembles an early-20th-century ballroom, but this club is hardly sedate. It throws theme nights such as "Sexy Fridays," as well as Chippendales male reviews and Latin dance parties. Watch for occasional rock concerts with bands such as the Killers. ✉ *279 Tremont St., Theater District* ☎ *617/338–7699* ⊕ *www. roxyboston.com* Ⓣ *Boylston.*

Rumor wants guests to dance, dance, dance, with all types of DJs spinning throughout the week. Options include house on Tuesday, hip-hop and house on Friday, and house, hip-hop, Latin, and Latin house on weekends. ✉ *100 Warrenton St., Theater District* ☎ *617/422–0045* ⊕ *www.rumorboston.com* ⌧ *Varies by DJ/night, expect a $10 minimum* Ⓣ *NE Medical Center*

Umbria in the Financial District, attracts a mature, upscale crowd that ranges from mid-twenties to over-forties. Dress accordingly: no sneakers or caps. Wander among the five floors for formal Italian or informal dining, an "ultralounge," and a nightclub featuring R&B, techno, and international tunes. ✉ *295 Franklin St., Downtown* ☎ *617/338–1000* ⊕ *www.umbriaristorante.com* Ⓣ *South Station.*

Venu brings Miami's South Beach to Boston. A warm energy distinguishes this club from the city's other dark, techno-industrial spots. The crowd is diverse—stylish international students mix with young downtown suits cutting loose on their off-hours. Local DJs spin Top 40 and international tunes. Friday offers house, Latin, and hip-hop DJs, and Saturday features Top 40, rock, and mashups. ✉ *100 Warrenton St., Theater District* ☎ *617/338–8061* ⊕ *www.venuboston.com* Ⓣ *Boylston, Arlington.*

MUSIC CLUBS

BLUES AND R&B CLUBS

★ **The Cantab Lounge/Third Rail** hums every night with live Motown, rhythm and blues, folk, or bluegrass. The Third Rail bar, downstairs, holds poetry slams, open-mike readings, bohemia nights, and improv comedy. It's friendly and informal, with a diverse under-forty crowd. ✉ *738 Massachusetts Ave., Cambridge* ☎ *617/354–2685* ⊕ *www.cantab-lounge. com* ⊟ *No credit cards* Ⓣ *Central.*

Harpers Ferry, noisy and crowded, is known for its live rock and blues acts and has played host to the likes of Bo Diddley and B.B. King. If music's not your thing, turn to the pool tables or darts. ✉ *158 Brighton Ave., Allston* ☎ *617/254–9743* ⊕ *www.harpersferryboston.com* Ⓣ *Harvard Ave. on Green Line's B train.*

Johnny D's Uptown is a restaurant–cum–music hall where every seat is a good seat. It lines up Cajun, country, Latin, jazz, blues, and more. Come early for Southern and Mediterranean bistro food. On weekends it hosts a popular jazz brunch. ✉ *17 Holland St., Somerville* ☎ *617/776–9667 recorded info, 617/776–2004* ⊕ *www.johnnyds uptown.com* Ⓣ *Davis.*

JAZZ CLUBS

Clubs often alternate jazz with other kinds of music; always call ahead for program information and times.

The Beehive is a café and nightclub in the basement of the Boston Center for the Arts' Cyclorama building. While you'll find mostly jazz acts booked here, there's also the occasional cabaret or burlesque act, too. ✉ *541 Tremont St., South End* ☎*617/423–0069* ⊕*www.beehiveboston. com* ☉ *5 PM–2 AM.*

Regattabar is host to some of the top names in jazz, including Sonny Rollins and Herbie Hancock. Tickets for shows are $15–$35. Even when there's no entertainment, the large, low-ceiling club is a pleasant (if expensive) place for a drink. ✉*Charles Hotel, 1 Bennett St., Cambridge* ☎*617/661–5000 or 617/395–7757* ⊕*www.regattabarjazz.com* Ⓣ*Harvard.*

★ **Ryles Jazz Club** uses soft lights, mirrors, and greenery to set the mood for first-rate jazz. The first-floor stage is one of the best places for new music and musicians. Upstairs is a dance hall staging regular tango, salsa, and merengue nights, often with lessons before the dancing starts. Ryles also holds occasional open-mike poetry slams and a Sunday jazz brunch (call for reservations). It's open nightly, with a cover charge. ✉*212 Hampshire St., Cambridge* ☎*617/876–9330* ⊕*www.ryles.com* Ⓣ*Bus 69, 83, or 91.*

Scullers Jazz Club hosts well-known acts such as Wynton Marsalis, Diana Krall, and Tony Bennett. Shows are Tuesday through Sunday nights; tickets are $18–$50 per show, more with dinner included; advance tickets are advised. ✉*Doubletree Guest Suites hotel, 400 Soldiers Field Rd., Allston* ☎*617/562–4111* ⊕*www.scullersjazz.com* Ⓣ*BU West, Bus 47, or CT2.*

Fodor'sChoice **Wally's Café** is a rare gem for blues and jazz fans. Founded in 1947, the ★ club continues to play host to big names such as Branford Marsalis and Chick Corea but is still best known for performances by local bands. Wally's has a more-diverse crowd than most other Boston clubs, and brings in both South End and Roxbury locals and lots of college students, especially those from Berklee College of Music. It's open every night of the year and there's no cover. ■TIP➜ **Get here early if you want a seat.** ✉*427 Massachusetts Ave., South End* ☎*617/424–1408* ⊕*www. wallyscafe.com* Ⓣ*Massachusetts Ave.*

ROCK CLUBS

Great Scott books an impressive lineup of local and visiting indie rock bands, with live music nearly every night of the week. The crowd typically consists of Allston hipsters, Boston University students, and the lonely sports fan. ✉*1222 Commonwealth Ave., Allston* ☎*617/566–9014* ⊕*www.greatscottboston.com* Ⓣ*Harvard Ave.*

Green Street Grill is the place for both a meal and music. Start with spicy Caribbean food, then stick around for the night's show, which might be jazz, Latin, folk, or serious rock. There's usually no cover charge. ✉*280 Green St., Cambridge* ☎*617/876–1655* ⊕*www.greenstreetgrill. com* Ⓣ*Central.*

Hard Rock Cafe, formerly in the Back Bay, relocated to Faneuil Hall in mid-2007. It now inhabits the former space of the Rack, a popular nightclub that closed its doors. With a significantly larger space to work with, the Hard Rock now books rock shows, private parties, and still offers an extensive bar and restaurant. Expect to see a cover band or two

5

MADE IN BOSTON

MUSICIANS FROM BOSTON INCLUDE:	
Aerosmith	Letters to Cleo
Boston (go figure . . .)	Lori McKenna
Buffalo Tom	Jo Dee Messina
The Cars	Mighty Mighty Bosstones
Paula Cole	Mission of Burma
Dresden Dolls	Morphine
Dropkick Murphys	New Edition
Godsmack	New Kids on the Block
Guster	Pernice Brothers
Juliana Hatfield	The Pixies
Patty Larkin	Donna Summer
The Lemonheads	James Taylor
	Yo-Yo Ma

during an evening here, particularly on weekend nights. ⊠ *22–24 Clinton St., Faneuil Hall* ☎ *617/424–7625* ⊕ *www.hardrock.com/boston* ▭ *N/A for drinks/dinner, shows will vary* ☽ *Sun.–Thurs. 11 AM–1 AM, Fri. and Sat. 11 AM–2 AM.* Ⓣ *Haymarket, Government Center*

Harpers Ferry is a rock and blues club where not only local rock bands take the stage, but also legends like Steven Tyler and Joe Perry (⇨ *Blues & R&B Clubs, above*). ⊠ *158 Brighton Ave., Allston* ☎ *617/254–9743* ⊕ *www.harpersferryboston.com* Ⓣ *Harvard Ave.*

Lizard Lounge is a low-key nightspot that often features more-experimental and local cult bands. Seven nights a week see folk, rock, acid jazz, and pop, sometimes mixed with cabaret, burlesque shows, or poetry readings. Martinis are a house specialty; upstairs, the Cambridge Common restaurant serves excellent burgers and comfort food (sweet potato fries, basket of tater tots). ⊠ *1667 Massachusetts Ave., between Harvard and Porter Sqs., Cambridge* ☎ *617/547–0759* ⊕ *www.lizard loungeclub. com* Ⓣ *Harvard, Porter.*

★ **The Middle East Restaurant & Nightclub** manages to be both a Middle Eastern restaurant and one of the area's most eclectic rock clubs, with three rooms showcasing live local and national acts. Local phenoms the Mighty Mighty Bosstones got their start here. Music-world celebs often drop in when they're in town. There's also belly dancing, folk, jazz, and even the occasional country-tinged rock band. ⊠ *472–480 Massachusetts Ave., Cambridge* ☎ *617/497–0576 or 617/864–3278* ⊕ *www.mideastclub.com* Ⓣ *Central.*

Midway Café, in Jamaica Plain, books a mix of live rock bands, DJs, and hip-hop artists for an eclectic set any night of the week. There's also a lesbian dance party and "queeraoke" each Thursday night. ⊠ *3496*

Washington St., Jamaica Plain ☎*617/524–9038* ⊕*www.midwaycafe. com* T*Green St., Forest Hills.*

Fodor'sChoice
★
Paradise Rock Club is a small place known for hosting big-name talent like U2, Coldplay, and local stars such as the Dresden Dolls. Two tiers of booths provide good sight lines anywhere in the club, as well as some intimate and out-of-the-way corners, and four bars quench the crowd's thirst. The 18-plus crowd varies with the shows. The newer Paradise Lounge, next door, is a more-intimate space to experience local, often acoustic songsters, as well as literary readings and other artistic events. It serves dinner. ✉*967–969 Commonwealth Ave., Allston* ✥*Near Boston University* ☎*617/562–8800 or 617/562–8814* ⊕*www.thedise.com* T*Pleasant St.*

T. T. the Bear's Place schedules live rock nightly, showcasing the hottest local bands and on-the-rise alternative bands such as Dear Leader and the Rudds. Separate rooms make it easy to concentrate on the music, chat around the bar, or relax over a game of pool. Monday night is usually acoustic night. It closes at 1 AM. ✉*10 Brookline St., Cambridge* ☎*617/492–2327* ⊕*www.ttthebears.com* T*Central.*

5

SALSA CLUBS

An Tua Nua is an Irish pub that, however improbably, hosts one of the city's most popular salsa nights each Wednesday. Arrive early for a lesson with local experts Johnny and Kelly, then put your new moves to the test on the packed dance floor. ✉*835 Beacon St., Boston University* ☎*617/262–2121* ⊕*www.salsaboston.com/antuanua/* T *Fenway, Kenmore, St. Mary St.*

Havana Club at the Greek American Political Club in Central Square has a 5,400-square-foot ballroom dance floor, a rotating cast of DJs and live bands, and (usually) free food such as burritos or nachos. Typically, 400 people show up to dance, creating a lively scene for dancers at any level. The club is open for salsa on Friday and Saturday (open for private functions other nights). ✉*288 Green St., Cambridge* ☎*617/312–5550* ⊕*www.havanaclubsalsa.com* T*Central.*

Ryles is home to one of the city's friendliest salsa scenes, **Temporada Latina**. It's held Thursday nights with newcomers and experts dancing the night away (often together). Dancing starts at 9:30; arrive at 8 for the lesson. ✉*212 Hampshire St., Cambridge* ☎*617/876–9330* ⊕*www. ryles.com/dancing.cfm* T*Bus 68 or 69.*

THE ARTS

DANCE

Boston Dance Alliance serves as a clearinghouse for local dance information. Visit its Web site for upcoming performances and details about Boston dance companies and venues. ✉*19 Clarendon St., South End* ☎*617/456–6295* ⊕*www.bostondancealliance.org.* T*Back Bay*

BALLET

★ **Boston Ballet,** the city's premier dance company, performs at the Citi Performing Arts Center from October through May. In addition to a world-class repertory of classical and high-spirited modern works, it presents an elaborate signature *Nutcracker* during the holidays at the restored downtown Opera House. ✉ *19 Clarendon St., South End* ☎ *617/695–6950* ⊕ *www.bostonballet.org.* Ⓣ *Back Bay.*

José Mateo's Ballet Theatre is a troupe building an exciting, contemporary repertory under Cuban-born José Mateo, the resident artistic director-choreographer. The troupe's performances include an original *Nutcracker,* and take place October through April at the **Sanctuary Theatre,** a beautifully converted former church at Massachusetts Avenue and Harvard Street in Harvard Square. ✉ *400 Harvard St., Cambridge* ☎ *617/354–7467* ⊕ *www.ballettheatre.org* Ⓣ *Harvard.*

CONTEMPORARY

Dance Complex presents varied dance styles by local and visiting choreographers at Odd Fellows Hall, an intimate space that draws a multicultural crowd. Works range from classical ballet to contemporary and world dance. Recent performances have included video and spoken word. ✉ *536 Massachusetts Ave., Central Sq., Cambridge* ☎ *617/547–9363* ⊕ *www.dancecomplex.org* Ⓣ *Central.*

FOLK/MULTICULTURAL

★ **Art of Black Dance and Music** performs the music and dance of Africa, the Caribbean, and the Americas at venues including the **Strand Theatre,** at Columbia Road and Stoughton Street in Dorchester, and local area universities. ☎ *617/666–1859* ⊕ *www.abdm.com* Ⓣ *Andrew, then 16 or 17 bus; Ruggles, then 15 bus.*

Cambridge Multicultural Arts Center presents local and visiting arts programs, ethnic music, and dance performances. Two galleries showcase the visual arts. ✉ *41 2nd St., Cambridge* ☎ *617/577–1400* ⊕ *www. cmacusa.org* Ⓣ *Lechmere.*

Folk Arts Center of New England promotes participatory international folk dancing and music for adults and children, as well as traditional New England contra dancing at locations throughout the greater Boston area. ✉ *42 W. Foster St., Melrose* ☎ *781/662–7476 recorded info, 781/662–7475* ⊕ *www.facone.org.* Ⓣ *No stop; Venues vary*

World Music presents the biggest names in traditional dance and music from around the globe; regular performers include Africa's Ladysmith Black Mambazo and Ireland's Mary Black, and its annual Boston Flamenco Festival has become a winter highlight. Its CRASHArts series offers more-daring, contemporary fare. Performances take place at the Somerville Theatre in Davis Square, Berklee Performance Center, and other venues around Boston. ✉ *720 Massachusetts Ave., Cambridge* ☎ *617/876–4275* ⊕ *www.worldmusic.org* Ⓣ *Central.*

FILM

With its large population of academics and intellectuals, Boston has its share of discerning moviegoers and movie houses, especially in Cambridge. Theaters at suburban malls, downtown, and at Fenway have better screens, if less-adventurous fare. The *Boston Globe* has daily listings in the "Living/Arts" and "Sidekick" sections, and both the *Boston Herald* Friday "Scene" section and the *Boston Phoenix* "Arts" section list films for the week. Movies cost $8–$11. Many theaters have half-price matinees, but theaters sometimes suspend bargain admissions during the first week or two of a major film opening.

★ **Boston Public Library** regularly screens free family, foreign, classic, and documentary films in the Rabb Lecture Hall. ⊠*700 Boylston St., Copley Sq., Back Bay* ☎*617/536–5400* ⊕*www.bpl.org* Ⓣ*Copley.*

Brattle Theatre shows classic movies, new foreign and independent films, themed series, and directors' cuts. Tickets sell out every year for its acclaimed Bogart festival, scheduled around Harvard's exam period; the Bugs Bunny Film Festival in February; and *Trailer Treats,* an annual fund-raiser featuring an hour or two of classic and modern movie previews in July. It also has holiday screenings such as *It's a Wonderful Life* at Christmas. ⊠*40 Brattle St., Harvard Sq., Cambridge* ☎*617/876–6837* ⊕*www.brattlefilm.org* Ⓣ*Harvard.*

The Coolidge Corner Theatre has an eclectic and frequently updated bill of art films, foreign films, animation festivals, and classics, as well as an intimate 45-seat video-screening room for more-experimental offerings. It also holds book readings, concerts, and popular midnight cult movies. ⊠*290 Harvard St., Brookline* ☎*617/734–2501, 617/734–2500 recorded info* ⊕*www.coolidge.org* Ⓣ*Coolidge Corner.*

Harvard Film Archive screens works from its vast collection of classics and foreign films that are not usually shown at commercial cinemas. Actors and directors frequently appear to introduce newer work. The theater was created for student and faculty use, but the general public may attend regular screenings for $8 per person. ⊠*Carpenter Center for the Visual Arts, 24 Quincy St., Cambridge* ☎*617/495–4700* ⊕*hcl. harvard.edu/hfa/* Ⓣ*Harvard.*

The Institute of Contemporary Art, Boston screens art films, foreign-film award winners, experimental movies, and documentaries. ⊠*100 Northern Ave., Waterfront* ☎*617/478–3100* ⊕*www.icaboston.org/ programs/film/* Ⓣ*South Station, Courthouse, World Trade Center.*

Kendall Square Cinema is devoted to first-run independent and foreign films. There are nine screens and a concession stand with choices such as cappuccino and homemade cookies. Note that 1 Kendall Square stands where Hampshire runs into Broadway, not near the Kendall Square T stop. The free Galleria Mall shuttle runs directly from the T stop to the theater every 20 minutes, Monday–Saturday 9–7, and Sunday noon–7. ⊠*1 Kendall Sq., Cambridge* ☎*617/499–1996* ⊕*www.landmarktheatres. com* Ⓣ*Kendall/MIT.*

The Museum of Fine Arts screens international and avant-garde films, works by local filmmakers, and films connected to museum exhibitions in Remis Auditorium. ⊠*465 Huntington Ave., Fens* ☎*617/369–3306 box office* ⊕*www.mfa.org/film* Ⓣ*Museum of Fine Arts, Ruggles.*

MUSIC

For its size, Boston has a great diversity and variety of live music choices. New York has more events, but 10 times the population. Most of the year the music calendar is crammed with classical, pop, and rock events. Jazz, blues, folk, and world-music fans have plenty to keep them busy as well. *(See also Music Clubs in Nightlife, above.)* Supplementing appearances by nationally known artists are performers from the area's many colleges and conservatories, which also provide music series, performing spaces, and audiences.

The jewel in Boston's musical crown is the multifaceted Boston Symphony Orchestra, which performs at Symphony Hall October through early May and at Tanglewood Music Center in Lenox, Massachusetts, from late June through and August. A favorite of television audiences, the Boston Pops presents concerts of "lighter music" from May to July and during December.

But pop orchestral arrangements and the warhorses of the 19th-century symphonic repertoire aren't Boston's only classical-musical offerings today. The city has emerged as the nation's capital of early-music performance. Dozens of small groups, often made up of performers who have one foot in the university and another on the concert stage, are rediscovering pre-18th-century composers, whose works they play on period instruments, often in small churches where the acoustics resemble the venues in which some of this music was first performed. **The Cambridge Society for Early Music** (☎617/489–2062 ⊕*www.csem.org*) helps promote early-music performances and deserves much of the credit for early music's preeminence in Boston's musical scene.

If you're a die-hard early-music devotee, plan to visit Boston in odd-number years, when the biennial **Boston Early Music Festival** (☎617/661–1812 ⊕*www.bemf.org*) takes over the city for a week in June.

CONCERT HALLS

★ **Bank of America Pavilion** gathers up to 5,000 people on the city's waterfront for summertime concerts. National pop, folk, and country acts play the tentlike pavilion from about mid-June to mid-September. ⊠*290 Northern Ave., South Boston* ☎617/728–1600 ⊕*www.bankofamerica pavilion.com* Ⓣ*South Station.*

Berklee Performance Center, associated with Berklee College of Music, is best known for its jazz programs, but it's also host to folk performers such as Joan Baez and pop and rock stars such as Andrew Bird, Aimee Mann, and Henry Rollins. ⊠*136 Massachusetts Ave., Back Bay* ☎617/747–2261 box office, 617/747–8890 recorded info ⊕*www. berkleebpc.com* Ⓣ*Hynes/ICA.*

The Boston Opera House hosts plays, musicals, and traveling Broadway shows, but also has booked diverse performers such as David Copperfield, B.B. King, and Pat Metheny. The occasional children's production may schedule a run here as well. ⊠ *539 Washington St., Downtown* ☎617/259–3400 ⊕*www.bostonoperahouse.com* Ⓣ*Boylston, Chinatown, Downtown Crossing, Park Street.*

Hatch Memorial Shell, on the bank of the Charles River, is a wonderful acoustic shell where the Boston Pops perform their famous free summer concerts (including their traditional Fourth of July show, broadcast live nationwide on TV). Local radio stations also put on music shows and festivals here April through October. ⊠ *Off Storrow Dr. at embankment, Beacon Hill* ☏ *617/626–4970* ⊕ *www.mass.gov/ dcr/hatch_events.htm* Ⓣ *Charles/MGH, Arlington.*

Fodor's Choice
★
The Isabella Stewart Gardner Museum holds concerts in its beautiful Tapestry Room—young artist showcases and chamber music every Sunday—as well as an "after hours" series the third Thursday of each month. It also hosts a "composer portrait series," which highlights the work of a particular composer. The charge is in addition to the museum admission. ⊠ *280 The Fenway, Fens* ☏ *617/278–5156 box office, 617/566–1401 recorded info* ⊕ *www.gardnermuseum.org* Ⓣ *Museum of Fine Arts.*

The Institute of Contemporary Art, Boston hosts experimental musicians, with some performances in partnership with World Music/CRASHArts. Expect the unexpected—concerts here could contain a mix of disparate instruments, fusions of melody and spoken word, or electronica mashups. ⊠ *100 Northern Ave., Waterfront* ☏ *617/478–3100* ⊕ *www. icaboston.org/programs/performance* Ⓣ *South Station, Courthouse, World Trade Center.*

The Museum of Fine Arts has jazz, blues, and folk concerts in its outdoor courtyard every Wednesday evening from late June through August (bring a blanket and a picnic). During the rest of the year, the action moves inside to the Remis Auditorium on various nights of the week. ⊠ *465 Huntington Ave., Fens* ☏ *617/369–3300* ⊕ *www.mfa.org/concerts* Ⓣ *Museum of Fine Arts.*

★ **New England Conservatory's Jordan Hall** is one of the world's acoustic treasures, and is ideal for chamber music yet large enough to accommodate a full orchestra. The Boston Philharmonic and the Boston Baroque ensemble often perform at the relatively intimate 1,000-seat hall. ⊠ *30 Gainsborough St., Back Bay* ☏ *617/585–1260 box office* ⊕ *concerts. newenglandconservatory.edu* Ⓣ *Symphony.*

Sanders Theatre provides a jewel box of a stage for local and visiting classical, folk, and world-music performers. "The Christmas Revels," a traditional, participatory Yule celebration, delights families here each December. ⊠ *Harvard University, 45 Quincy St., Cambridge* ☏ *617/496–2222* ⊕ *www.fas.harvard.edu/tickets* Ⓣ *Harvard.*

Fodor's Choice
★
Symphony Hall, one of the world's best acoustical settings—if not *the* best—is home to the Boston Symphony Orchestra (BSO) and the Boston Pops. The BSO is led by the incomparable James Levine, who's known for commissioning special works by contemporary composers, as well as for presenting innovative programs such as his two-year Beethoven/ Schoenberg series. The Pops concerts, led by conductor Keith Lockhart, take place in May and June and around the winter holidays. The hall is also used by visiting orchestras, chamber groups, soloists, and many local performers. Rehearsals are sometimes open to the public, with tickets sold at a discount. ⊠ *301 Massachusetts Ave., Back Bay* ☏ *617/266–1492* ⊕ *www.bostonsymphonyhall.org* Ⓣ *Symphony.*

TD Banknorth Garden hosts concerts by big-name artists from Celine Dion to U2, ice shows, and, of course, Bruins and Celtics games. ⊠ *100*

Legends Way, Old West End ☎617/624–1000 ⊕*www.tdbanknorth garden.com* Ⓣ*North Station.*

Tsai Performance Center, associated with Boston University, presents many free classical concerts by both student and professional groups. The New England Philharmonic and Boston Musica Viva are regular guests in the 500-seat theater. ✉*685 Commonwealth Ave., Fens* ☎617/353–6467, 617/353–8725 *box office* ⊕*www.bu.edu/tsai* Ⓣ*Boston University East.*

CHORAL GROUPS

It's hard to imagine another city with more active choral groups than Boston. Many outstanding choruses are associated with Boston schools and churches.

The Boston Cecilia, which dates from 1876, holds regular concerts at Jordan Hall and other venues, and is especially noted for its period-instrument performances of Handel. ☎617/232–4540 ⊕*www.boston cecilia.org.*

Boston Gay Men's Chorus seeks to "create a more-tolerant society through the power of music." Their repertoire ranges from holiday favorites to show tunes, chamber selections to pop hits. They perform at Symphony Hall, Jordan Hall, the Cutler Majestic Theatre, and other venues around town. ☎617/542–7464 ⊕*www.bgmc.org.*

Boston Secession is a professional vocal ensemble that's trying to modernize the choral experience with both virtuoso singing and creative, thematic programs such as "Handel in the Strand" and the annual anti-Valentine "(un)Lucky in Love." ☎617/499–4860 ⊕*www.boston secession.org.*

Cantata Singers perform music dating from the 17th century to the present at various venues in Boston. ☎617/868–5885 ⊕*www.cantata singers.org.*

CHURCH CONCERTS

Boston's churches have outstanding music programs. The Saturday *Boston Globe* and the Friday *Boston Herald* list performance schedules.

★ **Emmanuel Music** holds concerts at Emmanuel Church, known as "the Bach church" for its Holy Eucharist services on Sunday at 10 AM. The concert series, which is performed by a professional chamber orchestra and chorus, is one of Boston's hidden gems, and runs weekly from September to May. ✉*15 Newbury St., Back Bay* ☎617/536–3356 ⊕*www.emmanuelmusic.org* Ⓣ*Arlington.*

Trinity Boston presents a free half-hour organ or choir recital Friday at 12:15, as well as seasonal choral concerts, in the vaulted neo-Romanesque interior of Copley Square's Trinity Church. ✉*Trinity Church, 206 Clarendon St., Copley Sq., Back Bay* ☎617/536–0944 ⊕*www.trinityboston.org* Ⓣ*Back Bay/South End, Copley.*

CONCERT SERIES

The Bank of America Celebrity Series presents about 50 events annually—renowned orchestras, chamber groups, recitalists, vocalists, and dance companies—often at Symphony Hall or Jordan Hall. Regulars include Yo-Yo Ma and the Alvin Ailey American Dance Theater. ✉*20 Park*

Frugal Fun

The nightlife and arts options we list are worth their weight in gold. Yet if you're feeling the pinch, you can be entertained without dropping a dime.

Nosh on gratis appetizers at the **Fritz Lounge** during happy hour on weekdays.

See a film at the **Boston Public Library**.

Go baroque—not broke—with classical concerts at the **Tsai Performance Center**.

Head to **Trinity Church** for free Friday organ or choir recitals at 12:15 PM.

Get down to blues and jazz at **Wally's Café** jazz club.

Buy a coffee or smoothie, and surf wireless Internet for free at **Trident Booksellers & Café**.

See art in the making: check out one of the weekend **Boston Open Studios** (⊕ *www.cityofboston.gov/arts/ visual/openstudios.asp*) in neighborhoods throughout the city. Summer brings even more free activities:

Bop along with the **Boston Pops** (☎ *617/266–1200 or 888/266–1200* ⊕ *www.bso.org*) at the Hatch Memorial Shell.

In July and August, the Commonwealth Shakespeare Company brings you **Shakespeare in the Park** in Boston Common.

From April to September, the Hatch Shell on the Esplanade is busy with free concerts, movie showings, and more, all part of the **Esplanade Summer Events** (☎ *617/626–1250* ⊕ *www.mass.gov/dcr/hatch_events. htm*). Perennial favorites include the Boston Pops' Fourth of July concert and "Free Friday Flicks" outdoor movie screenings.

Cinephiles can catch "Movies by Moonlight": classic films shown waterside as part of the Boston Harbor Hotel's outdoor **Summer in the City Series** (☎ *617/439–7000* ⊕ *www. bhh.com*). Other weekly offerings include swing dancing, soul singing, and blues concerts staged on a barge anchored behind the hotel.

5

Plaza, Suite 1032, Downtown ☎ *617/482–2595, 617/482–6661 box office* ⊕ *www.celebrityseries.org.*

EARLY-MUSIC GROUPS

Boston Camerata, founded in 1954, has become a worldwide favorite thanks to its popular recordings. It performs a series of medieval, Renaissance, and baroque concerts at various venues. ☎ *617/262–2092* ⊕ *www.bostoncamerata.org.*

Boston Early Music Festival focuses on medieval, baroque, and Renaissance music. Throughout the year, concerts, master classes, and lectures take place at churches and concert halls throughout Boston. Every other year in June, a fully staged opera is performed. Past productions have included Conradi's *Ariadne* (1691) and Mattheson's 1710 opera *Boris Goudenow.* ☎ *617/661–1812* ⊕ *www.bemf.org.*

★ **Handel & Haydn Society,** America's oldest music organization, has a history of performances that dates from 1815. It presents instrumental and choral performances at Symphony Hall. The group's holiday-season performances of Handel's *Messiah* are especially popular. ☎*617/266–3605 or 617/262–1815* ⊕*www.handelandhaydn.org.*

ORCHESTRAS

★ **Boston Philharmonic** is headed by the charismatic Benjamin Zander, whose informal preconcert talks help audiences better understand what they're about to hear. Most performances take place at Harvard's Sanders Theatre or the New England Conservatory's Jordan Hall. ☎*617/236–0999* ⊕*www.bostonphil.org.*

Boston Pops perform a mix of American standards, movie themes, and contemporary vocal numbers during May and June at Symphony Hall, followed by outdoor concerts at the Hatch Memorial Shell throughout July. The extremely popular outdoor concerts are free. ☎*617/266–1200, 888/266–1200 box office* ⊕*www.bostonpops.org.*

Boston Symphony Orchestra presents more than 250 concerts annually. The season at Symphony Hall runs from October to early May. In July and August, the activity shifts to the orchestra's beautiful summer home at the Tanglewood Music Center in Lenox, Massachusetts. ☎*617/266–1200, 888/266–1200 box office* ⊕*www.bso.org.* Ⓣ*Symphony*

OPERA

Boston Lyric Opera stages four full productions each season at Citi Performing Arts Center, which usually include one 20th-century work. Recent highlights have included Puccini's *La Boheme* and Englebert Humperdinck's *Hansel and Gretel.* ☎*617/542–4912, 617/542–6772 audience services office* ⊕*www.blo.org.* Ⓣ*Boylston*

Opera Boston draws a connoisseur crowd with its fully staged performances of little-known or rarely seen works such as Handel's *Semele* or Verdi's *Ernani.* Shows are at the Cutler Majestic Theatre at Emerson College. ☎*617/451–3388* ⊕*www.operaboston.org.* Ⓣ*Boylston*

THEATER

In the 1930s Boston had no fewer than 50 performing-arts theaters; by the 1980s, the city's downtown Theater District had all but vanished. Happily, in the late 1990s several historic theaters saw major restoration, opening to host pre-Broadway shows, visiting artists, and local troupes. More recently, the glorious renovation of the Opera House in 2004 has added new light to the district. Meanwhile, established companies such as the Huntington Theatre Company, near Northeastern University, and the American Repertory Theatre, in Cambridge, continue to offer premieres of works by major writers, including David Mamet, August Wilson, and Don DeLillo.

MAJOR THEATERS

The Charles Playhouse was formerly a church, a YWCA, a Prohibition-era speakeasy, and a nightclub. These days it plays host to the *Blue Man Group,* a loud, messy, exhilarating trio of playful performance artists painted vivid cobalt. (Warning: don't dress up, especially if you're sitting close to the stage.) ✉*74 Warrenton St., Theater District* ☎

617/426–6912 Blue Man Group
⊕*blueman.com/tickets/boston*
T*Boylston.*

Citi Performing Arts Center, formerly the Wang Center for the Performing Arts and the Shubert Theatre, is a performance space complex dedicated to both large-scale productions (at the former Wang) and more-intimate shows (at the former Shubert). Expect names such as *Riverdance* and other nationally touring Broadway shows, popular comedians, and the occasional ballet. ✉*270 Tremont St., Theater District* ☎*617/482–9393* ⊕*www. citicenter.org* T*Boylston.*

The Colonial Theatre has ornate red wallpaper, intricately carved balconies, and stately marble columns that evoke its turn-of-the-20th-century glamour. Visiting stars from W. C. Fields to Fanny Brice to Katharine Hepburn have trod its boards. More recently, the theater welcomed Broadway productions *The Producers* and *Avenue Q.* ✉*106 Boylston St., Back Bay* ☎*617/880–2460 day* ⊕*www.broadwayacrossamerica.com* T*Boylston.*

The Huntington Theatre Company, Boston's largest resident theater company, consistently performs a high-quality mix of 20th-century plays, new works, and classics under the leadership of dynamic artistic director Nicholas Martin, and commissions artists to produce original dramas. ✉*Boston University Theatre, 264 Huntington Ave., Back Bay* ☎*617/266–0800 box office* ⊕*www.huntingtontheatre.org* T*Symphony* ✉*Calderwood Theatre Pavilion, Boston Center for the Arts, 527 Tremont St., South End* ☎*617/426–5000* ⊕*www.bcaonline.org* T*Back Bay/South End, Copley.*

★ **The Opera House** features lavish musical productions such as *The Lion King* and Boston Ballet's *The Nutcracker.* The meticulously renovated 2,500-seat, beaux arts building has $35 million worth of gold leaf, lush carpeting, and rococo ornamentation. ✉*539 Washington St., Downtown Crossing, Chinatown* ☎*617/880–2495 or 617/259–3400* ⊕*www.broadwayinboston.com* T*Boylston, Chinatown, Downtown Crossing, Park Street.*

Stuart Street Playhouse regularly books traveling productions such as *I Love You, You're Perfect, Now Change* and *Menopause, The Musical* for long-running engagements. Originally a movie theater, the reconstituted performance space has been showing live performances since 1996. ✉*200 Stuart St., in Radisson Hotel Boston, Theater District* ☎*617/426–4499* ⊕*www.stuartstreetplayhouse.com* T*Boylston.*

SMALL THEATERS AND COMPANIES

★ **American Repertory** stages experimental, classic, and contemporary plays, often with unusual lighting, stage design, or multimedia effects. Its home at the Loeb Drama Center has two theaters; the smaller also

---

BEST ALFRESCO ARTS EVENTS

■ The Boston Pops at the Hatch Memorial Shell

■ Summer rock shows at the Bank of America Pavilion

■ Shakespeare in the Park on the Boston Common

■ Summer concerts at the Museum of Fine Arts' Calderwood Courtyard

■ Live music on summer evenings in Copley Square

5

holds productions by the Harvard-Radcliffe Drama Club. A modern theater space down the street, called the Zero Arrow Theatre, has a more-flexible stage design for electrifying contemporary productions. ⊠*64 Brattle St., Harvard Sq., Cambridge* ☎*617/547–8300* ⊕*www. amrep.org* Ⓣ*Harvard.*

★ **Boston Center for the Arts** houses more than a dozen quirky, low-budget troupes in six performance areas, including the 300-seat Stanford Calderwood Pavilion, two black box theaters, and the massive Cyclorama, built to hold a 360-degree mural of the Battle of Gettysburg (the painting is now in a building at the battlefield). The experimental Pilgrim Theater, multiracial Company One, gay/lesbian Theatre Offensive, Irish-American Súgan Theatre troupe, and contemporary Speak-Easy Stage Company put on shows here year-round. ⊠*539 Tremont St., South End* ☎*617/426–5000* ⊕*www.bcaonline.org* Ⓣ*Back Bay/ South End, Copley.*

Harvard's Hasty Pudding Theatricals at Harvard University calls itself the "oldest collegiate theatrical company in the United States." It produces one show annually, which plays in Boston in February and March and then goes on tour. The troupe also honors a famous actor and actress each year with an awards ceremony and a parade (in drag) through Cambridge. Recent honorees include Charlize Theron and Christopher Walken. Performances are scattered around Cambridge and Harvard Square. ⊠*Harvard Sq., Cambridge* ☎*617/495–5205* ⊕*www.hasty pudding.org* Ⓣ*Harvard.*

Sports and the Outdoors

WORD OF MOUTH

"Anyone who tells you the bleachers at Fenway are really rowdy has not been there in many years. But, some things to know. First, Boston fans are passionate and knowledgeable about baseball. If there is a bad call or play, they will be quite vocal—and possibly use some language that is not old-fashioned refined Boston. Second, rows are long; you will have to stand multiple times to allow fans in/out to buy beer and food. It gets annoying. Third, there is no shade out there and therefore no protection from sun, rain—dress acordingly."

—gail

Updated
by Bethany
Cassin
Beckerlegge

Everything you've heard about the zeal of Boston fans is true; here, you root for the home team. You cheer, and you pray, and you root some more. "Red Sox Nation" witnessed a miracle in 2004, with the reverse of the curse and the first World Series victory since 1918.

Then in 2007 they proved it wasn't just a fluke with another Series win. In 2008 the Celtics ended their 18-year NBA championship drought with a thrilling victory over longtime rivals the LA Lakers. And despite the sting of their first Super Bowl loss (in recent memory) earlier in '08, the Patriots are still a remarkable force to be reckoned with.

Bostonians' long-standing fervor for sport is equally evident in their leisure-time activities. Harsh winters keep locals wrapped up for months, only to emerge at the earliest sign of oncoming spring, striving to push back the February blues through feverish exercise. Once the mercury tops freezing and the snows begin to thaw, Boston's extensive parks, paths, woods, and waterways teem with sun worshippers and athletes—until the bitter winds bite again in November, and that energy becomes redirected once again toward white slopes, frozen rinks, and sheltered gyms and pools.

Most public recreational facilities, including skating rinks and tennis courts, are operated by the **Department of Conservation & Recreation** (*DCR* ✉ *251 Causeway St., Suite 600, North End* ☎ *617/626–1250* ⊕ *www. mass.gov/dcr*). The DCR provides information about recreational activities in its facilities and promotes the conservation of Massachusetts parks and wilderness areas.

The **Appalachian Mountain Club** (✉ *5 Joy St., Beacon Hill* ☎ *617/523–0655* ⊕ *www.outdoors.org* Ⓣ *Park St.*) makes a helpful first stop for anyone with questions about the great outdoors. Its bookstore has maps and guides about hiking and other active pursuits in the Northeast and Mid-Atlantic. The club also runs workshops and organized hiking, paddling, biking, and skiing trips throughout New England. Programs fill up fast, so advance reservations are essential. Fees are higher for nonmembers. A one-year individual membership starts at $50; discounted family, youth, and senior memberships are available. The club is open weekdays 9–5.

BEACHES

Although nearly 20 years of massive cleanup efforts have made the water in Boston Harbor safe for swimming, many locals and visitors still find city beaches unappealing since much better beaches are a short drive or train ride away.

If you're using public transportation to get around, you have several choices. Just north of the city, **Revere Beach** (✉ *Revere Beach Blvd., Revere02151*), the oldest public beach in America, has faded somewhat since its glory days in the early 20th century when it was a Coney Island–type playground, but it still remains a good spot to people-watch and catch some rays. The sand and water are less than pristine, but on hot summer days the waterfront is still packed with colorful local characters and Bostonians looking for an easy city escape. Most of the beach's former amusements are gone, but you can still catch concerts on the bandstand in summer. Take the Blue Line to the Revere Beach Station; one-way fares are $1.70.

WORD OF MOUTH

"Crane's Beach is excellent, arguably the best in the area assuming it isn't greenhead fly season when you go (they bite!). Wingaersheek Beach in Gloucester and Singing Beach in Manchester-by-the-Sea are other good Cape Ann area beaches." — bachslunch

'WICH WAY TO THE BEACH?

The huge, juicy roast beef sandwiches served at **Kelly's Roast Beef** (✉ *410 Revere Beach Blvd., Revere* ☎ *781/284–9129* ⊕ *www.kellysroastbeef. com*), a local institution since 1951, is the sole reason some Bostonians make the trek to Revere. Other menu favorites include the fried clams and hand-breaded onion rings. It's open from 5 AM to 2:30 AM Sunday through Thursday, and until 3 AM Friday and Saturday.

Singing Beach (✉ *Beach St., Manchester-by-the-Sea*), 32 mi north of Boston in a quiet Cape Ann town, gets its name from the musical squeaking sound its gold-color sand makes when you step on it. The beach is popular with both locals and out-of-towners in summer. It's also worth a visit in fall, when the crowds have gone home and you'll have the splendid shores all to yourself. There's a snack bar at the beach, but it's worth taking a 10-minute stroll up Beach Street into town to get a cone at Captain Dusty's Ice Cream (60 Beach Street). Because there's no public parking at the beach, the easiest way to get here is by Rockport commuter rail train from North Station to the Manchester stop, which is a 15-minute walk from the beach. From downtown Boston, the train takes 45 minutes and costs $6.75 each way.

Sandy Cape Cod and the rocky North Shore are studded with New England beach towns, each with its favorite swimming spot. **Nantasket Beach** (✉ *Rte. 3A, Hull*), a 45-minute drive from downtown Boston, has cleaner sand and warmer water than most local beaches. Take Route 3A South to Washington Boulevard, Hingham, and follow signs to Nantasket Avenue. Part of the 1,200-acre Crane Wildlife Refuge, **Crane Beach** (✉ *Argilla Rd., Ipswich* ☎978/356–4354), an hour's drive to the north of Boston in the 17th-century village of Ipswich, has 4 mi of sparkling white sand that serves as a nesting ground for the threatened piping plover. From Route 128 North (toward Gloucester), follow signs for Route 1A North, 8 mi to Ipswich. The well-groomed beaches of **Plum Island** (✉*Plum Island Blvd., Newburyport*) are worth the effort to find a parking space. The water is clear and blue, but quite cold. From I–95 follow Route 113 East (becomes Route 1A South) 3½ mi to Newbury. Then, take a left on Rolfe's Lane and a right on to the Plum Island Turnpike.

PARKS

Comprising 34 islands, the **Boston Harbor Islands National Park Area** is somewhat of a hidden gem for nature lovers and history buffs, with miles of lightly traveled trails and shoreline and several little-visited historic sites to explore. The focal point of the national park is 39-acre Georges Island, where you'll find the partially restored pre–Civil War Fort Warren that once held Confederate prisoners. Other islands worth visiting include Peddocks Island, which holds the remains of Fort Andrews, and Lovells Island, a popular destination for campers. Lovells, Peddocks, Grape, and Bumpkin islands allow camping with a permit from late June through Labor Day. There are swimming areas at the four camping-friendly islands as well, but only Lovells has lifeguards.

> **TOP 5**
>
> ■ Taking in a Red Sox game at Fenway Park, the nation's oldest ballpark—the experience can't be duplicated.
>
> ■ Running or biking along the Charles River or, better yet, sailing on it with Community Boating.
>
> ■ Seeing magnificent whales and their young close-up on a whale-watch boat tour.
>
> ■ Exploring the quiet, awe-inspiring trails and shorelines of the Boston Harbor Islands.
>
> ■ Strolling through the parks and gardens of the Emerald Necklace (including the Boston Common and Public Garden).

Pets and alcohol are not allowed on the Harbor Islands. The **National Park Service** (☎617/223–8666 ⊕*www.bostonislands.com*) is a good source for information about camping, transportation, and the like. To reach the islands, take the **Harbor Express** (☎617/222–6999 ⊕*www. harborexpress.com*) from Long Wharf (Downtown) or the Hingham Shipyard to Georges Island or Spectacle Island. High-speed catamarans run daily from May through mid-October and cost $14. Other islands can be reached by the free interisland water shuttles that depart from Georges Island.

As soon as the snow begins to recede, Bostonians emerge from hibernation. Runners, bikers, and in-line skaters crowd the **Charles River Reservation** (⊕*www.mass.gov/dcr*) at the Esplanade along Storrow Drive, the Memorial Drive Embankment in Cambridge, or any of the smaller and less-busy parks farther upriver. Here you can cheer a crew race, rent a canoe or a kayak, or simply sit on the grass, sharing the shore with packs of hard-jogging university athletes, in-line skaters, moms with strollers, dreamily entwined couples, and intense academics, often talking to themselves as they sort out their intellectual—or perhaps personal—dilemmas.

The **Hatch Memorial Shell** (☎617/626–4970 Ⓣ*Charles/MGH*) on the Esplanade holds free concerts and outdoor events all summer.

The six large public parks known as Boston's **Emerald Necklace** stretch 5 mi from the Back Bay Fens through Franklin Park, in Dorchester. Frederick Law Olmsted's design heightened the natural beauty of the Emerald Necklace, which remains a well-groomed urban masterpiece.

Locals take pride in and happily make use of its open spaces and its pathways and bridges connecting rivers and ponds. The **Emerald Necklace Conservancy** (☎617/522–2700 ⊕*www.emeraldnecklace.org*) maintains a regular calendar of nature walks and other events in the parks. Rangers with the **Boston Parks & Recreation Department** (✉*1010 Massachusetts Ave.* ☎*617/635–4505* ⊕*www.cityofboston.gov/parks/parkrangers*) lead tours highlighting the area's historic sites and surprising ecological diversity. The sumptuously landscaped **Arnold Arboretum** (✉*125 Arborway, Jamaica Plain* ☎*617/524–1718* ⊕*www.arboretum.harvard.edu* Ⓣ*Forest Hills*) is open all year to joggers and in-line skaters. Volunteer docents give free walking tours in spring, summer, and fall.

Cambridge's historic **Mt. Auburn Cemetery** (✉*580 Mt. Auburn St., Mt. Auburn, Cambridge* ☎*617/547–7105* ⊕*www.mountauburn*.org Ⓣ*Harvard, then Bus 71 or 73 to Mount Auburn St. at Aberdeen Ave. stop*) is known as one of the best birding spots in the area, and also has walking paths, gardens, and unique architecture. You can also see the graves of distinguished New Englanders such as Oliver Wendell Holmes, Henry Wadsworth Longfellow, and Mary Baker Eddy, among many others.

SPORTS

BASEBALL

Fodor'sChoice
★

Hide your Yankees cap and practice pronouncing "Fenway Pahk." Boston is a baseball town, where the crucible of media scrutiny burns hot, fans regard myth and superstition as seriously as player statistics, and grudges are never forgotten. The **Boston Red Sox** (✉*Fenway Park, The Fenway* ☎*877/733–7699 tickets, 617/226–6666 tours* ⊕*www. bostonredsox.com*) made history in 2004, crushing the Yankees in the American League Championship after a three-game deficit and then sweeping the Cardinals in the World Series for their first title since 1918. More than 3 million fans from "Red Sox Nation" celebrated the championship team and the reversal of the "Curse of the Bambino" with a victory parade through the streets of Boston and down the Charles River. And as icing on the cake, they did it again in 2007, this time defeating the Colorado Rockies in another historic sweep. The Red Sox ownership has committed to staying in the once-threatened Fenway Park for the long term, so you can still watch a game in the country's oldest active ballpark and see (or, for a premium price, get a seat on top of) the fabled "Green Monster" (the park's 37-foot-high left-field wall) and one of the last hand-operated scoreboards in the major leagues. Baseball season runs from early April to early October. The play-offs continue several more weeks, and postseason buzz about contracts, trades, and injuries lasts all winter long.

DID YOU KNOW?

The longest measurable home run hit inside Fenway Park—502 feet—was batted by legendary Red Sox slugger Ted Williams on June 9, 1946. A lone red seat in the right-field bleachers marks the spot where the ball landed.

6

BASKETBALL

★ The **Boston Celtics** (✉*TD Banknorth Garden, Old West End* ☎*617/624–1000, 617/931–2222 Ticketmaster* ⊕*www.celtics.com*) have won the National Basketball Association (NBA) championship 17 times since 1957, more than any other franchise in the NBA. The mystique of the Celtics' former glory days keeps fans coming back year after year in hopes that a championship banner might again be hoisted above the court. And in 2008, after a solid defeat of longtime rivals the LA Lakers, fans got their wish and witnessed the not-a-moment-too-soon end of an 18-year championship dry-spell. Basketball season runs from October to April, and play-offs last until mid-June.

BICYCLING

★ It's common to see suited-up doctors, lawyers, and businessmen commuting on two wheels through Downtown; unfortunately, bike lanes are few and far between. Boston's dedicated bike paths are well used, as much by joggers and in-line skaters as by bicyclists. The **Dr. Paul Dudley White Bike Path,** about 17 mi long, follows both banks of the Charles River as it winds from Watertown Square to the Museum of Science. The **Pierre Lallement Bike Path** winds 5 mi through the South End and Roxbury, from Copley Place to Franklin Park. The tranquil **Minuteman Bikeway** courses 11 mi from the Alewife Red Line T station in Cambridge through Arlington, Lexington, and Bedford. The trail, in the bed of an old rail line, cuts through a few busy intersections—be particularly careful in Arlington Center.

> **ON YER BIKE!**
>
> Boston may be dubbed America's Walking City, but it's a fine place for pedal-pushing, too. **Boston Bike Tours** (☎*617/308–5902* ⊕*www.bostonbiketours.com*) offers a variety of themed excursions on weekends from spring through fall. Most outings cover about 10–12 mi. It costs about $35 a person ($24 if you bring your own bike). No reservations needed: just show up at the Visitor Information Center on the Boston Common at 10 AM for the morning option, or 2 PM for the afternoon outing. You bring the adrenaline, they bring the bikes, helmets, and water.

For other path locations, consult the **Department of Conservation & Recreation** (*DCR* ⊕*www.mass.gov/dcr*) Web site.

The **Massachusetts Bicycle Coalition** (*MassBike* ✉*171 Milk St., Suite 33, Downtown* ☎*617/542–2453* ⊕*www.massbike.org*), an advocacy group working to improve conditions for area cyclists, has information on organized rides and sells good bike maps of Boston and the state. Thanks to MassBike's lobbying efforts, the MBTA now allows bicycles on subway and commuter-rail trains during nonpeak hours. **Community Bicycle Supply** (✉*496 Tremont St., at E. Berkeley St., South End* ☎*617/542–8623* ⊕*www.communitybicycle.com*) rents cycles from April through October, at rates of $25 for 24 hours. **Back Bay Bicycles** (✉*362 Commonwealth Ave., Back Bay* ☎*617/247–2336* ⊕*www.backbaybicycles.com*) has mountain bike rentals for $35 per day and road bikes for $55 per day. Staff members also lead group mountain bike rides on nearby trails.

BOATING

Except when frozen over, the waterways coursing through the city serve as a playground for boaters of all stripes. All types of pleasure craft, with the exception of inflatables, are allowed from the Charles River and Inner Harbor to North Washington Street on the waters of Boston Harbor, Dorchester inner and outer bays, and the Neponset River from the Granite Avenue Bridge to Dorchester Bay.

Sailboats can be rented from one of the many boathouses or docks along the Charles. Downtown, public landings and float docks are available at the **Christopher Columbus Waterfront Park** (✉ *Commercial St., Boston Harbor, North End* ☎ *617/635–4505*) with a permit from the Boston harbormaster. Along the Charles, **boat drop sites** are at **Clarendon Street** (✉ *Back Bay*), the **Hatch Shell** (✉ *Embankment Rd., Back Bay*), **Pinckney Street Landing** (✉ *Back Bay*), **Brooks Street** (✉ *Nonantum Rd., Brighton*), **Richard T. Artesani Playground** (✉ *Off Soldiers Field Rd., Brighton*), **Charles River Dam, Museum of Science** (✉ *Cambridge*), and **Watertown Square**(✉ *Charles River Rd., Watertown*).

The **Charles River Watershed Association** (☎ *781/788–0007* ⊕ *www. charlesriver.org*) publishes a 32-page canoe and kayaking guide with detailed boating

LESSONS AND EQUIPMENT

★ From May to October, **Boston University** (✉ *Soldier's Field Rd.* ☎ *617/353–2748* ⊕ *www.bu.edu/fitrec*) offers beginner to advanced rowing and sailing programs. From May through mid-November, you can rent a canoe, kayak, paddleboat, rowboat, or rowing shell from **Charles River Canoe & Kayak Center** (✉ *2401 Commonwealth Ave., Newton* ☎ *617/965–5110* ⊕ *www.paddleboston.com*). There are a variety of canoeing and kayaking classes for all skill levels, as well as organized group outings and tours. The Canoe & Kayak Center's **kiosk** (✉ *Soldiers' Field Rd. near Eliot Bridge, Allston*) rents canoes and kayaks and is open Thursday evening, Friday afternoon, and weekends early May through mid-October. It's open weekdays only for group appointments. **Community Boating** (✉ *21 David Mugar Way, Beacon Hill* ☎ *617/523–1038* ⊕ *www. community-boating.org*), near the Charles Street footbridge on the Esplanade, is the host of America's oldest public sailing program. From April through October, $89 nets you a 30-day introductory membership, beginner-level classes, and use of sailboats and kayaks. Full memberships grant unlimited use of all facilities; splash around for 60 days for $175 or all season long for $240. Experienced sailors short on time can opt for a one-day sailboat rental for $75.

Community Rowing (✉ *Daly Memorial Skating Rink, Nonantum Rd., Brighton* ☎ *617/779–8267* ⊕ *www.communityrowing.org*) teaches introductory to competitive adult and youth rowing courses. Private lessons are also available. From April to October, the **Jamaica Pond Boat House** (✉ *Jamaica Way and Pond St., Jamaica Plain* ☎ *617/522–5061*)

6

Thar She Blows

Ships depart regularly for whale-watching excursions from April or May through October, from coastal towns all along the bay. Humpbacks, finbacks, and minkes feed locally in season, so you're sure to see a few—and on a good day you may see dozens. Bring warm clothing, as the ocean breezes can be brisk; rubber-soled shoes are a good idea.

The **New England Aquarium** (⊠ *Central Wharf at end of Central St., Downtown* ☎ *617/973–5200* ⊕ *www.neaq.org*) runs daily whale-watching cruises from Central Wharf. The trip, with an aquarium staff whale expert on board, lasts three to four hours. The high-speed catamarans of **Boston Harbor Cruises** (⊠ *Long Wharf next to aquarium, Downtown* ☎ *877/733–9425* ⊕ *www.boston harborcruises.com*) glide to the whaling banks in half the time of some

other cruises, allowing nearly as much whale time in only a three-hour tour.

The old fishing port of Glouces-ter is Massachusetts Bay's hot spot for whale-sighting trips. **Cape Ann Whale Watch** (⊠ *Rose's Wharf, 415 Main St., Gloucester* ☎ *800/877–5110* ⊕ *www.caww.com*) has run whale-watch tours since 1979. Tours with **Captain Bill's Deep Sea Fishing/ Whale Watch** (⊠ *24 Harbor Loop, Gloucester* ☎ *978/283–6995 or 800/339–4253* ⊕ *www.captbilland sons.com*) make use of knowledgeable naturalists from the Whale Center of New England.

South of Boston, whale-watch trips leave from Plymouth and loca-tions around Cape Cod. **Capt. John Boats** (⊠ *10 Town Wharf, Plymouth* ☎ *508/746–2643 or 800/242–2469* ⊕ *www.captjohn.com*) sends out sev-eral daily whale-watch cruises from Plymouth Town Wharf.

provides lessons and equipment for rowing and sailing on its name-sake pond.

EVENTS

In mid-October more than 7,500 male and female athletes from
★ all over the world compete in the annual **Head of the Charles Regatta** (☎ *617/868–6200* ⊕ *www.hocr.org*). Thousands of spectators line the banks of the Charles River with blankets and beer (although the police disapprove of the latter), cheering on their favorite teams and generally using the weekend as an excuse to party. Limited free parking is avail-able, but the chances of finding an open space close to the race route are slim, so take public transportation if you can. During the event, free shuttles run between the start and end point of the race route on both sides of the river.

FISHING

Efforts to clean up the city's waterways have heightened the popular-ity of recreational fishing in and around Boston. For saltwater fishing, locals cast their lines from the **John J. McCorkle Fishing Pier** on Castle Island off Day Boulevard in South Boston and **Tenean Beach** and **Victory**

Road Park off Morrissey Boulevard in Dorchester. The **Boston Harbor Islands National Park Area** (☎*617/223–8666* ⊕*www.bostonislands.com*) is also known for great fishing, although no public piers are available.

You can try to catch freshwater fish in **Jamaica Pond** (✉*Jamaica Way and Pond St., Jamaica Plain*), Turtle Pond in **Stony Brook Reservation** (✉*Turtle Pond Pkwy., Hyde Park*), Quarter Mile Pond and Dark Hollow Pond in **Middlesex Fells Reservation** (✉*Off Rte. 93, Stoneham*), or Houghton's Pond in **Blue Hills Reservation** (✉*Off Rte. 128, Milton*).

Nonresidents can purchase a three-day Massachusetts fishing license for $23.50 at the **MassWildlife Boston Office** (✉*251 Causeway St., North End* ☎*617/626–1590* ⊕*www.mass.gov/dfwele*), Brookline Town Hall, and some sporting-goods stores around the city. No license is required for recreational ocean angling.

FOOTBALL

Since 2002, Boston has been building a football dynasty, starting with the **New England Patriots'** (✉*Gillette Stadium, Rte. 1, off I–95 Exit 9, Foxborough* ☎*617/931–2222 Ticketmaster* ⊕*www.patriots.com*) come-from-behind Super Bowl victory against the favored St. Louis Rams. Coach Bill Belichick and heartthrob quarterback Tom Brady then brought the team two more Super Bowl rings, in 2004 and 2005, and have made Patriots fans as zealous as their baseball counterparts. The team's heartbreaking Super Bowl loss in 2008 has only increased fan fervor for coming seasons. Exhibition football games begin in August, and the season runs through the play-offs in January. The state-of-the-art Gillette Stadium is in Foxborough, 30 mi southwest of Boston.

With the only Division 1A football program in town, the **Boston College Eagles** (✉*Alumni Stadium, Chestnut Hill* ☎*617/552–4622*) play against some of the top teams in the country.

Built in 1903, Harvard Stadium is the oldest concrete stadium in the country and the home of the **Harvard University Crimson** (✉*Harvard Stadium, N. Harvard St. and Soldiers Field Rd., Allston* ☎*877/464–2782*), who went undefeated in 2001 and 2004. The halftime shows of the Harvard Band make any game worth the trip.

GOLF

Although you'll need to know someone who knows someone who *is* someone to play at Brookline's **Country Club,** one of the nation's top-rated private courses, anyone can use the public courses in Boston, which are among the best in the country.

Donald Ross crafted the 6,009-yard, par-70 **Franklin Park Golf Course** (✉*1 Circuit Dr., Dorchester* ☎*617/265–4084*) in the early 1900s. It's open year-round, weather permitting. Greens fees without a cart are $14 for 9 holes and $23 for 18 holes on weekdays, and $16 and $29, respectively, on weekends. (You can play 9 holes only after 1 PM on weekends.) If you're not a Boston resident, the course ups the ante by $2 to $5; charges for a golf cart tend to run about $16 to $26 more. Club rentals run $10 for 9 holes and $12 for 18 holes. The course is part of a delightful city park with picnic facilities and jogging courses. Festivals and other outdoor activities take place all year.

The hilly **George Wright Golf Course** (✉ *420 West St., Hyde Park* ☎ *617/364– 2300*) is more challenging than the other Donald Ross–designed course at Franklin Park. The par-70, 6,096-yard course is open for the season starting in April each year. Weekend 18-hole greens fees are $42; weekday fees are $36. Tee times are necessary on weekends.

The **Massachusetts Golf Association** (✉ *300 Arnold Palmer Blvd., Norton* ☎ *800/356–2201* ⊕ *www.mgalinks.org*) represents 400 clubs in the state and has information on courses that are open to the public.

HIKING

With the Appalachian Trail just two hours' drive from Downtown and thousands of acres of parkland and trails encircling the city, hikers will not lack for options in and around Boston.

☾ ★ A 20-minute drive south of Boston, the **Blue Hills Reservation** (✉ *695 Hillside St., Milton* ☎ *617/698–1802*) encompasses 7,000 acres of woodland with about 125 mi of trails, some ideal for cross-country skiing in winter, some designated for mountain biking the rest of the year. Although only 635 feet high, Great Blue Hill, the tallest hill in the reservation, has a spectacular view of the entire Boston metro area. It's open daily, and maps are available for purchase at the reservation headquarters or the Blue Hills Trailside Museum. To get there, take Route 93 South to Exit 3, Houghton's Pond.

☾ The **Blue Hills Trailside Museum** (✉ *1904 Canton Ave., Milton* ☎ *617/333– 0690*), which is managed by the Massachusetts Audubon Society, organizes hikes and nature walks. Open Wednesday through Sunday 10–5, the museum has natural-history exhibits and live animals. Admission is $3. Take Route 93 South to Exit 2B and Route 138 North.

Just a few miles north of Boston, the 2,575-acre **Middlesex Fells Reservation** (☎ *617/727–5380*) has well-maintained hiking trails that pass over rocky hills, across meadows, and through wetland areas. Trails range from the quarter-mile Bear Hill Trail to the 6.9-mi Skyline Trail. Mountain bikers can ride along the reservation's fire roads and on a designated loop trail. This sprawling reservation covers area in Malden, Medford, Stoneham, Melrose, and Winchester. To get to the western side of the reservation from Boston, take Route 93 North to Exit 33, and then take South Border Road off the rotary.

Easily accessible from downtown Boston, the **Boston Harbor Islands National Park Area** is seldom crowded. The park maintains walking trails through diverse terrain and ecosystems (⇨ *Parks, above*).

Rangers with the **Boston Parks & Recreation Department** (✉ *1010 Massachusetts Ave.* ☎ *617/635–7383* ⊕ *www.cityofboston.gov/parks/park rangers*) lead walks through the Emerald Necklace parks.

Excellent hiking footpaths crisscross the 475-acre **Stony Brook Reservation** (✉ *Turtle Pond Pkwy.* ☎ *617/333–7404*), which spans Hyde Park and West Roxbury.

HOCKEY

Boston hockey fans are informed, vocal, and extremely loyal. Despite frequent trades of star players, disappointing losses, high ticket prices, and the complete lockout of the 2004–05 season, the stands are still packed at Bruins games. That said, local college hockey teams tend to give spectators more to celebrate at a much more reasonable price.

The **Boston Bruins** (⊠ *TD Banknorth Garden, 100 Legends Way, Old West End* ☎ *617/624–1000, 617/931–2222 Ticketmaster* ⊕ *www.boston bruins.com*) are on the ice from September until April, frequently on Thursday and Saturday evenings. Play-offs last through early June.

Boston College, Boston University, Harvard, and Northeastern teams face off every February in the **Beanpot Hockey Tournament** (☎ *617/624– 1000*) at the TD Banknorth Garden. The colleges in this fiercely contested tournament traditionally yield some of the finest squads in the country.

ICE SKATING

The Department of Conservation & Recreation operates more than 20 **public ice-skating rinks** (☎ *617/626–1250* ⊕ *www.mass.gov/dcr*); hours and season vary by location. Call for a complete list of rinks and their hours of operation.

Thanks to a refrigerated surface, the **Boston Common Frog Pond** (⊠ *Beacon Hill* ☎ *617/635–2120* ⊕ *www.bostoncommonfrogpond.org*) transforms into a skating park from November to mid-March, complete with a warming hut and concession stand. Admission is $4 for adults; kids 13 and under skate free. Skate rentals cost $8 and lockers are $1. Frog Pond hours are Monday 10–5, Tuesday through Thursday and Sunday 10–9, and Friday and Saturday 10–10.

Skaters flock to the frozen waters of the lagoon at **Boston Public Garden.** Ice on one side of the bridge is theoretically reserved for figure skating and the other for faster-paced ice hockey, though most ignore the rule during slow times.

Outside the city, try the skating rink in **Larz Anderson Park** (⊠ *23 Newton St., Brookline* ☎ *617/739–7518*), at the top of a wooded hill. Admission for Brookline residents is $4; nonresidents pay $7. Skate rentals are $5. The rink is open from December through early March.

SKATE RENTALS

Beacon Hill Skate Shop (⊠ *135 Charles St., off Tremont St., near Wang Center for the Performing Arts, South End* ☎ *617/482–7400*) rents skates for use in the Frog Pond and Public Garden for $10 per hour or $20 per day. A credit card is required; call in advance and they'll have the skates sharpened and ready for you.

RUNNING AND JOGGING

Boston's parks and riverside pathways almost never lack for joggers, even in the worst weather. Paths on both sides of the Charles River are the most crowded and best maintained, particularly along the **Esplanade.**

The Boston Marathon

Though it missed being the first U.S. marathon by one year (the first, in 1896, went from Stamford, Connecticut, to New York City), the Boston Marathon is arguably the nation's most prestigious. Why? It's the only marathon in the world for which runners have to qualify; it's the world's oldest continuously run marathon; it's been run on the same course since it began. Only the New York Marathon compares with it for community involvement. Spectators have returned to the same spot for generations, bringing their lawn chairs and barbecues.

Runners compete in the world's oldest, and most prestigious, marathon.

Held every Patriots' Day (the third Monday in April), the marathon passes through Hopkinton, Ashland, Framingham, Natick, Wellesley, Newton, Brookline, and Boston; only the last few miles are run in the city proper. The first marathon was organized by members of the Boston Athletic Association (BAA), who in 1896 had attended the first modern Olympic games in Athens. When they saw that the Olympics ended with a marathon, they decided the same would be a fitting end to their own Spring Sports Festival, begun in the late 1880s.

The first race was run on April 19, 1897, when Olympian Tom Burke drew a line in the dirt in Ashland and began a 24.5-mi dash to Boston with 15 men. For most of its history, the race concluded on Exeter Street outside the BAA's clubhouse. In 1965 the finish was moved to the front of the Prudential Center, and in 1986 it was moved to its current location, Copley Square. The race's guardian spirit is the indefatigable John A. Kelley, who ran his first marathon shortly after Warren G. Harding was sworn in as president. Kelley won twice—in 1935 and 1945—took the second-

place spot seven times, and continued to run well into his eighties, finishing 58 Boston Marathons in all. Until his retirement in 1992, his arrival at the finish signaled the official end of the race. A double statue of an older Kelley greeting his younger self stands at the route's most strenuous incline— dubbed "Heartbreak Hill"—on Commonwealth Avenue in Newton.

Women weren't allowed to race until 1972, but in 1966 Roberta Gibb slipped into the throngs under a hooded sweatshirt; she was the first known female participant. In 1967 cameras captured BAA organizer Jock Semple screaming, "Get out of my race," as he tried to rip off the number of Kathrine Switzer, who had registered as K. Switzer. But the marathon's most infamous moment was when 26-year-old Rosie Ruiz came out of nowhere to be the first woman to cross the finish line in the 1980 race. Ruiz apparently started running less than 1 mi from the end of the course, and her title was stripped eight days later. Bostonians still quip about her taking the T to the finish.

Watch out for in-line skaters and bikers. At **Castle Island** in South Boston, skaters and joggers zip past strolling lovebirds and parents pushing jogging strollers. The wooded 1½-mi-long loop around **Jamaica Pond** is a slightly less-crowded option.

For equipment and information on local running routes, contact the **Bill Rodgers Running Center** (⊠ *Faneuil Hall Marketplace, Government Center* ☎ *617/723–5612* ⊕ *www.billrodgers.com*).

EVENTS

Fodor'sChoice
★

Every Patriots' Day (the third Monday in April), fans gather along the Hopkinton–to–Boston route of the **Boston Marathon** (⇨ *Close-Up box in this chapter*) to cheer on more than 20,000 runners from all over the world. The race ends near Copley Square in the Back Bay. For information, call the **Boston Athletic Association** (☎ *617/236–1652* ⊕ *www. bostonmarathon.org*).

In October women runners take the spotlight on Columbus Day for the **Tufts Health Plan 10K for Women** (☎ *888/767–7223 Registration* ⊕ *www. tufts-healthplan.com/tufts10k*), which attracts 7,000 participants and 20,000 spectators. Four American records have been set at this race since it began in 1977.

SKIING

CROSS-COUNTRY

From mid-December to March, the **Weston Ski Track** (⊠ *200 Park Rd., Weston* ☎ *781/891–6575* ⊕ *www.skiboston.com*) provides cross-country skiers and snowshoers with 9 mi of groomed, natural trails and a snowmaking area with a lighted 1-mi ski track. Rentals and basic instruction are available.

DOWNHILL

The closest downhill skiing to Boston is at the **Blue Hills Ski Area** (⊠ *Blue Hills Reservation, 4001 Washington St., Canton* ☎ *781/828–5070* ⊕ *www.ski-bluehills.com*). It has 60 acres of skiing terrain and 10 trails to choose from. There's a snow sports school, equipment rentals, and a restaurant. Off-peak and group rates are available. Take Route 93 South to Exit 2B and Route 138 North.

On weekends and holidays, serious skiers and snowboarders head north to the mountain resorts along I–93 in New Hampshire. The first big resort off the interstate, **Waterville Valley Resort** (⊠ *Rte. 49, off I–93 Exit 28, Waterville Valley, NH* ☎ *603/236–8311 or 800/468–2553*), is one of the state's most popular ski destinations with 52 trails and a terrain park with a 400-foot half pipe.

Nearby **Loon Mountain Resort** (⊠ *Off I–93 Exit 32, Lincoln, NH* ☎ *603/745–8111 or 800/229–5666* ⊕ *www.loonmtn.com*) has 53 trails spanning more than 2,100 vertical feet and six terrain parks. Farther north in Franconia Notch, the historic **Cannon Mountain Resort** (⊠ *Off I–93 N Exit 34A, B, or C, Franconia, NH* ☎ *603/823–8800* ⊕ *www.cannonmt. com*) is the site of North America's first aerial tramway and home to the New England Ski Museum. There are 60 trails and nine lifts. **Ski**

6

NH (☎*603/745–9396 or 800/887–5464* ⊕*www.skinh.com*) is a good source for local ski information.

The **Berkshires** (✉*135 mi west of Boston along I–90 and Rte. 2* ⊕*www. berkshires.org*) region in western Massachusetts offers a little bit of Aspen on the East Coast, with tony ski resorts, fine dining, and an upscale atmosphere for those able to take a daylong or weekend ski trip. For details on the various resorts in the Berkshires, go to www. berkshireskiing.com.

SOCCER

New England's major-league soccer team, **New England Revolution** (✉*Gillette Stadium, Foxborough* ☎*877/438–7387, 617/931–2222 Ticketmaster* ⊕*www.nerevolution.com*), plays from late March to late October.

On any clear weekend morning, pickup games at most of Boston's parks, especially the fields at the western end of **Back Bay Fens Park** and at **Mayor Thomas W. Danehy Park** near the Alewife transit center in Cambridge, become meeting places for amateur soccer players and fans.

TENNIS

The **Department of Conservation & Recreation** (☎*617/626–1250* ⊕*www. mass.gov/dcr*) maintains more than 25 public tennis courts throughout the greater Boston area. These operate on a first-come, first-served basis. Lighted courts are open from dawn to 10 PM; other courts are open from dawn to dusk.

Some of Boston's most popular lighted courts are those at **Charlesbank Park** (✉*Storrow Dr. opposite Charles St., Beacon Hill*), **Marine Park** (✉*Day Blvd., South Boston*), and **Weider Playground** (✉*Dale St., Hyde Park*).

Shopping

WORD OF MOUTH

"The South End and Charles St in Beacon Hill have the most independent boutiques (clothing and housewares, etc.). There's also been several stores that have opened in the North End in the last couple of years, mostly clothing boutiques. Newbury St. has a mix of chains and independent stores but is worth checking out as it's the main shopping thoroughfare of the city."

—wyatt92

Updated
by Bethany
Cassin
Beckerlegge

Shopping in Boston is a lot like the city itself: a mix of clas-sic and cutting-edge, the high-end and the handmade, and international and local sensibilities. Though many Bosto-nians think too many chain stores have begun to clog their distinctive avenues, there remains a strong network of idio-syncratic gift stores, handicrafts shops, galleries, and a growing number of savvy, independent fashion boutiques. For the well-heeled, there are also plenty of glossy interna-tional designer shops.

Boston's shops are generally open Monday through Saturday from 10 or 11 until 6 or 7 and Sunday noon to 5. Many stay open until 8 PM one night a week, usually Thursday. Malls are open Monday through Saturday from 9 or 10 until 8 or 9 and Sunday noon to 6. Most stores accept major credit cards and traveler's checks. There's no state sales tax on clothing. However, there's a 5% luxury tax on clothes priced higher than $175 per item; the tax is levied on the amount in excess of $175.

MAJOR SHOPPING DISTRICTS

Boston's shops and department stores are concentrated in the area bounded by Quincy Market, the Back Bay, and Downtown. There are plenty of bargains in the Downtown Crossing area. The South End's gentrification creates its own kind of consumerist milieus, from house-wares shops to avant-garde art galleries. In Cambridge you can find lots of shopping around Harvard and Central squares, with independent boutiques migrating west along Massachusetts Avenue (or Mass Ave., as the locals and almost everyone else calls it) toward Porter Square and beyond.

BOSTON

Pretty **Charles Street** is crammed beginning to end with top-notch antiques stores such as Judith Dowling Asian Art, Eugene Galleries, and Devonia as well as a handful of independently owned fashion boutiques whose prices reflect their high Beacon Hill rents. River Street, parallel to Charles Street, is also an excellent source for antiques. Both are easy walks from the Charles Street T stop on the Red Line.
Copley Place (⊠*100 Huntington Ave., Back Bay* ☏*617/369–5000* Ⓣ*Copley*), an indoor shopping mall in the Back Bay, includes such high-end shops as Christian Dior, Louis Vuitton, and Gucci, anchored by the pricey but dependable Neiman Marcus and the flashy, over-priced Barneys. A skywalk connects Copley Place to the **Prudential Center** (⊠*800 Boylston St., Back Bay* ☏*800/746–7778* Ⓣ*Copley, Prudential*

Center). The Pru, as it's often called, contains moderately priced chain stores such as Ann Taylor and the Body Shop.

Downtown Crossing (✉ *Washington St. from Amory St. to about Milk St., Downtown* ⓣ *Downtown Crossing, Park St.*) is a pedestrian mall with a Macy's and a handful of decent outlets. Millennium Place, a 1.8-million-square-foot complex with a Ritz-Carlton Hotel, condos, a massive sports club, a 19-screen Loews Cineplex, and a few upscale retail stores, seems to be transforming the area, as promised, from a slightly seedy hangout to the newest happening spot.

Faneuil Hall Marketplace (✉ *Bounded by Congress St., Atlantic Ave., the Waterfront, and Government Center, Downtown* ☎ *617/523–1300* ⓣ *Government Center*) is a huge complex that's also hugely popular, even though most of its independent shops have given way to Banana Republic, Crate & Barrel, and other chains. The place has plenty of history, one of the area's great à la carte casual dining experiences (Quincy Market), and carnival-like trappings: pushcarts sell everything from silver jewelry to Peruvian sweaters, and buskers carry out crowd-pleasing feats such as balancing wheelbarrows on their heads.

★ **Newbury Street** (ⓣ *Arlington, Copley, Hynes/ICA*) is Boston's version of New York's Fifth Avenue. The entire street is a shoppers' paradise, from high-end names such as Brooks Brothers to tiny specialty boutiques such as Diptyque. Upscale clothing stores, up-to-the-minute art galleries, and dazzling jewelers line the street near the Public Garden. As you head toward Mass Ave., Newbury gets funkier and the cacophony builds, with skateboarders zipping through traffic and garbage-pail drummers burning licks outside the hip boutiques. The best stores run from Arlington Street to the Prudential Center. Parallel to Newbury Street is **Boylston Street**, where a few standouts, such as Shreve, Crump & Low, are tucked among the other chains and restaurants.

South End (ⓣ *Back Bay/South End*) merchants are benefiting from the ongoing gentrification that has brought high real-estate prices and trendy restaurants to the area. Explore the chic home-furnishings and gift shops that line Tremont Street, starting at Berkeley Street. The MBTA's Silver Line bus runs through the South End.

TOP 5

■ Head to **Louis Boston** for exquisitely made clothing and personalized attention.

■ Pick up a Red Sox hat at the T-shirt stand outside Fenway Park on a game day.

■ Make an appointment with designer Daniela Corte to buy one of her signature custom-made wrap dresses.

■ Pick up a slew of Danish-designed tableware and home decor (that no one else will have!) at **Lekker** in the South End.

■ Hit **Charles Street** to troll through the dozens of antiques shops.

7

CAMBRIDGE

CambridgeSideGalleria (⊠ *100 CambridgeSide Pl., Kendall Sq.* ☎ *617/621–8666* Ⓣ *Lechmere, Kendall/MIT via shuttle*) is a basic three-story mall with a food court. Macy's makes it a good stop for appliances and other basics; it's a big draw for local high-school kids. **Central Square** (⊠ *East of Harvard Sq.* Ⓣ *Central*) has an eclectic mix of furniture stores, used-record shops, ethnic restaurants, and small, hip performance venues. **Harvard Square** (Ⓣ *Harvard*) takes up just a few blocks but holds more than 150 stores selling clothes, books, records, furnishings, and specialty items.

The **Galleria** (⊠ *57 JFK St.* Ⓣ *Harvard*) has various boutiques and a few decent, independently owned restaurants. A handful of chains and independent boutiques are clustered in **Brattle Square** (⊠ *Behind Harvard Sq.* Ⓣ *Harvard*).

Porter Square (⊠ *West on Mass Ave. from Harvard Sq.* Ⓣ *Porter*) has distinctive clothing stores, as well as crafts shops, coffee shops, natural-food stores, restaurants, and bars with live music.

DEPARTMENT STORES

★ **Barneys New York.** The hoopla (not to mention the party) generated by this store's arrival was surprising in a city where everything new is viewed with trepidation. But clearly Boston's denizens have embraced the lofty, two-story space because it's filled with cutting-edge lines like Comme des Garçons and Nina Ricci, as well as a few bargains in the second-level Co-op section. ⊠ *100 Huntington Ave., Back Bay* ☎ *617/385–3300* Ⓣ *Copley*.

Lord & Taylor. This is a reliable, if somewhat overstuffed with merchandise, stop for classic clothing by such designers as Anne Klein and Ralph Lauren, along with accessories, cosmetics, and jewelry. ⊠ *760 Boylston St., Back Bay* ☎ *617/262–6000* Ⓣ *Prudential Center*.

Macy's. Three floors offer men's and women's clothing and shoes, housewares, and cosmetics. Although top designers and a fur salon are part of the mix, Macy's doesn't feel exclusive; instead, it's a popular source for family basics. ⊠ *450 Washington St., Downtown* ☎ *617/357–3000* Ⓣ *Downtown Crossing*.

Neiman Marcus. The flashy Texas-based retailer known to many as "Needless Markup" has three levels of swank designers such as Gaultier, Gucci, Ferragamo, and Calvin Klein, as well as cosmetics and housewares. ⊠ *5 Copley Pl., Back Bay* ☎ *617/536–3660* Ⓣ *Back Bay/South End*.

Saks Fifth Avenue. The clothing and accessories at Saks runs from the traditional to the flamboyant. It's a little pricey, but an excellent place to find high-quality merchandise, including shoes and cosmetics. ⊠ *Prudential Center, 1 Ring Rd., Back Bay* ☎ *617/262–8500* Ⓣ *Prudential Center*.

BLITZ TOURS

Study the T map (*see* inside back cover) before plunging into one of the following shopping tours. You're almost always better off leaving your car behind than trying to navigate congested city streets and puzzle out parking arcana.

ANTIQUES

Avid antiques shoppers have their work happily cut out for them. Plan to spend at least three hours on Charles Street, which has more than 30 stores on five blocks. Start at the north end of the street, in Beacon Hill right over the walking bridge from the Charles/MGH T stop. Bargain hunters should check out **Reruns Antiques** and the jumble of dealers inside the **Boston Antique Co-op.** Other favorite stops include **Tierney Trading, Eugene Galleries, Marika's,** a tangle of American and European objets d'art, and furniture with a smattering of Japanese prints. At the corner of Mt. Vernon Street, turn right and then left onto River Street—some small but intriguing galleries are on this block. Turn left on Chestnut Street to return to Charles Street; on the corner, up a flight of stairs, is the engrossing **Devonia: Antiques for Dining.** From here, continue along Charles Street to Beacon Street and cut through the Public Garden to Newbury Street to reach the **Brodney Gallery.** For more reasonably priced choices, hop on the Green Line to the **Cambridge Antique Market,** near the Lechmere stop.

BEANTOWN BAHGAINS

Thriftiness is considered one of the highest moral virtues in New England—even when buying luxury items. At **DSW** you can always find high-end designer shoes for both sexes at decent prices. Several shops full of watches and jewelry at reduced prices (some barely above wholesale) are found along Washington Street. If vintage is your thing, Newbury Street is dotted with consignment shops lined with gently worn Prada, Gucci, Burberry, and their ilk. Look first in **Second Time Around,** or try across the river in Harvard Square at **Oona's.** Both are also known to carry more-daring labels such as Chloé and Catherine Malandrino for women, and Ermenegildo Zegna for men.

BOOKS

Boston is a bibliophile's dream. For rare, antique, or just plain unusual books, start at **Ars Libri Ltd.** in the South End, a few blocks away from the Back Bay T stop. From here, head to Newbury Street (turn right on Waltham Street, walk three blocks, and cross Tremont Street, then pick up Clarendon Street to Newbury Street) for a break at the **Trident Booksellers & Café,** one of the city's first bookstore-cafés, almost directly across the street. Alternatively, from Ars Libri follow Waltham to Tremont Street, make a right, and head over the turnpike to reach West Street and the **Brattle Bookshop.** From here catch the Red Line T into Harvard Square to browse through the **Harvard Book Store** and, just around the corner, **Grolier Poetry Bookshop.**

7

SPECIALTY STORES

ANTIQUES

Newbury Street and the South End have some excellent (and expensive) antiques stores, but Charles Street—coincidentally, one of the city's oldest streets—is the place to go for a concentrated selection.

Autrefois Antiques. Come here to find French country and Italian 18th-, 19th-, and 20th-century furniture, mirrors, and lighting. ⊠ *130 Harvard St., Brookline* ☎ *617/566–0113* Ⓣ *Coolidge Corner.*

Boston Antique Co-op. This flea market–style collection of dealers occupies two floors, containing everything from vintage photos and paintings to porcelain, silver, bronzes, and furniture. ⊠ *119 Charles St., Beacon Hill* ☎ *617/227–9810 or 617/227–9811* Ⓣ *Charles/MGH.*

Brodney Gallery. In addition to plenty of porcelain and silver, Brodney claims to have the biggest selection of estate jewelry in New England. ⊠ *145 Newbury St., Back Bay* ☎ *617/536–0500* Ⓣ *Copley.*

Cambridge Antique Market. Off the beaten track this may be, but it has a selection bordering on overwhelming: five floors of goods ranging from 19th-century furniture to vintage clothing, much of it reasonably priced. There are two parking lots next to the building. ⊠ *201 Monsignor O'Brien Hwy., Cambridge* ☎ *617/868–9655* Ⓣ *Lechmere.*

Devonia: Antiques for Dining. Some of the fabulous china sets here are fit for a queen—some really were designed for royalty. Feast your eyes on tens of thousands of pieces of tableware, including, perhaps, the custom-made set of Baccarat once owned by the Sultan of Brunei. ⊠ *43 Charles St., Beacon Hill* ☎ *617/523–8313* Ⓣ *Charles/MGH.*

★ **Eugene Galleries.** This store is chockablock with prints, etchings, old maps, and books; a 19th-century print of a Boston landmark, for instance, makes for a unique and lasting souvenir. ⊠ *76 Charles St., Beacon Hill* ☎ *617/227–3062* Ⓣ *Charles/MGH.*

Judith Dowling Asian Art. Judith Dowling's sophistication results from spareness and restraint. High-end Asian artifacts range from Japanese pottery to scrolls, Buddha figures, painted screens, cabinets, and other furnishings. ⊠ *133 Charles St., Beacon Hill* ☎ *617/523–5211.*

Marika's. Every available inch of space in this jam-packed store, including the walls, is used to display wares. That silver chafing dish might need a polish, and the telephone table may be slightly scratched, but such imperfections keep the prices reasonable. ⊠ *130 Charles St., Beacon Hill* ☎ *617/523–4520* Ⓣ *Charles/MGH.*

Reruns Antiques. Don't let its low prices and jumble-shop aspect fool you. Poke around Reruns and you may come up with a Hiroshige print, a 19th-century Moroccan lamp, or an Asmat ancestral figure. If you're in the mood for a history or an anthropology lesson, owner Tom Armstrong is glad to oblige. ⊠ *125 Charles St., Beacon Hill* ☎ No phone Ⓣ *Charles/MGH.*

ART GALLERIES

Although Newbury Street has the highest concentration of galleries in the city, a neighborhood in the South End, discordantly dubbed SoWa (for South of Washington), has emerged as a hot spot for contemporary artists.

★ **Alpha Gallery.** This gallery specializes in 20th-century and contemporary American and European painting, sculpture, and master prints. ✉*38 Newbury St., Back Bay* ☎*617/536–4465* Ⓣ*Arlington.*

Barbara Krakow Gallery. Krakow shows contemporary paintings, photographs, drawings, prints, and sculptures by emerging and established regional and international artists. ✉*10 Newbury St., 5th fl., Back Bay* ☎*617/262–4490* Ⓣ*Arlington.*

Bernard Toale Gallery. Toale's contemporary tastes tend toward more-experimental pieces, including sculpture, paintings, photographs, and works on paper. ✉*450 Harrison Ave., South End* ☎*617/482–2477* Ⓣ*New England Medical Center.*

Bromfield Art Gallery. A small, cooperative operation, Bromfield mounts monthlong shows of its members' work, including oil and acrylic paintings, charcoals, and pastels. ✉*450 Harrison Ave., South End* ☎*617/451–3605* Ⓣ*New England Medical Center.*

Childs Gallery. Childs carries paintings, prints, drawings, watercolors, and sculpture from the 1500s to the present. ✉*169 Newbury St., Back Bay* ☎*617/266–1108* Ⓣ*Copley.*

Copley Society of Boston. After more than a century, this nonprofit membership organization continues to present the works of well-known and aspiring New England artists. ✉*158 Newbury St., Back Bay* ☎*617/536–5049* Ⓣ*Copley.*

Gallery NAGA. Here are contemporary paintings, sculpture, and furniture displayed in a striking space: the Church of the Covenant. ✉*67 Newbury St., Back Bay* ☎*617/267–9060* Ⓣ*Arlington.*

Nielsen Gallery. Both established and aspiring artists show their representational and abstract paintings and prints. ✉*179 Newbury St., Back Bay* ☎*617/266–4835* Ⓣ*Copley.*

Rolly-Michaux. You'll find only the highest quality works here, from the likes of Moore, Calder, Picasso, Chagall, Miró, and Matisse. ✉*290 Dartmouth St., Back Bay* ☎*617/536–9898* Ⓣ*Copley.*

Samson Projects. A truly cross-cultural blend of exhibits, this gallery shows the experimental works of young contemporary artists. ✉*450 Harrison Ave., South End* ☎*617/357–7177* Ⓣ*New England Medical Center.*

Vose Galleries. Established in 1841, Vose specializes in 19th- and 20th-century American art, including the Hudson River School, Boston School, and American impressionists. The addition of works of contemporary American realism recognizes an area that is often overlooked by the trendier set. ✉*238 Newbury St., Back Bay* ☎*617/536–6176* Ⓣ*Copley, Hynes/ICA.*

7

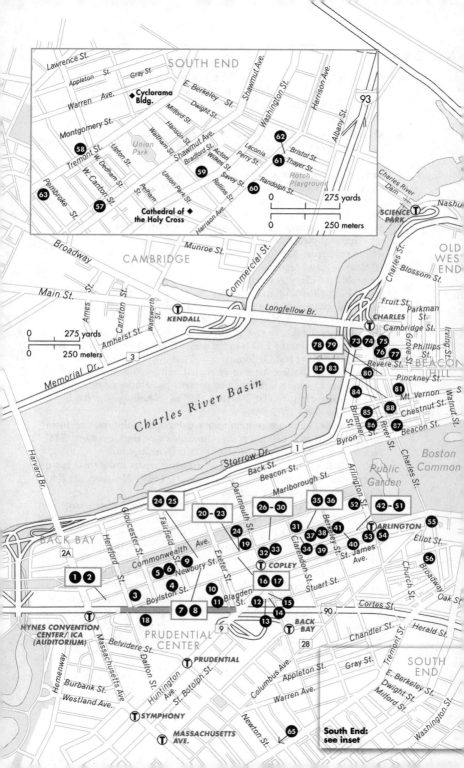

SOUTH END

Lawrence St.
Appleton St.
Gray St.
Warren Ave.
◆ Cyclorama Bldg.
E. Berkeley St.
Dwight St.
Milford St.
Hanson St.
Shawmut Ave.
Washington St.
Shawmut Ave.
Montgomery St.
Waltham St.
Bradford St.
Acton St.
Wilkes St.
Savoy St.
Laconia St.
Perry St.
Rollins St.
Randolph St.
Bristol St.
Thayer St.
Albany St.
Harrison Ave.
62
61
58
W. Dedham St.
Upton St.
Pelham St.
Union Park St.
59
60
Tremont St.
W. Canton St.
63
Pembroke St.
57
◆ Cathedral of the Holy Cross
Harrison Ave.
Union Park

0   275 yards
0   250 meters

Rotch Playground

SCIENCE PARK

Charles River Dam
Nashu

OLD WEST END

Broadway
Munroe St.
Commercial St.
Charles St.
Blossom St.
Fruit St.
Parkman St.
CHARLES
Cambridge St.

CAMBRIDGE

Main St.
Longfellow Br.

Ames St.
Carleton St.
Wadsworth St.
Amherst St.
KENDALL

73 74 75
78 79
76
77
Grove St.
Phillips St.
Revere St.
BEACON HILL
Irving St.
82 83
80
Pinckney St.
Memorial Dr.
84
81
Mt. Vernon St.
Walnut St.
85
88
Chestnut St.
86
87
Beacon St.
Brimmer St.
River St.

0   275 yards
0   250 meters

Charles River Basin

Storrow Dr.
Back St.
Beacon St.
Marlborough St.
Byron St.
Charles St.
Boston Common

Harvard Br.

Public Garden

24 25
20 – 23
26 – 30
35 36
52
42 – 51
55
BACK BAY
Gloucester St.
Fairfield St.
Hereford St.
Commonwealth Ave.
Dartmouth St.
Berkeley St.
Arlington St.
ARLINGTON
Eliot St.
2A
24
19
31
37 38 41
53 54
1 2
5 6
9
Newbury St.
32 33
34 39
40
56
3
4
Boylston St.
Exeter St.
16 17
COPLEY
Clarendon St.
St. James Ave.
Church St.
Broadway St.
Oak St.
10
Blagden St.
Stuart St.
7 8
11
12
15
HYNES CONVENTION CENTER/ ICA (AUDITORIUM)
18
PRUDENTIAL CENTER
13
14
BACK BAY
90
Cortes St.
Chandler St.
Herald St.
Tremont St.

Belvidere St.
Dalton St.
9
28
Columbus Ave.
Appleton St.
Gray St.
E. Berkeley St.
Dwight St.
Milford St.
Washington St.
SOUTH END
Hemenway St.
Burbank St.
Massachusetts Ave.
Huntington Ave.
St. Botolph St.
PRUDENTIAL
Warren Ave.
Newton St.
65
South End: see inset
Westland Ave.
SYMPHONY
MASSACHUSETTS AVE.

Boston Shopping

CHARLESTOWN

NORTH END

NORTH STATION

BOWDOIN

HAYMARKET

GOVERNMENT CENTER

GOV'T CTR

BOWDOIN

STATE

PARK

DOWNTOWN CROSSING

BOYLSTON

CHINATOWN

BOSTON

DOWNTOWN

SOUTH STATION

N.E. MEDICAL CENTER

Charlestown Br.

Washington

Hull St. Tileston St.

Prince St.

Salem St.

Margin St.

Endicott St.

Commercial St.

Charter St.

Hanover St.

North St.

Richmond St.

Clinton St.

Chatham St.

State St.

India St.

Causeway

Canal St.

Friend St.

Merrimac St.

New Chardon St.

New Sudbury St.

Hancock St.

Bowdoin St.

Somerset St.

Court St.

School St.

Park St.

Washington St.

Temple Pl.

West St.

Avon St.

Bedford St.

Summer St.

Snow Pl.

High St.

Purchase St.

Kirby St.

Milk St.

Broad St.

Pearl St.

Franklin St.

Federal St.

Congress St.

Devonshire St.

Tremont St.

Beach St.

Essex St.

Stuart St.

Kneeland St.

Tyler St.

Hudson St.

Harrison Ave.

Marginal Rd.

Broadway Bridge

Thayer St.

W. 4th St.

Dorchester Ave.

Atlantic Ave.

Fort Point Channel

Ted Williams Tunnel

KEY

🚇 Subway station

▬ Tunnel

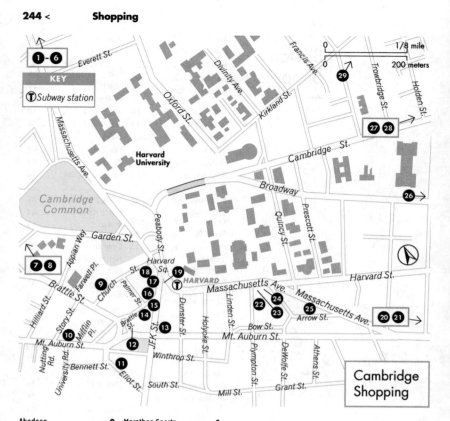

Cambridge
Shopping

BEAUTY

Beauty & Main. Cosmetics boutiques are supposed to be intimidating, right? Not this one. The informed, helpful staff at Beauty & Main preside over lines both popular (Laura Mercier) and lesser known (Darphin), encouraging customers to sample the wares. ✉ *30 Brattle St., Cambridge* ☎ *617/868–7171* Ⓣ *Harvard.*

Bella Sante. As pristine as it is serene, the beautifully designed Bella Sante is well stocked with high-end products and staffed by a well-trained crew. The locker room is stocked with thoughtful amenities such as body creams and just about any hair product you might need. ✉ *38 Newbury St., Back Bay* ☎ *617/424–9930* Ⓣ *Arlington.*

Exhale. This Zen-like sanctuary is deceptively bigger than it appears since the subterranean lower level houses a first-rate spa and yoga studio. Upstairs, you'll find holistic body and skin-care products. ✉ *28 Arlington St., Back Bay* ☎ *617/532–7095* Ⓣ *Arlington.*

James Joseph Salon. Sleek and modern yet utterly free of pretense, James Joseph has a fun, talented staff that gives customers exactly the cuts, color, and treatments they ask for. ✉ *30 Newbury St., Back Bay* ☎ *617/266–7222* Ⓣ *Arlington.*

Mario Russo Salon. It may be the most coveted cut in town, but Mario Russo and his expert staff retain a down-to-earth attitude as they provide excellent styling and color services. The manicures are equally good. ✉ *9 Newbury St., Back Bay* ☎ *617/424–6676* Ⓣ *Arlington.*

Michaud Cosmedix. Makeup artist Julie Michaud and her staff have worked hard to become Boston's go-to studio for natural-looking makeup application, brow grooming, waxing, and facials. ✉ *69 Newbury St., Back Bay* ☎ *617/262–1607* Ⓣ *Arlington, Copley.*

BOOKS

If Boston and Cambridge have bragging rights to anything, it's their independent bookstores, many of which stay open late and sponsor author readings and literary programs.

Inside the Prudential Center is **Barnes & Noble** (✉ *800 Boylston St., Back Bay* ☎ *617/247–6959* Ⓣ *Prudential Center* ✉ *660 Beacon St., Kenmore Sq.* ☎ *617/267–8484* Ⓣ *Kenmore*). The company now runs the Harvard Coop. **Borders** (✉ *10–24 School St., Downtown* ☎ *617/557–7188* Ⓣ *Government Center* ✉ *511 Boylston St., Back Bay* ☎ *617/236–1444*) is also prominent.

SPECIALTY

Ars Libri Ltd. The rare and wonderful books on display here make it easy to be drawn in. The airy space is filled with books on photography and architecture, out-of-print art books, monographs, and exhibition catalogs. ✉ *500 Harrison Ave., South End* ☎ *617/357–5212* Ⓣ *New England Medical Center.*

Ⓒ **Barefoot Books.** Don't come looking for the same old kids' books; Barefoot Choice foot is full of beautifully illustrated, creatively told reading for kids of all ★ ages. These are the kind of books that kids remember and keep as adults. ✉ *1771 Massachusetts Ave., Cambridge* ☎ *617/349–1610* Ⓣ *Porter.*

Brattle Bookshop. The late George Gloss built this into Boston's best used- and rare-book shop. Today, his son Kenneth fields queries from passionate book lovers. If the book you want is out of print, Brattle has it or can probably find it. ⊠*9 West St., Downtown* ☎*617/542–0210 or 800/447–9595* Ⓣ*Downtown Crossing.*

Calamus Bookstore. This friendly, informal store carries not only books, but also videos, music, and gifts for the gay, lesbian, bisexual, or transgender shopper. ⊠*92B South St., Leather District* ☎*617/338–1931* Ⓣ*South Station.*

Globe Corner Bookstore. Hands down, this is the best source for domestic and international travel books and maps. The store also has very good selections of books about New England and by New England authors. ⊠*90 Mt. Auburn St., Cambridge* ☎*617/497–6277 or 800/358–6013* Ⓣ*Harvard.*

Grolier Poetry Bookshop. Proprietor Louisa Solano is an outspoken proponent of all things poetic—and her dog, Jessie, is one of the friendliest shopkeepers in Harvard Square. The store, founded in 1927, carries in-print poetry from all eras and from all over the world. ⊠*6 Plympton St., Cambridge* ☎*617/547–4648* Ⓣ*Harvard.*

★ **Harvard Book Store.** The intellectual community is well served here, with a slew of new titles upstairs and used and remaindered books downstairs. The collection's diversity has made the store a frequent destination for academics. ⊠*1256 Massachusetts Ave., Cambridge* ☎*617/661–1515* Ⓣ*Harvard.*

Harvard Coop Society. Begun in 1882 as a nonprofit service for students and faculty, the Coop is now managed by Barnes & Noble. In addition to books and textbooks (many discounted), school supplies, clothes, and accessories plastered with the Harvard emblem are sold here, as well as basic housewares geared toward dorm dwellers. ⊠*1400 Massachusetts Ave., Cambridge* ☎*617/499–2000* Ⓣ*Harvard.*

Kate's Mystery Books. A favorite Cambridge haunt, Kate's is a good place to track down mysteries by local writers; look for authors in the flesh at the shop's frequent readings and events. ⊠*2211 Massachusetts Ave., Cambridge* ☎*617/491–2660* Ⓣ*Porter.*

Trident Booksellers & Café. Browse through an eclectic collection of books, tapes, and magazines; then settle in with a snack. It's open until midnight daily, making it a favorite with students. ⊠*338 Newbury St., Back Bay* ☎*617/267–8688* Ⓣ*Hynes/ICA.*

CLOTHING AND SHOES

The terminally chic shop on Newbury Street, the hip hang in Harvard Square, and everyone goes Downtown for the real bargains.

★ **Alan Bilzerian.** Satisfying the Euro crowd, this store sells luxe men's and women's clothing by such fashion darlings as Yohji Yamamoto and Ann Demeulemeester. ⊠*34 Newbury St., Back Bay* ☎*617/536–1001* Ⓣ*Arlington.*

Anne Fontaine. You can never have too many white shirts—especially if they're designed by this Parisienne. The simple, sophisticated designs are mostly executed in cotton and priced around $160. ⊠*318 Boylston St., Back Bay* ☎*617/423–0366* Ⓣ*Arlington, Boylston.*

Betsy Jenney. Ms. Jenney herself is likely to wait on you in this small, personal store, where the well-made, comfortable lines are for women who cannot walk into a fitted size-4 suit—in other words, most of the female population. The designers found here, such as Philippe Adec, Teenflo, and Nicole Miller, are fashionable yet forgiving. ⊠ *114 Newbury St., Back Bay* ☎ *617/536–2610* Ⓣ *Copley.*

Brooks Brothers. Founded in 1818, Brooks still carries the classically modern styles that made them famous—old faithfuls for men such as navy blazers, seersucker in summer, and crisp oxford shirts. Its Newbury Street store offers a similar vibe for women as well. ⊠ *46 Newbury St., Back Bay* ☎ *617/267–2600* Ⓣ *Arlington* ⊠ *75 State St., Government Center* ☎ *617/261–9990* Ⓣ *Government Center.*

Calypso. The women's and children's clothing here bursts with bright colors, beautiful fabrics, and styles so fresh you might need a fashion editor to help you choose. ⊠ *114 Newbury St., Back Bay* ☎ *617/421–1887* Ⓣ *Copley.*

Chanel. Located at No. 5 in honor of its famous perfume, this branch of the Parisian couture house carries suits, separates, bags, shoes, cosmetics, and, of course, a selection of little black dresses. ⊠ *5 Newbury St., Back Bay* ☎ *617/859–0055* Ⓣ *Arlington.*

Fodor'sChoice ★ **Daniela Corte.** Local designer Corte cuts women's clothes that flatter from her sunny Back Bay studio. Look for gorgeous suiting, flirty halter dresses, and sophisticated formal frocks that can be bought off the rack or custom tailored. ⊠ *91 Newbury St., Back Bay* ☎ *617/262–2100* Ⓣ *Copley.*

Dress. True to its name, this shop owned by two young local women carries a number of great party dresses as well as flattering tees, pretty tops, and shoes from emerging designers. ⊠ *221 Newbury St., Back Bay* ☎ *617/424–7125* Ⓣ *Copley, Hynes/ICA.*

DSW. Major discounts on high-quality (and big-name) shoes for men and women are what draw much of Boston to DSW, also known as Designer Shoe Warehouse. Everything from Nike to Prada can be found at varying discounts—sometimes up to 90% off. ⊠ *385 Washington St., Downtown* ☎ *617/556–0052* Ⓣ *Downtown Crossing.*

Giorgio Armani. This top-of-the-line Italian couturier is known for his carefully shaped jackets, soft suits, and mostly neutral palette. ⊠ *22 Newbury St., Back Bay* ☎ *617/267–3200* Ⓣ *Arlington.*

Grettaluxe. Drop by Copley's sassy little boutique and pick up the latest "it" pieces—from velour hoodies by Juicy Couture to the must-have Stella McCartney design du moment. There's also jewelry, handbags, and other accessories. ⊠ *Westin Hotel, 10 Huntington Ave., Back Bay* ☎ *617/266–6166* Ⓣ *Copley.*

Helen's Leather Shop. Choose from half a dozen brands of boots (Lucchese, Nocona, Dan Post, Tony Lama, Justin, and Frye); then peruse the leather sandals, jackets, briefcases, luggage, and accessories. ⊠*110 Charles St., Beacon Hill* ☎*617/742–2077* Ⓣ*Charles/MGH.*

Holiday. A stockpile of flirty and feminine getups—from dresses to denim—are the rage here. Cult lines such as Rock and Republic, Mint, Eberjey, and Tracy Reese are in regular rotation among the fashionable racks. ⊠*53 Charles St., Beacon Hill* ☎*617/973–9730* Ⓣ*Charles/ MGH.*

In the Pink. Don't be caught dead in Palm Beach this year without your Lilly Pulitzer resort wear, available here along with shoes, home decor, and children's clothing. ⊠*133 Newbury St., Back Bay* ☎*617/536–6423* Ⓣ*Copley.*

John Fluevog Shoes. Many club goers have at least one pair of these oh-so-hip shoes in their closets, perhaps because of the company's claim that their Angel soles repel all kinds of nasty liquids "and Satan." ⊠*302 Newbury St., Back Bay* ☎*617/266–1079* Ⓣ*Copley.*

Jos. A. Bank Clothiers. Like Brooks Brothers, Joseph Bank is well known to the conservatively well dressed everywhere. ⊠*399 Boylston St., Back Bay* ☎*617/536–5050* Ⓣ*Arlington.*

FodorśChoice ★ **Louis Boston.** Impeccably tailored designs, subtly updated classics, and the latest Italian styles highlight a wide selection of imported clothing and accessories. Visiting celebrities might be trolling the racks along with you as jazz spills out into the street from the adjoining Restaurant L. ⊠*234 Berkeley St., Back Bay* ☎*617/262–6100* Ⓣ*Arlington.*

Marc Jacobs. Only the third stateside outpost to be opened by this celebrated designer, this two-floor boutique includes both his younger, casual line and his elegant (and, of course, more expensive) collection. Look, too, for a well-edited sampling of MJ's high-end home accessories. ⊠*81 Newbury St., Back Bay* ☎*617/425–0707* Ⓣ*Copley.*

Matsu. This shop trends toward the funkier with edgy pieces from designers like Lilith and Rozae Nichols. Look for a well-edited jewelry selection as well as high-end handbags and accessories. ⊠*259 Newbury St., Back Bay* ☎*617/266–9707* Ⓣ*Copley, Hynes/ICA.*

Mint Julep. Cute dresses, playful skirts, and form-fitting tops make up the selection here. The Cambridge location is a little larger and easier to navigate, but Brookline houses the original. ⊠*6 Church St., Cambridge* ☎*617/576–6468* Ⓣ*Harvard* ⊠*1302 Beacon St., Brookline* ☎*617/232–3600* Ⓣ*Coolidge Corner.*

Queen Bee. Only clothes from the hottest, most youthful lines—Mint, Tibi, Shoshana—pass through this boutique's doors. Even if you wouldn't wear most of this stuff, it's fun just to see the latest and maybe pick up an accessory. ⊠*85 Newbury St., Beacon Hill* ☎*888/859–8005* Ⓣ*Arlington, Copley.*

Relic. This ultrahip subterranean shop sells designer denim such as Miss Sixty and Meltin' Pot. The interior is a work of art; a few local artists designed the space with pieces of metal culled from the city's Big Dig project and hand-painted wall murals. ⊠*116 Newbury St., Back Bay* ☎*617/437–7344* Ⓣ*Copley.*

Stil. Local designers such as Daniela Corte and Elaine Perlov share rack space with cutting-edge Scandinavian labels such as Rutzou and Bruun's Bazaar—all of it at surprisingly earthly prices. ⊠*Shops at Prudential Center, 800 Boylston St., Back Bay* ☎617/859–7845 Ⓣ*Copley.*

Toppers. Nothing old hat about this place, where you can cover your head in anything from a tam-o'-shanter to a 10-gallon. ⊠*151 Tremont St., Back Bay* ☎617/859–1430 Ⓣ*Back Bay.*

Wish. Everything a hip young woman could wish for, from designers such as Milly, Rebecca Taylor, and Nanette Lepore, can be found in this small but comfy addition to antiques row. ⊠*49 Charles St., Beacon Hill* ☎617/227–4441 Ⓣ*Charles/MGH.*

CRAFTS

Beadworks. Find beads of every color, texture, size, and material in the tiny bins in Back Bay's do-it-yourself jewelry store. The prices are reasonable, the staff is helpful and friendly, and there's a worktable to assemble your masterpiece in the center of the shop. ⊠*167 Newbury St., Back Bay* ☎617/247–7227.

Cambridge Artists' Cooperative. The ceramics, weavings, jewelry, and leather work here can be pricier than most, but they're all one-of-a-kind or limited edition. ⊠*59A Church St., Cambridge* ☎617/868–4434 Ⓣ*Harvard.*

Society of Arts & Crafts. More than a century old, this is the country's oldest nonprofit crafts organization. It displays a fine assortment of ceramics, jewelry, glass, woodwork, and furniture by some of the country's finest craftspeople. ⊠*175 Newbury St., Back Bay* ☎617/266–1810 Ⓣ*Copley.*

GIFTS

Black Ink. A wall full of rubber stamps stretches above unusual candles, cookie jars, and other home accessories and gift items. ⊠*101 Charles St., Beacon Hill* ☎617/723–3883 Ⓣ*Charles/MGH* ⊠*5 Brattle St., Cambridge* ☎617/497–1221 Ⓣ*Harvard.*

Buckaroo's Mercantile. It's Howdy Doody time at Buckaroo's—a great destination for the kitsch inclined. Find pink poodle skirts, lunch-box clocks, Barbie lamps, *Front Page Detective* posters, and everything Elvis. ⊠*5 Brookline St., Cambridge* ☎617/492–4792 Ⓣ*Central.*

★ **Diptyque.** The venerable Paris house has its flagship U.S. store right here on Newbury Street. The hand-poured candles, room sprays, and gender-neutral eau de toilettes are expensive, but each is like a little work of art—and just entering the calmly inviting store is like having a mini–aromatherapy session. ⊠*123 Newbury St., Back Bay* ☎617/351–2430 Ⓣ*Copley.*

The Flat of the Hill. There's nothing flat about this fun collection of seasonal items, toiletries, toys, pillows, and whatever else catches the fancy of the shop's young owner. Her passion for pets is evident—pick up a Fetch & Glow ball and your dog will never again have to wait until daytime to play in the park. ⊠*60 Charles St., Beacon Hill* ☎617/619–9977 Ⓣ*Charles/MGH.*

★ **Fresh.** You won't know whether to wash with these soaps or nibble on them. The shea-butter-rich bars come in such scents as clove-hazelnut and orange-cranberry. They cost $6 to $7 each, but they carry the scent to the end. ✉*121 Newbury St., Back Bay* ☎*617/421–1212* Ⓣ*Copley.*

★ **Nomad.** Low prices and an enthusiastic staff are just the beginning at this imports store; it carries clothing as well as Indian good-luck *torans* (wall hangings), Mexican *milagros* (charms), mirrors to keep away the evil eye, silver jewelry, and curtains made from sari silk. In the basement you'll find kilims, hand-painted tiles, and sale items. ✉*1741 Massachusetts Ave., Cambridge* ☎*617/497–6677* Ⓣ*Porter.*

Tibet Emporium. More upscale than your average imports store, Tibet Emporium goes beyond the usual masks and quilted wall hangings to offer beautifully delicate beaded silk pillowcases, pashmina wraps in every color imaginable, appliquéd and silk clothing, and finely wrought but affordable silver jewelry. ✉*103 Charles St., Beacon Hill* ☎*617/723–8035* Ⓣ*Charles/MGH.*

Tokai Japanese Gifts. Chopstick rests, origami paper, Yukata cotton robes, and high-end kimonos are among the wares here. ✉*1815 Massachusetts Ave., Cambridge* ☎*617/864–5922* Ⓣ*Porter.*

GROCERS

Cardullo's. This 50-year-old shop in Harvard Square purveys exotic imports, sandwiches to go, chocolates, breads, olive oils, cheeses, wines, and beer amid impressive clutter. ✉*6 Brattle St., Cambridge* ☎*617/491–8888 or 800/491–8288* Ⓣ*Harvard.*

Deluca's Market. Here's one neighborhood grocer that delivers the gourmet goods: an international cheese counter, homemade pâtés, fresh produce, and a snacks section that includes a dream team of cookies. ✉*11 Charles St., Beacon Hill* ☎*617/523–4343* Ⓣ*Charles/MGH* ✉*239 Newbury St., Back Bay* ☎*617/262–5990* Ⓣ*Copley.*

Savenor's. If you're looking for exotic game meats, you've come to the right place. Savenor's food market, once Julia Child's favorite butcher, carries buffalo rump, alligator tail, even rattlesnake. There are plenty of tamer choices, too, as well as outstanding cheeses, breads, and treats such as foie gras and smoked salmon. ✉*160 Charles St., Beacon Hill* ☎*617/723–6328* Ⓣ*Charles/MGH* ✉*92 Kirkland St., Cambridge* ☎*617/576–6328* Ⓣ*Central.*

HOME FURNISHINGS

A home-furnishings hot spot has emerged in the South End, but don't overlook the choice strip on Massachusetts Avenue in Cambridge.

Abodeon. New York decorators come to town just to shop this incredible collection of 20th-century modern housewares, both newly produced classic designs and pristine-condition vintage. You might come across a mint 1963 stove, a complete set of Jetson-esque dinnerware, or a Lucite dining set from the early 1970s. As a bonus, the back room contains more than 10,000 hard-to-find records. ✉ *E. 1731 Massachusetts Ave., Cambridge* ☎*617/497–0137* Ⓣ*Porter.*

★ **Bliss Home.** Funky and colorful home designs such as brightly patterned rugs by Angela Adams, gleaming barware by Alessi, gorgeous baby blankets, handmade pottery pet bowls, and beautifully sleek handbags by Ply fill this stylish shop. ✉225 *Newbury St., Back Bay* ☎617/421–5544 or 888/325–2547 Ⓣ*Copley*.

Gargoyles Grotesques & Chimeras. The space is so dark you can hardly see the objects for sale. But once your eyes adjust, they'll be rewarded with stained glass, architectural salvage, and devotional art perfect for a Gothic revival. ✉262 *Newbury St., Back Bay* ☎617/536–2362 Ⓣ*Copley*.

Kitchen Arts. There are so many gadgets, gizmos, and doodads here that it makes Williams-Sonoma look like a meagerly stocked cupboard. ✉215 *Newbury St., Back Bay* ☎617/266–8701 Ⓣ*Copley*.

Koo de Kir. Break out of the blond-wood school with this offbeat selection of furniture, lamps, candles, wine racks, table settings, and other urban necessities. ✉65 *Chestnut St., Beacon Hill* ☎617/723–8111 Ⓣ*Charles/MGH*.

★ **Lekker.** Dutch design with contemporary panache pervades South Washington Street's coolest home store—the best place to pick up bright oversize pillows, china, tables, Asian cabinets, and sleek, contemporary flatware. ✉1317 *Washington St., South End* ☎617/542–6464 Ⓣ*Back Bay/South End*.

London Lace. You may have spotted this company in the "resources" pages of glossy home-decor magazines. At the shop, it's hard to choose from among the exquisite curtains made from 120-year-old patterns. ✉470 *Shawmut Ave., South End* ☎617/267–3506 or 800/926–5223 Ⓣ*Massachusetts Ave*.

Mohr & McPherson. These stores are a visual exotic feast; cabinets, tables, chairs, and lamps from Japan, India, China, and Indonesia, as well as new and antique Oriental rugs, make up the impressive array. Also impressive are the high prices. ✉460 *Harrison Ave., Back Bay* ☎617/210–7900 Ⓣ*Arlington* ✉75 *Moulton St., Cambridge* ☎617/520–2000 Ⓣ*Alewife* ✉151 *Alewife Brook Parkway., Cambridge* ☎617/520–2112 Ⓣ*Alewife*.

Posh on Tremont. "Where do you get this stuff?" is something the owners hear often at Posh, a shop that somehow manages to be all things to all South End nesters. A pair of sleek silver candlesticks would be perfect for a contemporary loft, for instance, and a brownstone buyer could snap up vintage end tables. ✉557 *Tremont Ave., South End* ☎617/437–1970 Ⓣ*Back Bay/South End*.

Showroom. This industrial-looking shop has some of the finest modern furniture in town. Collections from Italian lines Flexform and Cappellini are set up in roomlike designs on the floor to give shoppers an accurate visual of their future interior design. ✉240 *Stuart St., Back Bay* ☎617/482–4805 Ⓣ*Arlington*.

7

JEWELRY

Brodney Gallery. Brodney sells the most estate jewelry in New England, and its wide selection of platinum filigree diamond rings ensures a steady stream of nervous male customers about to pop the question. ⊠*145 Newbury St., Back Bay* ☎*617/536–0500* Ⓣ*Copley.*

Dorfman Jewels. This elegant shop glows with first-class watches, pearls, and precious stones. ⊠*24 Newbury St., Back Bay* ☎*617/536–2022* Ⓣ*Arlington.*

★ **Shreve, Crump & Low.** Since 1796, Shreve has specialized in high-end treasures, including gems and handcrafted platinum rings, as well as high-quality antiques. But don't get the impression that you can't afford anything here: one of the store's best-selling items is a $95 ceramic pitcher called "The Gurgling Cod," in honor of the state fish. ⊠*440 Boylston St., Back Bay* ☎*617/267–9100* Ⓣ*Arlington.*

Small Pleasures. The antique and estate jewelry—from Victorian-era tourmaline cocktail rings to mint-condition pocket watches—that lines these cases should not be missed by vintage lovers. The staff is notably helpful and informed. ⊠*Copley Place, 142 Newbury St., Back Bay* ☎*617/267–7371* Ⓣ*Copley.*

Tiffany & Co. Fine service complements the finest in gems and precious metals as well as crystal, china, stationery, and fragrances. ⊠*100 Huntington Ave., Copley Pl., Back Bay* ☎*617/353–0222* Ⓣ*Copley.*

Twentieth Century Limited. Every kind of rhinestone concoction imaginable for the bauble babe in your life is here, as well as gently used 20th-century ladies' hats and pocketbooks. ⊠*73 Charles St., Beacon Hill* ☎*617/742–1031* Ⓣ*Charles/MGH.*

MUSIC STORES

As befitting a town with so many colleges and universities, live music of all kinds is never far away. Unfortunately, the market for recorded music has diminished over the years, and CD and record stores are disappearing along with it.

★ **Newbury Comics.** These local outposts for new rock and roll carry especially good lineups of independent pressings. Frequent sales keep prices down. ⊠*332 Newbury St., Back Bay* ☎*617/236–4930* Ⓣ*Hynes/ICA* ⊠*36 JFK St., Cambridge* ☎*617/491–0337* Ⓣ*Harvard* ⊠*Faneuil Hall Marketplace, North Bldg.* ☎*617/248–9992* Ⓣ*Government Center.*

ODDS AND ENDS

Grasshopper Shops. The souvenirs in this little collection of independently owned shops in historic Faneuil Hall are Boston-centric but not cheesy. The **Bostonian Society Museum Shop** (☎*617/720–3284*) has history books for children and adults. At **Explore Boston** (☎*617/725–1055*) you can buy saltwater taffy or a Boston-in-a-Box board game. **Out of Left Field** (☎*617/722–9401*) sells Red Sox gear. ⊠*Faneuil Hall Sq., Government Center* Ⓣ*Government Center.*

Kate Spade. Trendsetters go wild for Kate's colorful and classically whimsical handbags, as well as her shoes, PJs, accessories, and travel and cosmetics cases. ✉*117 Newbury St., Back Bay* ☎*617/262–2632* Ⓣ*Copley.*

Lannan Ship Model Gallery. Though a sign on the door says it's open by appointment only, a simple knock almost always gains you admission to this water rat's dream store—but call ahead to be sure. The 6,000-square-foot space looks like the attic of a merchant seaman: in addition to finished 18th- and 19th-century ship models ($200 to $100,000-plus) and vintage pond yachts, you can find lanterns, navigational instruments, and marine charts, prints, and oils. ✉*99 High St., Downtown* ☎*617/451–2650* Ⓣ*South Station.*

Out-of-Town News. Smack in the middle of Harvard Square is a staggering selection of the world's newspapers and magazines. The stand is open daily 6 AM–10:30 PM. ✉*0 Harvard Sq., Cambridge* ☎*617/354–1441* Ⓣ*Harvard.*

RUNNING GEAR

★ **Marathon Sports.** Marathon is known for its personalized service and advice for choosing the perfect shoe, whether you're a beginning walker or a serious runner. Many marathon runners find their way here before the Boston race each spring. ✉*1654 Massachusetts Ave., Cambridge* ☎*617/354–4161* Ⓣ*Harvard.*

THRIFT SHOPS

Garment District. This warehouselike building is crammed with vintage, used, and new clothing and accessories. Students crowd the store year-round, and everyone comes at Halloween for that perfect costume. ✉*200 Broadway, Cambridge* ☎*617/876–5230* Ⓣ*Kendall/MIT.*

Keezer's. Since 1895 this shop has been many a man's secret weapon for formal wear at an informal price. Pick up new or used suits, tuxedos, ties, shirts, and pants. ✉*140 River St., Cambridge* ☎*617/547–2455* Ⓣ*Central.*

Oona's. Crowded racks of cared-for, secondhand clothing for women and men are reason enough to browse through the multiple rooms of reasonably priced stock. A helpful staff and fun, eclectic vibe just make doing so that much more fun. ✉*1210 Massachusetts Ave., Cambridge* ☎*617/491–2654* Ⓣ*Harvard.*

Second Time Around. OK, so $700 isn't all that cheap for a used suit—but what if it's Chanel? Many of the items here, from jeans to fur coats, are new merchandise; the rest is on consignment. The staff takes periodic markdowns, ranging from 20% to 50% over a 90-day period. ✉*176 Newbury St., Back Bay* ☎*617/247–3504* Ⓣ*Copley* ✉*8 Eliot St., Cambridge* ☎*617/491–7185* Ⓣ*Harvard.*

TOYS

Ⓒ **Curious George.** Time can really slip away from you in this jungle of kids' books and gifts. Decorated with tropical plants, a fake hut, and tot-size chairs, and equipped with puzzles, toys, activity sets, and books of all kinds for all ages, this store is a wonderland for kids and a parent's salvation on a rainy day. ⊠*1 JFK St., Harvard Sq., Cambridge* ☎*617/498–0062* Ⓣ*Harvard.*

☾ **Henry Bear's Park.** The specialty at this charming neighborhood store is huggable bears and collectible dolls, although it also sells books, toys, and games. ⊠*361 Huron St., Cambridge* ☎*617/547–8424* Ⓣ*Porter* ⊠*19 Harvard St., Brookline* ☎*617/264–2422* Ⓣ*Brookline Village.*

☾ **Stellabella.** Creative toys are the draw here—books and games to stimulate kids' imaginations and get their brains going without relying on TV or violence. No gun or weapon toys are sold. ⊠*1360 Cambridge St., Cambridge* ☎*617/491–6290* Ⓣ*Central.*

Side Trips

WORD OF MOUTH

"The Peabody Essex Museum in Salem is a world class museum and if you are on the fence about including Salem, I would say it is worth the trip (but this is coming from me: with art background and a love of visiting museums wherever I am)."

—mamadadapaige

Updated
by Bethany
Cassin
Beckerlegge

History lies thick on the ground in the towns surrounding Boston—from Pilgrims to pirates, witches to whalers, the American Revolution to the Industrial Revolution. The sights outside the city are at least as interesting as those on Boston's Freedom Trail.

Visit Concord and Lexington, to the northwest of Boston, and that history class from high school may suddenly come rushing back to you. The state's coast from Boston to Cape Ann is called the North Shore, visited for its beautiful beaches, quintessential New England seaside communities, and the bewitching Salem. South of Boston lies more history in Quincy and Plymouth, and more seaside scenery at Cape Cod, Martha's Vineyard, and Nantucket. To the west is Pioneer Valley and the Berkshires, home to centuries-old towns, antiques shops, and rolling green hills.

ABOUT THE RESTAURANTS

Massachusetts invented the fried clam, and it's served in many North Shore and Cape Cod restaurants. Creamy clam chowder is another specialty. Eating seafood "in the rough"—from paper plates in seaside shacks—is a revered local custom. On the Cape, specialties from the Portuguese community like kale soup and linguiça sausage appear on some menus. At country inns in the Berkshires and the Pioneer Valley you'll find creative contemporary fare as well as traditional New England "dinners" strongly reminiscent of old England: double-cut pork chops, rack of lamb, game, Boston baked beans, Indian pudding, and the dubiously glorified "New England boiled dinner."

ABOUT THE HOTELS

While Boston has everything from luxury hotels to charming bed-and-breakfasts, the signature accommodation outside Boston is the country inn; in the Berkshires, where magnificent mansions have been converted into lodgings, the inns reach a very grand scale indeed. Less extravagant and less expensive are B&B establishments, many of them in private homes. On Cape Cod, inns are plentiful, and rental homes and condominiums are available for long-term stays. You'll want to make reservations for inns well in advance during peak periods: summer on the Cape and islands, and summer through winter in the Berkshires. Smoking has been banned in all Massachusetts hotels.

WHAT IT COSTS					
	¢	$	$$	$$$	$$$$
Restaurants	under $8	$8–$14	$15–$24	$25–$32	over $32
Hotels	under $75	$75–$150	$151–$225	$226–$325	over $325

For restaurants, prices are per person, for a main course at dinner. For hotels, prices are for two people in a standard double room in high season, excluding 12.45% tax and service charges.

TOP 5

■ **Early American History.** From Plimoth Plantation to Salem, Deerfield, Sturbridge Village, and Hancock Shaker Village, you can visit reenactment museums, preserved villages, homes, and inns where memories of Colonial history and personalities are kept alive.

■ **Seafaring Communities.** Set off on a whale watch from Gloucester, warm yourself after a windy coastal walk in Rockport with clam chowder, and admire the dedicated routine of fishermen along the North Shore.

■ **Revisit your Reading.** Nathaniel Hawthorne's *House of Seven Gables* still stands in Salem, the town that also served as the setting for *The Scarlett Letter.* Liberate yourself with a swim in Thoreau's Walden Pond. In Concord, see where both Louisa May Alcott and Ralph Waldo Emerson penned their thoughts.

■ **Cranberry Bogs.** An artist's dreamscape in every season—reds, greens, golds, and blues.

■ **The** *Mayflower II.* The story of the Pilgrims' Atlantic crossing comes alive here.

NORTHWEST OF BOSTON

Northwest of the city, Lexington and Concord embody the spirit of the American Revolution. These two quintessential New England towns enclose several historic homes and small museuems dedicated to some of the country's first substantial writers—Ralph Waldo Emerson, Nathaniel Hawthorne, Louisa May Alcott, and Henry David Thoreau. The town of Lowell, meanwhile, examines the story of the textile mills, canals, and other facets of the Industrial Revolution, and Sudbury is famous for its Henry Wadsworth Longfellow connection.

8

LEXINGTON

16 mi northwest of Boston.

Discontent within the British-ruled American colonies burst into action in Lexington in April 1775. On April 18, patriot leader Paul Revere alerted the town that British soldiers were approaching. The next day, as the British advance troops arrived in Lexington on their march toward Concord, the minutemen were waiting to confront the Redcoats in what became the skirmish of the Revolutionary War.

These first military encounters of the American Revolution are very much a part of present-day Lexington, a modern suburban town that sprawls out from the historic sites near its center. Although the downtown area is generally lively, with ice-cream and coffee shops, boutiques, and a great little movie theater, the town becomes especially animated each Patriots' Day (April 19 but celebrated on the third Monday in April), when costume-clad groups re-create the minutemen's battle maneuvers and Paul Revere rides again.

To learn more about the city and the 1775 clash, stop by the **Lexington Visitor Center** (⊠*1875 Massachusetts Ave.* ☎*781/862–2480*

PLANNING YOUR TRIP

BUDGETING YOUR TIME

Though Massachusetts is small compared to some states in the country, you could easily spend several weeks exploring it. If you have a few days, head to a town or two north and south of Boston, such as Concord, Plymouth, and Salem. Those who have a week may want to add on the Berkshires or spend the entire time relaxing at Cape Cod or Martha's Vineyard.

WHEN TO GO

The dazzling foliage and cool temperatures make fall the best time to visit western Massachusetts. Summer, especially late in the season when the water is a bit warmer, is ideal for visits to the beaches. Many towns save their best for winter—inns open their doors to carolers, shops serve eggnog, and lobster boats parade around Gloucester harbor adorned with lights. The off-season is the perfect time to try cross-country skiing, take a walk on a stormy beach, or spend a night by the fire, tucked under a quilt, catching up on books by Hawthorne or Thoreau.

GETTING THERE AND AROUND

Boston's Logan International Airport is the state's major airline hub. Flights also come into Manchester Boston Regional Airport in New Hampshire, 50 mi northwest of Boston, and TF Green International Airport in Providence, Rhode Island, 59 mi south of Boston.

Trains depart from Boston's North Station to the North Shore and from South Station to destinations south of the city. High-speed ferries and small commuter flights provide transportation to the islands. If you're driving to Cape Cod, avoid the Friday late-afternoon-to-early-evening summer rush, when traffic over the Sagamore Bridge can back up for several hours. Outside of Boston, you need a car to explore the state. Expect heavy traffic heading in and out of the city at rush hour, generally from 6 AM to 9 AM and 4 PM to 7 PM.

⊕ *www.lexingtonchamber.org* ⊗ *Apr.–Nov., daily 9–5; Dec.–Mar., daily 10–4*).

WHAT TO SEE

❸ **Battle Green.** It was on this two-acre triangle of land, on April 19, 1775, that the first confrontation between British soldiers, who were marching from Boston toward Concord, and the colonial militia known as the minutemen took place. The minutemen—so called because they were able to prepare themselves at a moment's notice—were led by Captain John Parker, whose role in the American Revolution is commemorated in Henry Hudson Kitson's renowned 1900 *Minuteman* statue. Facing downtown Lexington at the tip of Battle Green, the statue's in a traffic island and therefore makes for a difficult photo op.

❷ **Buckman Tavern.** While waiting for the arrival of the British on the morning of April 19, 1775, the minutemen gathered at this 1690 tavern. A half-hour tour takes in the tavern's seven rooms, which have been restored to the way they looked in the 1770s. Among the items on display is an old front door with a hole made by a British musket ball. ⊠ *1 Bedford St.* ☎ *781/862–1703* ⊕ *www.lexingtonhistory.org* ⊠ *$6;*

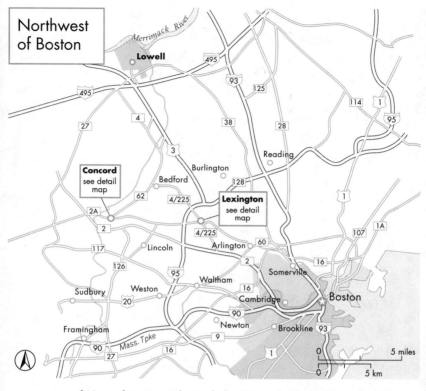

Northwest
of Boston

$10 combination ticket includes Hancock-Clarke House and Munroe Tavern ⊗ Apr.–Oct., daily 10–4.

❶ Hancock-Clarke House. On April 18, 1775, Paul Revere came here to warn patriots John Hancock and Sam Adams, who were staying at the house while attending the Provincial Congress in nearby Concord, of the advance of British troops. Hancock and Adams, on whose heads the British king had put a price, fled to avoid capture. The house, a parsonage built in 1698, is a 10-minute walk from Lexington Common. Inside are the pistols of the British major John Pitcairn as well as period furnishings and portraits. ✉ *36 Hancock St.* ☎ *781/862–1703* ⊕ *www.lexingtonhistory.org* ✉ *$6; $10 combination ticket includes Buckman Tavern and Munroe Tavern ⊗ Apr.–mid-June, weekends and mid-June–Oct., daily 10–4.*

❻ Minute Man National Historical Park. West of Lexington's center stretches this 1,000-acre, three-parcel park that also extends into nearby Lincoln and Concord (⇨ *Concord, What to See*). Begin your park visit at Lexington's **Minute Man Visitor Center** to see its free multimedia presentation, "The Road to Revolution," a captivating introduction to the events of April 1775. Then, continuing along Highway 2A toward Concord, you pass the point where Revere's midnight ride ended with his capture by the British; it's marked with a boulder and plaque, as well as

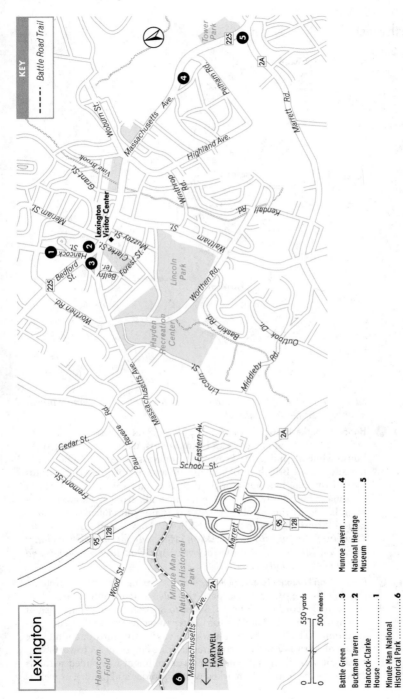

Lexington

KEY

- - - - Battle Road Trail

Lexington
Visitor Center

550 yards

500 meters

Battle Green **3**
Buckman Tavern **2**
Hancock-Clarke
House **1**
Minute Man National
Historical Park **6**

Munroe Tavern **4**
National Heritage
Museum **5**

TO
HARTWELL
TAVERN

an enclosure where rangers sometimes give educational presentations. You can also visit the 1732 **Hartwell Tavern** (open late May through October, daily 9–5), a restored drover's (driver's) tavern staffed by park employees in period costume; they frequently demonstrate musket firing or open-hearth cooking, and children are likely to enjoy the reproduction Colonial toys. ⊠*250 N. Great Rd., Lincoln* ☎*978/369–6993* ⊕*www.nps.gov/mima* ⊙*North Bridge Visitor Center, Apr.–Nov., daily 9–5; Dec.–Mar., daily 11–3. Minute Man Visitor Center, Apr.–Oct., daily 9–5; Nov., daily 9–4; closed Dec.–Mar.*

❹ **Munroe Tavern.** As April 19, 1775, dragged on, British forces met fierce resistance in Concord. Dazed and demoralized after the battle at Concord's Old North Bridge, the British backtracked and regrouped at this 1695 tavern, 1 mi east of Lexington Common, while the Munroe family hid in nearby woods. The troops then retreated through what is now the town of Arlington. After a bloody battle there, they returned to Boston. Tours of the tavern last about 30 minutes. ⊠*1332 Massachusetts Ave.* ☎*781/862–1703* ⊕*www.lexingtonhistory.org* ⊠*$6; $10 combination ticket includes Hancock-Clarke House and Buckman Tavern* ⊙*June–Oct., weekends and Apr.–mid-June, daily noon–4.*

❺ **National Heritage Museum.** View items and artifacts from all facets of American life, put in social and political context. An ongoing exhibit, "Lexington Alarm'd," outlines events leading up to April 1775 and illustrates Revolutionary-era life through everyday objects such as blacksmithing tools, bloodletting paraphernalia, and dental instruments, including a "tooth key" used to extract teeth. ⊠*33 Marrett Rd., Hwy. 2A at Massachusetts Ave.* ☎*781/861–6559* ⊕*www.monh.org* ⊠*Donations accepted* ⊙*Mon.–Sat. 10–5, Sun. noon–5.*

8

WHERE TO EAT

$–$$ ✕**Bertucci's.** Part of a popular chain, this family-friendly spot offers ☺ good Italian food—specialities include ravioli, calzones, and brick-oven pizzas. ⊠*1777 Massachusetts Ave.* ☎*781/860–9000* ▤*AE, D, DC, MC, V.*

CONCORD

About 10 mi west of Lexington, 21 mi northwest of Boston.

The Concord of today is a modern suburb with a busy center filled with arty shops, places to eat, and (recalling the literary history made here) old bookstores. Autumn lovers, take note: Concord is a great place to start a fall foliage tour. From Boston, head west along Route 2 to Concord, and then continue on to find harvest stands and apple-picking around Harvard and Stow.

WHAT TO SEE

❼ **Concord Museum.** The original contents of Emerson's private study, as ☺ well as the world's largest collection of Thoreau artifacts, reside in this 1930 Colonial-revival building just east of the town center. The museum provides a good overview of the town's history, from its original American Indian settlement to the present. Highlights include American Indian artifacts, furnishings from Thoreau's Walden Pond cabin,

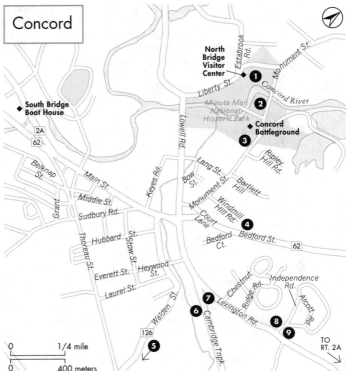

and one of the two lanterns hung at Boston's Old North Church to signal that the British were coming by sea. If you've brought the children, ask for a free family activity pack. ☒*200 Lexington Rd., entrance on Cambridge Tpke.* ☎*978/369-9763* ⊕*www.concordmuseum.org* ☒*$10* ⏱*Jan.–Mar., Mon.–Sat. 11–4, Sun. 1–4; Apr.–Dec, Mon.–Sat. 9–5, Sun. noon–5; June–Aug., daily 9–5.*

❶ **Minute Man National Historical Park.** Along Route 2A is a three-parcel ☺ park with 1,000 acres. The park contains many of the sites important to ★ Concord's role in the Revolution, including Old North Bridge, as well as two visitor centers, one each in Concord and Lexington (⇨ *Lexington, What to See*). Although the initial Revolutionary War sorties were in Lexington, word of the American losses spread rapidly to surrounding towns: when the British marched into Concord, more than 400 minutemen were waiting. A marker set in the stone wall along Liberty Street, behind the North Bridge Visitors Center, announces: ON THIS FIELD THE MINUTEMEN AND MILITIA FORMED BEFORE MARCHING DOWN TO THE FIGHT AT THE BRIDGE. The park's **North Bridge Visitor Center** (☒*174 Liberty St.* ☎*978/369-6993*) is open from April through October, daily 9–5; November, daily 9–4; and December through March, daily 11–3. ☒*Bounded by Monument St., Liberty St., and Lowell Rd.* ⊕*www.nps. gov/mima* ⏱*Grounds daily dawn–dusk.*

❸ Old Manse. The Reverend William Emerson, grandfather of Ralph Waldo Emerson, watched rebels and redcoats battle from behind his home, which was within sight of the Old North Bridge. The house, built in 1770, was occupied continuously by the Emerson family for almost two centuries, except for a 3½-year period during which Nathaniel Hawthorne rented it. Furnishings date from the late 18th century. Tours run throughout the day and last 45 minutes, with a new tour starting within 15 minutes of when the first person signs up. ⊠*269 Monument St.* ☎*978/369–3909* ▣*$8* ☉*Mid-Apr.–Oct., Mon.–Sat. 10–5, Sun. noon–5; last tour departs 4:30.*

❷ Old North Bridge. A half-mile from Concord center, at this bridge, the Concord minutemen turned the tables on the British on the morning of April 19, 1775. The Americans didn't fire first, but when two of their own fell dead from a redcoat volley, Major John Buttrick of Concord roared, "Fire, fellow soldiers, for God's sake, fire." The minutemen released volley after volley, and the redcoats fled. Daniel Chester French's famous statue *The Minuteman* (1875) honors the country's first freedom fighters. Inscribed at the foot of the statue are words Ralph Waldo Emerson wrote in 1837 describing the confrontation: BY THE RUDE BRIDGE THAT ARCHED THE FLOOD / THEIR FLAG TO APRIL'S BREEZE UNFURLED / HERE ONCE THE EMBATTLED FARMERS STOOD / AND FIRED THE SHOT HEARD ROUND THE WORLD. The lovely wooded surroundings give a sense of what the landscape was like in more rural times.

❽ Orchard House. The dark brown exterior of Louisa May Alcott's family home sharply contrasts with the light, wit, and energy so much in evidence inside. Named for the apple orchard that once surrounded it, Orchard House was the Alcott family home from 1858 to 1877. Here, Louisa wrote *Little Women,* based on her life with her three sisters; and her father, Bronson, founded his school of philosophy—the building remains behind the house. Because Orchard House had just one owner after the Alcotts left and because it became a museum in 1911, many of the original furnishings remain, including the semicircular shelf-desk where Louisa wrote *Little Women.* ⊠*399 Lexington Rd.* ☎*978/369–4118* ⊕*www.louisamayalcott.org* ▣*$9, tours free* ☉*Apr.–Oct., Mon.–Sat. 10–4:30, Sun. 1–4:30; Nov.–Dec. and Jan. 16–Mar., weekdays 11–3, Sat. 10–4:30, Sun. 1–4:30. Half-hr tours begin every 30 mins Apr.–Oct.; call for off-season schedule.*

❻ Ralph Waldo Emerson House. The 19th-century essayist and poet Ralph Waldo Emerson lived briefly in the Old Manse in 1834–35, then moved to this home, where he lived until his death in 1882. Here he wrote the *Essays.* Except for items from Emerson's study, now at the nearby Concord Museum, the Emerson House furnishings have been preserved as the writer left them, down to his hat resting on the newel post. You must join one of the half-hour-long tours to see the interior. ⊠*28 Cambridge Tpke., at Lexington Rd.* ☎*978/369–2236* ⊕*www.rwe.org/ emersonhouse* ▣*$7* ☉*Mid-Apr.–mid-Oct., Thurs.–Sat. 10–4:30, Sun. 1–4:30; call for tour schedule.*

❹ Sleepy Hollow Cemetery. In the Author's Ridge section of this cemetery are the graves of American literary greats Louisa May Alcott, Ralph

Literary Concord

The first wholly American literary movement was born in Concord, the tiny town west of Boston that, quite coincidentally, also witnessed the beginning of the American Revolution.

Under the influence of essayist and poet Ralph Waldo Emerson, a group eventually known as the Transcendental Club (but called the Hedges Club at the time) assembled regularly in Emerson's Concord home. Henry David Thoreau, a fellow townsman and famous proponent of self-reliance, was an integral club member, along with such others as pioneering feminist Margaret Fuller and poet Ellery Channing, both drawn to Concord simply because of Emerson's presence.

These are the names that have become indelible bylines in high school anthologies and college syllabi, but Concord also produced beloved authors outside the Transcendental movement. These writers include Louisa May Alcott of *Little Women* fame and children's book author Harriet Lothrop, pseudonymously known as Margaret Sydney. Even Nathaniel Hawthorne, whose various places of temporary residence around Massachusetts constitute a literary trail all their own, abided in Concord during the early and late portions of his career.

The cumulative inkwells of these authors have bestowed upon Concord a literary legacy unique in the United States, both for its influence on literature in general and for the quantity of related sights packed within such a small radius. From Alcott's Orchard House to Hawthorne's Old Manse, nearly all their houses remain standing, well preserved and open for tours.

Louisa May Alcott wrote *Little Women* while living at Orchard House in Concord.

The Thoreau Institute, within walking distance of a reconstruction of Thoreau's famous cabin in the woods at Walden Pond, is a repository of his papers and original editions. Emerson's study sits in the Concord Museum, across the street from his house. Even their final resting places are here, on Authors Ridge in Sleepy Hollow Cemetery, a few short blocks from the town common.

Various tours make the rounds of all of Concord's literary landmarks. The **Literary Trail of Greater Boston** (☎ *617/621–4020* ⊕ *www.literarytrailofgreaterboston.org*) offers trolley tours mid-June through mid-October. **Concord Bike Tours** (☎ *978/697–1897* ⊕ www.concordbiketours.com) guide you through the sites via two wheels, usually early April through November (weather permitting).

Waldo Emerson, Henry David Thoreau, and Nathaniel Hawthorne. Each Memorial Day, Alcott's grave is decorated in commemoration of her death. ⊠ *Bedford St. (Rte. 62)* ☎ *978/318–3233* ⊘ *Daily dawn–dusk.*

❺ ★ Walden Pond. For lovers of early American literature, a trip to Concord isn't complete without a pilgrimage to Henry David Thoreau's most famous residence. Here, in 1845, at age 28, Thoreau moved into a one-room cabin—built for $28.12—on the shore of this 100-foot-deep kettle hole formed by the retreat of an ancient glacier. Living alone for the next two years, Thoreau discovered the benefits of solitude and the beauties of nature. The essays in *Walden,* published in 1854, are a mixture of philosophy, nature writing, and proto-ecology. The site of the first cabin is staked out in stone. A full-size, authentically furnished replica of the cabin stands about ½ mi from the original site, near the Walden Pond State Reservation parking lot. Even when it's closed, you can peek through its windows. Now, as in Thoreau's time, the pond is a delightful summertime spot for swimming, fishing, and rowing, and there's hiking in the nearby woods. To get to Walden Pond State Reservation from the center of Concord—a trip of only 1½ mi—take Concord's Main Street a block west from Monument Square, turn left onto Walden Street, and head for the intersection of Routes 2 and 126. Cross over Route 2 onto Route 126, heading south for ½ mi. ⊠ *915 Walden St. (Rte. 126)* ☎ *978/369–3254* ⊕ *www.mass.gov/dcr/parks/ walden* ⊠ *Free, parking $5* ⊘ *Daily from 8* AM *until about ½ hr before sunset, weather permitting.*

❾ The Wayside. Nathaniel Hawthorne lived at the Old Manse in 1842–45, working on stories and sketches; he then moved to Salem (where he wrote *The Scarlet Letter*) and later to Lenox (*The House of the Seven Gables*). In 1852 he returned to Concord, bought this rambling structure called The Wayside, and lived here until his death in 1864. The subsequent owner, Margaret Sidney, wrote the children's book Five Little Peppers and How They Grew (1881). Before Hawthorne moved in, the Alcotts lived here, from 1845 to 1848. An exhibit center, in the former barn, provides information about the Wayside authors and links them to major events in American history. Hawthorne's tower-study, with his stand-up writing desk, is substantially as he left it. ⊠ *455 Lexington Rd.* ☎ *978/369–6993* ⊘ *Open by guided tour only, May–Oct., Fri.–Sun., at 11, 1, 3, and 4:30.*

8

WHERE TO EAT

$ ✕ La Provence. This little taste of France, a casual café and take-out shop opposite the Concord train station, makes a good stop for a light meal. In the morning you can start off with a croissant or a brioche, and at midday you can pick up sandwiches (perhaps pâté and cheese or French ham), quiches, or salads. Leave room for an éclair or a petite fruit tart. Just don't plan a late night here; the café closes at 7 PM during the week and at 5:30 on Saturday. ⊠ *105 Thoreau St.* ☎ *978/371–7428* ⊕ *www. laprovence.us* ⊟ *D, MC, V* ⊘ *Closed Sun.*

$$–$$$ ✕ Walden Grille. Chowders, salads and sandwiches are typical fare at this old brick firehouse-turned-dining room, but in a town with limited dining options, this isn't a bad choice. Start with the Philly spring rolls or crispy fried oysters. Sandwiches include run-of-the-mill burgers and BLTs, plus more creative options like the chicken curry roll-up. Entrées run the gamut from the maple-glazed salmon to the chicken potpie. ⊠*24 Walden St.* ☎*978/371–2233* ⊕*www.waldengrille.com* ▤*AE, D, MC, V.*

LOWELL

30 mi northwest of Boston.

Everyone knows that the American Revolution began in Massachusetts. But the Commonwealth, and in particular the Merrimack Valley, also nurtured the Industrial Revolution. Lowell's first mill opened in 1823; by the 1850s, 40 factories employed thousands of workers and produced 2 million yards of cloth every week.

WHAT TO SEE

Boott Cotton Mills Museum. About a 10-minute walk northeast from the National Park Visitor Center is this museum devoted to industrialization. The textile worker's grueling life is shown with all its grit, noise, and dust. You know you're in for an unusual experience when you're handed earplugs—they're for the re-created 1920s weave room, authentic down to the deafening roar of 88 working power looms. Other exhibits at the complex include weaving artifacts, cloth samples, video interviews with workers, and a large, meticulous scale model of 19th-century production. ⊠ *115 John St.* ☎*978/970–5000* ⊕*www.nps.gov/ lowe* ▦*$6* ⊙*Daily 9:30–4:30.*

Lowell National Historical Park. This park tracks the history of a gritty era when the power loom was the symbol of economic progress. It encompasses several blocks in the downtown area, including former-mills-turned-museums, a network of canals, and a helpful visitor center. Begin at the National Park Visitor Center where you can watch a multimedia presentation on the Industrial Age in Lowell. Several tours, including canal boat trips and guided walking and trolley tours, depart from here. ⊠*246 Market St.* ☎*978/970–5000* ⊕*www.nps.gov/lowe* ▦*Free* ⊙*Daily 9–5.*

THE NORTH SHORE

The slice of Massachusetts's Atlantic Coast known as the North Shore extends past Boston to the picturesque Cape Ann region just shy of the New Hampshire border. In addition to miles of woods and beaches, the North Shore's highlights include Marblehead, a stunningly classic New England sea town; Salem, which thrives on a history of witches, writers, and maritime trades; Gloucester, the oldest seaport in America; Rockport, rich with crafts shops and artists' studios; and Newburyport, with its redbrick center and clapboard mansions, and a handful of typical New England towns in between. Bustling during the short summer season and breathtaking during the autumn foliage, the North Shore is calmer (and colder) between November and June. Since many restaurants, inns, and attractions operate reduced hours, it's worth calling ahead off-season.

MARBLEHEAD

17 mi north of Boston.

Marblehead, with its narrow and winding streets, beautifully preserved clapboard homes, sea captains' mansions, and harbor, looks much the way the village must have when it was founded in 1629 by fishermen from Cornwall and the Channel Islands. One of New England's premier sailing capitals, Marblehead's Race Week—first held in 1889—continues to attract boats each July from along the Eastern seaboard. Parking in town can be difficult; lots at the end of Front Street or on State Street by the Landing restaurant are the best options.

WHAT TO SEE

The 1768 Jeremiah Lee Mansion. Marblehead's 18th-century high society is exemplified in this mansion run by the town's museum and historical society. Colonel Lee was the wealthiest merchant and ship owner in Massachusetts in 1768, and although few original furnishings remain, the unique hand-painted wallpaper and fine collection of traditional North Shore furniture provide clues into the life of an American gentleman. ⊠*161 Washington St.* ☎*781/631–1768* ⊕*www.marbleheadmuseum. org/LeeMansion.htm* ☒*$5* ☉*June–Oct., Tues.–Sat. 10–4.*

Abbott Hall. The town's Victorian-era municipal building, built in 1876, displays Archibald Willard's painting *The Spirit of '76*. Many visitors, familiar since childhood with this image of the three Revolutionary veterans with fife, drum, and flag, are surprised to find the original in an otherwise unassuming town hall. Also on site is a small naval museum exploring Marblehead's maritime past. ⊠*188 Washington St.* ☎*781/631–0000* ☒*Free* ☉*Call for hrs.*

Fort Sewall. Marblehead's magnificent views of the harbor, the Misery islands, and the Atlantic are best seen from this fort that was built in 1644 atop the rocky cliffs of the harbor. Used as a defense against the French in 1742 as well as during the War of 1812, Fort Sewall today is open to the public as community parkland. Barracks and underground quarters can still be seen, and Revolutionary War re-enactments by members of the modern-day Glover's Marblehead Regiment occur at the fort annually. ⊠*End of Front St.* ⊕*www.essexheritage.org/sites/ fort_sewall.shtml* ☒*Free* ☉*Daily, sunrise to sunset.*

WHERE TO EAT AND STAY

$–$$
SEAFOOD
✕**The Landing.** Decorated in nautical blues and whites, this pleasant restaurant sits right on Marblehead harbor, with a deck that's nearly in the water. The menu mixes classic New England fare (clam chowder, lobster, broiled scrod) with more contemporary dishes like the Asian stir-fry basket. Brunch is served on Sunday. The pub area has a lighter menu and local feel. ⊠*81 Front St.* ☎*781/639–1266* ▤*AE, D, DC, MC, V* ⊕*www.thelandingrestaurant.com.*

$$–$$$
Fodor'sChoice
★
▨**Harbor Light Inn.** Housed in a pair of adjoining 18th-century mansions in the heart of Old Town Marblehead, this elegant inn features many rooms with canopy beds, brick fireplaces, and jacuzzis. A soaring ceiling on the top floor reveals the original post-and-beam construction. Rates include continental breakfast buffet, and require two-night minimum

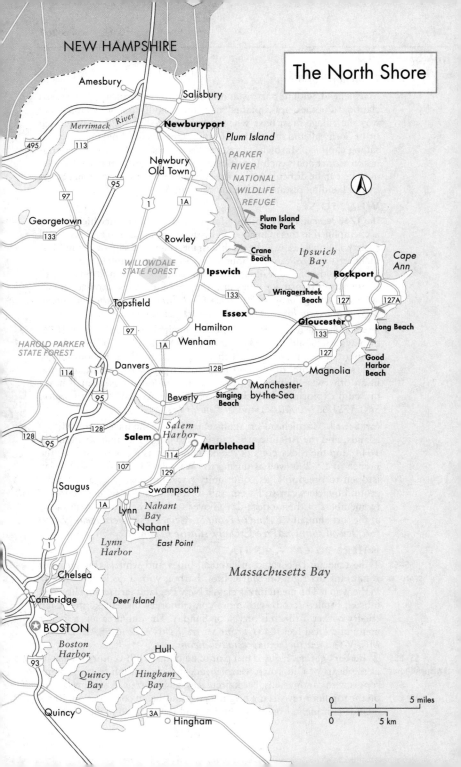

on weekends. **Pros:** nice location amid period homes. **Cons:** limited parking; many one-way and narrow streets make this town somewhat confusing to get around by car, and the inn tricky to find. ⌂*58 Washington St.* ☎*781/631–2186* ⊕*www.harborlightinn.com* ⟲*21 rooms* ⌂*In-room: VCR, Wi-Fi. In-hotel: Pool, no kids under 8, Wi-Fi, no-smoking rooms* ▤*AE, MC, V* ❍*CP.*

SALEM

16 mi northeast of Boston, 4 mi west of Marblehead.

Known for years as the "Witch City," Salem is redefining itself. Though numerous witch-related attractions and shops still draw tourists, there's much more to the city. But first, a bit on its bewitched past. The witchcraft hysteria emerged from the trials of 1692, when several Salem-area girls fell ill and accused some of the townspeople of casting spells on them. More than 150 men and women were charged with practicing witchcraft, a crime punishable by death. After the trials later that year, 19 people were hanged and one man was crushed to death.

Though the witch trials might have built Salem's infamy, it'd be a mistake to ignore the town's rich maritime and creative traditions, which played integral roles in the country's evolution. Frigates out of Salem opened the Far East trade routes and generated the wealth that created America's first millionaires. Among its native talents are writer Nathaniel Hawthorne, the intellectual Peabody Sisters, navigator Nathaniel Bowditch, and architect Samuel McIntire. This creative spirit is today celebrated in Salem's internationally recognized museums, waterfront shops and restaurants, galleries, and wide common.

To learn more on the area, stop by the **Regional Visitor's Center.** (⌂*2 Liberty St.* ☎*978/740–1650* ◷*Daily 9–5*) Innovatively designed in the Old Salem Armory, the center has exhibits, a 27-minute film, maps, and a gift shop.

WHAT TO SEE

❶ ★ House of the Seven Gables. Immortalized in Nathaniel Hawthorne's classic novel, this site itself is a literary treasure. Built in 1668 and also known as the Turner-Ingersoll Mansion, the house includes a secret staircase, a garret containing an antique scale model of the house, and some of the finest Georgian interiors in the country. Also on the property is the small house where Hawthorne was born in 1804; built in 1750, it was moved from its original location a few blocks away. ⌂*115 Derby St.* ☎*978/744–0991* ⊕*www.7gables.org* ▦*$12* ◷*Nov., Dec., and mid-Jan.–June, daily 10–5; July–Oct., daily 10–7.*

❷ Fodor'sChoice ★ **Peabody Essex Museum.** Salem's world-class museum celebrates maritime art, history, and the spoils of the Asian export trade. Its 30 galleries, housed in a contemplative blend of modern design, represent a diverse range of styles; ranging from American decorative and oceanic art to idea studios and photography. ⌂*East India Sq.* ☎*978/745–9500 or 866/745–1876* ⊕*www.pem.org* ▦*$15* ◷*Tues.–Sun. 10–5.*

❸ Salem Maritime National Historic Site. Near Derby Wharf, this 9¼-acre site focuses on Salem's heritage as a major seaport with a thriving overseas

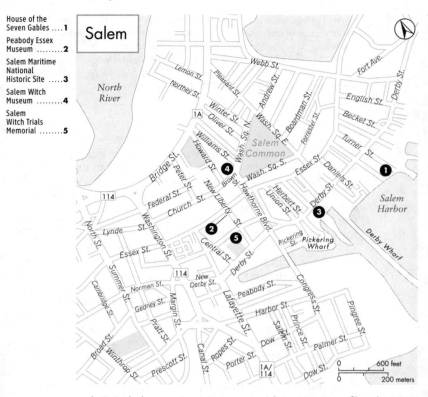

trade. It includes an orientation center with an 18-minute film; the 1762
home of Elias Derby, America's first millionaire; the 1819 Customs
House, made famous in Nathaniel Hawthorne's *The Scarlet Letter*; and
a replica of the *Friendship,* a 171-foot, three-masted 1797 merchant
vessel. There's also an active lighthouse dating from 1871, as well as
the nation's last surviving 18th-century wharves. The West India Goods
Store, across the street, is still a working 19th-century store with glass
jars of spices, teas, and coffees. ⊠*193 Derby St.* ☎*978/740–1660*
⊕*www.nps.gov/sama* ≊*Site free, tours $5* ☉*Daily 9–5.*

❹ Salem Witch Museum. An informative, if somewhat hokey, introduction
to the 1692 witchcraft hysteria, this museum has a short walk-through
exhibit, "Witches: Evolving Perceptions," that describes witch hunts
through the years. ⊠*Washington Sq. N* ☎*978/744–1692* ⊕*www.
salemwitchmuseum.com* ≊*$8* ☉*Sept.–June, daily 10–5; July–Aug.,
daily 10–7.*

❺ Salem Witch Trials Memorial. Dedicated by Nobel Laureate Elie Wiesel in
1992, this melancholy space—an antidote to the relentless marketing of
the merry-witches motif—honors those who died because they refused
to confess that they were witches. A stone wall is studded with 20 stone
benches, each inscribed with a victim's name, and sits next to Salem's
oldest burying ground. ⊠*Off Liberty St. near Charter St.*

The First Witch Trial

It was in Danvers, not Salem, that the first witch trial was born, originating with the family of Samuel Parris, a minister who moved to the area in 1680 from Barbados, bringing with him two slaves, including one named Tituba. In 1691 Samuel's daughter, Betty, and niece, Abigail, began having "fits." Tituba, who had told Betty and Abigail stories of magic and witchcraft from her homeland, baked a "witch cake" to identify the witches who were harming the girls. The girls in turn accused Tituba of witchcraft. After three days of "questioning," which included beatings from Samuel and a promise from him to free her if she cooperated, Tituba confessed to meeting the devil (in the form of a black hog or dog). She also claimed there were other witches in the village, confirming the girls' accusations against Sarah Good and Sarah Osborne, but she refused to name any others. Tituba's trial prompted the frenzy that led to the deaths of 20 accused "witches."

ARTS AND ENTERTAINMENT

THEATER **Cry Innocent: the People Versus Bridget Bishop.** This show, the longest continuously-running play north of Boston, transports audience members to Bridget Bishop's trial of 1692. After hearing historical testimonies, the audience cross-examines the witnesses and must then decide the verdict. Actors respond in character revealing much about the Puritan frame of mind. Each show is different and allows audience members to play their "part" in history. ⊠ *Old Town Hall, 32 Derby Sq.* ☎ *978/867–4767* ⊕ *www.gordon.edu/historyalive* ⊠ *$9* ⊗ *Jun.-Oct., showtimes vary.*

WHERE TO EAT & STAY

$$–$$$ ✕ **The Lyceum Bar & Grill.** Always a hit for classy fare, the restaurant takes
SEAFOOD advantage of its historic building where Alexander Graham Bell made
Fodor'sChoice the first long-distance phone call. The "local ingredients, global flavors"
★ philosophy is seen best in the panko crusted fish 'n' chips, oysters, and lobster crepe. Jazz is played most weekends. ⊠ *43 Church Street St.* ☎ *978/745–7665* ⊕ *www.lyceumsalem.com* ⊟ *AE, D, MC, V* ⊗ *No dinner Sun. (brunch only).*

$–$$ ⊞ **Amelia Payson House.** Built in 1845, this Greek-revival house is a comfortable bed-and-breakfast near all the historic attractions. With high ceilings, floral-print wallpaper, and marble fireplaces, the four guest rooms are delicate and feminine. **Pros:** spotless, cozy and decorated in period furniture. **Cons:** no children under 14, telephones and Internet connection are not available in guest rooms (though easily accessed in a common room). ⊠ *16 Winter St.* ☎ *978/210–9814* ⊕ *www.amelia paysonhouse.com* ⊅ *4 rooms* ⊘ *In-hotel: Parking (no fee), Wi-Fi, no-smoking rooms* ⊟ *AE, D, MC, V* ⊗ *Closed Nov.–Mar.* ⊠ *CP.*

$–$$$ ⊞ **The Hawthorne Hotel.** Elegantly restored, this full-service landmark hotel celebrates the town's most famous writer. The historic hotel and tavern is within walking distance from the town common, all museums, and the waterfront. Across the street is Nathaniel's statue and

8

a fine gifts shop named after his wife, Sophia (Peabody), located in the couple's former home. **Pros:** lobby is historic and lovely, parking available behind hotel, easy walking access to all the town's features. **Cons:** many rooms are small, management sometimes too busy to give personal attention. ⊠*18 Washington Sq. W* ☎*978/744–4080* ⊕*www. hawthornehotel.com* ⇆*93 rooms* ⚄*In-room: Wi-Fi. In-hotel: public Wi-Fi, no-smoking rooms* ⊟ *AE, D, MC, V.*

GLOUCESTER

37 mi northeast from Boston, 8 mi northeast from Manchester.

On Gloucester's fine seaside promenade is a famous statue of a man steering a ship's wheel, his eyes searching the horizon. The statue, which honors those "who go down to the sea in ships" was commissioned by the town citizens in celebration of Gloucester's 300th anniversary in 1923. The oldest seaport in the nation (with some of the North Shore's best beaches) is still a major fishing port. Sebastian Junger's 1997 book, *A Perfect Storm,* was an account of the fate of the *Andrea Gail,* a Gloucester fishing boat caught in "the storm of the century" in October 1991. In 2000 the book was made into a movie, filmed on location in Gloucester.

WHAT TO SEE

Hammond Castle Museum. Inventor John Hays Hammond Jr. built this structure in 1926 to resemble a "medieval" stone castle. Hammond is credited with more than 500 patents, including ones associated with the organ that bears his name. The museum contains medieval-style furnishings and paintings, and the Great Hall houses an impressive 8,200-pipe organ. From the castle you can see "Norman's Woe Rock," made famous by Longfellow in his poem "The Wreck of the Hesperus." ⊠*80 Hesperus Ave., south side of Gloucester off Rte. 127* ☎*978/283–2080 or 978/283–7673* ⊕*www.hammondcastle.org* ☜*$9* ⊗*May.–early June, weekends and mid-June–Oct., daily. Call for hrs.*

Rocky Neck. The town's creative side thrives in this neighborhood, the first-settled artists' colony in the United States. Its alumni include Winslow Homer, Maurice Prendergast, Jane Peter, and Cecilia Beaux. ⊠*Rocky Neck Ave. at E. Main St.* ⊕*www.rockyneckartcolony.org* ⊗*Galleries 10–10 in summer.*

The Cape Ann Historical Association. Downtown in Captain Elias Davis 1804 house, this is Gloucester's surprise museum and gallery. It reflects the town's commitment to artists and has the world's largest collection by maritime luminist Fitz Henry (Hugh) Lane. There's also an excellent exhibit on Gloucester's maritime history. ⊠*27 Pleasant St.* ☎*978/283–0455* ⊕*www.capeannmuseum.org* ☜*$8* ⊗*Tues.–Sat. 10–5, Sun. 1–4.*

SPORTS AND THE OUTDOORS

BEACHES Gloucester has the best beaches on the North Shore. From Memorial Day through mid-September, parking costs $15 to $20 on weekdays and $20 to $25 on weekends, when the lots often fill by 10 AM. **Good Harbor Beach** (⊠*Easily signposted from Rte. 127A*) is a huge, sandy, dune-backed beach, with showers and snack bar, and a rocky islet just offshore. For excellent sunbathing, visit **Long Beach** (⊠ *Off Rte. 127A on Gloucester-Rockport town line*). **Wingaersheek Beach** (⊠ *Exit 13 off Rte. 128*) is a well-protected cove of white sand and dunes, with the white Annisquam lighthouse in the bay.

BOATING Consider a sail along the harbor and coast aboard the 65-foot schooner **Thomas E. Lannon** (⊠ *63 Rear Rogers St., Seven Seas Wharf* ☎ *978/281–6634* ⊕ *www.schooner.org*) crafted in Essex in 1996 and modeled after the great boats built a century before. From mid-May through mid-October there are several two-hour sails, including those that let you enjoy the sunset or participate in a lobster bake.

WHERE TO EAT AND STAY

$$ ✕ **Franklin Cape Ann.** This contemporary nightspot offers bistro-style AMERICAN chicken, roast cod, and steak frites, perfect for the late-night crowd (it's open until midnight). Live jazz is on tap most Tuesday evenings. Look for the signature martini glass over the door. ⊠ *118 Main St.* ☎ *978/283–7888* ⊟ *AE, D, MC, V* ⊗ *No lunch.*

$-$$$ ✕ **Passports.** With an eclectic lunch and dinner menu—hence the name— SEAFOOD Passports is a bright and airy café with French, Spanish, and Thai dishes, as well as (of course) lobster sandwiches. The fried calamari and house haddock are favorites here, and there's always local art hanging on the walls for patrons to buy. Occasionally there are wine tastings. ⊠ *110 Main St.* ☎ *978/281–3680* ⊟ *AE, D, MC, V.*

$ 🏨 **Cape Ann's Marina Resort.** This year-round hotel and spa less than a mile from Gloucester comes alive in summer. Two restaurants, a whale-watch boat, and deep-sea fishing excursions are available from the premises. The rooms all have balconies and water views. The Gull restaurant is closed November to mid-April. **Pros:** guests get a free river cruise during summer stays. **Cons:** "Resort" is a bit of a misnomer, as the hotel is surrounded by parking lots, with no walking path to or from town. ⊠ *75 Essex Ave.* ☎ *978/283–2116 or 800/626–7660* ⊕ *www.capeann marina.com* ⭿ *31 rooms* ♿ *In-room: Kitchen (some). In-hotel: Restaurant, pool, no elevator, no-smoking rooms* ⊟ *AE, D, DC, MC, V.*

$-$$ 🏨 **Cape Ann Motor Inn.** On the sands of Long Beach, this three-story, shingled motel has no-frills rooms except for the balconies and ocean views. Half have well-furnished kitchenettes. The Honeymoon Suite is pricier but has a full kitchen, fireplace, whirlpool bath, king-size bed, and private balcony. **Pros:** exceptional view from every room. **Cons:** summer season can be loud and crowded. ⊠ *33 Rockport Rd.* ☎ *978/281–2900 or 800/464–8439* ⊕ *www.capeannmotorinn.com* ⭿ *30 rooms, 1 suite* ♿ *In-room: No a/c, kitchen (some). In-hotel: Some pets allowed, no-smoking rooms* ⊟ *AE, D, MC, V* ⊠*CP.*

8

ROCKPORT

41 mi northeast of Boston, 4 mi northeast of Gloucester on Rte. 127.

Rockport, at the very tip of Cape Ann, derives its name from the local granite formations. Many Boston-area structures are made of stone cut from its long-gone quarries. Today, the town is a tourist center with a well-marked, centralized downtown that is easy to navigate and access on foot. Unlike typical tourist-trap landmarks, Rockport's shops sell quality arts, clothing, and gifts, and its restaurants serve seafood, or home-baked cookies rather than fast food. Walk past shops and colorful clapboard houses to the end of Bearskin Neck for an impressive view of the Atlantic Ocean and the old, weather-beaten lobster shack known as "Motif No. 1" because of its popularity as a subject for amateur painters and photographers.

WHERE TO EAT AND STAY

$–$$
SEAFOOD
✕**Brackett's Ocean View.** A big bay window in this quiet, homey restaurant gives an excellent view across Sandy Bay. The menu includes chowders, fish cakes, and other seafood dishes. ⊠*25 Main St.* ☎*978/546–2797* ▭*AE, D, DC, MC, V* ✆*Closed Nov.–mid-Apr. Closed Mon.–Tues.*

¢–$$
AMERICAN
✕**The Greenery Restaurant and Café.** This spot has become a local institution because it is one of Rockport's only restaurants open year-round. In-season, the second floor opens to accommodate the boom of tourists. Stop in for a sandwich or pastry from the bakery or dine in the back room surrounded by bay windows overlooking the harbor. Breakfast is served daily until 4 PM. ⊠*15 Dock Sq.* ☎*978/546–9593* ✍*Reservations not accepted* ▭*AE, MC, V.*

¢–$$
SEAFOOD
✕**Portside Chowder House.** This casual seafood spot has big picture windows overlooking the harbor. Its popularity means that the wait for tables and food can be long. Chowder is the house specialty; it also serves lobster rolls, salads, burgers, and sandwiches. ⊠*7 Tuna Wharf* ☎*978/546–7045* ▭*AE, MC, V* ✆*No dinner Mon.–Thurs. Dec.–Mar.*

$–$$
★
⌂**Addison Choate Inn and Periwinkle Cottage.** Just a minute's walk from both the center of Rockport and the train station, this 1851 inn sits in prime location. The sizable and beautifully decorated rooms have their share of antiques and local seascape paintings, as well as pine floors and large bathrooms; the captain's room contains a canopy bed, handmade quilts, and Oriental rugs. In the third-floor suite, huge windows look out over the rooftops to the sea. Two spacious stable-house apartments have skylights, cathedral ceilings, and exposed wood beams. Rates include afternoon tea. **Pros:** proximity to the ocean, shopping and train station. **Cons:** only one bedroom on the first floor. ⊠*49 Broadway* ☎*978/546–7543 or 800/245–7543* ⊕*www.addison choateinn.com* ⇌*6 rooms, 2 apartments* ⌂*In-room: No TV. In-hotel: Restaurant, Wi-Fi, no elevator, no-smoking rooms* ▭*MC, V* ✆*Closed Jan.–Mar.* ¶|*CP.*

$
Fodor's Choice
★
⌂**Sally Webster Inn.** This inn was named for a member of Hannah Jumper's "hatchet gang," teetotalers who smashed up the town's liquor stores in 1856 and turned Rockport into the dry town it remains today. Sally lived in this house for much of her life, and the poshly decorated guest rooms are named for members of her family. Caleb's room is a romantic retreat with a four-poster bed and floral quilts, and William's room has a crisply nautical theme. Other rooms have pine wide-board floors, nonworking brick fireplaces, rocking chairs, and four-poster, brass, or canopy beds. **Pros:** homey atmosphere in an excellent location with attentive staff. **Cons:** only two rooms have fireplaces. ⊠*34 Mt. Pleasant St.* ☎*978/546–9251 or 877/546–9251* ⊕*www.sallywebster.com* ⇌*8*

rooms ♿In-room: No TV, Internet access in main room. In-hotel: No elevator, no-smoking rooms ▭*MC, V* ☉*Closed Jan.* ⏐◎⏐*CP.*

ESSEX

30 mi northeast of Boston, 12 mi west of Rockport. Head west out of Cape Ann on Rte. 128, turning north on Rte. 133.

The small, seafaring town of Essex, once an important shipbuilding center, is surrounded by salt marshes and is filled with antiques stores and seafood restaurants.

WHAT TO SEE

⟳ **Essex Shipbuilding Museum.** Still an active shipyard, this museum traces the evolution of the American schooner, which was first created in Essex. The museum sometimes offers shipbuilding demonstrations. One-hour tours take in the museum's many buildings and boats, especially the *Evelina M. Goulart*—one of only seven remaining Essex-built schooners. ⊠*66 Main St. (Rte. 133)* ☎*978/768–7541* ⊕*www. essexshipbuildingmuseum.org* ⊡*$8* ☉ *June–Oct., Wed.–Sun. 10–5; Nov.–May, Sat. and Sun. 10–5.*

SHOPPING

Chebacco Antiques (⊠*38 Main St.* ☎*978/768–7371*), open every weekend, concentrates on lighting and country furniture, as well as Staffordshire plates and sterling silver. Open only on weekends, **Howard's Flying Dragon Antiques** (⊠*136 Main St.* ☎*978/768–7282*) is a general antiques shop that carries statuary and glass.

WHERE TO EAT

$–$$$ ✕**Woodman's of Essex.** According to local legend, this is where Law-
Fodor's Choice rence "Chubby" Woodman invented the first fried clam back in 1916.
★ Today this sprawling wooden shack with indoor booths and outdoor picnic tables is *the* place for seafood in the rough. Besides fried clams, you can tuck into clam chowder, lobster rolls, or the popular "downriver" lobster combo. ⊠*121 Main St. (Rte. 133)* ☎*978/768–2559 or 800/649–1773* ⊕*www.woodmans.com* ▭*AE, MC, V.*

IPSWICH

36 mi north of Boston, 6 mi northwest of Essex.

Quiet little Ipswich, settled in 1633 and famous for its clams, is said to have more 17th-century houses standing and occupied than any other place in America; more than 40 were built before 1725. Information and a booklet with a suggested walking tour are available at the **Visitor Information Center** (⊠*Hall Haskell House, 36 S. Main St.* ☎*978/356–8540* ☉*Memorial Day–Oct., Mon.–Sat. 9–5, Sun. noon–5*).

WHAT TO SEE

Great House at Castle Hill. This 59-room Stuart-style mansion, built in 1927 for Richard Crane—of the Crane plumbing company—and his family, is part of the Crane Estate, a stretch of more than 2,100 acres along the Essex and Ipswich rivers, encompassing Castle Hill, Crane Beach, and the Crane Wildlife Refuge. Although the original furnishings were sold at auction, the mansion has been elaborately refurnished in period style; photographs in most of the rooms show their original appearance. The Great House is open for one-hour tours and also hosts concerts and other events. ⊠*Argilla Rd.* ☎*978/356–4351* ⊕*www. thetrustees.org* ☒*Tours $10* ⊙*June–Oct., Wed.–Sat.; call for hrs.*

SPORTS AND THE OUTDOORS

BEACHES

★

Crane Beach, one of New England's most beautiful beaches, is a sandy, 4-mi-long stretch backed by dunes and a nature trail. Public parking is available, but on a nice summer weekend, it's usually full before lunch. There are lifeguards and changing rooms. Check ahead before visiting mid-July to early-August, when greenhead flies terrorize sunbathers. ⊠*Argilla Rd.* ☎*978/356–4354* ⊕*www.thetrustees.org* ☒*Beach free. Parking $15 weekdays, $22 weekends mid-May–early Sept.; $7 early Sept.–mid-May* ⊙*Daily 8–sunset.*

HIKING

The Massachusetts Audubon Society's **Ipswich River Wildlife Sanctuary** has trails through marshland hills, where there are remains of early Colonial settlements as well as abundant wildlife. Make sure to grab some birdseed and get a trail map from the office. Enjoy bridges, man-made rock structures, and other surprises on the Rockery Trail. ⊠*87 Perkins Row, southwest of Ipswich, 1 mi off Rte. 97, Topsfield* ☎*978/887–9264* ⊕*www.massaudubon.org* ☒*$4* ⊙*Office May–Oct., Tues.–Sun. 9–5; Nov.–Apr., Tues.–Fri. 9–4, Sat.–Sun. 10–4. Trails Tues.–Sun. dawn–dusk.*

WHERE TO EAT

¢–$
SEAFOOD
Fodor'sChoice
★

✕**Clam Box.** Shaped like a giant fried clam box, this small roadside stand is the best place to sample Ipswich's famous bivalves. Since 1938, locals and tourists have been lining up for clams, oysters, scallops, and onion rings. ⊠*246 High St. (Rte. 1A)* ☎*978/356–9707* ⊕*www.ipswichma. com/clambox* ⌂*Reservations not accepted* ▭*No credit cards* ⊙*Closed mid-Dec.–Feb.*

$$–$$$
SEAFOOD

✕**Stone Soup Café.** It may look like nothing more than a simple storefront, but this cheery café in the center of town is booked days in advance for dinner. There are two seatings of eight tables a night for lobster bisque, porcini ravioli, or whatever contemporary fare the chef is inspired to cook from the day's farm-stand finds. If you can't book ahead, stop in for breakfast or lunch. ⊠*0 Central St., off Rte. 1A* ☎*978/356–4222* ⌂*Reservations essential* ▭*No credit cards* ⊙*No dinner Sun.–Wed., breakfast but no lunch Sun.*

NEWBURYPORT

38 mi north of Boston, 12 mi north of Ipswich on Rte. 1A.

Newburyport's High Street is lined with some of the finest examples of Federal-period (roughly, 1790–1810) mansions in New England. The city was once a leading port and shipbuilding center; the houses were built for prosperous sea captains. Although Newburyport's maritime significance ended with the decline of the clipper ships, the town was revived in the 1970s. Today, the town bustles with shops, restaurants, galleries and a waterfront park and boardwalk. The civic improvements have been matched by private restorations of the town's housing stock, much of which dates from the 18th century, with a scattering of 17th-century homes in some neighborhoods.

Newburyport is walker-friendly, with well-marked restrooms and free parking all day down by the water.

A stroll through the **Waterfront Park & Promenade** offers a view of the harbor as well as the fishing and pleasure boats that moor here. A causeway leads from Newburyport to a narrow piece of land known as Plum Island, which harbors a summer colony (rapidly becoming year-round) at one end.

WHAT TO SEE

Custom House Maritime Museum. Built in 1835 in Greek-revival style, this museum contains exhibits on maritime history, ship models, tools, and paintings. ⊠ *25 Water St.* ☎ *978/462–8681* ⊕ *www.customhousemaritime museum.org* ◫ *$7* ⊙ *Thurs.–Sat. 11–4, Sun. noon–4.*

SPORTS AND THE OUTDOORS

Parker River National Wildlife Refuge. On Plum Island, this 4,662-acre refuge of salt marsh, freshwater marsh, beaches, and dunes is one of the few natural barrier beach–dune–salt marsh complexes left on the Northeast coast. Here you can bird-watch, fish, swim, and pick plums and cranberries. The refuge is a popular place in summer, especially on weekends; cars begin to line up at the gate before 7 AM. There's no restriction on the number of people using the beach, but only a limited number of cars are let in; no pets are allowed in the refuge. ⊠ *6 Plum Island Tpk.* ☎ *978/465–5753* ⊕ *www.parkerriver.org* ◫ *$5 per car, bicycles and walk-ins $2* ⊙ *Daily dawn–dusk. Beach usually closed during nesting season in spring and early summer.*

BEACH
♻
★ **Salisbury Beach State Reservation.** Relax at the long sandy beach, or play at the amusement area and nearby arcades. From Newburyport center, follow Bridge Road north, take a right on Beach Road, and follow it until you reach State Reservation Road. ⊠ *Rte. 1A, 5 mi northeast of Newburyport, Salisbury* ☎ *978/462–4481* ◫ *Beach free, parking $7.*

NIGHTLIFE

The **Grog** (⊠ *13 Middle St. 01950* ☎ *978/465–8008* ⊕ *www.thegrog. com*) hosts blues, rock bands, and salsa lessons several nights weekly.

SHOPPING

Todd Farm Flea Market. A New England tradition since 1971, the Todd Farm Flea Market features up to 240 vendors from all over New England and New York. It's open every Sunday from mid-April through late November, though its busiest months are May, September, and October. Merchandise varies from antique furniture, clocks, jewelry, recordings, and tools to fishing rods, golf accessories, honey products, cedar fencing, vintage toys, and seasonal plants and flowers. Antique hunters often arrive before the sun comes up for the best deals. ⊠ *303 Main St. Rowley, off of Route 1A* ☎ *978/948–3300* ⊕ *www.toddfarm. com* ⊙ *Apr.–Nov., Sun. 5 AM–3 PM.*

WHERE TO EAT AND STAY

$$–$$$ ✕**Glenn's.** A block from the waterfront parking lot, Glenn's offers cre-
SEAFOOD ative combinations from around the world, with the occasional New
England twist. The ever-changing menu might include sesame-crusted
yellowfin tuna or house-smoked baby-back ribs. There's live jazz or
blues on Sunday. ⊠*44 Merrimac St.* ☎*978/465–3811* ▭*AE, D, DC,
MC, V* ⊗*Closed Mon. No lunch.*

$–$$ 🏨**Clark Currier Inn.** Once the home of the 19th-century sea captain
★ Thomas March Clark, this 1803 Federal mansion has been beautifully
restored. Guest rooms are spacious and furnished with antiques. Rates
include afternoon tea. **Pros:** easy to find, it is close to shopping and
the oceanfront. Perfect for couples or persons on business looking for
a peaceful and quiet experience. **Cons:** quiet atmosphere may not be a
good fit for families. ⊠*45 Green St.* ☎*978/465–8363* ⊕*www.clark
currierinn.com* ⇦*8 rooms* ⌂*In-room: Some TVs. In-hotel: No kids
under 10, no elevator, no-smoking rooms* ▭*AE, D, MC, V* ⦿*CP.*

SOUTH OF BOSTON

People all over the world travel south of Boston to visit Plymouth for
a glimpse into the country's earliest beginnings. The two main stops
are the Plimoth Plantation, which re-creates the everyday life of the
Pilgrims; and the Mayflower II, which gives you an idea of how frightening the journey across the Atlantic must have been. As you may guess,
November in Plymouth brings special events focused on Thanksgiving.
Farther south, New Bedford reveals the world of whaling.

**EN
ROUTE** While driving from Boston to Plymouth, you can easily make a stop at
Quincy, where sites pay tribute to the nation's second and sixth presi-
dents. The **Adams National Historic Park** (⊠*Carriage house, 135 Adams
St.; visitor center and bookstore, 1250 Hancock St.* ☎*617/770–1175*
⊕*www.nps.gov/adam* 🎟*$5* ⊗*Tours 9:15–3:15 daily mid-Apr.–mid-
Nov.*) contains the birthplace, home, and grave of both John Adams
and his son John Quincy Adams.

PLYMOUTH

40 mi south of Boston.

On December 26, 1620, 102 weary men, women, and children dis-
embarked from the *Mayflower* to found the first permanent European
settlement north of Virginia. Today, Plymouth is characterized by narrow streets, clapboard mansions, shops, antiques stores, and a scenic
waterfront. To mark Thanksgiving, the town holds a parade, historic-
house tours, and other activities. Historic statues dot the town, including depictions of William Bradford, Pilgrim leader and governor of
Plymouth Colony for more than 30 years, on Water Street; a Pilgrim
maiden in Brewster Gardens; and Massasoit, the Wampanoag chief who
helped the Pilgrims survive, on Carver Street.

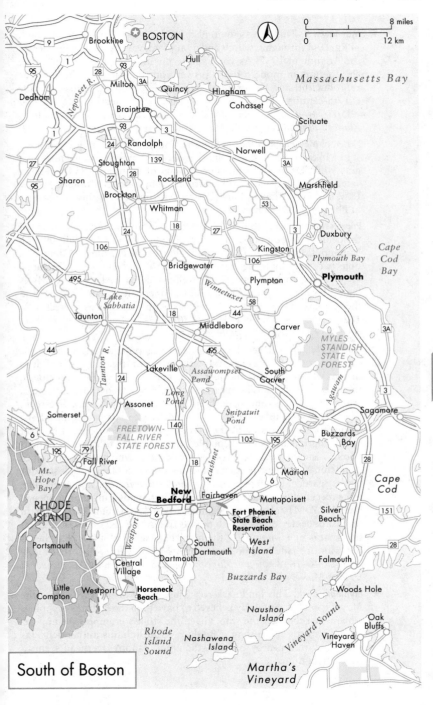

South of Boston

8

WHAT TO SEE

★ **Mayflower II.** This seaworthy replica of the 1620 *Mayflower* was built in England through research and a bit of guesswork, then sailed across the Atlantic in 1957. As you explore the interior and exterior of the ship, sailors in modern dress answer your questions about both the reproduction and the original ship, while costumed guides provide a 17th-century perspective. Plymouth Rock is nearby. ⊠*State Pier* ☎*508/746–1622* ⊕*www.plimoth.org* ✉*$10, $28 with admission to Plimoth Plantation* ⊙*Late Mar.–Nov., daily 9–5.*

National Monument to the Forefathers. The largest freestanding granite statue in the United States, this allegorical monument stands high on a grassy hill. Designed by Hammet Billings of Boston in 1854 and dedicated in 1889, it depicts Faith, surrounded by Liberty, Morality, Justice, Law, and Education and includes scenes from the Pilgrims' early days in Plymouth. ⊠*Allerton St.*

Pilgrim Hall Museum. From the waterfront sights it's a short walk to one of the country's oldest public museums. Established in 1824, Pilgrim Hall Museum transports you back to the time of the Pilgrims' landing with objects carried by those weary travelers to the New World. Included are a carved chest, a remarkably well-preserved wicker cradle, Myles Standish's sword, John Alden's Bible, American Indian artifacts, and the remains of the *Sparrow Hawk,* a sailing ship that was wrecked in 1626. ⊠*75 Court St. (Hwy. 3A)* ☎*508/746–1620* ⊕*www.pilgrimhall. org* ✉*$7* ⊙*May–Dec., daily 9:30–4:30.*

♻ **Plimoth Plantation.** Over the entrance of this popular attraction is the
Fodor'sChoice   caution: YOU ARE NOW ENTERING 1627. Believe it. Against the backdrop
★   of the Atlantic Ocean, and just 3 mi south of downtown Plymouth, this Pilgrim village has been carefully re-created, from the thatch roofs, cramped quarters, and open fireplaces to the long-horned livestock. Throw away your preconception of white collars and funny hats; through ongoing research, the Plimoth staff has developed a portrait of the Pilgrims that's more complex than the dour folk in school textbooks. Listen to the accents of the "residents," who never break out of character. You might see them plucking ducks, cooking rabbit stew, or tending garden. Feel free to engage them in conversation about their life, but expect only curious looks if you ask about anything that happened after 1627. "Thanksgiving: Memory, Myth & Meaning," an exhibit in the visitor center, offers a fresh perspective on the 1621 harvest celebration that is now known as "the first Thanksgiving." Note that there's not a lot of shade here in the summer. ⊠*137 Warren Ave. (Hwy. 3A)* ☎*508/746–1622* ⊕*www.plimoth.org* ✉*$24, $28 with Mayflower II* ⊙*Late Mar.–Nov., daily 9–5.*

★ **Plymouth Rock.** This landmark rock, just a few dozen yards from the *Mayflower II,* is popularly believed to have been the Pilgrims' stepping-stone when they left the ship. Given the stone's unimpressive appearance—it's little more than a boulder—and dubious authenticity (as explained on a nearby plaque), the grand canopy overhead seems a trifle ostentatious.

Sparrow House. Built in 1640, this is Plymouth's oldest structure. It is among several historic houses in town that are open for visits. You can peek into a pair of rooms furnished in the spartan style of the Pilgrims' era. The contemporary crafts gallery also on the premises seems somewhat incongruous, but the works on view are high quality. ⊠42 Summer St. ☎508/747–1240 ⊕www.sparrowhouse.com 🎫House $2, gallery free ⊙Thurs.–Tues. 10–5.

WHERE TO EAT AND STAY

$$ ✕**Blue-eyed Crab Grille & Raw Bar.** Grab a seat on the outside deck over-
SEAFOOD looking the water at this friendly, somewhat funky (plastic fish dangling from the ceiling), fresh fish shack. If the local Island Creek raw oysters are on the menu, go for them! Otherwise start with thick crab bisque full of hunks of floating crabmeat or the steamed mussels. Dinner entrées include seafood stew with chorizo and sweet potatoes and the classic fish-and-chips. Locals come for the brunch specials, too, like grilled shrimp and poached eggs over red-pepper grits, the lobster omelet, and banana-ginger pancakes. ⊠170 Water St. ☎508/747–6776 ⊕www. blueeyedcrab.com ▤D, MC, V ⊙No lunch Tues.–Thurs.

$–$$ 🏨**Best Western Cold Spring.** Walk to the waterfront and downtown Plymouth from this clean, family-friendly, two-story motel. Rooms, some with balconies and ocean views, are minimalist, with white walls, dark carpeted floors, and contemporary furniture. **Pros:** half-mile from Plymouth Rock and Mayflower II, some of the best wallet-pleasing rates in the area, friendly owners. **Cons:** basic rooms with not much character. ⊠188 Court St. ☎508/746–2222 or 800/678–8667 ⊕www.bestwestern massachusetts.com ➩56 rooms ⊘In-room: Ethernet. In-hotel: Pool, laundry facilities, public Internet, parking (no fee), no-smoking rooms ▤AE, D, DC, MC, V.

$$ 🏨**John Carver Inn & Spa.** This three-story, Colonial-style redbrick building is steps from Plymouth's main attractions. The public rooms are lavish, with period furnishings and stylish drapes. The guest rooms include six "environmentally sensitive" options with filtered air and water and four-poster beds; others are a bit dark and drab (time for refurbishing!). The suites have fireplaces and whirlpool baths. There's also an indoor pool with a Mayflower ship model and a waterslide. **Pros:** waterfront setting. on-site amenities include theme pool, restaurant, spa. **Cons:** pool is noisy and often overcrowded; some rooms need updating. ⊠25 Summer St. ☎508/746–7100 or 800/274–1620 ⊕www.johncarverinn. com ➩79 rooms, 6 suites ⊘In-room: Wi-Fi. In-hotel: Restaurant, bar, pool, gym, spa, laundry facilities, public Wi-Fi, parking (no fee), no-smoking rooms ▤AE, D, DC, MC, V.

NEW BEDFORD

45 mi southwest of Plymouth, 50 mi south of Boston.

In 1652 colonists from Plymouth settled in the area that now includes the city of New Bedford. The city has a long maritime tradition, beginning as a shipbuilding center and small whaling port in the late 1700s. By the mid-1800s, it had developed into a center of North American whaling. Today, New Bedford has the largest fishing fleet on the East

8

Coast. Although much of the town is industrial, the restored historic district near the water is a delight. It was here that Herman Melville set his masterpiece, *Moby-Dick*, a novel about whaling.

WHAT TO SEE

New Bedford Whaling Museum. Established in 1903, this is the world's largest museum of its kind. A highlight is the skeleton of a 66-foot blue whale, one of only three on view anywhere. An interactive exhibit lets you listen to the underwater sounds of whales, dolphins, and other sea life—plus the sounds of a thunderstorm and a whale-watching boat—as a whale might hear them. You can also peruse the collection of scrimshaw, visit exhibits on regional history, and climb aboard an 89-foot, half-scale model of the 1826 whaling ship *Lagoda*—the world's largest ship model. A small chapel across the street from the museum is the one described in *Moby-Dick*. ⊠ *18 Johnny Cake Hill* ☎ *508/997–0046* ⊕ *www.whalingmuseum.org* ☑ *$10* ⊙ *Mon.–Sat. 9–4, Sun. noon–4.*

New Bedford Whaling National Historical Park. The city's whaling tradition is commemorated at this park that takes up 13 blocks of the waterfront historic district. The park visitor center, housed in an 1853 Greek-revival building that was once a bank, provides maps and information about whaling-related sites. Free walking tours of the park leave from the visitor center at 10:30, 12:30, and 2:30 in July and August. ⊠ *33 William St.* ☎ *508/996–4095* ⊕ *www.nps.gov/nebe* ☑ *Free* ⊙ *Daily 9–5.*

Rotch-Jones-Duff House & Garden Museum. For a glimpse of upper-class life during New Bedford's whaling heyday, head one-half mile south of downtown to this 1834 Greek Revival mansion. Amid a full city block of gardens, it housed three prominent families in the 1800s and is filled with elegant furnishings from the era including a mahogany piano, a massive marble-top sideboard, and portraits of the house's occupants. A free self-guided audio tour is available. ⊠ *396 County St.* ☎ *508/997–1401* ⊕ *www.rjdmuseum.org* ☑ *$5* ⊙ *Mon.–Sat. 10–4, Sun. noon–4.*

WHERE TO EAT

$–$$
PORTUGUESE

✕ **Antonio's.** Expect the wait to be long and the dining room to be loud, but it's worth the hassle to sample the traditional fare of New Bedford's large Portuguese population at this friendly, unadorned restaurant. Dishes include hearty portions of pork and shellfish stew, *bacalau* (salt cod), and grilled sardines, often on plates piled high with crispy fried potatoes and rice. ⊠ *267 Coggeshall St., near intersection of I–195 and Hwy. 18* ☎ *508/990–3636* ⊟ *No credit cards.*

$–$$$
SEAFOOD

✕ **Davy's Locker.** A huge seafood menu is the main draw at this spot overlooking Buzzards Bay. Choose from more than a dozen shrimp preparations, or a choice of healthful entrées—dishes prepared with olive oil, vegetables, garlic, and herbs. For landlubbers, chicken, steak, ribs, and the like are also available. ⊠ *1480 E. Rodney French Blvd.* ☎ *508/992–7359* ⊟ *AE, D, DC, MC, V.*

SIDE TRIPS ESSENTIALS

To research prices, get advice from other travelers, and book travel arrangements, visit www.fodors.com.

TRANSPORTATION

BY BOAT

Marblehead is one of the North Shore's pleasure-sailing capitals, but the town has long waiting lists for mooring space. The harbormaster can inform you of nightly fees at public docks when space is available.

Contact Marblehead harbormaster (☎ 781/631-2386).

BY BUS

The Massachusetts Bay Transportation Authority, or MBTA, operates buses to Lexington from Alewife station in Cambridge. Buses 62 and 76 make the trip in 25 minutes. The Cape Ann Transportation Authority, or CATA, provides local bus service in the Gloucester, Rockport, and Essex region. The Coach Company bus line runs a commuter bus between Newburyport and Boston on weekdays. The ride takes 1–1¼ hours. MBTA buses leave for Marblehead and Salem daily from Central Square in Cambridge, and on weekdays in the early morning and evenings from Boston's Haymarket Station and Downtown Crossing. Travel time is about ½ hour from Cambridge and 1–1¼ hours from Boston. Look for numbers 441, 442, 448, or 449 for Marblehead and 455 or 459 for Salem. American Eagle Motorcoach offers service from Boston to New Bedford. Plymouth & Brockton links Plymouth and the South Shore to Boston's South Station with frequent bus service. From the Plymouth bus depot, you can take the Plymouth Area Link buses to the town center or to Plimoth Plantation.

Contacts American Eagle Motorcoach (☎ 800/453-5040). **Cape Ann Transportation Authority** (☎ 978/283-7916 ⊕ www.canntran.com). **Coach Company** (☎ 800/874-3377 ⊕ www.coachco.com). **MBTA** (☎ 800/392-6100 ⊕ www.mbta.com). **Plymouth & Brockton** (☎ 508/746-0378 ⊕ www.p-b.com). **Plymouth Area Link** (☎ 800/483-2500 ⊕ www.gatra.org/pal.htm).

BY CAR

From Boston to Lexington, pick up Memorial Drive in Cambridge, and continue to the Fresh Pond Parkway, then to Route 2 West. Exit Route 2 at Routes 4/225 if your first stop is the National Heritage Museum; from Routes 4/225, turn left on Mass Ave. For Lexington center, take the Waltham Street–Lexington exit from Route 2. Follow Waltham Street just under 2 mi to Mass Ave.; you'll be just east of the Battle Green. The drive takes about 30 minutes. To reach Concord by car, continue west on Route 2. Or take Interstate 90 (the Massachusetts Turnpike) to Interstate 95 North, and then exit at Route 2, heading west. Driving time is 40–45 minutes.

The fastest way to reach Sudbury from Boston is the Massachusetts Turnpike westbound, then Interstate 95 North to Route 20 (head west for Sudbury). Allow about 40–50 minutes to reach Sudbury.

8

Lowell lies near the intersection of Interstate 495 and Route 3. From Boston, take Interstate 93 North to Interstate 495. Go south on Interstate 495 to Exit 35C, the Lowell Connector. Follow the Lowell Connector to Exit 5B, Thorndike Street. Travel time is 45 minutes to an hour.

The primary link between Boston and the North Shore is Route 128, which splits off Interstate 95 and follows the coast northeast to Gloucester. To pick up Route 128 from Boston, take Interstate 93 North to Interstate 95 North to Route 128. If you stay on Interstate 95, you'll reach Newburyport. A less-direct route is Route 1A; once you're north of Lynn, you'll pass through several pretty coastal towns. Beyond Beverly, Route 1A travels inland toward Ipswich and Essex; at this point, Route 127 follows the coast to Gloucester and Rockport.

From Boston to Salem or Marblehead, follow Route 128 to Route 114 into Salem and on to Marblehead. A word of caution: this route is confusing and poorly marked, particularly returning to Route 128. An alternative route to Marblehead: follow Route 1A North, and then pick up Route 129 North along the shore through Swampscott and into Marblehead. It's possible to take Route 1A to Salem from Boston, but it's a very slow drive, and as the road turns inland, you miss the shore views that you get along Route 129.

Driving from Boston to Salem takes about 35–40 minutes; to Gloucester or to Newburyport, about 50–60 minutes. Many of the smaller roads connecting the North Shore communities (Routes 1A, 133, 127) do double duty as the towns' main streets.

If you don't have a car, Marblehead, Salem, Rockport, and Newburyport are the most accessible of the North Shore towns; many of the historic sights, museums, and shops are within walking distance. Attractions in the other North Shore communities are more spread out and are better explored by car.

To get to Plymouth, take the Southeast Expressway Interstate 93 South to Route 3 (toward Cape Cod); Exits 6 and 4 lead to downtown Plymouth and Plimoth Plantation, respectively. To reach New Bedford from Boston, follow Interstate 93 to Route 24 South to Route 140 South, and continue to Interstate 195 East. Allow about one hour from Boston to any of these three cities, about one hour from Plymouth to New Bedford.

BY TRAIN

The MBTA's commuter rail (the Purple Line) offers service to many of the towns mentioned in this chapter. For destinations north and west of the city, trains depart from North Station, and trains to Plymouth depart from South Station. Concord is a 40-minute ride on the Fitchburg line. The station is a short walk outside the town center. Lowell is a 45-minute ride on the Lowell line—catch a Lowell Regional Transit Authority bus from the station to downtown every 30 minutes on weekdays between 5:45 AM and 7:15 PM, and every half hour Saturday between 10:05 AM and 4:35 PM. On the North Shore, you can take the Newburyport/Rockport line to Salem (25–30 minutes), Gloucester (55–60 minutes), Rockport (70 minutes), Ipswich (50–55 minutes), and Newburyport (60–65 minutes). The stations at Salem, Gloucester,

Rockport, and Ipswich are within about ½ mi of the towns' historic sights. From the Newburyport station to downtown (about 1 mi), take the Merrimack Valley Regional Transit Authority Bus 51, but note that there's no Sunday service. Take the Middleborough/Lakeville line to Plymouth (50 minutes).

Contacts Lowell Regional Transit Authority (☎ *978/452–6161* ⊕ *www.lrta. com*). **MBTA** (☎ *800/392–6100* ⊕ *www.mbta.com*). **Merrimack Valley Regional Transit Authority** (☎ *978/469–6878* ⊕ *www.mvrta.com*).

BUSINESS HOURS

PHARMACIES

CVS pharmacies in Plymouth and New Bedford are open 24 hours. The CVS pharmacy in Concord is open nightly until 10, as are Walgreens pharmacies throughout the region.

Late-Night and 24-Hour Pharmacies CVS (✉ *199 Sudbury Rd., Concord* ☎ *978/371–0688* ✉ *8 Pilgrim Hill Rd., off Rte. 44, Plymouth* ☎ *508/747–1465* ✉ *1145 Kempton St., near Rte. 140, New Bedford* ☎ *508/999–3241* ⊕ *www. cvs.com*). **Walgreens** (✉ *201 Main St., Gloucester* ☎ *978/283–7361* ✉ *60 Bedford St., Lexington* ☎ *781/863–1111* ⊕ *www.walgreens.com*).

CONTACTS AND RESOURCES

EMERGENCIES
Police (☎ *911*).

Medical Emergencies Emerson Hospital (✉ *133 Old Rd., off Rte. 2, Concord* ☎ *978/369–1400*). **Jordan Hospital** (✉ *275 Sandwich St., Plymouth* ☎ *508/746–2000*). **Newton-Wellesley Hospital** (✉ *2014 Washington St., Rte. 16, Newton* ☎ *617/243–6000*). **St. Luke's Hospital** (✉ *101 Page St., New Bedford* ☎ *508/997–1515*).

VISITOR INFORMATION
Northwest and South of Boston Contacts Concord Visitor Center (✉ *58 Main St., Concord* ☎ *978/369–3120*). **Lexington Visitor Center** (✉ *1875 Massachusetts Ave., Lexington* ☎ *781/862–2480* ⊕ *www.lexingtonchamber.org*). **New Bedford Office of Tourism** (✉ *Waterfront Visitors Center, Pier 3, New Bedford* ☎ *508/979–1745 or 800/508–5353* ⊕ *www.ci.new-bedford.ma.us*). **Plymouth Visitor Information Center** (✉ *170 Water St., at Hwy. 44, Plymouth* ☎ *508/747–7533 or 800/872–1620* ⊕ *www.visit-plymouth.com*).

North Shore Contacts Cape Ann Chamber of Commerce (✉ *33 Commercial St., Gloucester* ☎ *978/283–1601* ⊕ *www.capeannvacations.com*). **Destination Salem** (✉ *54 Turner St., Salem* ☎ *978/741–3252 or 877/725–3662* ⊕ *www.salem.org*). **Ipswich Visitor Information** (✉ *36 S. Main St., Ipswich* ☎ *978/356–8540* ⊕ *www.ipswichma.com*). **Marblehead Chamber of Commerce Information Booth** (✉ *Corner of Pleasant and Spring Sts., Box 76, Marblehead* ☎ *781/639–8469* ⊕ *www.visitmarblehead.com*). **Rockport Chamber of Commerce** (✉ *33 Commercial St., Gloucester* ☎ *978/546–6575* ⊕ *www. rockportusa.com*).

Travel Smart Boston

GETTING HERE AND AROUND

Boston is a mix of old and new that comes together in a seemingly endless array of narrow and twisting one-way streets that radiate away from Boston Harbor in the east. As you travel north, downtown gives way to the concrete jungle of Government Center, and then to the bustling streets of the North End. Head generally southwest from here and you'll encounter the Old West End—home of the "Gah-den"— and Beacon Hill. The Back Bay's grid of streets runs southwest from the base of Beacon Hill and to the south of the Back Bay is the eclectic and historic South End. Head west from here and you'll encounter the retail wonderland of Prudential Center, and then the Fenway, home to many of Boston's art museums as well as the beloved Red Sox.

The Charles River serves as a natural dividing line between Boston and neighborhoods to the north, including Cambridge, Somerville, and Charlestown. The Four Point Channel separates South Boston—which is, you guessed it, to the south of Boston—and neighboring Dorchester from the city proper.

The best form of transportation within Boston or Cambridge/Somerville is the MBTA system, or the T, as it's known locally. Five separate lines run through the entire city and out toward the outlying suburbs. The system of underground trains, aboveground trolleys, and buses will take you to every major point of interest. A car is only necessary for getting out of town.

■TIP→ Ask the local tourist board about hotel and local transportation packages that include tickets to major museum exhibits or other special events.

▌ AIR TRAVEL

Flying to Boston takes about 1 hour from New York, 1½ hours from Washington, DC, 2¼ hours from Chicago, 3¾ hours

from Dallas, 5½ hours from Los Angeles, 7½ hours from London, and 21–22 hours from Sydney (including connection time). Delta, US Airways, and jetBlue have many daily shuttle flights from New York and Washington.

■TIP→ The Boston Convention and Visitor Bureau's Web site, ⊕ www.bostonusa.com, has direct links to 19 airlines that service the city. You can book flights here, too.

Airlines & Airports Airline and Airport Links.com (⊕ www.airlineandairportlinks.com) has links to many of the world's airlines and airports.

Airline Security Issues Transportation Security Administration (⊕ www.tsa.gov) has answers for almost every question that might come up.

AIRPORTS

Boston's major airport, Logan International (BOS), is across the harbor from Downtown, about 2 mi outside the city center, and can be easily reached by taxi, water taxi, or subway (called the "T") via the Silver or Blue Line. Logan has five terminals, identified by letters A through E. A free airport shuttle runs between the terminals and airport hotels. Some airlines use different terminals for international and domestic flights. Most international flights arrive at Terminal E. Most charter flights arrive at Terminal D. A visitor center in Terminal C offers tourist information. Green Airport, in Providence, Rhode Island, and the Manchester Airport in Manchester, New Hampshire, are both about an hour from Boston.

Airport Information Green Airport (⊠ *Off I–95, Exit 13, Providence, RI* ☎ *888/268–7222 or 401/737–8222* ⊕ *www.pvdairport.com*). **Logan International** (⊠ *I–90 east to Ted Williams Tunnel* ☎ *800/235–6426* ⊕ *www. massport.com* Ⓣ *Airport*). **Manchester Airport** (⊠ *Off I–293/Rte. 101, Exit 2, Manchester, NH* ☎ *603/624–6556* ⊕ *www.flymanchester.com*).

FLIGHTS

Airline Contacts Alaska Airlines (☎ *800/252–7522* ⊕ *www.alaskaair.com*). **American Airlines** (☎ *800/433–7300* ⊕ *www.aa.com*). **Continental Airlines** (☎ *800/523–3273* ⊕ *www.continental.com*). **Delta Airlines** (☎ *800/221–1212* ⊕ *www. delta.com*). **jetBlue** (☎ *800/538–2583* ⊕ *www.jetblue.com*). **Northwest Airlines** (☎ *800/225–2525* ⊕ *www.nwa.com*). **Southwest Airlines** (☎ *800/435–9792* ⊕ *www.southwest.com*). **Spirit Airlines** (☎ *800/772–7117* ⊕ *www.spiritair.com*). **United Airlines** (☎ *800/864–8331* ⊕ *www. united.com*). **US Airways** (☎ *800/428–4322* ⊕ *www.usairways.com*).

GROUND TRANSPORTATION

RENTAL CARS AND TAXIS

For recorded information about traveling to and from Logan Airport, as well as details about parking, contact the airport's ground-transportation hotline. Traffic can be maddening; it's a good idea to take public transportation to and from the airport.

When driving from Logan to downtown Boston, the most direct route is by way of the Sumner Tunnel ($3.50 toll inbound; no toll outbound). On weekends and holidays and after 10 PM weekdays, you can get around Sumner Tunnel backups by using the Ted Williams Tunnel ($3.50 toll inbound; no toll outbound), which will steer you onto the Southeast Expressway south of downtown Boston. Follow the signs to I–93 northbound to head back into the downtown area.

Taxis can be hired outside each terminal. Fares to and from Downtown should be about $15–$18, including tip. Taxis must pay an extra toll of $5.25 and a $2

NAVIGATING BOSTON

■ Boston is a walkable city but since its streets were originally laid out as cow paths leading from the waterfront to spots around the city, they are sometimes tricky to navigate.

■ In most cases, address numbers are listed in even numbers on one side of the street and odds number on the opposite side.

■ Head toward Boston Common or the Public Garden. It's a central spot in the city and there are maps around the park to help direct you around the city. Or, if you're near the waterfront, head toward Quincy Market where there are also maps to help you navigate.

■ The Financial District and Downtown Crossing are part of Downtown. The streets here have no rhyme or reason and often run only one way. If you're walking through the area, be sure to bring a map.

■ In general, signage in Boston is hard to come by, especially on roadways. But the city has done a great job of posting street maps at major visitor points throughout the city. If you find yourself wandering around lost, your best bet is to ask for directions as most residents are familiar with how difficult it is to find your way around. If their directions seem complicated, ask them to write them down.

■ The public transportation system, the T, offers easy-to-read navigation guides and maps in every station. It stops at all major points of interest throughout the city and just beyond the city limits, too.

airport fee when leaving the airport (but not going in) that will be tacked onto your bill at the end of the trip. (Major traffic jams or taking a longer route to avoid traffic will add to the fare.)

Contacts Logan Airport Customer Information Hotline (☎ 800/235–6426). **Metro Cab** (☎ 617/782–5500). **Town Taxi** (☎ 617/536–5000).

SUBWAY

The Blue and Silver lines on the subway, commonly called "the T" (and operated by the MBTA), run from the airport to downtown Boston in about 20 minutes. The Blue Line is best if you're heading to North Station, Faneuil Hall, North End/Waterfront, or Back Bay (Hynes Convention Center, Prudential Center area). Take the Silver Line to South Station, Boston Convention and Exhibition Center, Seaport World Trade Center, Chinatown Theater, and South End areas. From North and South stations, you can reach the Red, Green, or Orange lines, or commuter rail. The T costs $2 for in-town travel if you're paying in cash or $1.70 if you purchase a CharlieCard (a prepaid stored-value card). *See Subway, Train, and Trolley Travel below for more information.* Free 24-hour shuttle buses connect the subway station with all airline terminals. Shuttle Bus 22 runs between the subway and Terminals A and B, and Shuttle Bus 33 runs between the subway and Terminals C, D, and E.

Contact MBTA (☎ 800/392–6100 or 617/222–3200, 617/222–5146 TTY ⊕ www.mbta.com).

BUSES OR SHUTTLE VANS

Several companies offer shared-van service to many Boston-area destinations. Logan/Boston Hotel Shuttle and Ace American provide door-to-door service to several major Back Bay and Downtown hotels. (Check their Web sites for a listing of hotels.) Reservations are not required, because vans swing by all terminals every 20 minutes to half hour. One-way fares are $14.50 per person. Easy

Transportation is also a shared-van service, which runs from the airport to the Back Bay Hilton, Radisson, and Lenox hotels from 7 AM to 10 PM. Star Shuttle operates shared vans from the airport to the Marriott Copley Place and Sheraton Copley, every hour on the half hour, from 5:30 AM to 11:30 PM. Logan Express buses travel from the airport to the suburbs of Braintree, Framingham, Peabody, and Woburn. One-way fares are $11.

Contacts Ace American (☎ 800/517–2281). **Easy Transportation** (☎ 617/869–7760). **Logan/Boston Hotel Shuttle** (☎ 617/765–5649). **Logan Express** (☎ 800/235–6426 ⊕ www.massport.com). **Star Shuttle** (☎ 617/230–6005).

▌ BOAT TRAVEL

ARRIVING BY BOAT

Rowes Wharf Water Taxi shuttles from Logan Airport to Rowes Wharf, Downtown for $10 per person. It operates daily year-round between 7 AM and 7 PM, and from April through October, 7AM to 10 PM, Monday to Saturday and 7AM to 8PM on Sunday.

Harbor Express water taxis takes passengers from Logan Airport to Long Wharf, Downtown ($10) and to Quincy and Hull on the South Shore ($12). Boats leave approximately every 40–45 minutes 6:20 AM–10:20 PM Monday through Thursday, 6:20 AM–11 PM Friday, 8:30 AM–10:30 PM Saturday, and 8:30 AM–9 PM Sunday.

City Water Taxi has an on-call boat service between the airport and 16 downtown locations that operates from 7 AM to 10 PM Monday through Saturday and 7 AM to 8 PM on Sunday year-round. One-way fares to or from the airport are $10, and round-trip tickets are $17.

Several boat companies make runs between the airport and downtown destinations. Take the free Shuttle Bus 66 from any terminal to the airport's ferry dock to catch Boston's water taxis.

GETTING AROUND BY BOAT

MBTA commuter boat service operates weekdays between several downtown harbor destinations and quite a few locations on the South Shore. One-way fares range from $1.70 to $12 depending on destination. Schedules change seasonally, so call ahead.

Information City Water Taxi (☎617/422–0392 ⊕ www.citywatertaxi.com). **Harbor Express** (☎ 617/222–6999 ⊕ www. harborexpress.com). **MBTA** (☎617/222–5000 ⊕ www.mbta.com). **Rowes Wharf Water Taxi** (☎617/406–8584 ⊕ www.roweswharfwater taxi.com).

▌ BUS TRAVEL

ARRIVING BY BUS

Greyhound has buses to Boston from all major cities in North America. Besides its main location at South Station, Greyhound has suburban terminals in Newton, Framingham, and Worcester. Peter Pan Bus Lines connects Boston with cities elsewhere in Massachusetts, Connecticut, New Jersey, New York, and Maryland.

Concord Coach heads to Maine and New Hampshire. C&J sends buses up the New Hampshire coast to Dover. All of the above-mentioned bus companies leave from South Station, which is connected to the Amtrak station. The station is clean and safe. Many bus lines also make stops at Logan Airport; check individual lines for up-to-date schedules.

The Fung Wah bus offers inexpensive (very) low-maintenance service between the Chinatown neighborhoods of Boston and New York. BoltBus offers cheap fares in shiny, new, Wi-Fi–equipped buses between Boston and New York, starting at just $1 (if you reserve early enough). Megabus also offers low fares, and offers service to Hartford as well as New York City. BoltBus and Megabus leave from South Station.

If you want to travel in style, the Limo-Liner provides luxury bus service (with

> ### COMMUTING WITH A VIEW
>
> The Rowes Wharf Water Taxi offers a stunning glimpse of the city's skyline as it makes seven-minute trips across Boston Harbor between Logan Airport and Rowes Wharf in downtown Boston.

television, movies, high-speed Internet, and food-and-drink service) between Boston's Hilton Back Bay and Manhattan's Hilton New York for $79 each way. This service is open to the general public, not just guests of the Hilton. Reservations are a good idea.

Fares and schedules for all buses except LimoLiner are posted at South Station, at many of the tourist kiosks, and online.

Major credit cards are accepted for all buses. You can usually purchase your tickets online.

Bus Information BoltBus (⊕ www.boltbus. com). **C&J** (☎800/258–7111 ⊕ www.ridecj. com). **Concord Coach** (☎800/639–3317 ⊕ www.concordcoachlines.com). **Fung Wah Bus** (☎617/345–8000 ⊕ www.fungwahbus. com). **Greyhound** (☎800/231–2222 ⊕ www. greyhound.com). **LimoLiner** (☎888/546–5469 or 339/502–6411 ⊕ www.limoliner.com). **Megabus** (☎877/462–6342 ⊕ www.megabus. com). **Peter Pan** (☎800/343–9999 ⊕ www. peterpanbus.com). **Plymouth & Brockton** (☎508/746–0378 ⊕ www.p-b.com).

Station Information South Station (✉700 Atlantic Ave., at Summer St., Downtown Ⓣ South Station).

GETTING AROUND BY BUS

Buses of the Massachusetts Bay Transportation Authority (MBTA) crisscross the metropolitan area and travel farther into suburbia than subway and trolley lines. Buses run roughly from 5:30 AM to 12:30 AM.

At this writing, fares are $1.50 if paying in cash, $1.25 if paying with a pre-purchased CharlieCard for trips within the city; you often pay an extra fare for longer lines that run to the suburbs. The

SmarTraveler information line provides service updates.

CharlieCards (prepaid stored-value fare cards), sold at all subway terminals, can be purchased with cash or with debit or credit cards. To pay the bus fare, either flash your pass or pay in cash when you enter. Drivers accept dollar bills but don't have change.

Bus Information MBTA (☎ 617/222–3200, 617/222–5146 TTY ⊕ www.mbta.com). **SmarTraveler** (☎ 617/494–5200 ⊕ www. smartraveler.com).

▌ CAR TRAVEL

Driving isn't easy in Boston. It's important to plan out a route in advance if you're unfamiliar with the city. There's a profusion of one-way streets, so always keep a detailed map handy. It's also a good idea to pay extra attention to other drivers. Boston drivers have a bad reputation, and you should watch out for those using the emergency breakdown lanes (illegal unless posted otherwise), passing on the right, or turning from the wrong lane.

While having a car can be convenient in Boston if you're planning day trips outside the city limits, driving in the city can be stressful since the roads and signage are not easy to maneuver. Parking can be hard to come by, especially during major events (the Boston Marathon, Red Sox games). If you do decide to rent a car, have a detailed map handy at all times.

GASOLINE

Gas stations are not plentiful in downtown Boston. Try Cambridge Street (behind Beacon Hill, near Massachusetts General Hospital), near the airport in East Boston, along Commonwealth Avenue or Cambridge Street in Allston/Brighton, or off the Southeast Expressway just south of downtown Boston.

Cambridge service stations can be found along Memorial Drive, Massachusetts Avenue, and Broadway. In Brookline, try Commonwealth Avenue or Boylston

Street. Gas stations with 24-hour service can be found at many exits off Route 3 to Cape Cod, suburban Route 128 and Interstate 95, and at service plazas on the Massachusetts Turnpike. Many offer both full and self-service.

PARKING

Parking on Boston streets is tricky. Some neighborhoods have strictly enforced residents-only rules, with just a handful of two-hour visitors' spaces; others have meters, which usually cost 25¢ for 15 minutes, with a one- or two-hour maximum. Keep a few quarters handy, as most city meters take nothing else.

Parking-police officers are ruthless—it's not unusual to find a ticket on your windshield five minutes after your meter expires. However, most on-street parking is free after 8 PM in the city and on Sunday. Repeat offenders who don't pay fines may find the "boot" (an immovable steel clamp) secured to one of their wheels.

Major public lots are at Government Center and Quincy Market, beneath Boston Common (entrance on Charles Street), beneath Post Office Square, at the Prudential Center, at Copley Place, and off Clarendon Street near the John Hancock Tower. Smaller lots and garages are scattered throughout Downtown, especially around the Theater District and off Atlantic Avenue in the North End. Most are expensive; expect to pay up to $8 an hour or $24 to park all day. The few city garages are a bargain at about $7–$11 per day. Theaters, restaurants, stores, and tourist attractions often provide customers with one or two hours of free parking. Most downtown restaurants offer valet parking.

ROAD CONDITIONS

Bostonians tend to drive erratically. These habits, coupled with inconsistent street and traffic signs, one-way streets, and heavy congestion, make it a nerve-wracking city to navigate. Many roadways in the city are under construction or in need of repairs. Potholes and manhole covers sticking up above the street are the most common hazards. In general, err on the side of caution.

ROADSIDE EMERGENCIES

Dial 911 in an emergency to reach police, fire, or ambulance services. If you're a member of the AAA auto club, call their 24-hour help bureau.

Emergency Services AAA (☎ 800/222–4357).

RENTING

Rates in Boston begin at about $40 a day and $200 or more a week for an economy car with air-conditioning, automatic transmission, and unlimited mileage. This doesn't include gas, insurance charges, or the 5% tax. All major agencies listed below have branches at Logan International Airport.

Major Agencies Alamo ☎ 877/222–9075 ⊕ www.alamo.com. **Avis** ☎ 800/331–1212 ⊕ www.avis.com. **Budget** ☎ 800/527–0700 ⊕ www.budget.com. **Hertz** ☎ 800/654–3131 ⊕ www.hertz.com. **National Car Rental** ☎ 877/222–9058 ⊕ www.nationalcar.com.

▌ SUBWAY, TRAIN, AND TROLLEY TRAVEL

The Massachusetts Bay Transportation Authority (MBTA)—or "T" when referring to the subway line—operates subways, elevated trains, and trolleys along five connecting lines. Trains operate from about 5:30 AM to about 12:30 AM. A 24-hour hotline and the MBTA Web site offer specific information on routes, schedules, fares, wheelchair access, and other matters. Free maps are available at the MBTA's Park Street Station information stand, open daily from 7 AM to 10 PM. They're also available online at ⊕ www. mbta.com.

GETTING AROUND ON THE SUBWAY

"Inbound" trains head into the city center and "outbound" trains head away from downtown Boston. If you get on the Red Line at South Station, the train heading toward Cambridge is inbound. But once you pass the Park Street station, the train becomes an outbound train. The best way to figure out which way to go is to know the last stop on the train, which is usually listed on the front of the train. So, from Downtown, the Red Line to Cambridge would be the Alewife train and the Green Line to Fenway would be the Boston College or Cleveland Circle train.

The Red Line originates at Braintree and Mattapan to the south; the routes join near South Boston and continue to suburban Arlington. The Green Line operates elevated trolleys in the suburbs that dip underground in the city center. The line originates at Cambridge's Lechmere, heads south, and divides into four routes that end at Boston College (Commonwealth Avenue), Cleveland Circle (Beacon Street), Riverside, and Heath Street (Huntington Avenue). Buses connect Heath Street to the old Arborway terminus.

The Blue Line runs weekdays from Bowdoin Square and weeknights and weekends from Government Center to the Wonderland Racetrack in Revere, north of Boston. The Orange Line runs from Oak Grove in north suburban Malden to Forest Hills near the Arnold Arboretum. The Silver Line consists of two transit lines. One connects Downtown Crossing and Boylston to Dudley Square. The other runs from South Station down the waterfront to City Point. Park Street Station (on the Common) and State Street are the major downtown transfer points.

FARES AND PASSES

T fares are $2 for adults paying in cash or $1.70 with a prepurchased CharlieCard. There are CharlieCard dispensing machines at almost every subway stop. Children under age 11 ride free and senior citizens pay 60¢. An extra fare is required outbound on the most distant Red Line stops (for example, the fare each way from Braintree is $2.50). Fares on the commuter rail—the Purple Line—vary widely; check with the MBTA.

One-day ($9) and seven-day ($15) passes are available for unlimited travel on subways, city buses, and inner-harbor ferries. You must pay a double fare if you're headed to some suburban stations such as Braintree; pay the second fare as you exit the station. Buy passes at any full-service MBTA stations. Passes are also sold at the Boston Common Visitor Information Center (⇨ *Visitor Information*) and at some hotels.

TICKET/PASS	PRICE
Single Fare	$2
Day Pass	$9
Weekly Pass	$15
Monthly Unlimited Pass	$59

Contact MBTA (☎ 800/392–6100 or 617/222–3200, 617/222–5854 TTY ⊕ www.mbta.com).

TAXI TRAVEL

Cabs are available around the clock. You can also call for a cab or find them outside most hotels and at designated cab stands around the city that are marked by signs. Taxis generally line up in Harvard Square, around South Station, near Faneuil Hall Marketplace, at Long Wharf, near Massachusetts General Hospital, and in the Theater District. A taxi ride within the city of Boston starts at $2.60, and costs 40¢ for each 1/7 mi thereafter. Licensed cabs have meters and provide receipts. An illuminated rooftop sign indicates an available cab. If you're going to or from the airport or to the suburbs, ask about flat rates. Cabdrivers sometimes charge extra for multiple stops. One-way streets often make circuitous routes necessary and increase your cost.

Note that if you're in need of a cab at around 2 AM, when most bars close, hailing one can prove difficult and there will often be a 20 to 30 minute wait if you call for one. Heading to a cab stand is the most efficient late-night choice.

Taxi Companies Boston Cab Association (☎ 617/536–3200). **Independent Taxi Operators Association (ITOA)** (☎ 617/825–4000). **Metro Cab** (☎ 617/782–5500). **Town Taxi** (☎ 617/536–5000).

TRAIN TRAVEL

Boston is served by Amtrak at North Station, South Station, and Back Bay Station, which accommodate frequent departures to and arrivals from New York, Philadelphia, and Washington, DC. Amtrak's pricey high-speed Acela train cuts the travel time between Boston and New York from 4½ hours to 3½ hours. South Station is also the eastern terminus of Amtrak's *Lake Shore Limited,* which travels daily between Boston and Chicago by way of Albany, Rochester, Buffalo, and Cleveland. An additional Amtrak station with ample parking is just off Route 128 in suburban Westwood, southwest of Boston.

The MBTA runs commuter trains to points south, west, and north. Those bound for Worcester, Needham, Forge Park, Providence (RI), and Stoughton leave from South Station and Back Bay Station; those to Fitchburg, Lowell, Haverhill, Newburyport, and Rockport operate out of North Station.

Amtrak tickets and reservations are available at Amtrak stations, by telephone, through travel agents, or online. Amtrak schedule and fare information can be found at South Station, Back Bay Station, or the Route 128 station in suburban Westwood, as well as online. The 24-hour hotline is another good source for route, schedule, fare, and other information. Free maps are available at the MBTA's Park Street Station information stand.

Amtrak ticket offices accept all major credit cards, cash, traveler's checks, and personal checks when accompanied by a valid photo ID and a major credit card. You may pay on board with cash or a major credit card, but a surcharge may apply. MBTA commuter-rail stations generally accept only cash. You may also pay in cash on board commuter trains, but there may be a $1–$2 surcharge.

Amtrak has both reserved and unreserved trains. During peak times, such as a Friday night, get a reservation and a ticket in advance. Trains at nonpeak times are unreserved, with seats assigned on a first-come, first-served basis.

Train Information Back Bay Station (✉ *145 Dartmouth St., Back Bay*). **North Station** (✉ *Causeway and Friend Sts., North End*). **South Station** (✉ *Atlantic Ave. and Summer St., Downtown*).

ESSENTIALS

▮ COMMUNICATIONS

INTERNET

Most downtown hotels have started offering either free or fee-based wireless in their rooms and common areas. Call your hotel before arriving to confirm.

There are also a small number of Internet cafés on Newbury Street and scattered Downtown that charge a small fee ($2 and up) depending on how many minutes you use. Most Starbucks locations and locally based coffee shops, such as Espresso Royale, have Wi-Fi service.

Contacts Cybercafes (⊕ *www.cybercafes. com*) lists more than 4,000 Internet cafés worldwide. **WiFi Free Spot** (⊕ *www.wififree spot.com/mass.html*) lists hundreds of spots where you can connect to free Wi-Fi around the state.

▮ DAY TOURS AND GUIDES

Traveling to Boston on a package tour makes it quite convenient for those interested only in hitting the highlights or major historic sites such as the Freedom Trail, Faneuil Hall, the Bunker Hill Memorial, Quincy Market, and Harvard Square. If you're interested in exploring more neighborhoods, a tour will likely not give you access to these.

BOAT TOURS

Boston has many waterways that offer stunning views of the city skyline. Narrated sightseeing water tours generally run from spring through early fall, daily in summer, and on weekends in the shoulder seasons. (Labor Day weekend is often the cutoff point.) These trips normally last ¾–1½ hours and cost less than $20. Many companies also offer sunset or evening cruises with music and other entertainment.

The Boston Duck Tours, which gives narrated land-water tours on a World War II amphibious vehicle, are particularly popular. After driving past several historic sights, the vehicle dips into the Charles River to offer a view of the Boston skyline. These tours, costing $29.95 per person, run later than most, through late November.

June through September, you can relive the golden age of sail aboard the *Liberty Clipper*, a replica two-masted gaff-rigged schooner that operates midday harbor tours and romantic sunset cruises from Long Wharf.

Boston Harbor Cruises and Massachusetts Bay Lines have tours around the harbor. Trips with Boston Duck Tours and the Charles Riverboat Company are along the Charles River Basin.

Fees & Schedules Boston Duck Tours (⊠ *Departures from Prudential Center, Huntington Ave. in front of Shaw's supermarket; from New England Aquarium; and from Museum of Science* ☎ *617/267–3825* ⊕ *www.bostonducktours.com*). **Boston Harbor Cruises** (⊠ *1 Long Wharf* ☎ *877/733–9425 or 617/227–4321* ⊕ *www.bostonharbor cruises.com*). **Charles Riverboat Company** (⊠ *100 Cambridge Pl., Suite 320, Cambridge* ☎ *617/621–3001* ⊕ *www.charlesriverboat. com*). **Liberty Clipper** (☎ *617/742–0333* ⊕ *www.libertyfleet.com*).

Massachusetts Bay Lines (⊠ *60 Rowes Wharf* ☎ *617/542–8000* ⊕ *www.massbaylines. com*).

BUS TOURS

Bus tours, which cost around $25 and run daily from mid-March to early November, traverse the main historic neighborhoods in less than four hours. Reserve bus tours at least a day in advance. Boston Private Tours has customized tours in vans or limousines. Brush Hill has more traditional charter bus tours as well as smaller tours, with lots of prepackaged options and add-ons. One popular tour of theirs is 1½-hours and narrated.

Fees and Schedules Boston Private Tours (☎800/620–1136 ⊕www.bostonprivatetours. com). **Brush Hill Tours** (✉Transportation Bldg., 16 Charles St. S ☎800/343–1328 or 781/986–6100 ⊕www.brushhilltours.com).

TROLLEY TOURS

Narrated trolley tours, which usually cost $26 or so, don't require reservations and are more flexible than bus tours; you can get on and off as you wish. A full trip normally lasts 1½–2 hours. All trolleys run daily, though less frequently off-season. Because they're open vehicles, be sure to dress appropriately for the weather.

Old Town Trolley tours, usually focusing on history. include one that's 1½-hour and narrated.

Old Town Trolley (✉380 Dorchester Ave., South Boston ☎800/868–7482 or 617/269–7010 ⊕www.historictours.com/boston).

THEME TOURS

See how a brewery operates at the Boston Beer Museum & Samuel Adams Brewery; hear spine-tingling tales about Boston's famous cemeteries; or tour (for free) the offices and printing plant of the *Boston Globe*. These tours are often given a few days a week. Some organizations have special restrictions, such as an age limit for children. Many tours are free, but you'll often need to make a reservation at least a few days in advance and call ahead for schedules.

Beer Tours Boston Beer Museum & Samuel Adams Brewery (✉Boston Beer Company, 30 Germania St., Jamaica Plain ☎617/368–5080 ⊕www.samueladams.com).

Bike Tours Boston Bike Tours (✉Meet at Boston Common near Visitor Information Center ☎617/308–5902 ⊕www.bostonbiketours. com).

Children's Tours Boston by Little Feet (✉Meet at Samuel Adams statue in front of Faneuil Hall ☎617/367–2345 ⊕www.boston byfoot.com).

Gardens and Parks Tours Beacon Hill Garden Club Tours (✉Charles and Beacon

Sts., Beacon Hill ☎617/227–4392 ⊕www. beaconhillgardenclub.org). **Boston Park Rangers** (✉Parks and Recreation Dept. kiosk in Boston Common ☎617/635–4505 ⊕www. cityofboston.gov/parks).

History Tours Bay Colony Historical Tours (✉1 Cordis St., Charlestown ☎617/523–7303).

Movie Tours Boston Movie Tours (✉Meet at Shaw Memorial in front of State House ☎866/668–4345 ⊕www.bostonmovietours. net).

WALKING TOURS

Boston is the perfect city for walking tours, to explore topics ranging from history and literature to ethnic neighborhoods. Most tours cost less than $20 and last one to two hours. Guides prefer to keep groups at fewer than 20 people, so always reserve ahead. Several organizations give tours once or twice a day spring through fall and by appointment (if at all) in winter. Others run tours a few days a week, spring through fall.

The Women's Heritage Trail, the Freedom Trail, and the Black Heritage Trail can be completed as self-guided tours. Maps for the Women's Heritage Trail are available online and at the Old State House and the National Park Service Visitor Center. The Boston Common Visitor Information Center has maps of the Freedom Trail, which is indicated with a red line painted on the ground. The Freedom Trail and the Black Heritage Trail can also be completed with a ranger-led group. The Boston and Cambridge Centers for Adult Education lead in-depth educational tours on many topics, most of them centered around art, architecture, and literature.

Harvard Square is the starting point for free student-led campus tours.

Fees and Schedules Black Heritage Trail (☎617/725–0022 ⊕www.afroammuseum. org). **Boston by Foot** (✉77 N. Washington St. ☎617/367–2345 ⊕www.bostonbyfoot.com). **Boston Center for Adult Education** (✉122 Arlington St. ☎617/267–4430 ⊕www.bcae.

org). **Boston Common Visitor Information Center** (☎ *888/733-2678* ⊕ *www.bostonusa. com*).

Cambridge Center for Adult Education (✉ *42 Brattle St., Cambridge* ☎ *617/547-6789* ⊕ *www.ccae.org*). **Freedom Trail** (☎ *617/357-8300* ⊕ *www.thefreedomtrail.org*). **Harvard Campus Tours** (☎ *617/495-1573* ⊕ *www. hno.harvard.edu/guide/to_do/index.html*).

Historic New England (✉ *141 Cambridge St.* ☎ *617/227-3957* ⊕ *www.historicnewengland. org/about*). **North End Market Tour** (✉ *6 Charter St.* ☎ *617/523-6032* ⊕ *www.north endmarkettours.com*). **National Parks Service Visitor Center** (☎ *617/242-5642* ⊕ *www.nps. gov/bost*).

Women's Heritage Trail (⊕ *www.bwht.org*).

▌GEAR

The principal rule on Boston weather is that there are no rules. A cold, overcast morning can become a sunny, warm afternoon—and vice versa. Thus, the best advice on how to dress is to layer your clothing so that you can remove or add garments as needed for comfort. Rain often appears with little warning, so remember to pack a raincoat and umbrella. Because Boston is a great walking city—with some picturesque but uneven cobblestone streets—be sure to bring comfortable shoes. In all seasons, remember it's often breezier along the coast; always carry a windbreaker and fleece jacket or sweatshirt to the beach.

Boston Travel Agent Garber Travel (☎ *800/359-4272* ⊕ *www.garbertravel.com*).

▌HOURS OF OPERATION

Banks are generally open weekdays 9–4 or 5, plus Saturday 9 AM–noon or 1 PM at some branches. Public buildings are open weekdays 9–5.

Although hours vary quite a bit, most museums are open Monday through Saturday 9 or 10 AM–5 or 6 PM and Sunday noon–5 PM. Many are closed one day a week, usually Monday.

The major pharmacy chains—Brooks, CVS, and Walgreens—are generally open daily between 7 or 9:30 AM and 8 or 10 PM; independently owned pharmacies usually close earlier. Several pharmacies are open 24 hours a day.

Boston stores are generally open Monday through Saturday 10 or 11 AM–6 or 7 PM, closing later during the holiday-shopping season. Mall shops often stay open until 9 or 10 PM; malls and some tourist areas may also be open Sunday noon–5 or 6 PM.

▌MONEY

Prices are generally higher in Beacon Hill, the Back Bay, and Harvard Square than elsewhere. You're more likely to find bargains in the North End, Kenmore Square, Downtown Crossing, and Cambridge's Central Square. Many museums have one evening of free admission each week. There are no "happy hours" at any Boston bars due to a state law ("blue laws") that forbids promotions of discounted liquor.

ITEM	AVERAGE COST
Cup of Coffee	$1–$2
Glass of Wine	$6 and up
Glass of Beer	$3.50 and up
Slice of Pizza	$1.50–$2.50
One-Mile Taxi Ride	$3.50–$4
Museum Admission	$7–$15

Prices throughout this guide are given for adults. Substantially reduced fees are almost always available for children, students, and senior citizens.

CREDIT CARDS

Throughout this guide, the following abbreviations are used: **AE**, American Express; **D**, Discover; **DC**, Diners Club; **MC**, MasterCard; and **V**, Visa.

Reporting Lost Cards American Express (☎ *800/528-4800* ⊕ *www.americanexpress. com*). **Diners Club** (☎ *800/234-6377* ⊕ *www. dinersclub.com*). **Discover** (☎ *800/347-2683*

⊕ *www.discovercard.com*). **MasterCard**
(☎ *800/622-7747* ⊕ *www.mastercard.com*).
Visa (☎ *800/847-2911* ⊕ *www.visa.com*).

▌RESTROOMS

Public restrooms outside of restaurants, hotel lobbies, and tourist attractions are rare in Boston, but you'll find clean, well-lighted facilities at South Station, Faneuil Hall Marketplace, and the Visitor Information Center on Boston Common. Quarter-operated, self-cleaning public toilets can be found at Puopolo Park in the North End, near Faneuil Hall, at Central Wharf, and near the Boston Public Library.

Find a Loo The Bathroom Diaries (⊕ *www. thebathroomdiaries.com*) is flush with unsanitized info on restrooms the world over—each one located, reviewed, and rated.

▌SAFETY

With their many charming neighborhoods, Boston and Cambridge often feel like small towns. But they're both cities, subject to the same problems plaguing other urban communities nationwide. Although violent crime is rare, residents and tourists alike sometimes fall victim to pickpockets, scam artists, and car thieves. As in any large city, use common sense, especially after dark. Stay with the crowds and walk on well-lighted, busy streets. Look alert and aware; a purposeful pace helps deter trouble wherever you go. Take cabs or park in well-lighted lots or garages.

Store valuables in a hotel safe or, better yet, leave them at home. Keep an eye (and hand) on handbags and backpacks; do not hang them from a chair in restaurants. Carry wallets in inside or front pockets rather than back pockets. Use ATMs in daylight, preferably in a hotel, bank, or another indoor location with security guards.

Subways and trolleys tend to be safe, but it's wise to stay on your guard. Stick to routes in the main Boston and Cambridge tourist areas—generally, the downtown stops on all lines, on the Red Line in Cambridge, on the Green Line through the Back Bay, and on the Blue Line around the New England Aquarium. Know your itinerary and make sure you get on the right bus or train going in the right direction. Avoid empty subway and trolley cars and lonely station hallways and platforms, especially after 9 PM on weeknights. The MBTA has its own police officers; don't hesitate to ask them for help.

▌TIP→ **Distribute your cash, credit cards, IDs, and other valuables between a deep front pocket, an inside jacket or vest pocket, and a hidden money pouch. Don't reach for the money pouch once you're in public.**

▌TAXES

Hotel room charges in Boston and Cambridge are subject to state and local taxes of up to 12.45%.

A sales tax of 5% is added to restaurant and take-out meals and to all other goods except nonrestaurant food and clothing valued at less than $175.

▌TIME

Boston is in the eastern time zone, 3 hours ahead of Los Angeles, 1 hour ahead of Chicago, 5 hours behind London, and 15 hours behind Sydney. Daylight saving time is observed.

▌TIPPING

In restaurants, the standard gratuity is 15%–20% of your bill. Many restaurants automatically add a 15%–20% gratuity for groups of six or more.

Tip taxi drivers 15% of the fare and airport and hotel porters at least $1 per bag. It's also usual to tip chambermaids $1–$3 daily. Hotel room-service tips vary and may be included in the meal charge. Masseuses and masseurs, hairstylists, manicurists, and others performing personal

FOR INTERNATIONAL TRAVELERS

CURRENCY

The dollar is the basic unit of U.S. currency. It has 100 cents. Coins are the penny (1¢); the nickel (5¢), dime (10¢), quarter (25¢), half-dollar (50¢), and the rare golden $1 coin and rarer silver $1. Bills are denominated $1, $5, $10, $20, $50, and $100, all mostly green and identical in size; designs and background tints vary. A $2 bill exists but is extremely rare.

CUSTOMS

Information U.S. Customs and Border Protection (⊕ www.cbp.gov).

DRIVING

Driving in the United States is on the right. Speed limits are posted in miles per hour (usually between 55 mph and 70 mph). In small towns and on back roads limits are usually 30 mph to 40 mph. Most states require front-seat passengers to wear seat belts; children should be in the back seat and buckled up. In major cities, rush hours are 7 to 10 AM and 4 to 7 PM. Some freeways have high-occupancy vehicle (HOV) lanes, ordinarily marked with a diamond, for cars carrying two people or more.

Highways are well paved. Interstates—limited-access, multilane highways designated with an "I–" before the number—are fastest. Interstates with three-digit numbers circle urban areas, which may also have other expressways, freeways, and parkways. Limited-access highways sometimes have tolls.

Gas stations are plentiful, except in rural areas. Most stay open late (some 24 hours). Along larger highways, roadside stops with restrooms, fast-food restaurants, and sundries stores are well spaced. State police and tow trucks patrol major highways. If your car breaks down, pull onto the shoulder and wait, or have passengers wait while you walk to a roadside emergency phone (most states). On a cell phone, dial *55.

ELECTRICITY

The U.S. standard is AC, 110 volts/60 cycles. Plugs have two flat pins set parallel to each other.

EMBASSIES

Contacts Australia ☎ 202/797–3000 ⊕ www.austemb.org. **Canada** ☎ 202/682–1740 ⊕ www.canadianembassy.org. **UK** ☎ 202/588–7800 ⊕ ukinusa.fco.gov.uk/eu.

EMERGENCIES

For police, fire, or ambulance, dial 911 (0 in rural areas).

HOLIDAYS

New Year's Day (Jan. 1); Martin Luther King Day (3rd Mon. in Jan.); Presidents' Day (3rd Mon. in Feb.); Memorial Day (last Mon. in May); Independence Day (July 4); Labor Day (1st Mon. in Sept.); Columbus Day (2nd Mon. in Oct.); Thanksgiving Day (4th Thurs. in Nov.); Christmas Eve and Christmas Day (Dec. 24 and 25); and New Year's Eve (Dec. 31).

MAIL

You can buy stamps and send letters and parcels in post offices. Stamp-dispensing machines can occasionally be found in airports, bus and train stations, office buildings, drugstores, convenience stores, and in ATMs. U.S. mailboxes are stout, dark-blue steel bins; pickup schedules are posted inside the bin (pull the handle). Mail parcels over a pound at a post office.A first-class letter weighing 1 ounce or less costs 42¢; each additional ounce costs 17¢. Postcards cost 27¢. Postcards or 1-ounce airmail letters to most countries cost 94¢; postcards or 1-ounce letters to Canada or Mexico cost 72¢.

To receive mail on the road, have it sent c/o General Delivery to your destination's main post office. You must pick up mail in person within 30 days with a driver's license or passport for identification.

Contacts **DHL** ☎*800/225–5345* ⊕*www. dhl.com*. **FedEx** ☎*800/463–3339* ⊕*www. fedex.com*. **Mail Boxes, Etc./The UPS Store** ☎*800/789–4623* ⊕*www.mbe.com*. **USPS** ⊕*www.usps.com*.

PASSPORTS AND VISAS

Visitor visas aren't necessary for citizens of Australia, Canada, the United Kingdom, or most citizens of EU countries coming for tourism and staying for under 90 days. A visa is $100, and waiting time can be substantial. Apply for a visa at the U.S. consulate in your place of residence.

Visa Information Destination USA ⊕*www.unitedstatesvisas.gov*.

PHONES

Numbers consist of a three-digit area code and a seven-digit local number. In Boston, the area code is 617; surrounding areas use 781, 508, or 978. Within many local calling areas, dial just seven digits. In others, dial "1" first and all 10 digits; this is true for calling toll-free numbers—prefixed by "800," "888," "866," and "877." Dial "1" before "900" numbers, too, but know they're very expensive.

For international calls, dial "011," the country code, and the number. For help, dial "0" and ask for an overseas operator. Most phone books list country codes and U.S. area codes. The country code for Australia is 61, for New Zealand 64, for the United Kingdom 44. Calling Canada is the same as calling within the United States (country code: 1).

For operator assistance, dial "0." For directory assistance, call 555–1212 or 411 (free at many public phones). To call "collect" (reverse charges), dial "0" instead of "1" before the 10-digit number.

Instructions are generally posted on pay phones. Usually you insert coins in a slot (usually 25¢–50¢ for local calls) and wait for a steady tone before dialing. On long-distance calls the operator tells you how much to insert; prepaid phone cards, widely available, can be used from any phone. Follow the directions to activate the card, then dial your number.

CELL PHONES

The United States has several GSM (Global System for Mobile Communications) networks, so multiband mobiles from most countries (except for Japan) work here. It's almost impossible to buy just a pay-as-you-go mobile SIM card in the U.S.—needed to avoid roaming charges—but cell phones with pay-as-you-go plans are available for well under $100. AT&T (GoPhone) and Virgin Mobile have the cheapest with national coverage.

Contacts **AT&T** ☎*888/333–6651* ⊕*www. att.com*. **Virgin Mobile** ☎*No phone* ⊕*www. virginmobileusa.com*.

services generally get a 15% tip. Theater ushers, museum guides, and gas-station attendants generally do not receive tips. Tour guides may be tipped a few dollars for good service. Concierges may be tipped anywhere from $5 to $20 for exceptional service, such as securing a difficult dinner reservation or helping plan a personal sightseeing itinerary.

TIPPING GUIDELINES FOR BOSTON	
Bartender	$1–$2 per drink
Bellhop	$1 to $5 per bag, depending on the level of the hotel
Hotel Concierge	$5 or more, if he or she performs a service for you
Hotel Doorman	$1–$2 if he helps you get a cab
Hotel Maid	1$–$3 a day (either daily or at the end of your stay, in cash)
Hotel Room-Service Waiter	$1 to $2 per delivery, even if a service charge has been added
Porter at Airport or Train Station	$1 per bag
Skycap at Airport	$1 to $3 per bag checked
Taxi Driver	15%–20%, but round up the fare to the next dollar amount
Tour Guide	10% of the cost of the tour
Valet Parking Attendant	$1–$2, but only when you get your car
Waiter	15%–20%, with 20% being the norm at high-end restaurants; nothing additional if a service charge is added to the bill
Other	Restroom attendants in more-expensive restaurants expect some small change or $1. Tip coat-check personnel at least $1–$2 per item checked unless there is a fee, then nothing.

▮ VISITOR INFORMATION

Contact the city and state tourism offices for general information, details about seasonal events, discount passes, trip planning, and attraction information. The National Park Service has a Boston office where you can watch an eight-minute slide show on Boston's historic sites and get maps and directions. The Welcome Center and Boston Common Visitor Information Center offer general information.

Contacts Boston Common Visitor Information Center (⊠ *148 Tremont St. where Freedom Trail begins, Downtown* ☎ *888/733–2678).* **Boston National Historical Park Visitor Center** (⊠ *15 State St., Downtown* ☎ *617/242–5642* ⊕ *www.nps.gov/bost).* **Cambridge Tourism Office** (⊠ *4 Brattle St., Harvard Sq., Cambridge* ☎ *800/862–5678 or 617/441–2884* ⊕ *www.cambridge-usa.org).* **Greater Boston Convention and Visitors Bureau** (⊠ *2 Copley Pl., Suite 105, Back Bay* ☎ *888/733–2678 or 617/536–4100* ⊕ *www.bostonusa.com).* **Massachusetts Office of Travel and Tourism** (⊠ *State Transportation Bldg., 10 Park Plaza, Suite 4510, Back Bay* ☎ *800/227–6277 or 617/973–8500* ⊕ *www.massvacation.com).*

ONLINE RESOURCES

Boston.com, home of the *Boston Globe* online, has news and feature articles, ample travel information, and links to towns throughout Massachusetts. The site for Boston's arts and entertainment weekly, the Boston Phoenix has nightlife, movie, restaurant, and arts listings. The Bostonian Society answers some frequently asked questions about Beantown history on their Web site. The iBoston page has some wonderful photographs of buildings that are architecturally and historically important.

All About Boston Boston.com (⊕ *www.boston.com).* **Boston Phoenix** (⊕ *www.bostonphoenix.com).* **Bostonian Society** (⊕ *www.bostonhistory.org).* **iBoston** (⊕ *www.iboston.org)*

Safety Transportation Security Administration *(TSA* ⊕ *www.tsa.gov).*

INDEX

NOTES

NOTES

NOTES

NOTES

NOTES

NOTES

NOTES

NOTES

ABOUT OUR WRITERS

Travel/outdoor recreation writers Diane Bair and Pamela Wright hit the road for publications like *National Geographic Traveler, Family Circle,* and the *Miami Herald,* but they agree with Dorothy: there's no place like home (especially when the Sox are in town!). They happily sleuth out the best beds (and minibars) in Boston for Fodor's.

Former Fodor's production editor, Bethany Cassin Beckerlegge, enjoyed getting back to her roots for this project. A native of Massachusetts, this Connecticut-based writer and editor rediscovered her favorite Beantown haunts and added a few new ones while updating *Boston 2010.* When not on assignment, Bethany and her husband Robb travel the coasts of Maine, New Hampshire, and Connecticut with their toddler, Andy.

When she's not traveling on assignment for *Fodor's* and assorted other publications, freelancer Susan MacCallum-Whitcomb makes her home in Halifax, Nova Scotia. But she remains proud of her New England roots. Susan's family has been bouncing back and forth across the Canada/U.S. border since 1662, and she returns to Boston as often as possible to visit two of her relatives—Anne Hutchinson and Mary Dyer—both of whom are immortalized in bronze outside the State House. Susan updated the Dining chapter for *Boston 2010.*